In Pursuit of Refinement

Maurie D. McInnis

Susan Ricci Stebbins

(signature)

J. Thomas Savage

Angel D. Mah

Wendell Garrott

In Pursuit of Refinement
CHARLESTONIANS ABROAD

1740–1860

Maurie D. McInnis in collaboration with

Angela D. Mack

with essays by
J. Thomas Savage, Robert A. Leath, and Susan Ricci Stebbins

Gibbes Museum of Art
with the cooperation of the Historic Charleston Foundation

University of South Carolina Press

FRONT COVER:

Mr. and Mrs. Ralph Izard, 1775
John Singleton Copley (American, 1738–1815)
Oil on canvas, 69 × 88 ½ in.
Museum of Fine Arts, Boston,
Edward Ingersoll Brown Fund

BACK COVER:

Cymon and Iphigenia, ca. 1780
Angelica Kauffman (Swiss, 1741–1807)
Oil on canvas, 24 ⅜ in. (diam.)
Carolina Art Association/Gibbes Museum of Art,
gift of Miss Alicia Hopton Middleton

FRONTISPIECE:

John Moultrie III and Family, ca. 1782
John Francis Rigaud (British, 1742–1810)
Oil on canvas, 77 ½ × 60 ⅛ in.
Carolina Art Association/Gibbes Museum of Art,
purchased from Colnaghi's with funds from the
Moultrie and Ball families

Book design by Jennie Malcolm
Composition by Running Feet Books
Printed in Canada

This volume accompanies the exhibition
In Pursuit of Refinement
Charlestonians Abroad, 1740–1860

Gibbes Museum of Art
Charleston, South Carolina
April 9–July 3, 1999

Angela D. Mack and J. Thomas Savage, Curators

© 1999 University of South Carolina
Published in Columbia, South Carolina, by the University of South Carolina Press
03 02 01 00 99   5 4 3 2 1

Library of Congress Cataloging-in-Publication Data

    In pursuit of refinement : Charlestonians abroad, 1740–1860 /
    Maurie D. McInnis . . . [et al.].
       p.   cm.
"Gibbes Museum of Art with the cooperation of the Historic Charleston Foundation."
    Includes bibliographical references and index.
    ISBN 1-57003-314-5 (hardcover)
    ISBN 1-57003-315-3 (pbk.)
1. Art, Modern—Collectors and collecting—South Carolina—Charleston—Exhibitions.
2. Art patronage—South Carolina—Charleston—Exhibitions   3. Art patrons—South
Carolina—Charleston—Portraits—Exhibitions   4. Charleston (South Carolina)—Social
life and customs—18th century—Exhibitions.   5. Charleston (South Carolina)—Social life
and customs—19th century—Exhibitions.   I. McInnis, Maurie D.   II. Gibbes Museum of
Art (Charleston, S.C.)   III. Historic Charleston Foundation (Charleston, S.C.)
    N5201.5.S6 I5 1999
    708.157'915—dc21
    98-58068

To Anna Wells Rutledge and George C. Rogers, Jr.

whose research led the way

Contents

Supporters

The exhibition and catalogue have been made possible with principal corporate sponsorship from

Carolina First

and with the generosity of the following:
(as of December 1, 1998)

CORPORATIONS
BellSouth
Disher Hamrick & Myers
SCANA Corporation/SCE&G
Jeffries Travis Realty Corporation

FOUNDATIONS
Nathan & Marlene Addlestone Foundation, Inc.
DeMuth Family Foundation
Joanna Foundation
The Post & Courier Foundation
John and Kathleen Rivers Foundation
Women's Council of the Carolina Art Association
The Jerry and Anita Zucker Family Foundation, Inc.

PATRONS
Anonymous
Mr. and Mrs. John J. Avlon
Ralph Blakely
Mr. and Mrs. Smith B. Coleman, III

Richard C. Dailey
Mr. and Mrs. Eric G. Friberg
Thomas Gromme
Mrs. Roger Hanahan
Robert M. Hicklin, Jr., Inc.
Thomas S. Kenan, III
Mrs. Anne Olsen
Mr. and Mrs. Thomas J. Parsell
Mr. W. Thomas Rutledge, Jr.
Dr. James Simpson
Mr. and Mrs. Stephen J. Ziff

FRIENDS
Dr. and Mrs. F. M. Ball
Hilary Cadwallader
Mr. and Mrs. John F. Maybank
Mr. and Mrs. Felix C. Pelzer

The Gibbes Museum of Art also acknowledges the support of:
South Carolina Arts Commission
South Carolina Humanities Council
South Carolina Department of Parks, Recreation, and Tourism

Lenders

Addison Gallery of American Art

Art Gallery of Nova Scotia, Halifax, Nova Scotia, Canada

Mr. Russell Dehon Blocker

Mr. and Mrs. R. Lowndes Burke

Mary H. Cadwalader

Dr. and Mrs. Price Cameron

The Campbell-Johnston Family, England

Carolina Art Association/Gibbes Museum of Art

Charleston Library Society

The Charleston Museum

The Chrysler Museum of Art

Mr. and Mrs. Edward E. Crawford

DAR Museum, National Society Daughters of the American Revolution

The Detroit Institute of Arts

Mr. Edward Drinker

Mr. John Drinker

Mr. Sandwith Drinker

Mr. Charles H. P. Duell

Mr. and Mrs. Peter S. Finnerty, Jr.

Fitzwilliam Museum, Cambridge, England

Gainsborough's House, Sudbury, England

The Reverend Robert Emmet Gribbin

Mrs. Theodore B. Guérard

Historic Charleston Foundation

Mr. Peter Jefferys, London, England

Miss Joanna S. Jenkins

Dr. Mitchell E. Levine

Mr. and Mrs. Edward Lining Manigault
Mr. and Mrs. Peter Manigault
Mr. Louis M. McElveen
The Metropolitan Museum of Art
Middleton Place Foundation
Miles Brewton House Collection
Mr. Benjamin Allston Moore, Jr.
Mr. Edward Murray
Musée Fabre, Montpellier, France
Museum of Fine Arts, Boston
The National Portrait Gallery, Smithsonian Institution
New College, Oxford, England
Elise Pinckney
Mr. and Mrs. John Julius Pringle
Mrs. Edmund Rhett
Mr. and Mrs. Robert Goodwyn Rhett
Viscount Ridley, Newcastle upon Tyne, England
The Rivers Collection Foundation
Mr. Carl Salter
Dr. and Mrs. Charlton deSaussure
Anne Jenkins Sawyers
South Caroliniana Library, University of South Carolina
South Carolina Historical Society
South Carolina State Museum
Special Collections, Robert Scott Small Library, College of Charleston
Tate Gallery, London, England
Mary and Joseph Torras
Mr. and Mrs. Arthur M. Wilcox
Anonymous Private Collections

Committees and Boards

HONORARY EXHIBITION COMMITTEE
Mr. and Mrs. Charles A. Atkins
Mr. and Mrs. John J. Avlon
Dr. and Mrs. F. M. Ball
Ms. Hilary Cadwallader
Mrs. Graham Daughtridge
Mr. Charles H. P. Duell
Mrs. William O. Hanahan, Jr.
Mr. and Mrs. Robert M. Hicklin, Jr.
Senator and Mrs. Ernest F. Hollings
Ambassador and Mrs. Phil Lader
Mr. and Mrs. Douglas B. Lee
Mr. and Mrs. Thomas J. Parsell
Mr. and Mrs. Felix C. Pelzer
Mrs. Mary Ramsay
The Honorable Joseph P. Riley, Jr.
Mr. and Mrs. John Rivers, Jr.
Representative and Mrs. Marshall Sanford
Mr. and Mrs. J. Rutledge Young, Jr.
Mr. and Mrs. Stephen J. Ziff

Preface

*T*he histories of the Carolina Art Association and the Historic
Charleston Foundation are closely intertwined. In the 1930s under
the leadership of Director Robert N. S. Whitelaw and Presidents
Thomas R. Waring, Albert Simons, and Harold A. Mouzon, the mission of the
association was expanded into various roles in community affairs. One of these
was the organization of the Historic Charleston Foundation, a group devoted
from its beginnings to the preservation of Charleston's irreplaceable architectural
heritage. Over the decades each organization has grown, prospered, and refined
its concepts of service to the city, its residents, and visitors.

It is a distinct privilege and pleasure to see the goals of both merge in the present relationship centered upon the scholarship and interests of our respective
curators. Through this collaboration, current research on Charleston's preeminent
place in America's early cultural history is presented in the exhibition *In Pursuit of
Refinement: Charlestonians Abroad, 1740–1860* and the accompanying catalogue.
This project is an ambitious undertaking not only in research but in the assembly
of over 140 objects from both private and public collections. This could be possible only through a unique partnership.

The impetus for this endeavor was mutual respect and a commitment to edu-
cate others to the artistic accomplishments of Charleston. Specifically, the initial
work of art historians Anna Wells Rutledge and Helen McCormack, who examined Charleston's colonial art and its connections to eighteenth-century European
sources, provided fertile ground for further research. This was accomplished by
Angela Mack, curator of collections at the Gibbes Museum of Art. From 1994 to
1996, she undertook a comprehensive survey of Charleston-related paintings
found in collections in Europe and across the United States. We are grateful to Mr.
and Mrs. Stephen Ziff for recognizing the potential of this project at its earliest
stage with necessary venture capital and to Carolina First for their support of its

implementation. The results of Mack's scholarship were shared and enthusiastically received by the Historic Charleston Foundation's curators Tom Savage and Robert Leath. Their research in the decorative arts, as well as the expertise of Maurie McInnis on neoclassicism in Charleston, presents a full picture of the economic, social, and cultural factors that found expression in portraits and interior furnishings.

The scholarship assembled in this catalogue is the first serious exploration of the art and portraiture that Charlestonians commissioned for themselves and the decorative arts they assembled for their houses in more than a quarter century. Much has been revealed since the pioneer chroniclers of Charleston decorative arts first published the results of their research in the decades that straddled World War II. The scope of scholarly inquiry has expanded as well since initial efforts to describe the tastes of early Charlestonians. That is why both the exhibition and the catalogue go well beyond describing what Charlestonians purchased, to explore the direction of their acquisition of art, silver, furniture, and other fine objects.

Once the doors of discovery were opened many passages were explored. The path of presentation was a complex course to set. A parameter of time was established by focusing upon colonial and antebellum Charleston's meteoric rise to wealth. Of necessity, the range of objects in the exhibition reflects their availability. The condition of several examples required conservation. The selection also reveals to an extent what was important to individuals within families. Only by private stewardship have many of these works remained for study and reflection.

This project demonstrates a unique legacy in early America during a critical period of self-definition. It is the intention of this exhibition and catalogue to establish Charleston's place within American art and cultural history by investigating Charlestonians' aesthetic taste, arts patronage, and persistent cultural connections with Europe even long after the country achieved political independence.

Paul Figueroa
Director, Gibbes Museum of Art

Carter Hudgins
Director, Historic Charleston Foundation

Acknowledgments

Numerous colleagues in Charleston and from across the United States and Europe have shared their knowledge and enthusiasm with me as project director and cocurator of this exhibition. I would like to express my profound gratitude to the many individuals who have helped in the research and organization of this exhibition and its catalogue.

At the Gibbes Museum of Art, I am especially grateful for the enthusiastic support of the director, Paul Figueroa. His pivotal role in organizing the 1978–79 exhibition and accompanying publication titled *Art in the Lives of South Carolinians* formed the basis for his steadfast promotion of this project. I am deeply indebted to him for his unwavering encouragement, invaluable suggestions, and tireless fund-raising efforts. I would also like to thank Carter Hudgins, director of the Historic Charleston Foundation and the Boards of Directors of the Gibbes Museum of Art and the Historic Charleston Foundation, particularly Doug Lee and Dianne Avlon who served as liaisons. I am also grateful for the involvement of the Honorary Committee.

As co-curator of this exhibition, Tom Savage began this journey with me and has been the guiding force behind the decorative arts component of the exhibition. His research has helped to make significant strides in understanding eighteenth-century Charleston patronage and consumerism and has led to numerous important acquisitions for the house museums of the Historic Charleston Foundation. Without him the decorative arts would not have been a part of this exhibition.

I wish to express my deepest gratitude to Maurie McInnis. As content editor and principal essayist for the catalogue and as a consultant to the exhibition, she was essential to this entire endeavor. Her research on the neoclassical style in early-nineteenth-century Charleston art and architecture has served as the cornerstone for much of this project.

I am especially grateful to the other principal essayists, Wendell Garrett for an insightful introduction, Robert Leath for his contributions in the area of ceramics and for sharing his knowledge of primary documents, and Susan Ricci Stebbins who agreed to share her years of research on John Izard Middleton. In addition, I would like to thank those individuals who contributed catalogue entries. Their knowledge and expertise has added a significant dimension to this volume.

Without the early encouragement and support of Theodore E. Stebbins, Jr., and Carrie Rebora Barratt, this exhibition would not have occurred. I am deeply indebted to them both for seeing the potential of this project. In addition, I wish to thank those individuals who were kind enough to share their knowledge with me, particularly Richard McNeal, whose work on the early-nineteenth-century collector Joseph Allen Smith gave me direction; Philip Mould and his staff at Historical Portraits, Ltd., Charlotte Bailey and Pierce Davies, who answered numerous questions regarding English portraiture and helped with several discoveries; Barbara Doyle, who was the source for much information relating to the Middleton family; and Mrs. Theodora Gregorie Warren for her genealogical assistance. I am particularly grateful to Lance Humphries, whose research on early nineteenth-century American collectors has proven invaluable to this exhibition and catalogue. I will always be deeply in his debt for his groundbreaking discoveries and his generosity in sharing them with me.

I would like to thank the staffs of the following research institutions: the South Carolina Historical Society, particularly Pete Rerig; the Charleston Library Society, particularly Pat Bennett; the South Caroliniana Library, University of South Carolina; the Perkins Library, Duke University; the Southern Historical Collection, University of North Carolina; the Library of Congress; the Historical Society of Pennsylvania; and the Newport Historical Society and the British Library. I also appreciate the efforts of the present and past staff members at Middleton Place, particularly Tracey Todd and Kris Kepford-Young. A special thanks to Jennie Ingram for her research assistance.

To those institutions and private collectors who generously agreed to lend objects to the exhibition I would like to express my sincerest appreciation, particularly to Charles Duell, Peter Manigault, and Joanna S. Jenkins, who helped to locate and secure works from other collections.

Mounting an exhibition of this diversity and scope is an immense enterprise that requires the expertise of many people behind the scenes. I would like to acknowledge the enthusiastic and tireless efforts of the staff of the Gibbes Museum of Art, particularly Scott Zetrouer, Greg Jenkins, India Hopper, and Stacey Brown, and interns Shirley Hughes and Emory Hubbard. I would also like to thank the staff at the Historic Charleston Foundation for their support and assistance, particularly Renee Marshall. In addition I am grateful for the design talents of Dan Gottlieb and Jennie Malcolm and the fabrication talents of John Jeffers and JMO Woodworks.

I must express my deep gratitude to Roberta Sokolitz for her role as editorial associate, Alex Moore and Catherine Fry at the University of South Carolina Press, and Steve Hoffius for their assistance in the editing and production phase of the catalogue.

Finally, I would like to acknowledge the patience, support, and encouragement of my family, Ben, Alex, Benjamin, and Anna. You are the source of my strength.

Angela D. Mack, Project Director
Curator of Collections, Gibbes Museum of Art

Abbreviations

CC	*Charleston Courier,* Charleston, S.C.
CG	*City Gazette,* Charleston, S.C.
CLS	Charleston Library Society, Charleston, S.C.
CM	*Charleston Mercury,* Charleston, S.C.
HCF	Historic Charleston Foundation
HSP	Historical Society of Pennsylvania, Philadelphia, Penn.
LC	Library of Congress, Washington, D.C.
MDP	Charles Izard Manigault, "Description of Paintings, at No. 6 Gibbes Street, Charleston, S.C., the property of Charles Manigault, 1867," private collection.
MPF	Middleton Place Foundation, Charleston, S.C.
PAFA	Pennsylvania Academy of the Fine Arts, Philadelphia, Penn.
SCG	*South-Carolina Gazette,* Charleston, S.C.
SCHM	*South Carolina Historical Magazine* and *South Carolina Historical and Genealogical Magazine*
SCHS	South Carolina Historical Society, Charleston, S.C.
SCL	South Caroliniana Library, University of South Carolina, Columbia, S.C.
SHC-UNC	Southern Historical Collection, University of North Carolina, Chapel Hill, N.C.

In Pursuit of Refinement

Introduction

WENDELL GARRETT

*T*he South remains the nation's most distinctive region, most notably perhaps in a cultural sense. The persistence of an identifiable and pervasive regional culture is particularly evident in the South's historic architecture and fine and decorative arts. No other part of the United States has projected such a clear-cut sectional image, and Southerners seem to be as conscious of their regional identity and regional exceptionalism as they are loyal to their traditions and culture. Even in colonial times Americans were far more aware of local diversities than similarities among the several regions of British America. In 1760, Benjamin Franklin informed British readers in a well-known pamphlet that no two separate colonies on the North American continent seemed to be much alike. Rather, Franklin emphasized that the colonies were "not only under different governors, but have different forms of government, different laws, different interests, and some of them different religious persuasions and different manners."[1]

During the years encompassed by this volume—from the 1740s to the eve of the Civil War—Charleston dominated the intellectual and commercial life of what is now known as the Old South. The city was a center of the British Empire because it was a crossroads of trade on the main Atlantic highway. These years were Charleston's golden age in political power, art, literature, and science. The city gave South Carolina its leaders and decided questions for the rest of the colony and state. It was the great port of entry for immigrants headed for the early frontier and the market for the products they brought back to sell. It was a place of fashion and aristocratic pretensions.

The "great port town" of Charles Town was conceived by the Lord Proprietor Anthony Ashley Cooper as a true metropolis, "where we will oblige all ships . . . to unload all their goods and to take in all their loading." When the peninsular site between the Ashley and Cooper rivers was occupied in 1680, Ashley Cooper envisioned a city of unprecedented size for an English North American colony and

Figure 1 A View of Charles Town, *1773, Thomas Leitch. Oil on canvas. Courtesy of the Museum of Early Southern Decorative Arts.*

advised the governor "to have the streets laid out as large, orderly, and convenient as possible and when that is done the houses which shall hereafter be built on each side those designed streets, will grow in beauty with the trade and riches of the town."[2]

In 1740, many of the city's 6,300 inhabitants were displaced by a devastating fire that destroyed most of the area south of Broad Street, and the rebuilding that followed enhanced prospects for architectural refinement. Public buildings became more emphatically civic and increasingly sophisticated (fig. 1). Josiah Quincy admitted in 1773 that the city's maritime commerce surpassed that of his hometown of Boston: "Charleston appeared situated between two large spacious rivers . . . which here empty themselves into the sea. . . . The town struck me very agreeably [and] the new Exchange which fronted the place of my landing made a most noble appearance. . . . The numbers of inhabitants and appearance of the buildings far exceeded my expectation."[3]

In America as in England, class distinctions were communicated through elegance of dress and manners and appropriateness of architecture and furnishings. The traveler Joseph Bennett wrote in 1740 of Boston, "both ladies and gentlemen dress and appear as gay, in common, as courtiers in England on a coronation or birthday." William Eddis, after a few years in Annapolis, wrote in 1771 that he was almost inclined to believe that a new mode spread more rapidly among "polished and affluent" Americans than among "many opulent" Londoners. Also in 1771 Charles Carroll of Carrollton ordered a complete set of furniture from his London agent for a room in his Annapolis house.[4] When Josiah Quincy of Massachusetts dined with Miles Brewton in Charleston in 1773, he was profoundly impressed: "The grandest hall I ever beheld, azure blue satin window curtains, rich blue paper with gilt, mashee borders, most elegant pictures, excessive grand and costly looking glasses. . . . At Mr. Brewton's sideboard was very magnificent plate: a very exquisitely wrought Goblet, most excellent workmanship and singularly beautiful."[5] With its exterior architectural design, interior furnishings, extensive slave quarters, and landscaped garden that extended over several town lots, Brewton's was the most nearly perfect gentry home in Charleston, and certainly one of the most distinguished in America.

Charleston's increasing refinement was the result of the burgeoning commerce of the colony. At the beginning of the eighteenth century, exports from South Carolina accounted for only three percent of the value of goods sent from America to Great Britain, but by 1770 that number had risen to twenty-nine percent. At first these goods were naval stores. By 1720 rice became the principal crop, to be later supplemented by indigo and sea island cotton.[6] The labor to produce these crops came from enslaved Africans, who by 1708 comprised a majority of the colony's residents. Slaves from West Africa with knowledge of rice culture were particularly in demand, and by 1770 Africans and African-Americans accounted for more than seventy-eight percent of the Lowcountry's residents. On the eve of the American Revolution, the South Carolina Lowcountry was by any standard of measurement the wealthiest area in British North America, if not the entire world (fig. 2).[7]

An oligarchy of merchants and planters ruled the town and, to a great extent, the province. The importance of family in the society and culture of Charleston cannot be overestimated, and marriage was the cement of the new society. The natural alliances were among the families of the mercantile elite and Lowcountry planters. In Charleston these separate groups became unified through intermarriage. What drew them to Charleston was a common social life. Charleston was for the planters very much as London was for the British landed gentry. Every planter felt he should have a Charleston house, and most did; it was the center of trade, law, schooling, craftsmen, and transport to Europe, and, most important, of social intercourse. And every merchant aspired to become a planter, for that became the avenue to wealth and social status.

It is a dangerous anachronism to suppose that colonial America was a democracy or was struggling toward democracy in the modern sense. Not so. Colonial values and politics were indebted to the norms of Hanoverian England—a highly structured Christian monarchy grounded in a landed aristocracy. In Massachusetts not only did the founders belong to Britain's landed gentry but also as good Puritans they considered their superior station divinely ordained. In the words of their first governor, John Winthrop, "God Almighty in His most holy and wise providence hath so disposed of the condition of mankind as in all times some must be rich, some poor; some high and eminent in power and dignity, others mean in subjection."[8] As the decades progressed, the aristocracy retained its primacy, and families with fortunes newly made on land and sea won admittance to the circle of the ruling elite. The progression was especially notable in the colonial South. The Virginia patrician William Fitzhugh spoke for the southern aristocracy in avowing that his children had "better be never born than ill-bred." To William Byrd II it was nothing short of a "tragical Story" when a well-born Virginia girl in 1732 played "so senceless a Prank" as to marry her uncle's overseer, "a dirty Plebian."[9]

Throughout America colonial leadership was an oligarchy whose members asked deferential voters to embrace their politics as well as their social superiority and superior judgment. This governing aristocracy possessed the wisdom and capacity to provide cultural leadership and set standards of taste through its patronage of artists and craftsmen. In South Carolina the Lowcountry elite was not a rigid caste in the eighteenth century; it was always at the center of power and quite willing to enlist new members from among rising professionals, energetic

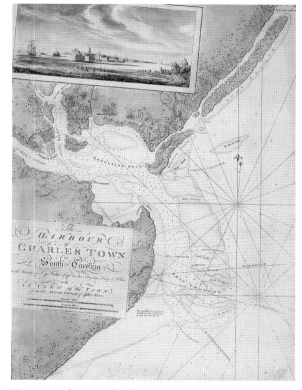

Figure 2 Harbour in Charles Town in South Carolina, *1777, J. F. W. Des Barres. Courtesy of the Carolina Art Association/ Gibbes Museum of Art.*

tradesmen, and skilled craftsmen. What kept the society open was the variety of avenues to new wealth.

To be sure, in the crisis of the American Revolution, loyalties were divided. While many became fervent patriots, some of the colonial gentry sided ardently with Britain, or exhibited only a lackluster patriotism. However, the well-informed Thomas McKean of Pennsylvania, himself a signer of the Declaration of Independence, wrote John Adams that in retrospect almost two-thirds of the country's "influential characters" had favored the American cause.[10] By 1763, the Carolina oligarchy was highly self-confident and had won its claim to power. This local aristocracy was immensely rich and secure because of the removal of the French and Spanish from America's expanding frontier. The men who became the greatest patriots in Charleston were outstanding examples of this new assertiveness. Henry Laurens was busy buying plantations in South Carolina and Georgia and building a town house amid a four-acre garden. Thomas Lynch, the successful rice planter from the banks of the Santee, married the daughter of the colonial treasurer, Jacob Motte. John Rutledge, fresh from studies in London, became the leading lawyer almost overnight. Christopher Gadsden, who made one fortune by 1761, closed his stores at the Cheraws and Georgetown and began to build the largest wharf in America and to develop a suburb just north of town.

The Revolution reversed Americans' loyalty to the king of England with astonishing abruptness. As John Adams put it, "The radical change in the principles, opinions, sentiments, and affections of the people was the real American Revolution."[11] Yet the rejection of Britain was tempered by ambivalence, and it may be that this selective attitude toward the colonial past helps to explain the difference between American and English arts in general and the uniqueness of southern decorative arts in Charleston in particular. The national consciousness that flourished in the early years of the Republic may be interpreted positively as the expression of a cultural identity distinct from England's or negatively as a deplorable example of cultural insularity. "Before the Revolution," Jedidiah Morse maintained in the preface to his *American Universal Geography* (1793), "Americans seldom pretended to write or to think for themselves. We humbly received from Great Britain our laws, our manners, our books, and our modes of thinking; and our youth were educated as the subjects of the British king, rather than as the citizens of a free and independent republic."[12]

Charleston's cultural milieu was a product of the traditions of her people, of the education of her youth, of the reading and writing of her adults, and of the pleasures of her citizens. Among the professional groups, the clergy and medical doctors contributed dynamic elements to the intellectual life of the city. There were private schools established by trusts or organizations, such as the South Carolina Society and the Friendly Society. Many sons of the leading citizens were sent to the mother country for their education, and when they returned to Charleston, the boys brought back things English—the manners, the accent, the clothes, the new styles of the day. The center of the intellectual life of the city was the Charleston Library Society, which was organized in 1748 by seventeen citizens hoping "to save their descendants from sinking into savagery."[13] Charleston had a theater as early as 1735, when the Dock Street Theater first opened. The St. Cecilia Society, also founded in 1735, held regular public concerts before the Revolution. When Benjamin Franklin wrote his friend Mary Stevenson in London in 1763, "'tis said, the Arts delight to travel Westward," he was reiterating a theory that had its roots in classical antiquity and remained an important tenet for scholars throughout the Renaissance. The theory was reaffirmed during the eighteenth-century Enlightenment by prophets of progress who were convinced that the North American continent was destined to become the future habitat for the arts and sciences.[14]

The effect of the War of American Independence abroad was to make Europeans believe that they lived in a rare era of momentous change. The success of the Revolution coinciding with the climax of the Enlightenment proved to them that the rights of man and the social contract, of liberty and equality, of responsible citizenship and popular sovereignty, of freedom of thought and speech, of separation of powers and written constitutions could now be made actual among real people. This created the belief in Europe that certain key doctrines were achieving their first realization in the United States. Indeed, many Europeans said that America would some day predominate over Europe. The Venetian ambassador to Paris observed in 1783: "If only the union of the [American] Provinces is preserved, it is reasonable to expect that, with the favorable effects of time, and of European arts and sciences, it will become the most formidable power in the world."[15]

Charleston's population growth in the antebellum period was much slower than in many cities in the North. In 1775, Charleston's 12,800 residents made it the fourth-largest city in America. By 1860, the 40,000 inhabitants ranked only 22nd.

The Lowcountry market economy was cyclical in the antebellum period, but it still provided ample opportunities for the creation of wealth, and planting was the principal means of achieving prosperity. By 1860, free whites in the Lowcountry were still about three times wealthier, per free capita, than the national average, but they were not as well off as their ancestors had been in 1775. Most of this accumulated wealth was in human property, with about two-thirds of a slave owner's wealth invested in slaves and about one-third in land and buildings.[16]

Just as the country gentry of England maintained town houses in London, Carolina planters spent much of their year in Charleston, called the most brilliant of American cities by Crèvecoeur.[17] Their long sojourns in the city, away from their rice estates, made these tidewater planters not only more sophisticated but also more closely knit in their views. The society of this opulent city practiced what Thorstein Veblen would have called conspicuous leisure, consumption, and display. When the duc de la Rochefoucauld traveled in the southern states in 1795–96, he noted that a Charleston gentleman seldom had fewer than twenty servants in his domestic establishment and that the children had Negro maids and body servants to wait upon them.[18] Of this planter aristocracy, President George Washington wrote during his southern journey of 1791: "The inhabitants are wealthy—Gay—and hospitable."[19] The American Republic was a nation and the American people were profitably engaged in the vulgar business of acquiring and spending—and Charleston's economic prosperity was in part the product of the peculiarly intense worldwide cotton demand between 1820 and 1860. James K. Polk would make the boastful pronouncement in 1848 that the United States was "a sublime spectacle to the world" and

Americans "the most favored people on the face of the earth." In the more restrained judgment of Nathaniel Hawthorne, "a commonplace prosperity" made it possible for most dwellers in his "dear native land" to live in "broad and simple daylight" such as no land had ever enjoyed.[20] This generation of Americans in general and Charlestonians in particular went in search of something to which all but a few men aspire; they found a larger portion of it than all but a few will ever know.

Most of the planter aristocracy moved within the penumbra of urban life and the rich modes of intellectual discourse it offered. In Charleston there was the Conversation Club, which met every few weeks for papers to be read and old Madeira to be consumed. During the first half century of national experience, a number of Charlestonians were taking the intellectual Grand Tour and making the cultural pilgrimage to Europe. There were lines of communication open between the South and the continent of Europe. The first doctoral degree granted to an American was awarded to Philip Tidyman of Charleston at Göttingen in 1800.[21] Hugh Swinton Legaré was writing on August von Schlegel in 1830, contemporaneously with the Scottish reviewers. By 1870, Paul Hamilton Hayne looked back on antebellum Charleston as a vanished Eden with Legaré at its center: "A brief half century ago, and culture, refinement, hospitality, wit, genius, and social virtue, seem to have taken up their lasting abode therein. A constellation of distinguished men—writers, politicians, lawyers, and divines—gave tone to the whole society, brightened and elevated the general discourse of men with men, and threw over the dull routine of professional and commercial labor, the lustre of art, and the graces of a fastidious scholarship."[22]

The city's beauty and distinctive architectural character were observed and commented upon repeatedly in travelers' accounts. In the 1820s, Charleston impressed the English actress Fanny Kemble as having an air of genteel decay and eccentricity: "The city is the oldest I have yet seen in America. . . . The appearance of the city is highly picturesque, a word which can apply to none other of the American towns. . . . It is in this respect a far more aristocratic city than any I have yet seen in America, inasmuch as every house seems built to the owner's particular taste; and in one street you seem to be in an old English town, and in another in some continental city of France or Italy."[23] The New Englander Charles Eliot Norton, the translator of Dante, also drew that analogy between the South and Italy when writing from Charleston in 1855: "The climate, the southern habits, the social arrangements, all give a picturesqueness in their separate ways, and there is a fine air of age, and dusty decay which invests whole streets with the venerableness of the past.—It is like Italy in the feeling that belongs to it,—and ought to have painters and poets."[24]

In the long view of history, the new nation, as well as busy, prosperous, and cosmopolitan seaports such as Charleston, then in full flower, was in rapid transition in the early-nineteenth century. At a speed and in a manner that startled the nations from which they and their ancestors had come, Americans moved from apparent insignificance to acknowledged prominence, from shaky beginnings to solid achievements. This "empire of liberty"—of which John Adams, Thomas Jefferson, and their Charleston compatriots Henry Laurens, Ralph Izard, Arthur Middleton, and Charles Cotesworth Pinckney dreamed and spoke—was dedicated to the values of personal liberty, the security of constitutionalism, the rightness of republicanism, the virtue of private property, and above all the high destiny and glorious future of the United States. In *Redburn* (1849) Herman Melville gave this cosmopolitan belief its noblest expression when Americans were deeply divided about the meaning of their history. "We are not, a nation, so much as a world," this mystic believed. "For who was our father and our mother? Or can we point to any Romulus or Remus for our founders? Our ancestry is lost in the universal paternity, and Caesar and Alfred, St. Paul and Luther, and Homer and Shakespeare are as much ours as Washington who is as much the world's as ours. We are the heirs of all time and with all nations we divide our inheritance."[25]

NOTES

1. Leonard W. Labaree, ed., *The Papers of Benjamin Franklin* (New Haven: Yale University Press, 1966), 9:90.

2. Ashley Cooper to John Yeamans, 15 December 1671, *Collections of the South Carolina Historical Society* (Charleston: South Carolina Historical Society, 1897), 5:360–62, quoted in Kenneth Severens, *Charleston: Antebellum Architecture and Civic Destiny* (Knoxville: University of Tennessee Press, 1988), p. 3.

3. *Memoir of the Life of Josiah Quincy, Junior, of Massachusetts Bay: 1744–1775* (Boston: Little, Brown, 1875), pp. 70–71.

4. Quoted in Wendell Garrett, "Editorial," *The Magazine Antiques* 133 (January 1988), p. 231.

5. Quoted in George C. Rogers, Jr., *Charleston in the Age of the Pinckneys* (Norman: University of Oklahoma Press, 1969), p. 70.

6. Walter Edgar, *South Carolina: A History* (Columbia: University of South Carolina Press, 1998), pp. 150–53.

7. Peter A. Coclanis, *The Shadow of a Dream: Economic Life and Death in the South Carolina Low Country, 1670–1920* (New York: Oxford University Press, 1989), pp. 64–65, 112, 121.

8. Perry Miller, ed., *The American Puritans: Their Prose and Poetry* (New York: Columbia University Press, 1982), p. 79.

9. Quoted in Garrett, "Editorial," 133:231.

10. Quoted in Garrett, "Editorial," 133:231.

11. Quoted in Wendell Garrett, "Editorial," *The Magazine Antiques* 123 (May 1983), p. 1013.

12. Quoted in Garrett, "Editorial," 123:1013.

13. Rogers, *Charleston,* p. 99.

14. Quoted in Wendell Garrett, "Editorial," *The Magazine Antiques* 133 (March 1988), p. 661.

15. Quoted in Wendell Garrett, "Editorial," *The Magazine Antiques* 134 (July 1988), p. 115.

16. Edgar, *South Carolina,* pp. 285–87.

17. J. Hector St. John de Crèvecoeur, *Letters from an American Farmer,* ed. Albert E. Stone (New York: Viking Penguin, 1986), pp. 166–67.

18. Duc de la Rochefoucauld, *Travels through the United States of America* (London, 1799), 1:557, quoted in Clement Eaton, *The Growth of Southern Civilization, 1790–1860* (New York: Harper and Brothers, 1961), p. 7.

19. Eaton, *Growth of Southern Civilization,* p. 6.

20. Clinton Rossiter, *The American Quest, 1790–1860: An Emerging Nation in Search of Identity, Unity, and Modernity* (New York: Harcourt Brace Jovanovich, 1971), p. 5.

21. Michael O'Brien, *Rethinking the South: Essays in Intellectual History* (Baltimore: Johns Hopkins University Press, 1988), p. 49.

22. O'Brien, *Rethinking the South,* p. 58.

23. Jonathan H. Poston, *The Buildings of Charleston: A Guide to the City's Architecture* (Columbia: University of South Carolina Press, 1997), p. 23.

24. Quoted in O'Brien, *Rethinking the South,* p. 110.

25. Herman Melville, *Redburn, White-Jacket, Moby-Dick,* notes by G. Thomas Tanselle (New York: Library of America, 1983), p. 185.

"To Blend Pleasure with Knowledge"
The Cultural Odyssey of Charlestonians Abroad

ROBERT A. LEATH AND MAURIE D. MCINNIS

"My aim will be to blend pleasure with knowledge, miscere utile dulci, *to make as far as I can the acquaintance of distinguished men of the day, and to lay up a store of information which may assist in giving me useful and honorable occupation during the remainder of my life."[1]*

Mitchell King to Joel Roberts Poinsett, 1840

Shortly after their arrival in London in 1753, the Pinckneys of Charleston were received at Kew Palace by Augusta, the princess of Wales, with other members of the British royal family. In a letter to a Charleston friend expressing her excitement with their situation, Eliza Lucas Pinckney described in intimate detail the experience of her family dressing in their finest clothes and riding in their carriage to the palace. She was particularly interested in observing the princess and her attendants, the social arrangements and interior decoration of the palace, the intricate steps of court etiquette, and the princess's fine manners and conduct toward the Pinckneys during their private audience (fig. 3). Mrs. Pinckney wrote:

> We had the Honor not long since to carry our little girl, to present the Princess Augusta with some birds from Carolina. It was attended with great difficulty as the attendance about the Princess was extreamly causious who they admit to her presence. We mentioned our desire to see the Royal family and to have our little girl present the birds. . . . We accordingly went in full dress, and were desired to sit in a parlour where we were received by an old lady, a foreigner, till the Princess should know we were there . . . we went through 3 or 4 grand rooms of the Princess of Wales appartment till we arrived at her dressing room where we were received in a manner that surprized us, for tho' we had heard

Figure 3 Her Royal Highness Augusta, Princess of Wales, *ca. 1756, J. B. Vanloo, "Pinxt."; B. Baron, "Sculpt." Courtesy of the Colonial Williamsburg Foundation.*

how good a woman the Princess of Wales was, and how very affable and easy, her behavior exceeded every thing I had heard or could imagine. . . . This, you'll imagine must seem pretty extraordinary to an American.[2]

Eliza Lucas Pinckney, identifying herself as an American, revealed the special fascination that England held for colonial Charlestonians. She was delighted that the princess took such a special interest in the family and their lives in Charleston. The princess asked about Carolina generally, the comforts and discomforts of their voyage to England, and their opinion of the colony's royal governor, its constitution and laws. Prince William asked even more direct questions of Mr. Pinckney, about his slaves, how many children he had, where he intended to place them in school now that he was in England, and what he "designed to bring them up to." As the conversation progressed, the topics became even more personal, as Mrs. Pinckney recounted:

> She asked me many little domestick questions as did Princess Augusta among which if I suckled my children. I told her I had attempted it but my constitution would not bear it. . . . I told her we had Nurses in our houses. . . . Princess Augusta was surprized at the suckling blacks; the Princess stroak'd Harriott's cheek, said it made no alteration in the complexion. . . . She resumed her inquiries after Carolina . . . of our houses, of what they were built, our wines and from whence we had them, our manner of eating and dressing turtle, one of which she was to have for dinner next day . . . of our manufactures and concerning silk . . . to all which we answered her Royal Highness in the clearest manner we could; and when the Princess would engage Mr. Pinckney at a little distance, and she wanted to ask him a question she would call in a familiar obliging manner, Mr. Pinckney is such a thing so and so?[3]

Not all Charlestonians had such intimate encounters with European royalty, but these were the cultural exchanges that Carolinians sought during their travels abroad. Endowed with the tremendous wealth that flowed from South Carolina's economic boom during the mid-eighteenth century, Charleston's elite created a society that extolled the virtues of European culture. Even after the American Revolution, Europe remained Charleston's cultural fountainhead, perhaps more than it did for any other American city.

Through their education and travels, upper-class Charlestonians were intimately acquainted with Europe—their ancestral homeland. As the antebellum period progressed, Charleston intellectuals solidified the connections between the two worlds. They emphasized the special parallels that existed between the ancient and modern European societies and their own southern culture. Both the worlds of the English country gentry and Charleston's merchant-planter elite were based upon an agrarian economy. Both were governed by the public service of a citizen gentry within a democratic republican framework. Both cultures were founded on a hierarchical class system supported by hereditary servitude. While in Europe this servitude was based on peasant tenantry, in Charleston servitude became institutionalized in the form of racial slavery.[4]

Some of these parallels were admittedly superficial, but the European ideal became part of the process by which Charlestonians wrote their history and shaped their culture. During the seventeenth and eighteenth centuries, many Charlestonians had genuine connections to the British gentry. By the nineteenth century, however, the close cultural affinity of Charlestonians for England gave rise to the notion that, as the younger sons of British dukes and earls, virtually all of their seventeenth-century ancestors had waded ashore to America in lace-lined silks and satins. For antebellum Charlestonians, a look through the prism of Anglo-European elite culture became a defining vision.

Many Americans undertook the cultural odyssey of European travel, but there are several important distinctions that make Charlestonians a unique subset within this group. First, the number of Charlestonians with the money and leisure to dedicate to extended travel was greater, and they differed in the degree to which they identified with European society and wished to emulate European manners. Second, Charleston's elite controlled an even greater share of the local social, political, and economic power than did the upper class in other American cities; thus they had a greater impact on the general tone of their city. In fact, they celebrated their stratified society. As one Charlestonian commented: "The possession of an inferior population, and of various castes, makes us, to a certain extent, an aristocracy. Our manners are decidedly those of an aristocracy . . . we would not wish them to be, otherwise."[5] Finally, the rhythm of life in the Lowcountry lent itself to European travel, as it created languishing months during the summer when all who could afford it escaped the intense heat. As Charleston's rice planters grew increasingly rich, they employed full-time overseers to manage their plantations, making them essentially absentee landlords with time available for extensive travel. Likewise, for Lowcountry merchants, the fall was the busy season for shipping, while the summer was generally a time of leisure. This essay explores the ways in which Charlestonians encountered European culture during their travels and how this knowledge, exposure, and perception shaped their cultural identity.

Education Abroad

For most Americans, knowledge of the European world began with a classical education formed on English models and sometimes undertaken in England. Charleston enjoyed the distinction of sending more of its sons abroad to complete their education than any other American city either before or after the Revolution. After completing their preliminary studies at home, many Charlestonians were sent to finish their education at Britain's finest public schools, such as Eton and Westminster, followed by university at Oxford or Cambridge. By the 1760s, there were twice as many Charlestonians engaged in the study of law at London's Inns of Court as students from all the other colonies combined.[6] Charles Cotesworth Pinckney recalled that those in England for their schooling before the Revolution included Walter and Ralph Izard, Thomas Lynch, Paul Trapier, Edward and John Rutledge, Jacob Read, John Hume, John Moultrie, Arthur and Thomas Middleton, Thomas Heyward, Charles and William Henry Drayton, John Faucheraud Grimké, Alexander Garden, and Benjamin Stead. He added, "There may be other Carolinians who were educated in England about the time of the Revolution, that I do not at present recollect."[7]

Such an educational experience was particularly valued because it provided instruction superior to that offered in America and allowed young Charlestonians to associate with the sons of the British aristocracy. Under the rigors of a classical education, preliminary instruction in Greek and Latin was followed by an extensive reading of classical history, oratory, and mythology, followed by a steady examination of modern European history and literature. Ultimately such an education, and the social and cultural training that was an integral part of it, prepared young Charlestonians for their roles as the future governing class in Carolina. The main focus of a classical education was not simply to acquire skills or prepare for a profession, but rather to contemplate "heroical models of excellence" drawn from antiquity. A classical education was expected to create "accomplished, elegant and learned men" who were prepared to govern.[8]

The minutiae of studying William Blackstone's laws of England, and Greek and Latin grammar, however, did not always occupy the single-minded attention of these young Charlestonians during their student years abroad. Other aspects of student life sometimes came equally into play. Weighing the prospects of his own son's education, Henry Laurens complained that young William Loughton Smith of Charleston was too often seen "rambling the streets" of London.[9] Thus Laurens decided to send his son to Calvinistic Geneva instead. Similarly, a school holiday in Bath found John Rutledge dancing with "nymphs," while one of his classmates spent his time in London with "a few handsome fallen angels of the other Sex and with a few good devils of [his] own."[10] William Hasell Gibbes described a raucous evening with Thomas Pinckney and Jacob Read at Covent Garden in London, "the rendezvous for Bucks and disorderly spirits," where, after a round of late-night drinking, they kicked the waiters down the stairs and were arrested at two o'clock in the morning. Gibbes gave a lively account of their adventure: "We drew our swords, which were more for show than service, and defended ourselves heroically, but were overpowered, disarmed and taken prisoners, with broken swords, black eyes and bruises and conducted to the 'Round House.' . . . A Tavern of genteel fame, was attached to this Midnight asylum and we had a polite message from the keeper that we could be supplied with whatever refreshments we wished from Champagne . . . to humble Porter. . . . Early in the morning we were . . . conducted amidst the shouts and scoffings of Chimney sweeps . . . and other blackguards who mounted behind the Coach to Sir John Fielding, the famous City Magistrate, for examination."[11] After a brief trial, they were quickly released on their own recognizance in exchange for promises of future good behavior.

By the late eighteenth century, London was seen by many Charlestonians as offering too many temptations for young men and other European cities, especially Edinburgh and Geneva, grew in popularity as educational centers. That, combined with the development of universities in America, resulted in a decline in the numbers of Charlestonians educated in England. Although the practice of sending sons abroad was not as widespread in the antebellum period as it had been during the eighteenth century, many families continued the tradition. Charged with the responsibility of caring for his half brothers, John Ball desired to send them to Europe, because "as your Guardian and very near relation I am anxious that you should all become useful & respectable citizens." Significantly, to a Charlestonian in 1824, becoming a "useful and respectable citizen" still necessitated schooling in Europe and not in the North or at home.[12] Writing in 1828, Charleston's leading antebellum intellectual, Hugh Swinton Legaré, described the tradition and its effects: "Many, perhaps it would be more accurate to say most, of our youth of opulent families, were educated at English Schools and Universities. There can be no doubt that their attainments in polite literature were very far superior to those of their contemporaries at the North, and the standard of scholarship in Charleston, was, consequently, much higher than in any other city on the continent."[13]

The classical component of that scholarship was particularly important because it taught respect for certain principles on which the United States was founded—most especially liberty. It is curious that such close connections did not lead directly to loyalty to England during the Revolution. In fact, the opposite proved true, as the principles of classical republicanism, Whig politics, and civic virtue created many of South Carolina's most ardent Revolutionary leaders. Charles Cotesworth Pinckney proudly recalled that of the prerevolutionary students in England, "[John] Hume was the only one who joined in the British Cause."[14]

Even for women, a classical education held much greater acceptance in Charleston. In 1841, Harriott Horry Rutledge preferred the study of Latin and ancient history to playing with dolls because "it has life and spirit in it as no 'pretty smiling doll' ever did."[15] In the South, educated women were almost entirely drawn from the privileged planter and merchant classes and did not seek outside employment. Consequently, in the antebellum period, the South showed the greatest support of higher education for elite women of any region in the country, while many northern women were seen as threats because they sought higher education in order to pursue teaching as a profession.[16] For both men and women in the South, a classical education was emblematic of elevated social status.

Education was equally valued for spreading the civilized aspects of Anglo-European culture, for creating "elegant and learned men," and then bringing them home to Charleston for positions of social as well as political leadership. Placing Charleston's youths within the sphere of the British gentry allowed them to acquire the manners and mores of the British governing class, as illustrated in the portrait of Sir Matthew White Ridley and Charles Cotesworth Pinckney, painted during their years together at Christ Church College, Oxford, in the 1760s (cat. 5). The portrait illustrates the close cultural affinity that developed between British aristocrats and their Charleston counterparts, as the two men ponder the lessons and aesthetics of a classical bust in the foreground. Ridley's father was a member of the British Parliament, his uncle was a baronet, and Ridley acquired both his uncle's baronetcy and the Ridley family's property, Blagdon, after his uncle's death in 1763.[17] Similarly, at Eton, Paul Trapier formed a lasting friendship with Sir William Windham and later named one of his sons William Windham Trapier in his honor. During Trapier's visits to Felbrigg Hall, the Windham estate, he would have studied the room specially created to house the family's collection of Dutch landscapes and ancient Roman views, pictures acquired by Sir William's father during his European travels in the 1740s and 1750s[18] (fig. 4). Exposure to such trappings of European gentility provided Charlestonians with the taste and knowledge they needed to expand their own travels once they completed their education abroad.

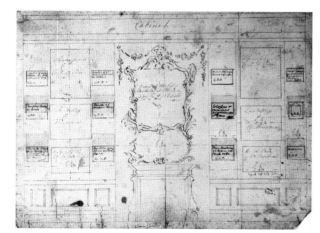

Figure 4 Design for the Cabinet at Felbrigg Hall, *ca. 1751, James Paine and William Windham. Courtesy of the National Trust of Great Britain. This drawing shows the arrangement of the Grand Tour pictures in the cabinet at Fellbrig Hall, installed in the mid-eighteenth century.*

CHARLESTONIANS AS CULTURAL TOURISTS

In 1802, South Carolina Governor John Drayton described Charlestonians as "too much prejudiced in favour of British manners, customs, and knowledge to imagine that elsewhere anything of advantage could be obtained."[19] Such a statement might not be surprising about an English colony prior to the Revolution, but Charlestonians were unique in the degree to which they adhered to English cultural precedents long after their political break with the mother country. Many had been educated there; most of their domestic luxury goods came from there; most of their agricultural products were sold there; and most looked to the English gentry for models of cultural refinement. Their private and public libraries were filled with the latest English publications and reviews; their tables set with English ceramics and silver; their sofas upholstered with English fabrics; and their amusements fashioned after English pastimes. This favor for British culture continued well into the nineteenth century, although other European traditions came increasingly into play, especially as travel and interest in the ancient world increased. Notions of European refinement became integral to the genteel life sought by Charlestonians traveling abroad and contributed to their ideals of civilized society at home in America.

Travel had its educational component, but it was most highly valued for the social refinement it provided. Knowledge of the latest manners and customs, familiarity with European landmarks, and the ability to discuss works of European art and literature became important cultural assets in upper-class Charleston society. European travel familiarized Charlestonians with European art and architecture, providing them a visual fluency that symbolized their connection to European culture. Travel to Europe required a substantial commitment of time as well as money, but as one Charlestonian noted, "it is not much more of an undertaking than going with one's family to the North, with all the advantage of novelty, intellectual improvement, of permanent advantage."[20] The opportunities for "intellectual improvement" were so compelling that another Charlestonian, Alicia Hopton Russell Middleton, writing from Paris, suggested in 1835: "I am astonished that persons who leave Charleston in the Summer do not come here instead of going to the North—it is so easy to come in May or June and return in Oct."[21] Many considered an extended European tour, often lasting as long as two to three years, an essential component to completing their education. For both men and women, it was in Europe that they could acquire the cultural refinements necessary to secure their upper-class status.

While some suggested that trips to Europe were no more complicated than traveling to the North, the reality was fraught with difficulties. In the eighteenth and nineteenth centuries the passage by ship from Charleston to Europe usually lasted at least five or six weeks. Alicia Middleton's thoughts were certainly shared by many as she described her ship as a "prison" in which she was to be "shut up" for more than a month: "the very idea is terrifying." Unfortunately, her predictions came true and her travel diary recounts the troubles they encountered with storms at sea, widespread illness, horrible food, and other uncomfortable aspects of the voyage.[22] Once on land, travel by horse-drawn carriage over rocky rural roads could be equally disagreeable. The greatest problems were encountered in the small towns where tourists were obliged to stop as they moved from one city to another. Along these routes they were often forced to stay in rustic inns that fell far short of their expectations. Ralph Izard Middleton, traveling with his mother Alicia, colorfully recounted the horrors of one of these establishments. Writing his brother from a small village in France, Middleton complained there was "nothing in the world to do but catch fleas and write letters . . . even whilst writing I am forced to hold a handkerchief to my nose so as in some measure to protect my olfactory from one of the most awful compound smells of kitchen, stable and necessary rooms. . . . Too often I am obliged to renounce even this frail barrier and employ both hands in the capture of a scoundrel flea."[23]

While this exhibition focuses on the surviving portraits and material objects that document Charleston's enthusiasm for European culture, these goods provide only part of a less tangible story. Antebellum Charlestonians were extremely well educated about European civilization, and while traveling abroad they eagerly sought to immerse themselves in social and cultural events. Attending dinners, balls, teas, musical concerts, the theater, and the opera was an important aspect of their pursuit of refinement. More than immersion, their goal was to acquire European manners. Before his first trip abroad in 1831, Nathaniel Russell Middleton received instruction from his mother on how to manage his cutlery in the European manner, how to bow instead of shaking hands while greeting, and how not to use "sir" or "m'am" in conversation as he might at home.[24] The opportunities for cultural missteps were many. As Charles Izard Manigault explained to Russell's younger brother, Izard, "the great object of us Americans was not to appear Gothic," but he comforted his younger fellow Charlestonian by advising him that he had "only to observe people and do as they did."[25]

Peter Manigault's letters home to his family in the 1750s provide perhaps the best picture of an American in Europe for the first time. The son of Charleston's richest prerevolutionary merchant, Manigault was sent to complete his education at London's Inns of Court and to explore the cultural opportunities of his years abroad. First, he learned the primary importance of fashion in order to gain admittance to the cultural endeavors he sought (fig. 5). Shortly after his arrival, Manigault and a Charleston friend, William Henry Drayton, suffered embarrassment at the hands of an usher in one of London's high-church establishments: "they wont even give one a Seat in Church, without a good suit of Clothes on, as I can witness; For one Sunday Evening, I went with Billy Drayton to hear the celebrated Mr. Foster. I was drest quite plain, my Friend had a Laced Waistcoat and hat. He, or rather his Laced Waistcoat, was introduced into a pew, while I, that is, my plain Clothes, were forced to stand up, during the whole time of divine Service, in the Isle."[26]

In Paris, Manigault was horrified at the amount of makeup worn by the Parisian ladies: "The Ladies every one of them paint to a great Degree, & tis so much the Fashion that a Lady is reckoned ridiculous without it. They don't call it Painting, but softin it into 'putting on' 'their Red.' . . . All the Concerns of Life seem to be centered in Dress; and a Man that goes abroad at all must murder the whole morning, in qualifying himself to look like a Monkey in the Afternoon."[27] By the time his portrait was painted by Allan Ramsay, however, Manigault could assure his mother that he had learned his lesson and that the silk and lace depicted in his portrait were "exactly like

Figure 5 Following the Fashion, *1794, James Gillray. Courtesy of the Library of Congress. This satirical print emphasizes the importance of fashion among European society, drawing the clear distinction between "St. James giving the ton" and "Cheapside aping the mode."*

the Ruffles I had on when I was drawn, you see my Taste in Dress by the Picture, for everything there is what I have had the Pleasure of wearing often."[28]

Properly attired, Manigault began his pursuit of refinement by enrolling in dancing lessons to prepare for the summer assemblies at Chelsea. He informed his mother that his first time dancing the minuet in public his knees had trembled "in such a Manner" that he thought he would be unable to complete the dance. He reassured her, however, "as I have a great Inclination to be a good Dancer, [I] am resolved to continue learning a few Months longer . . . in Order to compleat myself in that genteel Science." Once acclimated to the intricacies of European culture, Manigault set out voraciously to acquire it. Musical concerts and plays occupied prodigious amounts of his time. "The plays are now come in," wrote the young Manigault, "which makes London the pleasantest place in the World, and the Resort of all People of Fashion."[29]

Charlestonians often traveled together while abroad and enjoyed their cultural attainments as a group. Mary Stead Pinckney described her pleasing "little society of the boulevards" with the Middletons, the Rutledges, and the Horrys in Paris during the 1790s. Together they attended the art gallery at the Louvre, the operas and plays at the Théatre de la rue Feydeau, the porcelain factories at Sevres and Angoulême, the impressive cabinetmaking shop of Henri Jacob, the royal gardens at Versailles and Mousseau, the various milliners and dressmakers engaged in creating the latest neoclassical fashions, and all the other cultural pleasures that Parisian society had to offer.[30]

In the late eighteenth century the definition of a European trip expanded for Charlestonians. Previously they focused on extended residences in London with occasional jaunts through the British countryside to fashionable British resort towns such as Bath, or to Paris. Just before the American Revolution, however, Charlestonians began to augment their travels with ventures to southern Europe, especially Italy. In so doing they were again participating in a cultural ritual established by the eighteenth-century British aristocracy. The Grand Tour was an essential component to the proper education of an English gentleman, and it became a distinguishing mark for nineteenth-century Charlestonians as well. In Europe, the Grand Tour smoothed the rough edges of provincialism and added the luster necessary for a polished demeanor.

One of the most important aspects of the Grand Tour was developing an appreciation of the fine arts. Charlestonians prepared for their overseas travel by studying books and prints of the places they intended to visit. Ralph Izard, for example, acquired an extensive library of travel books on France, Germany, and Italy (cat. 129). Rarely did the books and prints suggest reality. "I find the buildings [here in Paris] absolutely finer in reality than in print," wrote Alicia Middleton in 1835.[31] Lewis Reeves Gibbes at first was unimpressed with Paris: "Upon first viewing the exterior of their Public Buildings, my feeling was rather that of disappointment than of admiration." He ascribed this, however, to his lack of exposure to grand buildings and great architecture. He revealed that as his exposure increased, his opinion changed: "It was not until after . . . I had more carefully studied . . . the elaborate and exquisite architecture of such buildings as The Madeleine, L'Arc de Triumphe, the colonnade and

Southern Facade of the Louvre, the curious construction of the three concentric domes of the Pantheon, the stately dome and spire of the Invalides, the imposing front of Notre-Dame, that I really felt their magnificence, a feeling which is only increased, the oftener I view them." Gibbes's comments illustrate the intangible process of cultural assimilation that transformed the mind set of Charlestonians abroad.[32]

Visiting the palaces and mansions of the European aristocracy was one of Charlestonians' most popular activities for it was in the private homes that they encountered the reality of gentry life and culture that they hoped to acquire and carry home with them. Touring the duke of Marlborough's palace at Blenheim in 1801 (fig. 6), John Blake White was struck by the picturesque landscape as he approached: "The magnificent Palace of Blenheim, embowered amidst lofty oaks—a beautiful chinese bridge, which is boldly thrown across an artificial Lake . . . across a rich & luxuriant valley, added to many other beautiful objects which catch the eye & compose indeed a most enchanting prospect." White also noted in his journal (cat. 122) that he was impressed by the monumental scale of the palace and noted the humorous epitaph of the British wit Joseph Addison for the architect, Sir John Vanbrugh—"Lay heavy on him Earth, for he has laid many a heavy load on thee." Once inside, the young Charleston artist examined every room, taking careful notes on the paintings by Peter Paul Rubens and Anthony Van Dyke, the sculptures by John Michael Rysbrack, and the architectural frescos by Louis LaGuerre.[33]

Touring Marlborough's estate in 1837, William Ravenel exclaimed, "I had no idea of a Palace until I entered this mansion." The first aspect of Blenheim that struck him was the scale, "spacious in the extreme," but he was most impressed by the scope of the duke's painting collection. It was on such visits that Charlestonians were likely introduced to the idea of collecting art. Describing his tour in a letter to his wife, he wrote, "you are then carried from room to room all of which are literally filled with magnificent paintings of every description—the sides of the rooms are covered with paintings—many of these cost immense sums—The Duke is very fond of fine pictures & music & is said to be quite a cultivated man . . . his library is spacious & beautifully arranged—& in it a beautiful statue of Queen Anne—who bestowed the title on one of this family. . . . This Palace . . . cost upwards of £500,000." Ravenel's comments reflect the importance British aristocrats placed upon learning, art, and music—the liberal attainments that served as evidence of refinement.[34] Returning home to their plantations and town houses, Charlestonians tried to recreate a similar statement of status, wealth, and refinement inspired by what they had seen when traveling—albeit on an American scale.

While abroad many Charlestonians developed their appreciation for painting and honed their skills of connoisseurship. A taste for the fine arts was an important signifier of social standing and taste, so in preparation for their travels, many studied the recommended literature on the subject. Consequently, their comments frequently reflect their absorption of the eighteenth- and nineteenth-century canons of good taste, with Old Master paintings forming the core of their commentary. Despite their homework, the travelers sometimes found themselves unprepared for the pictorial wealth they encountered. Initially they were often overwhelmed by the magnitude,

Figure 6 View of Blenheim Park, *1752, J. Boydell, "Delin & Sculp." Courtesy of Colonial Williamsburg Foundation.*

Figure 7 View of the Grand Gallery, Louvre, *1796, Hubert Robert. Courtesy of the Musée du Louvre, Paris. This painting shows the Grand Gallery of the Louvre in 1796, three years after it was opened to the public by the revolutionary government. The gallery is crowded with both tourists and artists copying the Old Masters.*

often citing the limitations of an "untutored eye." In France after an 1835 visit to the picture gallery, Alicia Middleton commented in her journal, "I found looking at so many confusing & came away without a clear recollection of more than three or four." By the time she had reached Italy, however, Alicia wrote self-assuredly of her opinions on the major works of art she observed, although as a devout Episcopalian, she continued to find works with nudity somewhat embarrassing. Alicia wrote, "We go to the different galleries, look at beautiful pictures and statues which would have horrified us at home," later commenting, "I am just beginning to see some beauty in statuary in spite of naked truth."[35] As their exposure increased and they felt themselves at ease with the magnitude of European collections, they found their earlier unease transformed into exuberance. Henry Middleton compared his visit to the Louvre (fig. 6) to a religious epiphany: "I confess I was completely lost in admiration. I felt as if that moment was the commencement of a new 'Sight'—what the religionists call a revival. It seemed as if a new sense of enjoyment has been suddenly developed and one worth all the rest. . . . I was all 'eye' and took in 'sights' that might create a soul."[36] Thus Henry Middleton and other Charlestonians who traveled to Europe found their aesthetic senses transfigured by their encounter with European art and architecture. It was a transformation that could occur only in front of the art works themselves. As Mary Stead Pinckney explained to a friend still in Charleston, "They must be seen. How can any written account convey to you an idea . . . the grace and beauty of the heads of Guido."[37] It was this transformation, this "commencement of a new 'Sight,'" that was the final goal of their cultural odyssey.

In Italy, Charlestonians encountered the remains of ancient civilizations that resonated with their classical learning. The archeological discoveries in 1748 of the cities of Herculaneum and Pompeii, both buried by the eruption of Mount Vesuvius in A.D. 79, added Naples to the already popular destinations of Venice, Florence, and Rome. In 1775, Ralph and Alice DeLancey Izard of Charleston were among the first Americans to visit the classical sites near Naples. Excavations of Pompeii and Herculaneum excited modern imaginations, and rediscovered artifacts greatly expanded eighteenth-century knowledge of the ancient world. The Izards were obviously impressed by these insights into the ancient world. Izard wrote, "We have received great pleasure from our tour. . . . I have met with nothing that seems so extraordinary to me as the neighborhood of this place. . . . The beautiful pieces of antiquity . . . that have been found in them, surpasses all imagination."[38] His enthusiasm for the ancient world is clearly expressed by the painting he commissioned from John Singleton Copley (cat. 12). On one level the painting serves as an emblematic expression of the benefits of a Grand Tour. Seated at a highly polished porphyry table, the Izards are surrounded by glories of European civilization. The Roman Colosseum, perhaps the most famous symbol of ancient Rome, sits in the background. Beside them is a Greek vase and an ancient sculptural group. Thus the painting communicates the learning, erudition, and connoisseurship of the Izards and unambiguously sets them apart as distinguished Americans on the Grand Tour. The Izards' deep interest in the classical world is evidenced by their decision to extend their journey to the Greek city of Paestum in southern Italy. Copley also joined the Izards in touring Paestum. He wrote, "This place I am glad to have seen, though I should not have extended my Tour so far, had not Mr. Izard invited me to accompany him their [*sic*] from Naples."[39] Paestum was onsidered a "desolate, malaria-ridden area," too "out of the way" for most travelers, but of great interest to serious antiquarians.[40]

In the nineteenth century, the region around Naples grew in popularity as a tourist destination. In addition to viewing the ruins of Pompeii, travelers were drawn to the beauty of the Bay of Naples and the sublime qualities of the volcano, Mount Vesuvius. According to Alicia Middleton, this was the only part of Italy that "exceeded my expectations."[41] In 1830 Charles Izard Manigault stood at the summit of Vesuvius and commemorated his enthusiasm by purchasing a series of gouaches of the area, including one of Mount Vesuvius erupting (cat. 58). Manigault was no stranger to travel for he went to Europe five times with his family between 1828 and 1855.[42] The trip in 1830 appears to be the first one that carried him to Naples, where the excavated sculptures and artifacts from Herculaneum and Pompeii were displayed. Unlike many of the collections in Rome and Florence, most of the works in Naples remained relatively unknown even in the first half of the nineteenth century, and those Charlestonians who traveled there were able to speak authoritatively of the recently excavated Roman art, thus acquiring a further badge of distinction.

Florence and Rome were also popular destinations for Charleston travelers. Both cities possessed significant collections of Old Master paintings and ancient art, especially at the Musei Vaticani and Musei Capitolini in Rome and the Tribuna in Florence. An additional attraction of Florence in the mid-nineteenth century was that Charlestonian Francis Kinloch resided there. In 1831 this aspiring artist and connoisseur moved to Florence where he studied sculpture with Horatio Greenough. Kinloch often acted as guide and companion to visiting friends from Charleston. Ann Middleton commented that he had been "exceedingly kind and attentive," and Alicia Middleton remarked that he was "unwearied in his kindly attentions." These attentions included escorting the Middletons to the many galleries and museums in town where they especially appreciated his knowledge and familiarity with the history of art.[43]

In Rome Charlestonians could learn most about ancient art and architecture. The list of Roman monuments popular in the eighteenth and nineteenth centuries is not greatly changed today. Leading the list were the Pantheon, the Colosseum, and the Roman Forum (then known as the Campo Vaccino). Many Charlestonians purchased souvenir works of art—paintings, watercolors, prints, and micromosaics—that served as visual reminders of their visit to the Eternal City. Their travels also extended to the Roman Campagna including Tivoli where Hadrian's villa was located. Ralph Izard Middleton described their visit: "We were conducted all over the ruins and to the different temples . . . and were also shown where some celebrated statues and mosaics had been taken from, of which the dying gladiator and Plinys doves are two that I remember for a wonder they are both in good preservation in the Capitol. Some of the frescoes in one of the temples are very well preserved . . . and when we were coming away, we all came to the conclusion that Hadrian must have been a man of great taste."[44] Charlestonians, like their British contemporaries, sought those Grand Tour experiences that would make them, likewise, men and women "of great taste."

Figure 8 Tribuna degli Uffizi, *1772, Johann Zoffany. Courtesy of the Royal Collection of Her Majesty Queen Elizabeth II. This painting shows the Uffizi thronged with connoisseurs and young men on the Grand Tour, many gathered around the* Venus de' Medici.

Italy was the most obvious and important destination for Charlestonians who wished to hone their connoisseurship skills. Perhaps most suggestive of the emotive power of studying works of art in person is Charles Izard Manigault's assessment of the Neapolitan sculpture collection: "It is while viewing such specimens of the arts as these that we are gradually led on to admire what at first appears to us a cold & innanimate art & end in coinciding in the conviction that marble can be made almost 'to speak.'"[45] In his writing on other sculptures in Naples, Manigault revealed his familiarity with the opinions of English tastemakers and the leading authorities, but he was confident enough in his own opinions to disagree. Firsthand experience of the masterpieces of European art distinguished Charleston's elite from most other nineteenth-century Americans.

Their concern with matters of taste and their skills in connoisseurship led to extensive discussions of the most famous works of art, such as *Venus de' Medici* (fig. 8). The date of its discovery is unknown, but after installation in the Tribuna in Florence in the late seventeenth century, its fame continued to grow. By the eighteenth century, the Medici sculpture was revered as the most beautiful Venus and one of the half-dozen finest antique statues to have survived. By the nineteenth century, however, modish travelers were inclined to discount something that previously had been so ardently worshiped. Increasingly, alterations to the arms and head were questioned. Charlestonians Ralph Izard Middleton and Charles Izard Manigault were confident enough in their own connoisseurship, however, to go against prevailing opinion. For Middleton, the changes to the arms and head were not sufficient to detract from the sublime beauty of the statue. In 1835 he wrote of the "loveliness of her charms," and while acknowledging that the arms were certainly replaced and maybe even the head, he still pronounced her "the finest statue existing."[46] Manigault was even more exultant in his praise, ignoring contemporary criticism: "the Venus de Medici is an undisguised display of all that is beautiful in the human form . . . [with] an unconscious air of any improper thought connected with this full display of all that is admirable & enchanting in the female form."[47]

By the mid-nineteenth century, elite Charlestonians such as Ralph Izard Middleton and Charles Izard Manigault had developed their affinity for European culture on many different levels: first through their studies of language, art, and literature, and later through their extensive travels. In Europe, Charlestonians learned the language of refinement, how to talk and dress like aristocrats, how to think like connoisseurs and cognoscenti, and how to pepper their conversation with the artistic and literary allusions that separated them from the common man. By 1834 an English visitor to Charleston observed: "the Planters formed a kind of landed aristocracy, who associated chiefly among themselves & considered merchandize as belonging to a rank decidedly below their own. . . . In many respects they were entitled to these claims of superiority, their estates were hereditary & themselves the descendants of the original settlers, they were generally wealthy & had received excellent educations & in the cultivation of the mind & manners decidedly took the lead."[48]

Thus assimilating European customs, habits, and taste, Charlestonians returned with an enhanced identification with Europe and the ancient world. Their travels had transformed their ideas about scale and grandeur and expanded their appreciation for art and architecture. Education and travel provided Charleston's upper class the link to European aristocracy and the intellectual framework that made antebellum Charleston a unique place in the realm of American material culture.

Notes

1. Mitchell King to Joel Roberts Poinsett, 21 May 1840, Henry D. Gilpin Papers, Joel Roberts Poinsett Section, HSP.

2. Harriott Horry Rutledge Ravenel, *Eliza Lucas Pinckney* (New York: Charles Scribner's Sons, 1928), pp. 144–49.

3. Ravenel, *Eliza Lucas Pinckney,* pp. 149–53.

4. Slavery in the British West Indies was abolished in 1833.

5. "Domestic Improvement," *Southern Literary Journal* 3, no. 1 (January 1838): 2–3.

6. George C. Rogers, Jr., *Charleston in the Age of the Pinckneys* (Norman: University of Oklahoma, 1969), p. 99.

7. Charles Cotesworth Pinckney, letter, 8 September 1819, Pinckney Papers, LC.

8. Hugh Swinton Legaré, "Classical Learning," *Southern Review* 1 (February 1828): 18, 35.

9. Henry Laurens to Rev. Richard Clarke, 6 April 1771, Henry Laurens letterbook, 1767–71, SCHS.

10. John Brown Cutting to John Rutledge, 4 February 1787, John Rutledge Papers, SHC-UNC.

11. "William Hasell Gibbes' Story of His Life," Arney R. Childs, ed., *SCHM* 50 (1949): 61.

12. John Ball, Jr., to Hugh Swinton Ball, Comingtee, S.C., 5 January 1824, John Ball, Jr. and Sr., Papers, Duke University.

13. Legaré, "Classical Learning," p. 3.

14. Pinckney, letter.

15. Harriott Horry Rutledge to Mrs. Edward C. Rutledge, 17 September 1841, Harriott Horry Rutledge Papers, Duke University, quoted in Jane H. Pease and William H. Pease, *Ladies, Women and Wenches: Choice and Constraint in Antebellum Charleston and Boston* (Chapel Hill: University of North Carolina Press, 1990), p. 77.

16. Christie Anne Farnham, *The Southern Education of the Southern Belle: Higher Education and Student Socialization in the Antebellum South* (New York: New York University Press, 1994), pp. 2–5, 31–32.

17. *Debrett's Peerage and Baronetage with her Majesty's Warrant Holders,* 1976 ed., pp. 963–64.

18. Paul Trapier, "Notices of Ancestors and Relatives, Paternal and Maternal," *Transactions of the Huguenot Society of South Carolina* 58 (1953): 33.

19. John Drayton, *A View of South-Carolina* (Charleston: W. P. Young, 1802), p. 217.

20. Charles Izard Manigault to O[liver] H[ering] Middleton, Paris, 10 November 1828, Manigault Family Papers, SCL.

21. Alicia Hopton Russell Middleton to Eweretta Barnewall Middleton, Paris, 25 July 1836, Cheves-Middleton Papers, SCHS.

22. Alicia Hopton Russell Middleton, travel journal, 10 May 1835, p. 3, Middleton Family Papers, SCL.

23. Ralph Izard Middleton to Nathaniel Russell Middleton, Roanne, France, 28 March 1836, Middleton Family Papers, SCHS.

24. Alicia Hopton Russell Middleton to Nathaniel Russell Middleton, 1 July 1831, Middleton Family Papers, SCL.

25. Ralph Izard Middleton to Nathaniel Russell Middleton, Paris, 4 July 1835, Middleton Family Papers, SCHS.

26. Peter Manigault to Gabriel Manigault, London, 20 February 1750, quoted in "Peter Manigault's Letters," Mabel L. Webber, ed., *SCHM* 32 (April 1931): 121–22.

27. Peter Manigault to Ann Ashby Manigault, 15 March 1753, Paris, in *SCHM* 32 (April 1931): 121–22.

28. Peter Manigault to Gabriel Manigault, London, 15 April 1751, in "Peter Manigault's Letters," Mabel L. Webber, ed., *SCHM* 31 (October 1930): 277–78.

29. Peter Manigault to Ann Ashby Manigault, 1 November 1750, London, in "Peter Manigault's Letters," Mabel L. Webber, ed., *SCHM* 31 (July 1930), pp. 181–82.

30. *Letter-book of Mary Stead Pinckney, November 14th, 1796, to August 29th, 1797,* ed. Charles F. McCombs (New York: Grolier Club, 1946), pp. 21–59.

31. Alicia Hopton Russell Middleton to Nathaniel Russell Middleton, Paris, 24 July 1835, Middleton Family Papers, SCHS.

32. Lewis Reeves Gibbes to Henrietta A. Drayton, 8 May 1837, Gibbes-Gilchrist Papers, SCHS.

33. John Blake White, travel journal, 1800–1802, SCHS, pp. 22–24. See cat. 122.

34. William Ravenel to Eliza Butler Pringle Ravenel, Liverpool, 30 July 1837, William Ravenel Papers, SCHS.

35. Alicia Hopton Russell Middleton to Nathaniel Russell Middleton, Florence, 26 December 1835, Middleton Family Papers, SCHS. See cat. 135 for an example of an art handbook.

36. Henry Middleton, Jr., to Eliza Middleton, Paris, August 1835, Cadwalader Collection, HSP.

37. Mary Stead Pinckney to Margaret Izard Manigault, 5 October 1797, Manigault Papers, SCL.

38. Ralph Izard to George Dempster, Naples, 21 January 1775, quoted in Anne Izard Deas, ed., *Correspondence of Mr. Ralph Izard of South Carolina* (New York: Charles Francis, 1844), pp. 42–43.

39. John Singleton Copley to his mother, Parma, 25 June 1775, quoted in *Letters & Papers of John Singleton Copley and Henry Pelham, 1739–1776,* ed. Guernsey Jones (1914; reprint, New York: De Capo Press, 1970), p. 330.

40. Meyer Reinhold, *Classica Americana: The Greek and Roman Heritage in the United States* (Detroit: Wayne State University Press, 1984), p. 266. Reinholds's discussion of "American Visitors to Pompeii, Herculaneum, and Paestum" lists only four visitors to Herculaneum and Pompeii and only one to Paestum after the Izards and before 1815.

41. Alicia Hopton Russell Middleton to Nathaniel Russell Middleton, Naples, 26 February 1836, Middleton Family Papers, SCHS.

42. Charles Izard Manigault, "Reminiscences," Manigault Family Papers, SHC-UNC.

43. Ann Manigault Middleton to Nathaniel Russell Middleton, Florence, 7 November 1835, and Alicia Hopton Russell Middleton to Nathaniel Russell Middleton, Florence, 26 December 1835, Middleton Family Papers, SCHS.

44. Ralph Izard Middleton to Nathaniel Russell Middleton, Rome, 28 April 1836, Middleton Family Papers, SCHS. Hadrian's villa was another of the rediscovered sites of the ancient world that excited the nineteenth-century mind.

45. Charles Izard Manigault, travel journal, Florence, 7 November 1829, CLS.

46. Francis Haskell and Nicholas Penny, *Taste and the Antique: The Lure of Classical Sculpture, 1500–1900* (New Haven: Yale University Press, 1981), pp. 325–28; Ralph Izard Middleton to Nathaniel Russell Middleton, Florence, ca. 1835, Middleton Family Papers, SCHS. For the complete quotation see cat. 76.

47. Charles Izard Manigault, travel journal, Florence, 7 November 1829, CLS. For the complete quotation see cat. 76.

48. G. F. Fox, diary, Microfilm from England Series, Duke University.

Reflections of Refinement
Portraits of Charlestonians at Home and Abroad

ANGELA D. MACK AND J. THOMAS SAVAGE

*T*he portraiture commissioned by traveling eighteenth-century Charlestonians represents an extraordinary chapter in the history of American art patronage. Too often appearing as scattered and buried footnotes in the histories of both American and British painting, portraits commissioned abroad by American patrons have often been viewed as exceptions to the rule rather than part of the cultural landscape of American art. Since the early-nineteenth century, strong nationalistic tendencies toward the study of American art have "separated American artists and their patrons from their European counterparts."[1]

In the coastal South, however, and particularly in Charleston, divisions based on the nationality of artist or sitter are inappropriate. European-commissioned portraits of Charlestonians, when blended into the established context of native art from this region, enlighten rather than confuse an understanding of taste and patronage in the richest urban center in colonial America. It is only by crisscrossing the Atlantic as our forefathers did during the formation of this country that we can understand the contributions of Charleston's patrons to the history of art in this region and to the field of portrait painting before the Civil War.[2] The history that emerges is somewhat at odds with the textbook version of American art, but no less significant.

Throughout the period under discussion, nowhere in America was a predilection for European artistic values more evident than in Charleston. This was most evident in portraiture, the prevailing genre valued in art patronage. The faces of Charlestonians painted by the great names of British portraiture—Johann Zoffany, Allan Ramsay, Joshua Reynolds, George Romney, and Thomas Gainsborough—as well as portraits from the European periods of both Benjamin West and John Singleton Copley, graced the drawing rooms of local dwellings.

These paintings were very much at home in Charleston's grand houses whose interiors were richly furnished with imported decorations including English furniture and silver, as well as expensive British and French porcelain and textiles. This predilection for luxuries from abroad was a natural outgrowth of the business dealings of many successful colonial entrepreneurs in Charleston. Having made their fortunes through agriculture and commerce during the first half of the eighteenth century, these wealthy individuals began to think in terms of social advancement and refinement. The lifestyle and trappings of the English aristocracy and landed gentry served as their models in forming and consolidating what would become a Carolina aristocracy.[3] Central to the concept of an aristocracy were symbols and trappings of permanence: extensive land holdings, an imposing town and/or country house, and possessions that spoke to the taste, wealth, and intended or real stability of the established social order they represented. By the eighteenth century, portraits in England were seen as emblematic of family pride and status. In their visits to the great country houses of Britain, traveling Carolinians were party to the endemic British cult of ancestor worship, tangibly expressed in the long galleries and state rooms with a hierarchical display of relations and connections in portraiture that began to proliferate during the Tudor period. In emulating the English passion for portraiture, Charlestonians were not merely recording their visages, but also acquiring for themselves and their progeny visible signs of rank and grandeur with which to adorn their own seats.

While much is made of the stratification of the British class system, it must be remembered that the eighteenth century saw a new freedom with which persons of varying social ranks mixed in the coffee houses, clubs, pleasure gardens, and spa resorts of England. Here the grand and the good, the titled and the aspirant, and, as Daniel Defoe called them, "the middle sort, who live well" mixed as near equals. In this milieu, Charleston travelers were active participants in the social and cultural life of their temporary homes abroad, as evidenced by Peter Manigault's 1750 presence at the Knights of the Garter installation, Windsor; the 1753 visit of the Charles Pinckneys to Augusta, princess of Wales, at Kew Palace; and Alice DeLancey Izard's presentation at court in the early 1770s.

The relative ease with which Charlestonians maneuvered in society abroad is supported by the variety of portrait types commissioned from an equally diverse selection of British painters. The eighteenth century saw the expansion and consolidation of a range of genres formerly limited by patterns of patronage, which left artists dependent upon a few families or individuals for commissions. By the second quarter of the eighteenth century, new patrons included bankers, lawyers, clergymen, physicians, artists, musicians, and newly established town and country gentry. They increased the demand for portraits as well as landscapes, house and garden prospects and topographical views, fancy pictures, and history paintings. Charlestonians might have satisfied their pursuit of refinement in portraiture by limiting their choice to an easily transportable, bust-length souvenir canvas by a known painter. Instead, the body of commissions included diversity in portrait types, such as masterfully executed conversation pieces with multiple figures by Benjamin West and John Singleton Copley and full-length, life-size depictions by George Romney.

Among the earliest surviving portraits of Charlestonians abroad are those of members of the Crokatt, Smith, and Manigault families dating from the late 1740s.

These families not only serve as examples of the rise of aristocratic Anglo-American clans, but they epitomize the close connections that commonly existed, both socially and professionally, between Charleston and England at this early point in American history. These connections ultimately affected patronage choices that their descendants tried to emulate and surpass. Like many ambitious Charlestonians living during the first half of the eighteenth century, James Crokatt, the son of a Scottish immigrant, made his fortune in trade (cat. 1). A principal merchant in the Carolina Indian trade with connections in the West Indies and London, he apprenticed Benjamin Smith (1717–70) around 1735, providing him with the opportunity to learn the business. Benjamin Smith and his brother Thomas embraced commerce as a means to enhance their inherited fortunes, which were made by previous generations through agriculture.[4]

James Crokatt's successes in Charleston allowed him to become established as a merchant in London by 1738, where he also functioned as Smith's agent. By the late 1740s, Crokatt had amassed such wealth as to purchase Luxborough Hall near Chigwell in Essex.[5] By acquiring Luxborough Hall, Crokatt entered the world of the English landed gentry, which for some colonials was the ultimate attainment. Crokatt's new social status is captured in the conversation piece by Thomas Gainsborough portraying his son Charles, who was born in Charleston in 1730, his future son-in-law Peter Muilman, and an artist friend William Keable (cat. 1). Shortly after the Gainsborough portrait was painted and possibly at the behest of James Crokatt, William Keable painted at least two members of the Smith family who arrived in England in April 1749: Thomas (cat. 3) and his sister-in-law Mrs. Benjamin Smith (cat. 2), the wife of Crokatt's Charleston business associate.[6]

James Crokatt may have also suggested Keable to Peter Manigault (1731–73), another Charlestonian abroad. In a letter to his mother written four months after visiting with the Crokatts at Luxborough Hall,[7] Manigault makes clear his intention to patronize the noted artist Allan Ramsay instead of Keable. His reasons were clearly stated:

> And now a few Words concerning my Picture, which comes by this Opportunity. Tis done by one of the best Hands in England, and is accounted by all Judges here, not only an Exceeding good Likeness, but a very good Piece of Painting: The Drapery is all taken from my own Clothes, & the very Flowers in the Lace, upon the Hat, are taken from a Hat of my own; I desire Mr. Theus may see it, as soon as is convenient after it arrives. I was advised to have it drawn by one Keble, that drew Tom Smith, & several others that went over to Carolina, but upon seeing his Paintings, I found that though his Likenesses, (which is the easiest Part in doing a Picture,) were some of them very good, yet his Paint seemed to be laid on with a Trowel, and looked more like Plaistering than Painting, you may guess at the Difference between Ramsay, & Keble Painting, by the Difference of their Prices, What Ramsay demanded Four & Twenty Guineas for, T'other humbly hopes, you'll allow him Seven.[8]

Unfortunately, Manigault's portrait by Ramsay is known only through an early, undated photograph in the Gibbes Museum of Art archives (fig. 9). However, this

Figure 9 Peter Manigault, *1751, Allan Ramsay. Currently unlocated.*

Figure 10 Thomas Lamb of Rye, *1753, Allan Ramsay. Oil on canvas. Courtesy of the National Gallery of Scotland, Edinburgh.*

Figure 11 Elizabeth Wragg Manigault, *1757, Jeremiah Theus. Oil on canvas. Courtesy of The Charleston Museum.*

descriptive passage clearly indicates that Manigault's selection of Ramsay over Keable is based on firsthand knowledge of both artists. Undeterred by the far greater expense, which he felt worthy of note, and having formed a personal judgment of their comparative abilities, Manigault opted for the more celebrated artist who later achieved the exalted status of portrait painter to the king.[9] He invested well since few works by Keable are known to exist. It is likely that Manigault sought out or was directed to Ramsay by one of his London acquaintances. By 1751, Ramsay had been well established in the capital city for years and enjoyed considerable patronage from ducal as well as lesser households. Visiting Ramsay's studio in that same year, critic George Vertue pronounced his portraits "much superior in merit" to those by his contemporaries.[10]

The disappearance of the Manigault portrait is a significant loss not only for the history of South Carolina patronage but also for a reassessment of the development of Ramsay's French style, usually cited as commencing in 1753 with the portrait of *Thomas Lamb of Rye* (fig. 10). Alastair Smart in the catalogue of the landmark 1992 Ramsay exhibition, writes that the Lamb portrait "marks a significant stage in Ramsay's development of a type of three-quarter-length male portrait in which the sitter is represented in an attitude expressive at once of elegance and of a sort of non-chalant ease."[11] Clearly two years earlier, the pose and composition in the Manigault portrait are nearly identical to the later Lamb commission. They mark Ramsay's rejection of Italianate baroque conventions in favor of the French rococo style he adopted under the influence of William Hogarth and the French pastellist Maurice Quentin de La Tour.

In his letter to his mother, Manigault requested that the Ramsay painting be shown to artist Jeremiah Theus, thus alluding to the vital interchange that occurred between imported works of art and Charleston's resident artists. Referring to both the Keable portraits of the Smiths and his own by Ramsay, Manigault wrote: "As Theus will have an Opportunity of seeing both, I'll be extremely obliged to you, if you'll let me know his Judgment; you'll also tell me if you think any Part of it to[o] gay, the Ruffles are done charmingly, and exactly like the Ruffles I had on when I was drawn, you see my Taste in Dress by the Picture, for everything there, is what I have had the Pleasure of wearing often."[12]

Working as a portraitist in the vicinity of Charleston his entire life, Jeremiah Theus (1716–74) immigrated to America in 1735, settling with members of his family in Orangeburg Township. By 1740, he was advertising himself in the *South-Carolina Gazette* as a limner willing to decorate coaches and chaises and later offered to teach drawing. With little competition Theus enjoyed considerable success. Manigault's request that Theus provide a comparative assessment between the Smith portraits by Keable and his own portrait by Ramsay indicates that Theus's opinion was highly regarded. Manigault commissioned Theus to create a pendant portrait for the Ramsay painting in 1755 (fig. 11). One of the most ambitious of his career, the portrait of Elizabeth Wragg (1736–72), daughter of Joseph Wragg and Judith Du Bose, was painted to celebrate her marriage to Peter, after his return from England in December 1754.[13] The same size as Ramsay's portrait of her husband, it is one of only three large-scale (fifty-by-forty–inch) paintings known to have been painted by Theus.[14]

While little is known about Theus's training, his familiarity with contemporary British portraiture was acquired primarily through imported engravings and mezzotints from which he borrowed compositions freely, as did most colonial American limners. However, unlike other native portraitists of this period, he had the opportunity to see original works by European masters and was called upon to respond to at least one. Therefore, one might assume that in the case of the portrait of Elizabeth Wragg Manigault, Theus saw an opportunity to test his skills against the famed court painter Ramsay. The commission must have drawn every ounce of rococo excess from the brush of the provincial painter. While there is no documentation that the Manigaults were any less pleased with the Theus portrait when hung next to the Ramsay, Peter Manigault and Theus himself would have known that the latter was no artistic threat to the London master from Edinburgh. Theus may also have been called upon to match his skills against those of Keable. A portrait of Benjamin Smith in the collection at the Gibbes is attributed to Theus and has long been thought to be a copy after one by Keable (cat. 2). Smith is known to have been in England as early as 1752 and may well have had his portrait painted along with that of his wife and brother.[15]

Smith's half brother-in-law and future business partner, Miles Brewton, traveled to England and had his portrait painted by Joshua Reynolds in 1756 (cat. 4). While circumstances surrounding the commission are unknown, the sitter was only twenty-five years of age when he sat for the portrait, and therefore may have been completing his education. Reynolds returned to London in 1752 after completing his studies in Italy. His subsequent rise to fame as a portrait painter is well documented. As the first president of the Royal Academy, founded in 1769, he exerted great influence through his annual "Discourses on Art," and is considered the most successful British painter of the eighteenth century. The portrait of Miles Brewton is representative of Reynolds's standard bust-length images of the 1750s, what Ellis Waterhouse called "rather dull single heads" among the wealth of Reynolds's innovations that revolutionized taste in portraiture in mid-eighteenth-century Britain.[16] The Brewton portrait shares many stylistic similarities with the portrait of another colonist, Charles Carroll of Carrollton, painted seven years later (fig. 12). In both paintings Reynolds uses strong shadows and cool tonalities characteristic of his work at the time. In the portrait of Carroll, however, the sharp light and dark contrasts evoke a sense of spontaneity and movement achieved by more traditional means in the Brewton portrait by the use of a swirl of drapery that recalls the portraits of Godfrey Kneller (1646–1723). As with many of Reynolds's works, the red pigments that he used have faded, creating a paler face than was probably intended originally.

One of the most significant Carolina patrons of British artists was Ralph Izard (fig. 13), who had his portrait painted by Johann Zoffany (1733–1810) soon after completing his education at Cambridge in 1763.[17] The painting, which is unlocated and known only through a photograph, is typical of Zoffany's small-scale, full-length portraits. It depicts Ralph Izard "in the dress of a gentleman commoner of Trinity College, Cambridge," seated near the base of a tree holding an open book in one hand and handkerchief in the other. A tricorn hat is casually placed to one side, and "his favorite poodle" sits near his feet.[18] From a prominent and wealthy family, Ralph Izard was the fourth of his line in America. The founder Ralph Izard (son of Ralph

Figure 12 Charles Carroll of Carollton, 1763, Joshua Reynolds. Oil on canvas. Courtesy of the Yale Center for British Art.

Figure 13 Ralph Izard, Johann Zoffany before 1765. Currently unlocated.

Izard of London with lands in the counties of Middlesex and Surrey) was educated in England and came to Charleston in 1682. Through marriage, grants, and purchase, the family increased its wealth and landholdings throughout the Lowcountry. Ralph Izard's parents, Henry Izard (1717–48/9) and Margaret Johnson (1722–43), died when he was relatively young.[19] Thus orphaned, he was sent to England by his guardians at the age of twelve. A portrait of Ralph as a boy attributed to Jeremiah Theus is in a private collection.[20]

Born near Frankfurt, Zoffany traveled in Italy extensively before settling in London in 1760. The son of an important cabinetmaker and architect, he was trained in Germany as a rococo history painter. His experiences in Rome (1750–57) probably made him aware of career opportunities in England. Zoffany painted Izard's portrait just prior to attracting the patronage of the royal family for whom he produced a series of intimate, informal family portraits. Masterful groupings and a careful attention to detail characterize Zoffany's work throughout his career. His paintings provide a visual record of both domestic and social activities among the upper classes of eighteenth-century England.[21]

A few months after the Zoffany portrait was painted, Ralph Izard sat for another artist—this time the American Benjamin West, who had arrived in England in August of 1763 from his recent travels and studies in Italy. Izard commissioned the second of two versions of a conversation piece known today as *The Cricketers* (cat. 6). The original was probably painted for Chief Justice William Allen of Pennsylvania, the wealthiest man in that colony and an early patron of West, who was in England at the time the portraits were commissioned.[22] The painting depicts the full-length figures of Allen's two sons, James and Andrew, with three young friends in an outdoor setting with cricket bats positioned in the foreground. Izard is traditionally identified as the gentleman standing in profile near the center of the painting in a red coat and wearing a tricorn hat similar to the one in the Zoffany portrait. Again, his favorite poodle is depicted near his feet. The original group portrait is neither signed nor dated; however, Izard's version was signed and dated by the artist, a fact that may indicate his desire to chronicle the event. It may also have been of some importance to the artist since both versions represent West's early attempts at the conversation piece which was a distinctly English genre popular in the eighteenth century.

West's progression from rural Pennsylvania to the court of George III and presidency of the Royal Academy is a well-documented success story. From his first royal commission in 1769, his position at court brought him wealth, power, and opportunities granted to no other artist. He had not only established himself as the most advanced proponent of the neoclassical style, but also as the foremost history painter in England. At this time in his career, the Middleton family of Charleston became serious patrons.

With the exception of a few Philadelphians, the Middletons were the only other Americans West painted during his first decade of royal patronage, having no less than four major portraits executed while they either lived or traveled abroad.[23] Like many wealthy Charlestonians, the Middletons were comfortable on both sides of the Atlantic. William Middleton (1710–75), who is suggested to be the subject of one of the West portraits (Middleton Place Foundation), was born in South Carolina and inherited estates in both England and America.[24] In 1754, he moved to England where he resided for the rest of his life. His son Thomas Middleton (1753–79), who is thought to be the subject of another West portrait (see cat. 7, fig. 70), grew up in England but returned to South Carolina in 1774 to reside at the family estate, Crowfield, where he died.[25] William Middleton's younger brother Henry Middleton (1717–84) remained in America and served briefly as president of the Continental Congress. Through marriage he acquired Middleton Place in 1741, to which he added two wings to the existing three-story house and elaborately terraced gardens. He built one wing as an art gallery and library.[26]

Henry Middleton's son Arthur Middleton inherited Middleton Place from his mother in the 1760s. He received his education at Cambridge and the Middle Temple in London and is probably depicted, along with Ralph Izard, in West's *The Cricketers*. He returned to Europe and traveled extensively with his new wife, Mary Izard Middleton, between 1768 and 1771. Their son Henry was born in England on 28 September 1770. Shortly thereafter, West must have started the large family portrait that depicts Henry as an infant and was completed in 1772 after the Middletons returned to Charleston (cat. 8). Among all the Middleton portraits by West, this painting displays the most obvious references to Italian Renaissance masters, references that may have found equal support from Arthur Middleton himself who had just arrived in England with his family after their own travels to Italy. Upon its arrival in Charleston the portrait, which is sometimes referred to as "The Holy Family," probably hung in the art gallery of Middleton Place built by Arthur's father.

Another distinctive aspect of West's work for the Middletons is his use of "Vandyke" dress, the modish masquerade costume popular in England for dress balls and summer masquerades in the pleasure gardens of Vauxhall and Ranelagh. Attending a masquerade at Vauxhall Gardens in 1742, Horace Walpole noted "quantities of pretty Vandykes and all kinds of pictures walked out of their frames."[27] Whether or not the Middletons were fond of such diversions is not known. However, the Middleton portraits by West represent their fascination with the costume. Peter Manigault, by contrast, was not fascinated. To his mother Ann Manigault in Charleston, he wrote from London in November 1750, "The plays are now come in, which makes London the pleasantest place in the World, and the Resort of all People of Fashion, the Plays, I must confess are the only Diversions I like as, for Vaux Hall & Renelagh, they never took my fancy."[28]

The portrait of Arthur Middleton and family and possibly other Middleton portraits by West may have paved the way for the Charleston career of American artist Henry Benbridge (1743–1812), who like West was born in Pennsylvania and traveled to Italy to further his artistic career. However, unlike West, Benbridge returned to America in 1770, and by 1772 he had established himself in Charleston as successor to the aging Jeremiah Theus. Soon Benbridge began executing portraits in a manner that demonstrated his Italian training. Armed with important credentials and letters of introduction to the highest levels of society by both West and Benjamin Franklin, whom he painted while they were both in England, Benbridge chose to spend almost two decades living and working in Charleston,

Figure 14 Thomas Middleton of Crowfield, *1777, Henry Benbridge. Oil on canvas. Courtesy of the Historic Charleston Foundation.*

Figure 15 Mrs. Charles Cotesworth Pinckney, *ca. 1773/74, Henry Benbridge. Oil on canvas. Courtesy of the Carolina Art Association/Gibbes Museum of Art.*

where his style of painting obviously appealed to fashion-conscious Charlestonians. He ultimately owed to them much of his success as a portrait painter. In a letter from Charleston to his sister dated 21 February 1773, Benbridge gives some insight into his patrons: "Everything of news here is very dull, the only thing attended to is dress and disapation, & if I come in for share of their superfluous Cash, I have no right to find fault with them, as it turns out to my advantage."[29] A letter from Charles Willson Peale to Benbridge dated 1 May 1773, evidently in response to a letter from him, says, "It gives me pleasure to hear you find such encouragers of the Art, men that don't want to be courted to patronize merit."[30]

A direct allusion to the Arthur Middleton family portrait by West is found in Benbridge's 1777 Charleston painting of Thomas Middleton of Crowfield (fig. 14). The portrait depicts Thomas in "Vandyke" costume gesturing to his daughter Mary (b.1775) in a pose derived from the West group. The portrait of Mrs. Sarah Middleton Pinckney (d. 1784) (fig. 15), Arthur Middleton's sister, heralds Benbridge's neoclassical style in Charleston, but again with allusions to West.

Mrs. Pinckney's pose and classical Roman garb are taken from the painting of a Sibyl by Anton Raphael Mengs (1728–79) (fig. 16) copied by Benjamin West in 1762 and sent to his patron, Chief Justice William Allen of Pennsylvania. The picture was accessible to American painters in Philadelphia, where John Singleton Copley saw it in 1771. Whether Benbridge knew the Mengs work from his own Italian studies or through West's copy after it arrived in Philadelphia, or both, is a matter of speculation, but his choice of inspiration for the Pinckney portrait was an obvious reference to his own European artistic literacy.

Ralph Izard resumed his patronage abroad upon his return to England in 1771 with his wife Alice DeLancey Izard and three of their children. Within a year of settling in a fine and elegantly furnished house in London,[31] Alice Izard had her portrait painted by Thomas Gainsborough (cat. 11). Having painted Charles Crokatt's portrait earlier in his career, Gainsborough was already familiar to Charlestonians abroad. During the artist's Bath period he also executed portraits of Lady Sarah Izard Campbell, Ralph Izard's cousin, and her husband, Lord William Campbell, the last royal governor of South Carolina.[32] Gainsborough's approach to portraiture may have been a selling point to the Izards. His emphasis on likeness and his preference for contemporary costume was in keeping with Izard's prior portrait commissions. Alice DeLancey Izard is depicted as a young matron, in the latest English fashion, demure, yet sophisticated. Her somewhat somber expression may be the result of having lost their second son, Ralph, in the same year the portrait was executed.[33]

With political tensions rising between the American colonies and Great Britain, Ralph and Alice Izard decided to take an extensive tour of Europe that commenced in the summer of 1774. Before leaving, they had a miniature portrait done of their eldest daughter, Margaret Izard, whom they left behind (cat. 79). They chose Jeremiah Meyer, a German native who had studied in London and achieved the posts of miniature portrait painter to the queen and painter in enamel to the king in 1764. Meyer's light colors and precise technique were obviously favored by the Izards because he painted at least two other miniatures for them. One is of Ralph Izard himself, probably done around the same time as Margaret's portrait and known only through a drawing by Charles Deas published in a volume of his grandfather's correspondence. The other is a double-sided miniature of Anne and Elizabeth Izard, ca. 1783, possibly painted just prior to the family's return to America (cat. 80).

A miniature of Alice DeLancey Izard, signed and dated "1774 S," is attributed to Henry Spicer (1743–1804) (fig. 17).[34] Spicer, who worked principally in enamel, exhibited at the Royal Academy from 1774 to 1804. In 1774, he was appointed enamel painter to the prince of Wales. Compared to the portrait by Gainsborough, Spicer's depiction of Alice Izard is one of refined elegance enhanced by the formal qualities of her sumptuous costume and powdered hair. Set into the lid of an ornately tooled gold snuff box, the miniature has a jewel-like effect. A companion miniature of Ralph Izard may have been made at the same time.[35] It too was signed and dated, "1774 S," and was set in a gold snuff box which has been identified as the work of Louis Renard of Paris and dated 1774–75.[36] Perhaps the miniatures were executed in England just before the Izards' departure for the Continent; the settings may have been made in France after their arrival.

To this group—the portraits and miniatures by Zoffany, West, Gainsborough,

Figure 16 Sybil, *ca. 1762, Benjamin West. Oil on canvas. Courtesy of Ferens Art Gallery, Hull City Museum and Art Galleries.*

Figure 17 Alice DeLancey, *1774, attributed to Henry Spicer. Watercolor on ivory. Courtesy of the Carolina Art Association/Gibbes Museum of Art.*

Figure 18 Gabriel Manigault, *ca. 1794,*
Gilbert Stuart. Oil on canvas. Courtesy
of Mr. and Mrs. Peter Manigault.

Figure 19 Margaret Manigault, *1794,*
Gilbert Stuart. Oil on canvas. Courtesy
of the Albright-Knox Museum.

Figure 20 Gabriel Manigault, *1794,*
Gilbert Stuart. Oil on canvas. Courtesy
of the Albright-Knox Museum.

Spicer, and Meyer—the Izards hoped to add a portrait by John Singleton Copley, who arrived in England in 1774 and quickly made his way to Rome. In Florence, Izard sought out the artist and together they traveled to Naples in January 1775 (cat. 12). The double portrait of Ralph and Alice Izard represents the apex of Izard's patronage. Copley completed the painting in England. Because of financial difficulties resulting from the war, Izard never took possession of it before he died in Charleston in 1804. Even though the portrait did not make its way back to Charleston until 1831, early attempts were made by the family to retrieve it from the hands of Copley himself.[37] Once in Charleston it was recognized as one of the most important works in the city and was exhibited in the first exhibition of the Carolina Art Association in 1858.

Following in the footsteps of Benjamin West and Henry Benbridge, the American artist Gilbert Stuart arrived in London in 1775 and trained with West before establishing himself as an independent artist in 1782 with the exhibition of his portrait of William Grant of Congalton skating on the Serpentine (*The Skater,* National Gallery of Art, Washington, D.C.). Stuart's style combines the compositional facility of West with the fluid, painterly style of Gainsborough. Early in his career Stuart's artistic abilities attracted the notice of Joseph Manigault, the son of Peter and Elizabeth Wragg Manigault, whose portrait Stuart painted in England in 1785. Joseph had gone to England in 1781 to study law at the Middle Temple in London, as his father had done approximately thirty years earlier when his portrait was painted by Ramsay. The first of his clan to be painted by Stuart, Joseph started a trend of patronage in the family that would continue upon the artist's return to America in 1793. Joseph's brother Gabriel Manigault (1758–1809) and his wife Margaret Izard Manigault (1768–1824), Ralph and Alice DeLancey Izard's daughter, sat for their portraits in 1794 (figs. 18, 19, 20), as did Margaret's sister Anne Izard who married another prominent Charlestonian, William Allen Deas.[38]

In a letter dated 13 May 1794, Gabriel, residing in New York with his family, wrote to his brother Joseph in Charleston about his portrait by Stuart:

> It is now a long time since I promised you my Picture, if I should ever meet with a good painter. You know that no opportunity ever offered for performing my promise. At last a very good, and as unexpected [event] has occurred. No other than the very Stuart who drew your's eight or nine years ago. You will receive by Sheffield [captain of a coastal packet] a likeness he has taken of me. I hope you will find it a good one. I am told here that it is so. For the execution I can answer for him that he took great pains, for he is desirous that you should not think he is fallen off, and he says that this is one of his best Pictures. I am not altogether pleased with the coat, I should have preferred it plain (I think a spotted coat too youthful). But it is Stuart's choice, and I promised him that I would leave everything to him, on which condition he had assured me he would make a good picture (for I must inform you that it is his second attempt, and that his first failure was owing to my meddling too much in the business, which induced him to bargain with me that if I would leave him entirely to himself he would produce a good picture).[39]

While it is not clear from the letter who declared the first portrait of Gabriel Manigault "a failure," the letter suggests a certain level of connoisseurship on the part of the sitter that gave him the confidence to "meddle." It recalls the letter that Gabriel's father, Peter Manigault, wrote to his mother candidly comparing the abilities of Ramsay and Keable. However, in Gabriel's estimation, it seems that now the "good painter" is not only found in Europe, but on this side of the Atlantic as well, albeit in New York.

The Revolutionary War did not deter Charlestonians from having their portraits painted abroad. In some instances the war may have allowed such patronage to occur because of the roles that Charlestonians played in wartime politics and diplomacy, such as the activities of diplomat and statesman Henry Laurens, who was captured by the British off Newfoundland while on a diplomatic mission for the United States. Following his release from the Tower of London in 1781, he was painted by John Singleton Copley (cat.14). Commemorative in nature, the portrait emphasizes Laurens's role in the history of his new nation. While this painting never came to Charleston, it was widely circulated through a popular engraving by Valentine Green (1739–1813). Between 1783 and 1784, Laurens also posed for Benjamin West, who had planned to execute a series of paintings on the American Revolution following his own precedent of creating works based on contemporary historical events.[40] West chose to paint the Americans involved in the preliminary peace conference between Britain and America in Paris in 1782 (fig. 21). Despite the importance of the event and unlike West's historic *The Death of General Wolfe*, 1770 (National Gallery of Canada, Ottawa), it is in the style of a conversation piece, reminiscent of the earlier group of Americans abroad captured by West in *The Cricketers*.[41] Unfortunately, West's series on the Revolution never materialized and *Signers for Peace* was never finished.

For many Charlestonians, the longstanding tradition of travel abroad for business, study, or the Grand Tour was hardly interrupted by the Revolutionary War. While the political break with England was decisive, social, economic, and cultural connections remained strong. Mary Rutledge Smith arrived in London in early 1785 along with seven of her children, presumably for the purpose of furthering the education of those who were of age, and for her own enhancement. She was the wife of Roger Moore Smith, grandson of Thomas Smith, whose portrait was painted by William Keable decades earlier. Roger was born into one of the wealthiest aristocratic Charleston families with important ties to New England and Barbados.[42] While in London, Mrs. Smith sat numerous times between January and May 1786, for a full-length portrait by the artist George Romney (cat. 18).[43] Her youngest child Edward Nutt Smith was born on 20 July 1785 in London and is most probably the infant portrayed in Romney's painting.[44]

Even though Romney functioned independently of the Royal Academy, his reputation as a portrait painter was comparable to those of Reynolds and Gainsborough. He reached a peak of sophistication and popularity in the late 1770s. The influence of this portrait was felt in Charleston soon after Mrs. Smith returned to the city. The 1792 full-length portrait of Mary Brewton Motte Alston (1769–1838) by Edward Savage (1761–1817) owes an obvious artistic debt to

Figure 21 Signers for Peace, *ca. 1783, Benjamin West. Courtesy of the Henry Francis du Pont Winterthur Museum. The American participants are, from left to right, John Jay, John Adams, Benjamin Franklin, Henry Laurens, and William Temple Franklin, Benjamin's grandson, who served as the Americans' secretary. On the unfinished side would have been the British representatives.*

Figure 22 Mary Brewton Motte, *1792, Edward Savage. Oil on canvas. On loan to the Carolina Art Association/Gibbes Museum of Art from a private collection.*

Figure 23 General Charles Cotesworth Pinckney, *ca. 1795, James Earl. Oil on canvas. Courtesy of the Carolina Art Association/Gibbes Museum of Art.*

Romney's grand manner picture that introduced the full-length genre to Charlestonians (fig. 22).

Another "life-size" portrait by Romney is mentioned by Dr. Gabriel Manigault in his history of the Carolina Art Association published in 1894. The portrait of Pinckney Horry done while he was a student at one of the English universities was considered "one of Romney's best, and altogether a charming picture." It apparently was destroyed during the burning of Columbia, South Carolina, where it had been sent for safekeeping in 1865.[45]

As far as portrait commissions are concerned, the political division between Charleston and England during the Federal period is blurred, with grand examples of high-style English portraiture occupying the same spaces as the sober faces of Revolutionary War heroes, such as those painted by Rembrandt (1778–1860) and Raphaelle Peale (1774–1825), and James Earl (1761–96). The Peales were in Charleston in the winter of 1795–96, where they exhibited "portraits of those patriots who most distinguished themselves in securing the independence of these states, many of whom are now dead."[46] The portraits of local heroes Generals William Moultrie and Christopher Gadsden, Colonels William Washington and Lewis Morris, and Doctor David Ramsey were included. James Earl, who has often been confused with his more famous elder brother Ralph, also painted Charleston's heroes, including the portrait of General Charles Cotesworth Pinckney (fig. 23). Earl enrolled as a student at the Royal Academy and exhibited there in 1789. From 1794 to 1796 he was in Charleston, where he planned to stay until illness cut short his life and career.

After the turn of the century, Charlestonians had fewer portraits painted abroad. Changing travel habits, a relatively steady flow of European-trained artists to the city, and evolving attitudes toward the abilities of artists working in America and toward portraiture in general may all have contributed to a decline in commissions abroad. The increased number of portrait painters in American cities may have also influenced changing habits as evidenced by the continued Charleston patronage of Gilbert Stuart in Philadelphia and Washington, D.C., as well as other artists such as Henry Inman (1801–46) in New York.[47]

In the first two decades of the nineteenth century, northern itinerant artists who visited Charleston included such well-known artists as Alvan Fisher, John Vanderlyn, John Wesley Jarvis, Samuel L. Waldo, and miniaturist Edward Greene Malbone. London-trained portraitists Samuel F. B. Morse (1791–1872), who first came to Charleston in 1818 and was present intermittently until 1821, and Thomas Sully (1783–1872), who received Charleston commissions in the 1830s and 1840s, led the group in popularity.[48] In 1819, the city of Charleston commissioned Morse to paint a full-length portrait of President James Monroe to commemorate his visit there.[49] Along with Charlestonians Joel R. Poinsett, John S. Cogdell, and Charles Fraser, Morse was active in creating the South Carolina Academy of Fine Arts, which had its first exhibition in 1822.[50] Morse's portrait of Mrs. Emma Doughty Quash, ca. 1820–21 (fig. 24), is indicative of the portrait style popular among Charlestonians at this time. However, it stands in sharp contrast to the few portraits still being commissioned abroad. Compared with the contrived grouping of the family portrait of Charles Izard Manigault by Ferdinando Cavalleri painted in Rome in 1831 (cat. 21),

Figure 24 Mrs. Francis Dallas Quash, *ca. 1820/21, Samuel F. B. Morse. Oil on canvas. Courtesy of the Carolina Art Association/Gibbes Museum of Art.*

Figure 25 Charles Izard Manigault, *1817, Thomas Sully. Oil on canvas. Courtesy of the Carolina Art Association/Gibbes Museum of Art.*

Mrs. Quash conveys an air of comfortable ease that is achieved through Morse's painting style, rather than through compositional means.

Thomas Sully's portraits of Charlestonians are most directly associated with the high-fashion portraiture of his teacher in England, Sir Thomas Lawrence (1769–1830). Lawrence's work appealed to Sully despite the fact that his pictures appeared "too much loaded with paint, and the red and yellow overpowering."[51] On his return to Philadelphia Sully's work also displayed the influence of Gilbert Stuart, with whom he had spent about three weeks in Boston in 1807. Yet, for his Charleston commissions, as evidenced by the 1817 portrait of Charles Izard Manigault (fig. 25), Sully turned to the more dramatic style and mood of Lawrence.[52]

The grandly conceived full-length portrait of Mrs. Harriett Lowndes Aiken (1812–92) by George Whiting Flagg (1816–97) is perhaps the last of Charleston's antebellum portraits conceived in the Grand Tour mode (fig. 26). This portrait was painted in 1858, when Governor William Aiken and his wife returned from Europe. While abroad they had purchased paintings and sculptures for their splendid Charleston town house at 48 Elizabeth Street, to which they had just added an art gallery. Mrs. Aiken may well have admired the works of Francis Xavier Winterhalter (1806–73) while in Europe and certainly provided Flagg, whose father was a half brother of his teacher Washington Allston, the opportunity to paint an imposing portrait that echoed the effect of Romney's *Mrs. Mary Rutledge Smith* of seventy-two years earlier.

Figure 26 Mrs. Harriett Lowndes Aiken, *1858, George Whiting Flagg. Oil on canvas. Courtesy of the Historic Charleston Foundation.*

The propensity of the wealthiest Charlestonians to have their portraits painted while traveling abroad translated into the development of few successful native-born artists at home through the antebellum period. Yet by 1800, a body of work had accumulated in Charleston that was greatly admired by native-born artist Charles Fraser (1782–1860). As a miniaturist, Fraser painted the portraits of his fellow citizens for over fifty years. His popularity in this medium is unparalleled in Charleston. The final pages of his account book (Carolina Art Association/Gibbes Museum of Art) give some indication of his appreciation for the patronage of Charlestonians abroad. On one page, the epitaph from the tomb of English miniaturist Jeremiah Meyer is neatly transcribed, followed by an admiring comment by Fraser and a reference to a work by Meyer in Fraser's possession. On the next page are notes about Sir Joshua Reynolds's fees and comments about Reynolds's attitudes concerning the practice of painting on Sunday. The final page bears an apparent self-portrait, inscribed "CF 1819," the year after the account book was begun.[53] From these notations it is clear that even though Fraser did not study abroad, he admired England's grand-style portrait painters, whose work he was able to see and in many instances copy (cats. 9, 11, and 14).

In the foreword to *Artists in the Life of Charleston through Colony and State from Restoration to Reconstruction* (1949), still a definitive source of information on the art and artists of Charleston, Anna Wells Rutledge wrote, "Charleston's greatest contribution to American painting was timely patronage of men of ability and this discriminating appreciation may well be its most valid claim as a place of artistic importance."[54] The history of portrait painting in Charleston bears out this statement. These "men of ability" had the means, desire, and knowledge to commission work from some of the best-known portrait painters on both sides of the Atlantic and thus assembled a body of European works of art unparalleled in other American cities.

NOTES

1. Ellen G. Miles, ed., *The Portrait in Eighteenth-Century America* (Cranbury, N.J.: Associated University Presses, 1993), p. 9.

2. Susan L. Lively, "Going Home: Americans in Britain, 1740–1776" (Ph.D. diss., Harvard University, 1997).

3. George C. Rogers, Jr., *Evolution of a Federalist: William Loughton Smith of Charleston (1758–1812)* (Columbia: University of South Carolina Press, 1962), p. 24.

4. Rogers, *Evolution of a Federalist*, p. 9. For a thorough explanation of the economic rise of the factor or agent in Charleston society see Rogers, *Evolution of a Federalist*, chaps. 2–6.

5. Peter Manigault describes the estate in a letter to his mother dated 20 February 1750, "Peter Manigault's Letters," ed. Mabel L. Webber, *SCHM* 31 (1930): 272–73.

6. Henry Laurens to Nicholas Tooker, London, 4 April 1749, quoted in George C. Rogers, Jr., and David R. Chesnutt, eds., *The Papers of Henry Laurens* (Columbia: University of South Carolina Press, 1979), 1:235.

7. See letter dated 12 March 1750, where Manigault describes sitting for his portrait: "I have sat twice for my Picture, which is to be half Length, & that I shall begin to learn to Fence, as soon as I have done setting for my Picture." "Peter Manigault's Letters," ed. Webber, p. 273.

8. "Peter Manigault's Letters," ed. Webber, pp. 277–78.

9. Allan Ramsay painted a portrait of another Charlestonian, David Deas (1680–1757), in 1754. Currently unlocated, it is known through an early undated photograph in the Gibbes Museum of Art archives.

10. Alastair Smart, *Allan Ramsay 1713–1784* (Edinburgh: Scottish National Portrait Gallery, 1992), p. 10.

11. Smart, *Allan Ramsay*, p. 118.

12. "Peter Manigault's Letters," ed. Webber, p. 278.

13. "Extracts from the Journal of Mrs. Ann Manigault," ed. Mabel L. Webber, *SCHM* 20 (1919): 128. The sittings are documented in a journal kept by her mother-in-law, Mrs. Ann Ashby Manigault

(d. 1782). She and her husband, Gabriel, were painted by Theus at the same time (Metropolitan Museum of Art, New York).

14. The only other fifty-by-forty–inch portraits painted by Theus are of Mr. and Mrs. Barnard Elliott, Jr. (Carolina Art Association/Gibbes Museum of Art), probably executed to celebrate their marriage in 1766.

15. Rogers, *Evolution of a Federalist*, p. 33. The Theus portrait of Benjamin Smith was purchased by the Carolina Art Association from a family descendant in 1883 along with the portrait of Mrs. Benjamin Smith by Keable, and a portrait of their son William Loughton Smith by Gilbert Stuart.

16. E. K. Waterhouse, *Painting in Britain 1530–1790* (Harmondsworth: Penguin Books, 1954), p. 221.

17. Manigault, "Description of Paintings" (cat. 128); Victoria Manners and G. C. Williamson, *John Zoffany, R.A.: His Life and Works, 1733–1810* (London: John Lane, the Bodley Head, 1920) misdated Zoffany's arrival in London as 1765; thus, the portrait of Ralph Izard was painted after 1771 when he returned to England. Dr. Gabriel E. Manigault correctly states that the portrait was completed before 1765; see Clarence W. Bowen, ed., *The History of the Centennial Celebration of the Inauguration of George Washington as First President of the United States* (New York: D. Appleton, 1892), p. 476, illustration p. 101. Anna Wells Rutledge, *Artists in the Life of Charleston through Colony and State from Restoration to Reconstruction* (1949; reprint, Columbia: University of South Carolina Press, 1980), p. 116, reiterates that the portrait was painted when Izard was at Cambridge.

18. Dr. Gabriel E. Manigault, "Paper to Be Delivered before the Congress on Art of the Chicago Exposition," ca. 1893, Manigault Papers, SCHS.

19. George DeLancey Hanger, "The Izards: Ralph, His Lovable Alice and Their Fourteen Children," *Transactions of the Huguenot Society of South Carolina* 89 (1984), p. 72.

20. *Georgia Collects* (Atlanta: High Museum of Art, 1989), p. 206.

21. Sir Roy Strong, *The British Portrait 1660–1960* (Woodbridge, Suffolk: Antique Collectors Club, 1991), p. 20

22. Allen Staley, *Benjamin West, American Painter at*

the English Court (Baltimore: Baltimore Museum of Art, 1989), p. 31.

23. Helmut von Erffa and Allen Staley, *The Paintings of Benjamin West* (New Haven: Yale University Press, 1986), p. 26.

24. For a discussion on the identity of this portrait see cat. no. 659, von Erffa and Staley, *Benjamin West*, pp. 529–30.

25. For a discussion of the identity of this portrait see cat. no. 660, von Erffa and Staley, *Benjamin West*, p. 530.

26. Sarah Lytle, "Middleton Place," *The Magazine Antiques* 115 (April 1979), p. 779–93.

27. Aileen Ribeiro, "Fashion and Fantasy: The Use of Costume in Eighteenth-Century British Portraiture," in *The British Face: A View of Portraiture 1625–1850* (London: Colnaghi, 1986), p. 21.

28. "Peter Manigault's Letters," ed. Webber, p. 182.

29. Robert Stewart, *Henry Benbridge (1743–1812): American Portrait Painter* (Washington, D.C.: Smithsonian Institution, 1971), p. 19.

30. Stewart, *Henry Benbridge*, p. 20.

31. Hanger, "The Izards," pp. 74–75.

32. Waterhouse, *Gainsborough*, p. 58. The portrait of Lady Campbell has never been located. Lord Campbell married Sarah Izard in 1763 before his royal appointment as governor of Nova Scotia and then South Carolina. See cat. 10.

33. "Izard of South Carolina," ed., Langdon Cheves, *SCHM* 2, no. 3 (July 1901): 216.

34 The miniature of Alice Izard by Spicer was found missing from the Gibbes Museum of Art in 1987. Another version of this miniature (ca. 1774) is attributed to Piat-Joseph Sauvage (1744–1818) in C. P. B. Jefferys, "The Identification of a Previously Unrecorded Malbone Miniature in Newport," *Bulletin of the Newport Historical Society* 41, no. 129, pt. 1 (Winter, 1968): 22, illustration. This miniature is similar to the miniature attributed to Spicer, except for the more realistic facial features and the fact that the pearls around Alice's neck are replaced by a ribbon. Sauvage was a fashionable miniaturist and enamelist in France. He painted Louis XIV and was a member of the French Academy. Perhaps he copied the Spicer

miniature after the Izards arrived in Paris. In the early nineteenth century, Thomas Middleton, an amateur artist, copied the Sauvage version. See illustration in Martha Severens, *The Miniature Portrait Collection of the Carolina Art Association* (Charleston: Carolina Art Association, 1984), p. 97. George Flagg (1816–97) is also known to have made a copy of the Spicer or Sauvage miniature. MDP. An early twentieth-century copy of the Flagg painting is in the collection of a family descendant.

35. While no image of this work is known to exist, it is listed in the 11 July 1898 will of Dr. Gabriel E. Manigault. It is also described in correspondence in the object file for *Mr. and Mrs. Ralph Izard* (cat. 12), Museum of Fine Arts, Boston.

36. Object file, Museum of Fine Arts, Boston.

37. MDP.

38. Copy of a bill, "1794, 25th April. paid Mr. Stuart the Painter for three portraits at 50drs L35," Louis Manigault, family record, 1886, vol. 3, SCHS. See also "Buying British: Merchants, Taste, and Charleston Consumerism" in this volume.

39. Louis Manigault, family records, 1886, vol. 3, SCHS.

40. Staley, *Benjamin West*, p. 57.

41. Staley, *Benjamin West*, p. 59.

42. George C. Rogers, Jr., "Mary Rutledge Smith," unpublished manuscript, HCF files, p. 8.

43. Romney, sitters' book, as quoted in "Mrs. Roger Smith, a Painting by George Romney," HCF (1976).

44. Rogers, "Mary Rutledge Smith," p. 9.

45. Dr. Gabriel E. Manigault, "History of the Carolina Art Association," *Year Book, City of Charleston, S.C. 1894* (Charleston: 1895), p. 245.

46. *CG,* 3 December 1795.

47. William Loughton Smith (1758–1812), son of Benjamin and Anne Loughton Smith whose portraits by William Keable were discussed earlier, had his portrait painted by Gilbert Stuart in 1795. Stuart painted Thomas (1766–1843) and Sarah I'on (1778–1840) Lowndes and General John Roger Fenwick (1773–1842) in Washington, D.C., in the early 1800s. William May Wightman (1808–82), bishop of the Southern Methodist Episcopal Church, was painted by Henry Inman in 1840 in New York. These works

are part of the collection of the Carolina Art Association/Gibbes Museum of Art.

48. Paul J. Staiti, *Samuel F. B. Morse* (Cambridge: Cambridge University Press, 1989), p. 59.

49. Charleston City Council commissioned two other major portraits of presidents, the heroic painting of George Washington by John Trumbull (1756–1843) completed in 1792 and a portrait of President Andrew Jackson by John Vanderlyn (1775–1852) commissioned in 1824. Both portraits are now displayed in the Council Chamber of Charleston City Hall.

50. For more on the South Carolina Academy of Fine Arts see Paul J. Staiti, "The 1823 Exhibition of the South Carolina Academy of Fine Arts: A Paradigm of Charleston Taste?" in *Art in the Lives of South Carolinians,* ed. David Moltke-Hansen (Charleston: Carolina Art Association, 1979), vol. 1: psa2–11, and Maurie D. McInnis, "The Politics of Taste: Classicism in Charleston, South Carolina, 1815–1840" (Ph.D. diss., Yale University, 1996), chap. 2.

51. William Dunlap, *A History of the Rise and Progress of the Arts of Design in the United States* (New York: Dover Publications, 1969), vol. 2, pt. 1, p. 119.

52. Dorinda Evans, *Benjamin West and His American Students* (Washington, D.C.: Smithsonian Institution Press, 1980), p. 154.

53. Charles Fraser, account book, Carolina Art Association/Gibbes Museum of Art. Transcription published in Martha R. Severens and Charles L. Wyrick, Jr., *Charles Fraser of Charleston: Essays on the Man, His Art and His Times* (Charleston: Carolina Art Association, 1983), pp. 122–46.

54. Originally published in 1949 as pt. 2 of vol. 39 of the *Transactions of the American Philosophical Society.* Rutledge, *Artists in the Life of Charleston,* p. 101.

"Picture Mania"
Collectors and Collecting in Charleston

MAURIE D. McINNIS

*I*n 1858 while on the Grand Tour, Governor William Aiken decided to add an art gallery to his house in Charleston (fig. 27). Even at this point, few Americans had constructed specialized domestic art galleries. Aiken's decision reflects the centrality of the fine arts as a marker of cultural refinement in Charleston. Eighteenth-century Charlestonians' strong interest in painting is documented by their commissioning works of portraiture as acts of social distinction. In 1775 Ralph Izard requested John Singleton Copley to make a copy of a Madonna painting for him. His commission, though never fulfilled, revealed a direction that collecting would take in the nineteenth century when interest expanded beyond portraiture, and collecting pictures became important to those seeking the status of refined gentlemen.[1]

In collecting, as in other cultural matters, Charlestonians followed the lead of the English. Just as the British in the nineteenth century remained "irreclaimably of the old school in painting," so too did Charlestonians. Their collective tastes were nourished by eighteenth-century English writings that asserted moral virtues were gained by collecting the right pictures.[2] Jonathan Richardson succinctly described the links between connoisseurship and the benefit of mankind in his *Argument in Behalf of the Science of a Connoisseur* (1719): "Our walls . . . speak to us, and teach us History, Morality, Divinity; excite in us Joy, Love, Pity, Devotion, etc. If Pictures have not this good effect, it is our Fault in not Chuseing well. . . . If Gentlemen were Lovers of Painting . . . This would help to Reform Them, as their example, and influence would have the like Effect upon the common People."[3] Because the subject matter of pictures was valued most, Old Master paintings were revered and copies after them were collected for the abstract principles they illustrated. To be described as having a "picture mania" was a compliment to a gentleman. Collections in Charleston affirmed the canon of taste established by eighteenth-century English collectors—particularly seventeenth-century Italianate, Flemish, and Dutch paintings and contemporary

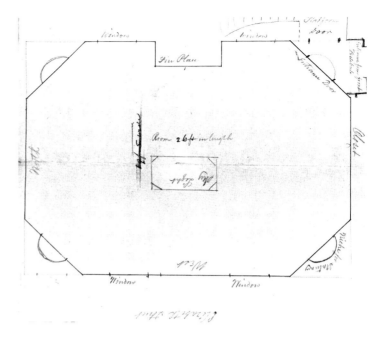

Figure 27 Floor plan for an art gallery, 1858, Aiken-Rhett House, 48 Elizabeth Street. Courtesy of The Charleston Museum.

images from the Grand Tour. Nineteenth-century Charleston collectors strove to assemble paintings that would demonstrate their breadth of knowledge in all of these areas. A painting collection became a mark of distinction, an important statement of taste. And taste was, after all, an important signifier of status. As class boundaries blurred and new wealth allowed many individuals to acquire large houses, plantations, and slaves, a painting collection, along with the ability to appreciate and discuss it, was a cultural tool to unify and identify Charleston's upper class.[4]

The topic of collecting in early nineteenth-century America awaits further study, for American art historians have been more interested in patrons who encouraged native artists. Collecting has historically been relegated to footnotes because it was often argued that early collectors acquired only copies and the work of third-rate artists.[5] In part this dismissal reflects changing late-nineteenth-century tastes as Old Master works fell out of favor. Later owners lost interest in the European paintings that once comprised early American collections. As a result of this neglect, many paintings are now in a lamentable condition and information about their provenance is usually lost. In Charleston the problem is compounded by the numerous fires that have taken their toll on both paintings and the documentation.

To dismiss these collectors of European paintings distorts our understanding of the growth of the fine arts in America. While many paintings today are no longer attributed to the artists they once were, it is important to recognize that these paintings played a vital role in artistic development in America. They established a corpus of fine arts where little had existed previously. They gave native artists access to examples of European fine arts. They broadened American taste for painting beyond the realm of portraiture while also establishing a tradition for buying, collecting, and

Figure 28 Friends and Amateurs in Musick, *1827, Thomas Middleton. Washdrawing with touches of white on paper. Courtesy of the Carolina Art Association/Gibbes Museum of Art.*

exhibiting works of art. Finally, they nurtured a public taste for the fine arts, which gave status to European paintings and, ultimately, to the work of contemporary American artists.[6]

A few collectors of the Federal era have received attention, notably Richard Codman of Boston, Thomas Jefferson of Virginia, and Robert Gilmor, Jr., of Baltimore (who was married to a Charlestonian).[7] The situation, however, was not as dire as the limited published scholarship suggests. By 1820 many Charleston collectors owned a broad range of history paintings, landscapes, genre scenes, portraits, and prints. The 1827 wash drawing *Friends and Amateurs in Musick* (fig. 28) by amateur artist Thomas Middleton (1791–1863) documents the broad interest in picture collecting among Charleston's elite. The drawing represents the dining room in the home of Thomas's brother, Arthur Middleton, a man generally not regarded in Charleston as a serious collector. Yet even he had a notable collection. The eight paintings depicted in *Friends and Amateurs* show the broad range of subject matter, styles, and national schools found in early-nineteenth-century Charleston homes. Just to the left of the center in Middleton's drawing, hanging over the sideboard, is the portrait of Arthur's father, Thomas Middleton (cat. 7), by Benjamin West. The painting hung in Arthur's house to proclaim Arthur's status as eldest son and heir in an important planting family. In the nineteenth century, portraits of ancestors gained a place of honor in the public entertaining spaces, bringing together the eighteenth-century fashion for European portraits with the nineteenth-century craze for collecting pictures. The large painting on the right appears to be a copy from Angelica Kauffman's *Departure of Telemachus,* a painting listed in the 1823 exhibition of the South Carolina Academy of Fine Arts in which Thomas Middleton was an associate.[8] Other paintings in this drawing remain unlocated, but works from the Italian and Dutch schools with mythological and Biblical paintings alongside a landscape, a seascape, and interior views represented many Charlestonian collections.

Opportunities to acquire European works of art increased after the French Revolution and the end of the Napoleonic Wars. Many European nobles found their financial situations precarious and were forced to disperse their collections. When they visited the palace of a Roman prince in 1830, Charles Izard Manigault observed that "this modern Prince would be glad to sell his Paintings & Statuary." For the most part, however, Charlestonians, like most nonaristocratic British collectors, were financially constrained. Manigault was frustrated at the sale of an art collection in Rome: "every thing that attracted our attention we found was a great price so that we came away without purchasing any thing."[9]

Assembling a distinguished collection, however, required more than just money, for the dangers of the picture trade were well known. Collector John Izard Middleton observed that auction sales in Paris were thronged by dealers who purchased paintings "of no particular excellence" and subjected the pictures to "expert professional restoration," before offering them for sale in Rome.[10] As a consequence, American collections were usually a mix of items. Copies after Old Masters, paintings believed to be from the school of an Old Master, and originals of lesser-known artists were found in Charlestonians' collections. Occasionally, some remarkably wonderful original works were purchased, like the drawings by Leonardo da Vinci (cats. 48 and 49) owned by Joseph Allen Smith (1769–1828), probably the most significant drawings owned by an American in the early-nineteenth century.

Charleston boasted a number of enlightened collectors and a stronger interest in paintings than in most other American cities. As early as 1784 Charlestonians talked of organizing an academy. They already supported a natural history museum (The Charleston Museum, founded 1773) and other institutions to spread the "refinement of knowledge." While such efforts bore no fruit until the founding of the South Carolina Academy of Fine Arts in 1822, they must have encouraged one of Charleston's (and America's) most notable early collectors, Joseph Allen Smith, also known as Allen Smith. In addition to the Leonardo drawings, Smith is best known for the extensive collection of paintings, prints, casts, and gems that he acquired in Italy and gave to the infant Pennsylvania Academy of the Fine Arts.[11]

Joseph Allen Smith was the youngest child of Benjamin Smith, a leading Carolina merchant (cat. 2). The greatest cultural influence on Smith was probably his half brother, William Loughton Smith, United States congressman and minister to Portugal. In 1786 William Smith married Charlotte Izard, the daughter of Ralph and Alice DeLancey Izard. Joseph Allen Smith himself also wed a daughter of the Izards, Charlotte Georgiana (1792–1832), but not until 1809, after fifteen years of European travel. Smith's passion for art was undoubtedly nurtured by his family's interest in painting (cats. 2, 3, 6, 11, 12 and 18).[12]

Details of Joseph Allen Smith's travels and collecting remain elusive, but it is clear that he was a remarkable American with wide acceptance in aristocratic European society. As a young man he was educated by a tutor in England; where he attended college is not known. He returned to Europe in 1792 and remained there until 1807, becoming one of the most widely traveled Americans, visiting not only Europe, but also Russia, Persia, and Greece. A rough itinerary of his travels includes the following: 1792–93, England and Portugal; 1794, France and Switzerland; 1794–97, Italy; 1797–98, Scotland, Ireland, and England; 1799–1800, England and France; 1802–3, Copenhagen, St. Petersburg, Moscow; 1803–4, Persia, Constantinople, and Greece; 1805, Russia; 1806–7, England.[13] In all of these countries he associated with the most distinguished circles. Robert Gilmor, Jr., recounted that "he was received in the best company at every court in Europe. . . . His person was fine, and his face handsome & expressive; he possessed great enthusiasm and vivacity, which combined with his extensive information . . . on art, literature & politics, rendered him not only one of the most agreeable but one of the most instructive of companions, and his society was eagerly sought by persons of the highest rank & the most distinguished talent."[14] In England and in some of his continental travels his companions were Lords Holland and Wycombe, "with whom he was almost a necessary companion." In Paris he was acquainted with Madame Récamier; in Russia he "was peculiarly a favorite of the Russian Emperor Alexander, with whom he dined in private, & who furnished him a guard . . . all over Russia and as far as Persia. Had he chosen to remain in Russia, he could have had any situation in the government that pleased him."[15]

While in Italy in the 1790s, Joseph Allen Smith was involved with the foremost artists, collectors, antiquarians, and dealers in the Italian art world. The most compelling record of Smith on the Grand Tour is a portrait by François-Xavier Fabre (cat. 19) that depicts Smith seated with Florence in the background. The painting not only documents his deep reverence for the fine arts and the classical world but also suggests the company he kept while in Italy. Fabre's portrait of Smith is derived from Wilhelm Tischbein's portrait of *Goethe in the Roman Campagna* (Frankfurt am Main, Städelsches Kunstinstitut und Städtische Galerie), and Smith himself suggested the arrangement. Perhaps he wanted to cast himself in the mold of the great author and fellow admirer of Italy, Goethe. Smith's friends, too, envisioned him in a classical mode, as Lord Wycombe called him "Smith the Aristotelian" and "Smith the Platonician."[16]

During his residence in Rome, he was acquainted with Gavin Hamilton and purchased items from him. He also patronized the city's most important engravers, Giovanni Volpato and Raffaello Morghen, and acquired from them prints and bound folios of Italy's art history, both ancient and modern. His goal was to assemble the "best representation [he] could of whatever was highly beautiful," in order to give his friends "some idea of the arts." Along those lines, he applied for and received permission, sometimes with "great difficulty," to have copies made in scagliola of the most famous sculptures including the *Apollo Belvedere, Belvedere Antinous, Capitoline Venus, Borghese Gladiator, Dying Gladiator,* and many others.[17]

In Naples Smith was a companion to William Hamilton and Wilhelm Tischbein. Hamilton, appointed British plenipotentiary to Naples in 1764, was an important collector of paintings and objects of virtu and antiquity, especially Greek vases. Smith's print collection included at least part of the published series of Hamilton's Greek

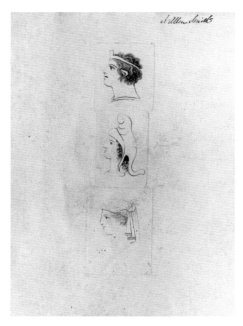

Figure 29 *Plate from* Collection of Engravings from Ancient Vases Mostly of Pure Greek Workmanship Discovered in Sepulchres in the Kingdom of the Two Sicilies, *1791–95. Courtesy of Dr. and Mrs. Price Cameron.*

Figure 30 *Venus Disarming Cupid. Courtesy of Dr. and Mrs. Price Cameron. This print of William Hamilton's favorite painting, believed to be by Correggio, was owned by Joseph Allen Smith.*

vases supervised by Tischbein: *Collection of Engravings from Ancient Vases Mostly of Pure Greek Workmanship Discovered in Sepulchres in the Kingdom of the Two Sicilies* (1791–95).[18] Volume four of the series lacked explanatory pages found in the first three volumes. Accordingly, Smith annotated his drawings with explanations of the mythological content as well as additional comments on the principal figures he knew in Naples. The most intriguing plate from Smith's collection is one that does not appear in other bound versions of the collection (fig. 29), but is clearly from the same project. The page is struck three times with three different profiles. Next to the rather unflattering physiognomies, he wrote the names "Tischbein, Hamilton, and Tischbein." Such jesting notations suggest Smith's close familiarity with Hamilton and Tischbein.

Sir William Hamilton frequently served as a dealer and advisor to other collectors, and it is tempting to speculate on the role that Hamilton might have played in helping Smith form his collection. Hamilton's favorite painting in his collection was *Venus Disarming Cupid,* a work he believed to be by Correggio, but is now attributed to Luca Cambiaso. A print of this painting, with Hamilton's name featured prominently, survives in Smith's collection (fig. 30). One of Smith's most prized paintings was *Dying Magdalene,* which he believed to be by Correggio (cat. 26). According to a family descendant, "[Smith] had succeeded in securing three Raphael's which he had reason to consider genuine. They were lost to him, however, through the seizure by one of the French generals and he was only able to retain a Correggio which was brought safely to America."[19] Other Smith purchases may have been influenced by Hamilton, such as the collection of gems that Smith donated to the Pennsylvania Academy. One of Smith's gifts is recorded as "Impressions of Antique Gems by Pichler, 6 cases." Giovanni Pichler was one of the leading exponents of the eighteenth-century revival of gem-carving and frequently was employed by Hamilton.[20]

One suspects, however, that Hamilton's influence was more profound. Hamilton enthusiastically supported the British Museum and spent most of his career as a collector and occasional dealer steering art works into public British collections. The concept of a public institution for the arts was unheard of in America, and Hamilton was likely instrumental in Smith's intention to found a public collection in America.[21]

Smith spent much of his time in Italy assembling a collection for shipment to the United States. His timing, however, was unfortunate. He left Italy just before it fell under French control and most of his collection was seized by the French. A full accounting of this collection was not taken, but it was described as "13 cases of valuable paintings—near 3,000 gems—some valuable statues, real antiques, & some copies, which he had himself superintended, of the most renowned statues of Rome, Florence, & Naples, of colossal size, & which he hoped to gratify his country men with."[22] Some of this collection was never recovered. Another part did not reach Philadelphia for more than fourteen years because of the vicissitudes of the Napoleonic Wars. A few cases were released around 1800 and were described by John Vaughan in 1804: "The above [items] form part of a collection which when in Italy Mr. Smith formed under the Idea, of collecting as accurate representations as he possibly could of those objects which were most admired, in the hopes that they might possibly be of some service to his countryman when they turn their thoughts to the study of Painting & Sculpture. For the object in view he deemed Philadelphia more central than Charleston & that his views would be better answered by placing them there. The remainder of the collection was taken by the French. Mr. Smith however hopes, it will one day be completed & enable his countrymen to form a just opinion of the Beauty of those productions of the arts which have been the Admiration of the Ages."[23] Among the first arrivals were plaster casts of antique statues, books, engravings, and more than 1500 impressions from gems. Apparently no paintings were included in the first shipment. Smith did not see the academy until 1807 after he returned to the United States and he was reportedly so pleased that he hoped also to donate the paintings he acquired in Italy, when they were released by the French.[24]

One case of paintings was released and en route to the United States when it was seized in 1812 by a British warship. The contents of the case were not listed, but it contained twenty-one paintings and fifty-two prints. Most of these were eventually given to the Pennsylvania Academy by British customs officers in Canada. Only a few of the paintings are known. They include three paintings thought to be by Salvator Rosa: *Mercury, Argus and Io* (cat. 25) and two landscapes (cats. 23 and 24). In the eighteenth and nineteenth centuries, Rosa was among the most popular seventeenth-century Italian artists, his fame increased by apocryphal stories linked with his life. He was especially revered for his wild and rugged mountainous landscapes, often with blasted trees and stormy skies. Connoisseurs deemed his work embodiments of the sublime.[25] Smith's gifts also include paintings by seventeenth-century Bolognese artists—Guido Reni, Bartolomeo Schidone, and Andrea Lucatelli—all of whom were held in the highest esteem as arbiters of taste, particularly valued for their focus on naturalism and the values of beauty, perfection, and harmony displayed in their art.[26]

Smith intended his collection to show the work of many artists and genres and to serve as a vehicle for ethical and artistic instruction. Celebrated examples of landscape painting were represented by the Rosa paintings, mythological subjects were featured in *Ganymede, Jove's Cupbearer* (fig. 31), *Petrarch's Laura* (fig. 32), and Bartolomeo Schidone's *Cupid with Vase* and *Cupid Musing.* Thanks to Smith, the American public had access, for the first time, to "objects most admired." These paintings were very popular in the Pennsylvania Academy's collection and were shown many times prior to 1850.[27]

After returning to America in 1807, Smith divided his time between Charleston and Philadelphia. While in the latter city he associated with other Charlestonians who resided there, especially with Alice Izard (cat. 11) and her family. As Alice Izard and her children had themselves spent many years abroad, it seems that in Smith they found a kindred spirit. Izard described their visits together: "the arrival of Mr. J. Allen Smith has brought us a frequent, & very agreeable companion. He calls without ceremony, & takes a plate of Hominy for breakfast and a potatoe in the evening. His manners are mild and gentle and unaffected, his conversation, interesting in the extreme. I am sorry to see that his health is not good. He says the want of it is occasioned by a fever he caught in the Morea which from all he has heard of the yellow fever, must be the same disorder."[28] The Izard women were charmed by Smith, the men less so. Alice Izard's son George mentioned the "copious Flow of Russian, Persian & Turkish anecdotes at Dinner," the result being a "prodigious sameness"

Figure 31 Ganymede, Jove's Cupbearer, *artist unknown. Purchased as Guido Reni by Joseph Allen Smith, given to the Pennsylvania Academy of the Fine Arts, deaccessioned. Present location unknown. Archival photograph courtesy of the Pennsylvania Academy of the Fine Arts, Philadelphia.*

Figure 32 Petrarch's Laura, *artist unknown. Purchased by Joseph Allen Smith, given to the Pennsylvania Academy of the Fine Arts, deaccessioned. Present location unknown. Archival photograph courtesy of the Pennsylvania Academy of the Fine Arts, Philadelphia.*

Figure 33 Temple of Castor and Pollux, *1796, Franz Kaiserman. Watercolor on paper. Purchased by Joseph Allen Smith. Courtesy of private collection.*

Figure 34 Interior of the Choir at the Capuchin Chapel, *François-Marius Granet. Courtesy of The Metropolitan Museum of Art, gift of L.P. Everary, 1880. All rights reserved.*

to his conversation. Despite George's misgivings, when Smith married the youngest Izard daughter, Charlotte Georgiana, in 1809, her brother remarked, "I am quite satisfied with the whole proceeding, as I believe him to be a man of honor."[29]

In addition to the works Smith collected for the Pennsylvania Academy, he retained some for his private collection. Years later, Gabriel E. Manigault, probably representing information given him by his father, Charles Izard Manigault, described Smith's Charleston collection as consisting of "about forty oil paintings and a large number of beautiful aquarelles, mostly of nude figures, which were kept in portfolios . . . a revelation to his untravelled friends."[30] He also maintained a private collection in Philadelphia. While there exists no complete list of his collections, surviving works suggest both its breadth and a different collecting focus from the objects he assembled for the Pennsylvania Academy of the Fine Arts. His private collection contained some seventeenth-century Italian paintings of religious and mythological subject matter, but the main focus was on Italy and antiquity. In addition to folios of Piranesi's engravings (cat. 130), he owned at least three works by the Swiss artist Franz Kaiserman (fig. 33 and cat. 55), who specialized in dramatic, large-scale watercolors of the ancient ruins in Rome. A number of gouaches in his collection featured the Bay of Naples and Mount Vesuvius. Small cabinet pictures inspired by the recently excavated fresco paintings at Pompeii (cat. 57) further document his interest in antiquity.

Undeniably, Smith's collection influenced other Charleston patrons. When John Izard Middleton (1785–1849) left for his Grand Tour in 1807, Joseph Allen Smith provided him with letters of introduction to several artists.[31] In 1823, Middleton, then living in Rome, lent sixty-three paintings to the Pennsylvania Academy of the Fine Arts, probably at Smith's suggestion. Given Middleton's artistic interest in landscape painting, it is not surprising that more than two-thirds of these paintings were landscapes. Most of the artists were not identified in the academy's documents, but works by Correggio, Vandewert, Polemburg, and Claude are mentioned, and the descriptions suggest other seventeenth-century paintings from the Dutch and Italian schools encompassing landscapes, marine views, and architectural scenes. Middleton's collection also included the work of contemporary European artists, including four by François-Marius Granet (1775–1849) who was best known for paintings featuring a powerful architectural motif, most commonly the inside of a church or monastery, onto which he grafted narrative material highlighted by atmospheric effect (fig. 34). Granet worked in Rome from 1802 to 1824, and it thus seems likely that Middleton purchased the paintings from the artist himself. These paintings were described as an interior of a cathedral, the "Lanthorn of Demosthenes at Athens," and two house interiors, one the entrance to Salvator Rosa's house.[32] Granet's paintings were particularly popular in Charleston, and a painting either by Granet or in the style of Granet appears in the watercolor *Friends and Amateurs in Musick* (fig. 28) directly over the mantle. The most important historical paintings sent by Middleton were the scenes of the Greek War of Independence by the German artist Franz Catel (cats. 36 and 37), making them the earliest images of the war exhibited in America.

The paintings Middleton sent to the Pennsylvania Academy were exhibited in 1824. Some were retained for exhibition with a few appearing in the catalogues of 1825,

1826, and a greater number in 1827. After that, according to a family descendant, the collection was split, with some of the paintings returned to Middleton in Paris and the remainder sent to Middleton Place, the primary family plantation outside Charleston.[33] Paintings listed at a partial inventory taken at the time of his death included Old Master paintings and copies, most notably a copy of Raphael's celebrated *Madonna della seggiola* (cat. 27), a Dutch landscape by Teneirs, and the work of eighteenth-century French artists Antoine Watteau and Nicolas Lancret.[34]

Middleton also owned some very important sculptures by contemporary artists including Rudolf Schadow and Lorenzo Bartolini (cat. 75). The most important of his sculptures was the colossal bust of *George Washington* by Giuseppe Ceracchi (cat. 74), which he likely acquired from the studio of Antonio Canova after the artist's death in 1822. Middleton died childless, and all of his paintings, sculptures, books, engravings, and Etruscan vases were left to his nephews in Charleston. Most were destroyed when Union troops burned Middleton Place in 1865.

Both Smith and Middleton had painting collections that were almost exclusively European, but other Charleston collectors both acquired European paintings and patronized American artists. Rice planter John Ashe Alston (1780–1831) was one of Charleston's most active patrons of native artists, and a partial list of his paintings suggests the breadth of his collection. While fulfilling the many requirements of a European collection of taste, Alston's personal predilections are revealed in the small number of seventeenth-century Italian paintings and the preference given to landscapes, genre scenes, still lifes, and the work of contemporary American artists. Of the forty-six paintings listed in the partial surviving list, twenty-one were landscapes exhibiting a wide range of subject matter. Like Smith and Middleton, Alston was fond of landscapes featuring either real or imagined places of classical antiquity, as thirteen of the twenty-one landscapes were of identifiable Italian sights. Thus landscapes depicting "Tomb of Cecilia Metella" and "part of the Coliseum," were likely *veduta* paintings of actual sites while the "Lake with ruins and figures" and "Column and Sea Port" were likely fictional *capriccio* combinations of classical elements. Paintings featuring classical ruins were popular in Charleston collections. Such works served not only as evocative reminders of travel, but also as cultural communicators of a patron's erudition and taste.[35]

Alston's collection also had a number of "Landscape marines," views of sea ports, and landscapes apparently in the Dutch tradition such as "Landscape with cattle." There were also three paintings identified as "School of Granet," after François-Marius Granet, whom John Izard Middleton also collected. Other examples that one might expect to find, such as religious and mythological works, were less common. The only religious works in this list were an image of the flagellation of Christ, a "Madonna and Bambino," in the manner of Schidone, and "Infant Jesus Sleeping," by Carlo Dolce, both of whom were popular baroque painters. Subjects drawn from mythology or ancient history were represented only by the "Rape of Proserpine."

Contemporaries remarked upon Alston's enthusiasm for paintings. One described him as having a "picture mania."[36] His collection was unusual for the number of paintings executed by contemporary American artists. These paintings, perhaps more than any others, demonstrate his true devotion to promoting art as both a collector and a patron. The taste for still life was little developed in America, and yet Alston owned at least six, four of which were by Raphaelle Peale. One of those survives (Toledo Museum of Art) and is inscribed on the back: "Painted for the Collection of John A. Alston, Esqr./ The Patron of Living American Artists."

Alston's collection of American paintings included two landscapes by Washington Allston, who was a distant cousin, Thomas Sully's *Washington Crossing the Delaware* and *Bonaparte as First Consul* and Benjamin West's *Venus and Cupid,* and at least seventeen portraits of family and friends by Samuel F. B. Morse.[37] He was a knowledgeable, demanding patron who instructed Morse to capture the genius of the Old Masters in his portrait of his daughter—"the learning of Michelangelo, the grace of Correggio, the coloring of Titian, but above all, I invoke the spirit of the divine Raphael to inspire you with the attitude."[38] Most of Alston's paintings have not survived.

Travel was a central feature of the refined lifestyle of the Lowcountry aristocrat, and paintings acquired in different locales were a powerful symbol. Charles Izard Manigault's collection represents another type of collection formed by a Charlestonian in the mid-nineteenth century. Unlike Alston's, which was personally assembled, Manigault's was acquired through inheritance and many years of travel. It differed greatly from Smith's, Middleton's, or Alston's. It was not as large and did not represent the others' range of interests and artistic erudition. In many ways, Manigault's collection more closely resembled that of other mid-nineteenth-century Charleston collectors, with a strong emphasis on portraiture and a sampling of all of the other kinds of paintings that were intended to compose a collection of good taste.

Manigault's collection contained many of the finest eighteenth-century portraits in Charleston, perhaps the finest such collection then held in America. His first major purchase was the portrait of his grandparents, Ralph and Alice DeLancey Izard, by John Singleton Copley (cat. 12). That painting held iconical status for Manigault, for it so consummately captured the Izards' cultured life and confirmed Manigault's status as their successor. To legitimate that visual mantle of succession, he commissioned a portrait of his own family overlooking the city of Rome. Painted by the Italian Ferdinando Cavalleri in 1831 (cat. 21), the portrait depicted a lineage that included Manigault, his wife, and his children. As soon as he received these paintings from Europe, Manigault entertained in order to display his fine new acquisitions.[39] The Copley painting hung "conspicuously" in Manigault's drawing room at his house on Gibbes Street, "surrounded by our numerous family portraits." These included a portrait of his grandfather Peter Manigault, by Allan Ramsay (fig. 9); his greatgrandparents Gabriel Manigault and Ann Ashby, by Jeremiah Theus; his grandmother Elizabeth Wragg Manigault, by Theus; his grandfather Ralph Izard, by Johann Zoffany (fig. 13); his father, Gabriel Manigault, by Gilbert Stuart. Those paintings he inherited. For ancestors for whom he did not have portraits, he commissioned copies, thus adding to his drawing room images of his wife's father, Nathaniel Heyward; her grandmother Elizabeth Heyward; and his grandmother Alice DeLancey Izard. Manigault also commissioned several portraits of his immediate family, including his children. Thus in Manigault's drawing room was a complete family history—a pictorial genealogy that not only affirmed Manigault's membership in Charleston's cultural elite but also bound him by blood ties to many branches of Charleston's cousinage.[40]

Manigault's art purchases spanned the 1830s to the 1850s—most made on his five European trips. Several reflected his preference for seventeenth-century baroque masters and religious painting, including *The Marriage of St. Catherine,* by an unidentified artist; *The Madonna of the Apple,* by Carlo Cignani (cat. 32); *The Little Spanish Madonna,* after Murillo; and *The Three Angels,* believed to be a remnant from a religious painting of Correggio. Manigault's *Madonna of the Apple* was purchased as an original by Cignani, the leading artist in late seventeenth-century Parma, whose work was valued for its harmonious style. The only history painting Manigault owned was *Louis XIV at the Siege of Namur,* which he purchased at auction in America in 1839 and considered "with the exception of some of my portraits, . . . the best painting I possess." The only Dutch interior genre scene he possessed was *Candlelight Picture,* thought to be by Schalcken. Manigault's commissions from American artists were all portraits except for Thomas Birch's *Sea Piece,* his first art purchase in 1827. His sculpture collection included a marble bust of *General Lafayette,* an American and Charleston hero, which he purchased from artist David D'Angers in 1829, and statues of *Hope* and *Faith,* bought in Rome in 1848.[41]

By the 1840s and 1850s, enthusiasm for the fine arts had spread and more Americans established painting collections. For the most part, collections in Charleston continued to be distinguished by Old Master paintings or copies after them, but Charlestonians also grew interested in the work of contemporary European artists. None of the collectors active in this period was as sophisticated as Smith, Middleton, or Alston, but they assembled a number of important collections.

One of the most distinctive was the collection of William Aiken, Jr. (1806–87). After completing his education at South Carolina College, Aiken made his first Grand Tour of Europe in 1826–28. The son of a successful Irish immigrant, Aiken was described by a contemporary as a gentleman with a "finished education, aided by an European tour and all the advantage of a princely fortune, which fortune, it is said, has nothing lessened under his prudent management."[42] An active politician, he served as governor (1844–46) and in the United States House of Representatives (1851–57). He became one of the wealthiest planters in the state with 878 slaves listed in the 1850 slave schedules and with property valued at more than $300,000 in the 1860 federal census. Aiken cemented his ties to Charleston's planter elite with his 1831 marriage to Harriett Lowndes; together they traveled to Europe in the 1840s and again in the 1850s.[43]

While the Aikens were in Europe in 1858, an art gallery was added to their home in Charleston. Aiken asked that the floor plan of the new art gallery (fig. 27) be mailed to him in Europe. Presumably, he wanted the measurements, so that he could plan his purchases while traveling. The most important acquisitions Aiken made were works of sculpture, and the floor plan specified three "niche[s] for statuary," and a skylight in the center of the room. At least five sculptures survive from the Aiken collection, most by artists working in Florence and Rome. The largest of the sculptures, too large to fit in one of the niches, is *Mary Magdelene,* signed "Firenze 1858" by D. Menconi, a little-known Italian sculptor working in Florence. The sculpture known as *First Grief* is unsigned. Two of Aiken's purchases were from popular American sculptors working in Florence. From Hiram Powers, Aiken ordered a bust of *Proserpine,* one of the sculptor's most popular ideal subjects. First produced in 1845, it has been estimated that as many as four dozen replicas were sold from Powers's studio at $400 apiece. For one of the niches in his new art gallery, Aiken also purchased *Shepherd Boy* from the American sculptor Edward Sheffield Bartholomew; it is signed and dated 1858. This was apparently a copy of the same subject that Bartholomew had previously executed for Enoch Pratt of Baltimore. Aiken and his wife were in Florence in November and December of 1857, where presumably they ordered this sculpture. Thus it may have been one of the last sculptures executed by Bartholomew, for in the spring of 1858 he became ill and died.[44]

In addition to contemporary works, the Aikens also purchased a reduced-scale copy of Canova's famous *Venus italica* (cat. 76). The original sculpture was completed in 1802, and it was immensely popular with those on the Grand Tour; no fewer than six full-size copies were commissioned from Canova during his lifetime. After Canova's death, other sculptors in Florence continued to produce copies. Interestingly, by the mid-nineteenth century, Canova had fallen from favor in the eyes of many connoisseurs, but not in the eyes of most on the Grand Tour who, like Aiken, continued to admire Canova's most famous work.[45]

The Aikens were interested in painting as well, for their library contained a number of books on artists and connoisseurship, including books purchased for their daughter Henrietta during their 1856–57 Grand Tour such as *Sacred and Legendary Art* and *Biographical Catalogue of the Principal Italian Painters* (cat. 135). While in Europe either on this trip or previous trips, the Aikens also acquired a number of paintings during their travels, although fewer of these have survived. A visitor to the Aikens' home in the late nineteenth century described the more notable ones. They included, according to her description, *Romeo and Juliet* by L. Terry; a bandit scene by Salvator Rosa purchased from the gallery of Prince Buonacorsi in Rome; a painting by David Teniers purchased from the gallery of Prince Torlonio in Rome; a *Flight into Egypt* by Carlo Marratti; and *Three Strolling Musicians* by Michelangelo. Only *Romeo and Juliet* was the work of a contemporary painter, a work commissioned by the Aikens that proved so popular that Terry asked to exhibit it in Rome for eighteen months before sending it to them.[46]

The collectors of the 1840s and 1850s revived the notion of a Charleston academy devoted to the exhibition of paintings. There had been a void since the demise of the South Carolina Academy of Fine Arts in the 1830s. There were some familiar families involved: Alston, Middleton, and Manigault. For the most part, however, this new group, the Carolina Art Association, was supported by a constituency broader in its social foundation than the South Carolina Academy of Fine Arts had been three decades earlier. Another important distinction was the different purpose that this institution was expected to serve. Instead of being designed to help young artists, as the South Carolina Academy had been, the Carolina Art Association was developed by several of its founders in the belief that a "picture gallery [w]as an important feature of modern city life."[47]

Exhibitions staged by the Carolina Art Association from 1858 to 1861 reveal the persistence of collecting habits in mid-nineteenth-century Charleston. While the collections assembled by Charlestonians included significant numbers of eighteenth- and nineteenth-century paintings including some American paintings, the 1858 Carolina Art Association exhibition still prioritized Old Master paintings. Nearly twenty percent of the paintings could be classified as Dutch, Flemish, or French baroque, while more than ten percent were Italian baroque. Perhaps the most interesting aspect of this exhibition is the number of new lenders listed who were not from families with a history of collecting. A fire in 1861 destroyed most of the collection of the Carolina Art Association, and the outbreak of the Civil War meant the institution, and indeed collecting in Charleston, could not recover for many years.

For Charlestonians in the first half of the nineteenth century, paintings were icons of status and cultural distinction. Through extensive collections that mixed European Old Masters and portraits of living and deceased family members, Charlestonians created the distinction that signaled membership in the city's aristocracy. Portraits were visual records of family lineage and social status, and European paintings were emblems of culture, refinement, wealth, travel, and education. It was true that anyone with enough money could assemble such collections, but the key was in knowing what to collect—and that is how one communicated one's refinement. In this sense art acted as a cultural identifier. Not all of Charleston's collectors were true connoisseurs, but many had an enthusiasm about the fine arts—a "picture mania"—that was part of Charleston's shared language of cultural values.

Notes

1. John Singleton Copley to his wife, Florence, 9 June 1775, quoted in Martha Babcock Amory, ed. *The Domestic and Artistic Life of John Singleton Copley, R.A.* (Boston: Houghton, Mifflin, 1882), p. 53.

2. Francis Haskell, *Rediscoveries in Art: Some Aspects of Taste, Fashion and Collecting in England and France* (London: Phaidon, 1976), p. 30.

3. Quoted in Ian Jenkins and Kim Sloan, *Vases and Volcanoes: Sir William Hamilton and His Collection* (London: British Museum, 1996), p. 78.

4. Iain Pears, *The Discovery of Painting: The Growth of Interest in the Arts in England, 1680–1768* (New Haven: Yale University Press, 1988), p. 179.

5. For a fuller treatment of this issue see Lance Humphries, "Robert Gilmor, Jr. (1774–1848), Baltimore Collector and American Art Patron" (Ph.D. diss., University of Virginia, 1998), especially chap. 1.

6. Wayne Craven, "Introduction: Patronage and Collecting in America, 1800–1835," in *Mr. Luman Reed's Picture Gallery: A Pioneer Collection of American Art,* ed. Ella M. Foshay (New York: Abrams, 1990), pp. 16–18.

7. For more on early American collectors see Craven, "Patronage"; Walter Liedtke, "Dutch Paintings in America: The Collectors and Their Ideals," in *Great Dutch Paintings from America* (The Hague: Waanders Publishers, 1990) pp. 14–59; and Liedtke, "Flemish Paintings in America: An Historical Sketch," in *Flemish Painting in America* (Antwerp: Fonds Mercator, 1992), pp. 11–28. Most of these essays are written from published sources and perpetuate assumptions about early collecting in America. This is an area where more primary research is needed. The excellent dissertation by Lance Humphries, "Robert Gilmor, Jr.," thoroughly explores Gilmor's collecting.

8. 1823 catalogue of the South Carolina Academy of Fine Arts. I wish to thank Susan Ricci Stebbins for her assistance on this issue.

9. Charles Izard Manigault, travel diary, February 1830, CLS.

10. Gabriel E. Manigault, "Paper to Be Delivered before the Congress on Art of the Chicago Exposition," ca. 1893, Manigault Family Papers, SCHS.

11. *SCG,* 5–7 February 1784, quoted in Anna Wells Rutledge, *Artists in the Life of Charleston through Colony and State from Restoration to Reconstruction* (1949; reprint, Columbia: University of South Carolina Press, 1980), p. 137. For more on the history of the South Carolina Academy of Fine Arts see Rutledge, *Artists in the Life of Charleston,* pp. 139–40, and Maurie D. McInnis, "The Politics of Taste: Classicism in Charleston, South Carolina, 1815–1840" (Ph.D. diss., Yale University, 1996), especially chap. 2.

12. For more on Smith's role and contributions to the Pennsylvania Academy of the Fine Arts see E. P. Richardson, "Allen Smith, Collector and Benefactor," *American Art Journal* 1, no. 2 (Fall 1969): 5–19; George C. Rogers, Jr., "Preliminary Thoughts on Joseph Allen Smith as the United States' First Art Collector," in *Art in the Lives of South Carolinians: Nineteenth-Century Chapters,* David Moltke-Hansen, ed. (Charleston: Carolina Art Association, 1979), pp. GR1–GR12; George C. Rogers, Jr., *Evolution of a Federalist: William Loughton Smith of Charleston (1758–1812)* (Columbia: University of South Carolina Press, 1962); and R. A. McNeal, "Joseph Allen Smith, 'American Grand Tourist,'" *International Journal of the Classical Tradition* 4, no. 1 (Summer 1997): 64–91.

13. The itinerary is extracted from Richardson, "Allen Smith"; Rogers, "Preliminary Thoughts on Joseph Allen Smith"; and an unpublished manuscript, private collection.

14. Robert Gilmor, Jr., "Family Record," fol. 62, n. 27, Maryland Historical Society, MS 2686.

15. Robert Gilmor, Jr., diary, SCL. I would like to thank Lance Humphries for bringing this and the preceding material to my attention.

16. Lord Wycombe to Lady Holland, Dublin, ca. 1798, Holland Papers, British Library.

17. Among the engravings and folios presented to the academy by Joseph Allen Smith was the folio *Principi del disegno* by Volpato and Morghen. Rogers, "Preliminary Thoughts on Joseph Allen Smith," p. GR-9, and an unpublished manuscript, private collection.

18. Jenkins and Sloan, *Vases and Volcanoes,* pp. 55–58. Few copies exist in the Southeast. The author has examined those at the Library of Virginia, Richmond.

19. Manigault, "Chicago Exposition."

20. Jenkins and Sloan, *Vases and Volcanoes,* p. 104.

21. Jenkins and Sloan, *Vases and Volcanoes,* pp. 80–82.

22. Mrs. Charles Cotesworth Pinckney to Mrs. Gabriel Manigault, Paris, 7 November 1797, Pinckney Papers, SCL, quoted in Richardson, "Allen Smith," p. 9.

23. Joseph Allen Smith Papers, PAFA, quoted in Richardson, "Allen Smith," p. 10.

24. A letter from Alice DeLancey Izard to Margaret Izard Manigault mentions Smith's intention to donate the paintings still in Italy; Mrs. Izard to Mrs. Manigault, 10 January 1808, Izard Family Papers, LC, quoted in Richardson, "Allen Smith," p. 11. A more detailed accounting of the fate of these pictures is given in Richardson, "Allen Smith," pp. 10–13.

25. In 1739 when crossing the Alps, Horace Walpole commented, "Precipices, mountains, torrents, wolves, rumblings—Salvator Rosa." Jane Turner, ed., *Dictionary of Art* (New York: Grove, 1996), 27:154. For more on Rosa's popularity in eighteenth-century England see John Sunderland, "The Legend and Influence of Salvator Rosa in England in the Eighteenth Century," *Burlington Magazine* 115 (December 1973): 785–89.

26. Robert Erich Wolf et al., *The Age of Correggio and the Caracci: Emilian Painting in the Sixteenth and Seventeenth Centuries* (Washington, D.C.: National Gallery of Art, 1986), pp. 325–26, 356–60.

27. Anna Wells Rutledge, ed., *Cumulative Record of Exhibition Catalogues for the Pennsylvania Academy of the Fine Arts, 1807–1870* (Philadelphia: American Philosophical Society, 1955), pp. 179, 186–87, 197. Reni's *Ganymede* was greatly admired by Thomas Sully who made a copy in 1822 for his own use (now in the collection of the Greenville County Museum of Art). Martha R. Severens, *Greenville County Museum of Art: The Southern Collection* (New York: Hudson Hills Press, 1995), p. 38.

28. Alice Izard to Henry Izard, New York, 3 December 1807, Izard Papers, SCL.

29. George Izard to Henry Izard, Farley, 25 July 1808 and 7 March 1809, Izard Papers, SCL.

30. G. E. Manigault, "History of the Carolina Art Association," *Year Book, City of Charleston, S.C. 1894* (Charleston: 1895), p. 247.

31. For more on John Izard Middleton see "John Izard Middleton" in this volume. The author wishes to thank Susan Ricci Stebbins for this information.

32. Edgar Munhall, *François-Marius Granet, Watercolors from the Musée Granet at Aix-en-Provence* (New York: Frick Collection, 1988). A number of Charleston artists made paintings in the style of Granet. These include Charles Fraser's *An Ancient Bath* (Carolina Art Association/Gibbes Museum of Art) and Henry Inman's *An Abbey Window* (Carolina Art Association/Gibbes Museum of Art).

33. Manigault, "Chicago Exposition."

34. Inventory of John Izard Middleton, Charleston County Inventories, vol. C (1850–54), pp. 230–31.

35. The "List of Pictures &c Belonging to the Estate of Col. J. A. Alston," unfortunately ends after the first page, although it is clear that it originally continued. Middleton Papers, SCHS. This list may have been drawn up to sell Alston's collection. An auction notice states that a catalogue was prepared. *CC,* 16 January 1838.

36. John Ashe Alston to Samuel F. B. Morse, Georgetown, 15 March 1820, Samuel F. B. Morse Papers, LC.

37. For more on Morse's years in Charleston see Paul Staiti, *Samuel F. B. Morse* (Cambridge: Cambridge University Press, 1989); Paul Staiti, "Samuel F. B. Morse in Charleston, 1818–1821," *SCHM* 79 (April 1978): 87–112; Paul Staiti, "John Ashe Alston: Patron of Samuel F. B. Morse," in *Art in the Lives of South Carolinians,* pp. PSa1–Psa13.

38. John A[she] Alston to Samuel F. B. Morse, Georgetown, 30 January 1819, Samuel F. B. Morse Papers, LC.

39. The dinner party given by Manigault where he displays the new paintings is described in cat. 21.

40. MDP.

41. MDP.

42. *South Carolinian,* 27 January 1841, quoted in Suzanne Cameron Linder, *Historical Atlas of the Rice Plantations of the ACE River Basin—1860* (Columbia: South Carolina Department of Archives and History, 1995), p. 290.

43. N. Louise Bailey, Mary L. Morgan, and Carolyn R. Taylor, eds., *Biographical Directory of the South Carolina Senate, 1776–1985* (Columbia: University of South Carolina Press, 1986): 1:40–46.

44. Wayne Craven, *Sculpture in America* (New York: Thomas Y. Crowell Company, 1968), pp. 115, 320–21.

45. Hugh Honour, "Canova's Statues of Venus," *Burlington Magazine* 111 (October 1972): 658–70, and Douglas Lewis, "The Clark Copy of Antonio Canova's *Hope Venus,*" in *The William A. Clark Collection* (Washington, D.C.: Corcoran Gallery of Art, 1978), pp. 105–15.

46. "Some Art Works in Charleston," newspaper clipping in the Claudia Rhett Papers, The Charleston Museum.

47. Manigault, "History of the Carolina Art Association," p. 248.

Buying British
Merchants, Taste, and Charleston Consumerism

J. THOMAS SAVAGE AND ROBERT A. LEATH

"Charles Town, the principal one in this province, is a polite, agreeable place. The people live very Gentile and very much in the English taste."[1]

Eliza Lucas to Mrs. Boddicott, 1740

*E*njoying the largest per capita income in British North America, Charleston society was more inclined to imitate British fashions than any other American city. Several factors contributed to this British bias among Lowcountry consumers. Foremost was the economic connection, a network of merchants in London and Charleston, upon whom South Carolinians depended to market their crops and from whom they obtained staples and luxury goods the colony could not produce. Second was the influx of British-trained artisans, a group replenished by immigration, who kept Charlestonians abreast of the latest British fashions and created the standards by which the products of local craftsmen were judged. The sobriquet "lately arrived from London" was a badge of distinction for sellers and buyers. Third was the impact of Charlestonians at home and abroad whose social status and cultural values were based more than a little on emulating their British cousins.

With the firm establishment by 1750 of the money crops rice and indigo, South Carolinians were poised to become full participants in the eighteenth-century consumer revolution. The Atlantic trade route, where new world crops were exchanged for old world luxuries, linked Charleston to Britain in social and economic ways. For the Charleston elite, the prevailing trade winds made travel and communication with their British relations easy and frequent. For the middle class, the transatlantic trade provided a steady stream of British-made luxury goods manufactured in the latest taste. In local society, emulation became a passport to refinement. Charleston's emerging aristocrats followed their peers in London, while the city's middle class mimicked their native elite. As historian Cary Carson has stated, "the consumer revolution would make comrades of ladies and gentlemen half a world away while leaving near but unequal neighbors worlds apart"[2] (fig. 35).

The Charleston economy was controlled by three principal figures: the British merchant, the Charleston factor, and the planter.[3] In London by the 1740s there were at least four merchant houses that specialized in the Carolina trade.[4] In their correspondence these businessmen used the telling term "friends" to describe their trading partners, indicating the close confidence and credit placed in those with whom they engaged in risky international speculations.

The most successful of the city's early merchants was undoubtedly James Crokatt (see cat. 1), described by one British observer as a "Scotch Jew Lately arrived from So. Carolina." Crokatt's success in the rice and indigo trade was such that by the 1740s he had departed the colony, purchased a fine country estate at Luxborough in Essex, and eventually retired to the lifestyle of an English country gentleman. Luxborough immediately became a center of hospitality for Charlestonians traveling abroad and London merchants with Carolina interests. Peter Manigault, impressed when he visited in 1750, remarked that with expenditures on his house and furnishings of more than 25,000 pounds sterling Crokatt had acquired "Grandour enough for his Money."[5]

Crokatt's model was emulated. During the heyday of his Charleston counting house, Crokatt's clerks included Henry Laurens (cat. 14) and Benjamin Smith (see cat. 2), two of the city's largest prerevolutionary traders. After their successful mercantile careers, Laurens and Smith established South Carolina's own version of the British country gentry, retiring from business to their plantations.

In many ways Benjamin Smith and his brother, Thomas (cat. 3), epitomized the colony's mercantile success. Born into one of South Carolina's founding families, they inherited small fortunes and through transatlantic trade turned them into large ones. After completing his clerkship under Crokatt, Benjamin went into business for himself and later partnered in one of Charleston's most successful trading establishments—Smith, Brewton and Smith—with his brother-in-law Miles Brewton (cat. 4), and his son Thomas Loughton Smith (1741–73). Thomas Smith formed an equally successful partnership with an English-born merchant, William Hopton (1712–86), in the firm Hopton and Smith. Hopton's clerkship in the Bristol Customs House before his arrival in Charleston in 1736 made him well versed in the rudiments of Britain's transatlantic trade.[6] Their firm supervised special commissions for imported goods, such as the British building materials ordered from James Crokatt for Charles Pinckney's elegant new Palladian mansion house on Colleton Square, completed around 1750.[7] Additionally, they brought the full array of British luxury goods to the local market for retail. In 1742 Hopton and Smith advertised a recent shipment of British goods, including ready-made clothing, jewelry, textiles, furniture, books, and other fashionable items: "JUST IMPORTED . . . from London, and to be sold by Hopton and Smith at their store next to Mr. Charles Shepheard's in Broad street, viz. All sorts of ready made Cloaths, shoes, stockings, gloves, hatts . . . a great variety of English and India silks, Lace and edgings, Lace lappets, Dutch and Genoa velvets,

Figure 35 A View of Charles Town, the Capital of South Carolina in North America, ca. 1770, *engraving by an unknown artist after an original painting by T. Mellish. Courtesy of the Carolina Art Association/Gibbes Museum of Art.*

gold and silver Lace . . . Gold and silver watches, silver tea spoons, buckles, and children's corals . . . gold ear rings, silver bitted swords and coutteaus, violins, flutes, mahogany and walnut fram'd sconces and pier glasses gilt and ornamented, a great variety of pictures and maps, books of History, Divinity, &c., bedsteads, beds, attrasses, quilts, cotton and fine chintz counterpains . . . and sundry other Goods."[8] Challenging traditional notions of the delay in transmission of style across the Atlantic, advertisements like Hopton and Smith's prove that the same sorts of goods commercially available in London were easily and expeditiously procured by Charleston consumers.

In 1766, Charleston's network of well-placed London merchants enabled St. Michael's Church to commission an impressive organ by Johann Snetzler (fig. 36), one of the most accomplished organ-builders in mid-eighteenth-century London. In May, the vestry wrote to James Crokatt's son Charles (cat. 1), enclosing a plan for the new organ by St. Michael's organist, Benjamin Yarnold, and instructing Crokatt to consult with Dr. William Boyce, master of the king's music and organist at the Chapel Royal.[9] In June 1768, Crokatt's brother-in-law and business partner, John Nutt, placed the new organ on board the *Polly and Betsey* and notified the vestry of the instrument's successful completion: "I have now the Pleasure to address you, with Invoice &ca of the Organ for St. Michael's Church, Charles Town, amounting with Charges to £528. . . . Mr. Snetzler who is now the most considerable, and the most reputable Organ Builder in England, assures me that this Piece of Work, is a very perfect one."[10] When it ordered a wrought-iron chancel rail and other church fittings in 1772, the vestry of St. Michael's again looked to England (fig. 37).[11] In completing their house of worship, Charleston's planters and merchants recreated a London city church complete with sights and sounds familiar to their British compatriots.

Likewise in their domestic spaces, one can trace the evolution of British taste among Charleston's merchant/planter elite. The British-educated Peter Manigault epitomized the informed Charleston consumer. Son of Gabriel Manigault, Charleston's wealthiest merchant and private banker, nineteen-year-old Peter set sail for England in 1750 to begin a four-and-a-half-year immersion in fashionable English society. During that time he read law at the Inner Temple in London and traveled extensively both in Britain and on the Continent. In his first year, he sat for one of Britain's foremost portraitists, Allan Ramsay, who produced an elegant three-quarter-length likeness now lost (fig. 9). Upon his return to Carolina in December 1754, he entered the South Carolina bar but left the law to enter the political arena, manage the business affairs of London firms with Carolina interests, and operate his plantations and the plantations of Ralph Izard (cat. 6 and 12) at Goose Creek.

For his new town house, completed by April 1771 and described in his will as "a large wooden House with a Cupola on the Top," Manigault wrote to Benjamin Stead, a transplanted Carolina merchant in London through whom Manigault marketed his crops, with a request for silver and furniture: "Having at last built myself a good House after having lived Sixteen Years in a very bad one I stand in need of some Plate & Furniture of which I inclose you a List. . . . I will be glad to have them out as soon as possible & the plainer the better so that they are fashionable. If a War send them not without convoy, & have them insured war or Piece. I think I may have enough in

Figure 36 St. Michael's Church, organ case, 1768, Johann Snetzler. Courtesy of St. Michael's Church, Charleston.

Figure 37 St. Michael's Church, altar rail, 1772, London. Courtesy of St. Michael's Church, Charleston. The wrought-iron altar rail was recently repainted in its original colors, Prussian blue with gilt accents, a popular scheme in eighteenth-century British churches.

Figure 38 Philadelphia high chest, ca. 1765–75. Mahogany with white pine and poplar secondary. Courtesy of the Philadelphia Museum of Art. Lauded as an "American" contribution to furniture design, when analyzed by eighteenth-century British standards, the Philadelphia high chest presents an anomaly: an archaic form, outdated in Britain by the 1730s, on which rococo elements have been superimposed.

your Hands to defray the Expence. If not you will advance what is wanting & I suppose the next Crop of Indigo will pay for it. I suppose you will think either my Wife or myself very extravagant. I should almost think so myself. If I had not seen [Miles] Brewton & [Thomas] L[oughto]n Smith's Bills for Furniture & Plate which I assure you, are twice as large."[12] Regrettably, Manigault's list does not survive but his letter records the nature of ordering consumer goods from England and outlines the rudiments of transatlantic trade in colonial South Carolina. Having built up capital by selling his indigo to Stead, Manigault could rely on Stead to purchase manufactured luxury goods on his account to send to Carolina.

Imported goods had an immediate impact on furniture produced locally. Richard Magrath, Charleston cabinetmaker "lately from London," seized an opportunity to notify customers of his ability to copy Peter Manigault's fashionable British-imported chairs. With the guarantee that his products were "as good as any imported from Europe," he offered on 9 July 1772, "carved chairs of the newest fashion, splat Backs, with hollow slats and commode fronts, of the same Pattern as those imported by Peter Manigault, Esq." Magrath advertised that he was producing another set of "Hollow-seated Chairs, the seats to take in and out," modeled after a second set of chairs recently imported "by the same gentleman, which have a light, airy Look, and make the sitting easy beyond expression."[13] Magrath's advertisement says a great deal about patterns of consumerism in eighteenth-century Charleston. The competition between locally produced wares and imported furniture was strong enough that Magrath employed name-dropping as a marketing technique. What better way to emulate the worldly and well-connected Mr. Manigault for those who had not traveled to Europe than to have copies of his London-made furniture?

The products of Charleston's native cabinetmakers are more clearly understood against the background of imported British furniture forms that set the standard for this emulation. Unlike northern furniture centers, where, by the 1770s, cabinetmakers represented three, four, and even five generations of native craftsmen, Charleston enjoyed a constant influx of British-trained artisans. The city avoided furniture forms that today have come to be seen as uniquely American. The high-chest form, for example, a ubiquitous and prized piece of furniture in the New England and Middle Atlantic colonies (fig. 38), was never produced in Charleston where the chest-on-chest or double-chest form was favored (fig. 39). This is not because local craftsmen were ignorant of the technology to produce such pieces. On the contrary, they knew that high chests were out-of-date in British urban centers by the 1730s. Naturally they did not construct such unfashionable objects for style-conscious Charlestonians. The city's cultural and economic ties to Britain, as well as the constant arrival of emigré British craftsmen, precluded the possibility of perpetuating of the outmoded high-chest form.

As in furniture, British-made silver and ceramics were highly prized by Charleston's consumers. A commonly understood means of displaying one's wealth since the Middle Ages, they were obvious symbols of cultural refinement. As a precious metal, silver denoted wealth, while fashionable forms connoted style and taste. The proper use of silver and ceramic objects in the evolving social rituals of the eighteenth century suggested membership among a sophisticated elite. By owning British silver and ceramics in the latest taste, Charleston's emerging aristocrats could vie with one another to set the most fashionable dinner and tea tables (cats. 94, 96, 112).

The demand for British silver and ceramics among Charleston patrons was not based on fashion alone, but also the finite supply available from local craftsmen. The shortage of local craftsmen was a sign of success. Many of them so benefited from the Lowcountry's booming economy that they left the ranks of "mechanicks" to become landowning gentlemen. Alexander Petrie exemplifies this pattern. Probably Charleston's best-known eighteenth-century silversmith, Petrie enjoyed great success in his craft and retired a wealthy man. When he died in 1768, his death notice in the *South-Carolina Gazette* reported, "On Sunday last died here Mr. Alexander Petrie, Silver-Smith, who had acquired a handsome Fortune, with a fair character, and had some Time ago retired from Business."[14] Like many Charleston craftsmen, Petrie had no desire to pass on his trade to the next generation. Instead, as he succeeded he bought land and slaves, sent his sons to school in England, and crafted marriages with prominent families to establish them as gentlemen.

Petrie's output indicates that he was capable of producing selected objects with the same skill and design awareness as his contemporaries in London. A coffee pot made by Petrie with rococo chasing (fig. 40) closely resembles standard British work. The demand for more elaborate symbols of refinement—epergnes, tea kitchens, and rococo salvers with elaborately cast borders—were more than likely beyond the capabilities of his provincial workshop (cats. 97, 99, 100). For these forms Charlestonians relied on imported pieces, which Petrie himself stocked to supplement his own work. Or they took advantage of travel abroad to make their own selections from the array of luxury goods available. Unlike the personal contact a patron might have enjoyed with Mr. Petrie, in London the consumer was far removed from the men and women involved in the fabrication of the object. However, the Charleston traveler would have delighted in the generously filled window displays of London's fashionable silver retailers whose shops were, by decree of the Goldsmith's Company, open only during daylight hours. The silver procured by Arthur and Mary Izard Middleton (cats. 100, 101, 102) dates to their period abroad and represents such personal selections made by Charlestonians traveling abroad.

In addition to silver and ceramics, styles of interior decoration were also dictated by Charleston's British taste. Josiah Quincy, Jr. (1744–75), a young Boston lawyer, left a tantalizing description of Miles Brewton's grand second-floor dining room (fig. 41), having visited there in 1773: "The grandest hall I ever beheld, azure blue satin window curtains, rich blue paper with gilt machee borders, most elegant pictures, excessive grand and costly looking glasses etc."[15] During the recent comprehensive restoration program at the Brewton House, physical evidence corroborated Quincy's description, documenting the rapid transmission of fashionable modes of British decoration to prerevolutionary Charleston. In addition to a fully intact papier-mâché ceiling scheme in the south parlor and a plaque depicting Apollo in the cove ceiling of the stair landing, four other British-imported papier-mâché borders were discovered. This easily exportable ornament was readily available in Charleston.[16] Paperhanger John Blott advertised in 1765, "Machie Ornament for ceilings &c. to imitate stoco work," and upholsterer Richard Fowler in 1771 listed among his newly imported

Figure 39 Charleston double chest, ca. 1765–75. Mahogany with cypress secondary. Courtesy of the Historic Charleston Foundation. Closely modeled on British prototypes, the double chest form favored in Charleston was virtually indistinguishable from contemporary British examples.

Figure 40 Coffee Pot, ca. 1760, Alexander Petrie. Silver. Courtesy of the Museum of Early Southern Decorative Arts.

textiles and decorations from London "Paper Hangings of the newest patterns . . . with rich double burnished gold machie borders."[17]

The "azure blue satin window curtains" described by Quincy were certainly of imported silk and probably took the form of festoons, curtains whose decorative appearance was achieved through drawing up the fabric with pulleys, cords, and rings. Rebecca Weyman, wife of Charleston upholsterer Edward Weyman, informed her customers in 1762 that she carried on "the business of making all kinds of bed or window-curtains, either festoon or otherwise."[18] Thomas Elfe, having secured an upholsterer from London, offered in 1751 "all sorts of festoons and window curtains to draw up, and pully rod curtains."[19] Expensive imported textiles were essential to the *toute ensemble* of the fashionable Charleston interior. Their specific presence in inventories attests to their importance. The second floor dining room of Lord William Campbell (cat. 10), South Carolina's last royal governor, was splendidly outfitted with rich textiles that included a settee, ten chairs, and two easy chairs all upholstered in "Crimson Silk Damask" and an imported "Large Green Worcester Carpet."[20]

The interiors of Charleston's most important colonial grandees were hardly provincial when compared with those of their London counterparts. In 1774, the auction of personal effects belonging to Sir Egerton Leigh, transplanted British baronet, judge of the vice admiralty court, and attorney general of South Carolina, included the furniture and upholstery textiles typical of an upper-class British interior: "elegant white and Gold Cabriole Sophas and Chairs, covered with blue and white Silk, Window Curtains to match; one other Set of Sophas and Chairs, covered with black and yellow Figures of Nuns Work in Silk, inlaid Commodes, Card Tables, Several Suits of handsome Chintz Cotton Window Curtains lined and ornamented with Silk Fringe and Tassels, a complete Set of Chintz Cotton Bed Curtains, a curious and superbe India Cabinet, a Rose Wood Desk and Book Case with Chinese Paintings on Glass very masterly executed, Carpets, Beds, Bedsteads, Toutenag Grates, etc." His other British luxury goods included an "elegant large Six-stop Organ, with Ten Barrels, containing near Four Score of the most approved Tunes, consisting of Airs, Minuets, Cotillions, Country Dances, Songs, and Marches." Additionally, he owned an ormolu-mounted musical clock by John Ellicott, clockmaker to King George III and London's most renowned clockmaker in the eighteenth century. His Italian pictures revealed British Grand Tour taste, including works attributed to well-known artists Veronese, Carladolsci, Jordano, Ghisolsi, Correggio, and Guido, as well as "several excellent Miniature Pictures, particularly one of Queen Elizabeth, done in the year 1574."[21] Auctions like these of the collection of an English-born connoisseur provided Charlestonians with another means of securing European luxuries, and dispersed British taste among a wider local audience.

After the Revolution, Charleston's desire for British goods persisted, as old mercantile connections were reestablished and British imports flooded a receptive local market. Advertisements placed by the city's leading postrevolutionary merchants— Nathaniel Russell (cat. 138), James Gregorie (cat. 105), Adam Tunno, and Daniel DeSaussure—mentioned goods similar to those advertised by Hopton and Smith a generation earlier, updated to the latest style. Seasoned by experiences abroad and traditional reliance on British products, Charleston shoppers knew and appreciated

Figure 41 Second floor dining room, Miles Brewton House, built in 1769.

the value of the name-brand object. A pianoforte by Clementi or Broadwood held special sway over the anonymous import. In 1784, a Charleston merchant advertised "A COMPLETE SET of ELEGANT MAHOGANY FURNITURE, made by SEDDON." The merchant felt certain that potential customers would respond to the names of Thomas and George Seddon, two of the most recognized London manufacturers of furniture for the elite and upper middle class. He specified, "this furniture was bespoke in London, and was originally intended for the use of a Private Family, who can at present dispense with it."[22]

Nearly forty years later, James Colbourn, another merchant, could make the same assumption about the sophistication of Charleston patrons when he advertised a complete set of London-made drawing-room furniture, "consisting of superfine green stripe Taberary Curtains, trimmed with gold lace, and enriched with gold coloured velvet and silk parisian fringe; a sett of drawing-room fancy Chairs, with carved backs and silk seats; green Tabouret Covers to the curtains and chairs. The above Furniture was made from designs, at the Manufactory of *Thos. And George Sedden*—uniting correctness with elegance, and permanence with grandeur."[23] How many merchants in other American cities could rely on their customers' familiarity with furniture makers operating in a city more than five thousand miles away?

Among the elite, Charleston's postrevolutionary interiors continued to be modeled on London style. The drawing room of Dr. Alexander Barron (d. 1819), for example, contained "London Made" cane-bottom sophas and chairs, satinwood card tables and tea tables, an English-made Brussels carpet with green baize cover, gilt-looking glasses and girandoles, a grand piano, a set of porcelain chimney ornaments, and window curtains and cornices "London Made."[24] When compared with the image of Mrs. Congreve and her daughters in their London drawing room (fig. 42), Barron's list suggests the camaraderie of style-conscious consumers on both sides of the Atlantic. Like many of Charleston's medical professionals, Dr. Barron had been educated abroad at the University of Edinburgh. He was president of the St. Andrew's Society, owned a plantation on the Ashley River, and occupied a grand double house in town. Even after political independence, Charlestonians continued to receive their social and fashion guidance from London.

The early-nineteenth century witnessed the retreat of the Carolina establishment into a genteel and select clique bound by common ancestry, inherited wealth, and a shared passion for the mannerly pastimes of balls, musicales, and tea parties. Reaffirming their cultural identity, elite Charlestonians still looked to England and their own past for models of deportment as well as their taste in architecture and furnishings. The increased leisure time for travel and connoisseurship in the nineteenth century was firmly rooted in mercantile fortunes established in the previous one. Many of the great travelers and patrons—Joseph Allen Smith, Mary Rutledge Smith, Alicia Hopton Russell Middleton—were the children of Charleston's most successful eighteenth-century merchants.

To construct their houses, Charleston's postrevolutionary elite turned to one of their own, Gabriel Manigault (figs. 18, 20), the grandson and namesake of the city's richest eighteenth-century merchant. Educated in Geneva, like his father Peter, Gabriel traveled extensively in Europe and read law in London. He possessed a large

Figure 42 Mrs. Congreve and Her Daughters, *ca. 1780, Philip Reinagle. Courtesy of the National Gallery of Ireland. The drawing room furnishings depicted by Reinagle are similar to those found in Charleston's upper-class interiors of the late eighteenth century.*

Figure 43 Painted Armchair, ca. 1800–1805, English. Courtesy of the Historic Charleston Foundation. Part of an extensive set of drawing room seating furniture originally owned by Thomas Wright Bacot (1765–1834), president of the Bank of South Carolina.

library of British pattern books and traveled within the distinguished architectural circles of Charles Bulfinch and John Macomb of New York, and Pierre-Charles L'Enfant. Himself an amateur gentleman-architect, Manigault promoted a derivative style of neoclassicism characterized by curved staircases, oval bays, circular basement windows, and applied classical ornament.[25] His best-known domestic commission was for the house of his brother Joseph (cats. 17, 42), completed in 1803.

To furnish his house on Meeting Street, Gabriel Manigault placed orders with Bird, Savage and Bird, the leading South Carolina trading firm in London with partners in Charleston, Beaufort, and Georgetown. That company provided "a connection of immense influence on both sides of the ocean" and, according to historian George Rogers, was "the best example of the immediate re-establishment of commercial ties after the Revolution."[26] In March 1800, Manigault wrote to Bird, Savage and Bird for "a few articles of furniture . . . such as is neat—1 Stuffed Sopha, not too deep in the seat . . . 16 painted cane bottom chairs, 2 of them with arms & all of them with cushions & covers to suit the curtains."[27] Two years later, the firm continued to supply Charlestonians with elegant British furniture by providing General Charles Cotesworth Pinckney (cat. 5) with "24 Tablet top Chairs with cane seats, japanned Puce ground stone colour ornaments yellow trellis in the boxes" and six "Chairs with scroll Elbows and caned seats japanned to match the above" (cat. 90).[28] As late as 1817, Pinckney imported an equally extensive set of rosewood seating furniture made by Gillows of Lancaster, England (cat. 91). In a letter to Pinckney's daughters, Isaac Coffin assured them that their new furniture was "all the fashion in the Houses of the first Nobility and Gentry in England . . . made by Mr. Gillow at Lancaster . . . the first Upholsterer in the Kingdom."[27] For their drawing rooms, where the greatest expense was lavished, Charlestonians exhibited an insatiable taste for imported British furniture (fig. 43) designed to impress their neighbors and to demonstrate that they were modish.

In addition to custom commissions, Charleston firms advertised "London made furniture" through the second decade of the nineteenth century, but disruptions to trade eventually forced Charlestonians to seek other sources for imported luxury goods. In the first two decades of the century, Charleston's market was rocked by British and French blockades, Jefferson's embargo, the nonintercourse acts, and the War of 1812. Furniture from New York, Philadelphia, Boston, Salem, and Providence flooded the local market, as northern cabinetmakers competed to fill the void created by the absence of British imports. But the decline in taste for British furniture was not due to the availability of other options alone. Protective tariffs imposed by Congress on imported furniture rose to a staggering thirty-three percent by 1822 and curtailed the profitability of fashionable British furniture in the Charleston marketplace. Merchant J. N. Cardozo recalled that by this time, "the class of merchants who grew out of the direct foreign trade of Charleston with the ports of Europe . . . had withdrawn from business or were dead . . . replaced by those who were connected with the indirect trade through Northern ports."[30]

Under the pressures of protective tariffs, Charleston's consumer patterns changed. The city's reliance on imported British goods ended as northern manufacturers supplied local markets. By 1820, furniture and silver from New York began to set new standards for good taste. The shopping sprees of Charlestonians abroad no longer included orders for entire suites of drawing-room furniture, but focused instead on paintings and sculpture and objets d'art, including micromosaics (cats. 143, 144), cameos (cat. 145), and plaster gems (cat. 146)—precious trinkets of sophistication. The occasional purchases, such as Robert F. W. Allston's complete set of London-made silver flatware, ordered from Britain's most fashionable mid-nineteenth-century manufacturer (cat. 111), represent lingering examples of Charleston's Grand Tour taste.

The desire of Charlestonians to buy British during the eighteenth and early-nineteenth centuries left its mark on the city's culture. From 1740 to 1860, Charlestonians enjoyed remarkable economic power and political importance. They became the richest Americans and used their wealth to become the most sophisticated. In both manners and possessions, Charlestonians engaged in the wholesale pursuit of refinement. Writing in 1773, a Charleston pundit summarized the city's consumer society:

> their whole Lives are one continued Race; in which everyone is endeavouring to distance all behind him, and to overtake or pass by, all before him; everyone is flying from his Inferiors in Pursuit of his Superiors, who fly from him with equal Alacrity . . . Every Tradesman is a Merchant, every Merchant is a Gentleman, and every Gentleman one of the Noblesse . . . The Sons of our lowest Mechanics are sent to the Colleges of Philadelphia, England, or Scotland, and there acquire, with their Learning, the laudable ambition of becoming Gentle-Folks. . . . Persons of small Fortune, Clerks and Apprentices, dress in every Respect equal to those of the first Rank and Eminence. . . . The Merchant leaves his Counting-house for the Ball-room, and the country Gentleman his Affairs for the Amusements of the Turf. . . . Every Planter of Distinction is impatient for an elegant carriage, Horses, Equipage, &c. and treads hard on the Heels of Quality, in Dress, and Expenses of every Kind.

He concluded, "we have no such Thing as common People among us: Between Vanity and Fashion, the Species is utterly destroyed." By importing British goods and modeling themselves after their British peers, Charlestonians had succeeded in creating the most Anglophilic urban culture in America.[31]

Notes

1. Eliza Lucas to Mrs. Boddicott, 2 May 1740, quoted in *The Letterbook of Eliza Lucas Pinckney, 1739–1762,* ed. Elise Pinckney (Columbia: University of South Carolina Press, 1997), p. 7.

2. Cary Carson, "The Consumer Revolution in Colonial British America, Why Demand?" in *Of Consuming Interests: The Style of Life in the Eighteenth Century,* eds. Ronald Hoffman, Cary Carson, and Peter J. Albert (Charlottesville: University Press of Virginia, 1994), p. 502.

3. For more on South Carolina's colonial economy and the role of the merchant see George C. Rogers, Jr., *Evolution of a Federalist: William Loughton Smith of Charleston (1758–1812)* (Columbia: University of South Carolina Press, 1962).

4. The leading Carolina trading firms in London were James Crokatt with son Charles Crokatt and son-in-law John Nutt; John Beswicke and Company; John Nickleson with brothers Richard and Thomas Shubrick; and Grubb and Watson. In 1763, the London city directory listed five firms under the heading "Carolina Merchants": James and Charles Crokatt and Company, John Beswicke and Company, Sarah Nickleson (the widow of John Nickleson), Richard Shubrick, and John Nutt. George C. Rogers, Jr., *Charleston in the Age of the Pinckneys* (Norman: University of Oklahoma Press, 1969), pp. 13–14.

5. Peter Manigault to Gabriel Manigault, 23 January 1750, in "Peter Manigault's Letters," ed. Mabel L. Webber, *SCHM* 31, no. 4 (October 1930): 272.

6. Deposition of William Hopton, 25 August 1785, case of Hopton v. Jones and Lutterback, Public Record Office, C12/983/8, London.

7. Invoice of James Crokatt to Charles Pinckney, 15 May 1746, Pinckney Family Papers, SCL.

8. *SCG,* 20 September 1742.

9. George W. Williams, *St. Michael's, Charleston, 1751–1951* (Columbia: University of South Carolina Press, 1951), pp. 219–20.

10. Williams, *St. Michael's,* pp. 222–23.

11. Williams, *St. Michael's,* pp. 171–75.

12. Peter Manigault to Benjamin Stead, 2 April 1771, quoted in "The Letterbook of Peter Manigault, 1763–1773," ed., Maurice A. Crouse, *SCHM* 70 (July 1969): 188–89.

13. *SCG,* 9 July 1772.

14. Milby Burton, *South Carolina Silversmiths 1690–1860* (Charleston: The Charleston Museum, 1968), p. 148.

15. "Journal of Josiah Quincy Junior, 1773," in Massachusetts Historical Society, *Proceedings* 49 (1916): 444–45.

16. J. Thomas Savage, with photography by N. Jane Iseley, *The Charleston Interior* (Greensboro, N.C.: Legacy Publications, 1995), pp. 11, 15.

17. *SCG,* 11 May 1765.

18. *SCG,* 22 October 1771.

19. *SCG,* 18 September 1762 and 7 January 1751. For more on the upholstery trade and imported textiles in Charleston see Audrey H. Michie, "Upholstery in All Its Branches: Charleston, 1725–1820," *Journal of Early Southern Decorative Arts* 11, no. 2 (November 1985): 21–84.

20. "Inventory of the Goods & Chattels Left in the House of His Excellency the Right Honorable Lord William Campbell, Charlestown, South Carolina," quoted in Graham Hood, *The Governor's Palace in Williamsburg: A Cultural Study* (Williamsburg, Va.: Colonial Williamsburg Foundation, 1991), pp. 307–13.

21. *SCG,* 6 June 1774.

22. *SCG,* 28–29 September 1784.

23. *CC,* 20 July 1820.

24. Inventory of Dr. Alexander Barron, 16 May 1819, Charleston County Inventories, Book F (1819–24), p. 53.

25. Beatrice Ravenel, *Architects of Charleston* (Charleston: Carolina Art Association, 1945), pp. 53–64.

26. Rogers, *Evolution of a Federalist,* p. 99.

27. Gabriel Manigault to Bird, Savage and Bird, 17 March 1800, Manigault Family Papers, SCL.

28. Invoice of Bird, Savage and Bird to Charles Cotesworth Pinckney, 2 July 1802, Pinckney-Means Papers, SCHS.

29. Isaac Coffin to the Misses Pinckney, 12 July 1817, Charles Cotesworth Pinckney Family Papers, LC.

30. Milby Burton, *Charleston Furniture 1700–1825* (Columbia: University of South Carolina Press, 1971), p. 8; see also Maurie D. McInnis and Robert A. Leath, "Beautiful Specimens, Elegant Patterns: New York Furniture for the Charleston Market, 1810–1840," in *American Furniture,* ed. Luke Beckerdite (Milwaukee: Chipstone Foundation, 1996), pp. 137–42.

31. *SCG,* 1 March 1773, quoted in Anna Wells Rutledge, *Artists in the Life of Charleston through Colony and State from Restoration to Reconstruction* (1949; reprint, Columbia: University of South Carolina Press, 1980), p. 117.

John Izard Middleton

"Talent Enough to Be One of the First Men in America"

SUSAN RICCI STEBBINS

"It is much more painful to leave the land of your fathers behind if you must cross the sea . . . it seems as if an abyss has opened up behind you, as if it might become forever impossible to return."[1]

Germaine Necker de Staël, *Corinne,* 1807

John Izard Middleton (1785–1849), a remarkable yet still little known Charlestonian, was a member of one of the city's most distinguished families. Best known today for his publication *Grecian Remains in Italy* (cat. 131), he devoted his life to aesthetic pursuits and to exploring the classical world. Middleton was a true figure of the Enlightenment—one of the first American archeologists and watercolorists, collector of paintings and books, amateur architect, and occasional botanist and writer. His travels took him across the length and breadth of Europe, in the process bringing him uniquely close to many of the leading European intellectuals and issues of the day. When Middleton finally chose not to return to America, settling in Paris for the last twenty-six years of his life, he became an early example of the special type of expatriate Henry James would later describe so well.

Only Charleston could have produced such a figure. And in Charleston, he could have come from only one of a handful of interconnected families with great wealth and keen interests in learning and the arts. The founder of the family in America, Edward Middleton (d. 1685), John Izard's great-great-grandfather, was the son of Henry Middleton of Twickenham, County Middlesex, England. Edward and his brother Arthur, wealthy landowners from Barbados, received large grants of land in Berkeley County north of Charleston around 1678. As successful planters, they became one of the leading colonial families of South Carolina, contributing to the governing of the colony from its founding in the 1670s to its emergence as a state after the War of Independence. Middleton's great-grandfather Arthur Middleton (1681–1737) served as lieutenant governor of the colony and president of the Royal Council, while his grandfather Henry Middleton (1717–84) became president of the Continental Congress and one of the largest landowners in South Carolina. It was he who established the family seat at Middleton Place on the Ashley River northwest of Charleston.[2]

John Izard's father Arthur Middleton (1742–87) (cat. 8) succeeded his father as delegate to the Continental Congress in 1776 and was a signer of the Declaration of Independence. In 1764 Arthur married Mary Izard, daughter of another prominent landowning Carolina family. Of their nine children, seven grew to maturity. John Izard Middleton was the youngest of the children who lived, and as the second son he received "his mother's large fortune" and her estate at Cedar Grove, across the river from Middleton Place.[3] He was fifteen years junior to his brother Henry Middleton (1770–1846), who inherited Middleton Place in 1787 and later served as governor, member of Congress, and as American minister to Russia.

Middleton's father died when he was only two, and he was brought up by his mother at both Middleton Place and Cedar Grove, surrounded by an extensive library and collection of watercolors, paintings, engravings, family portraits, miniatures, and other treasures brought back from Europe by his father and other family members.[4] Little is known about Middleton's youth, but he doubtless studied with a private tutor (as his brother Henry had) learning the classical curriculum then standard for young men aspiring to the values of the English gentleman, while also becoming accomplished in the arts. Judging from the praise given Henry as a youth (who was admired for "the boldness" of "his imitations and sketches") and given his family's interest in the arts, Middleton would also have been encouraged to learn the skills of drawing and watercolor.[5] By the age of fifteen, he was competent enough as a draftsman to make a finely rendered pencil drawing of an Ionic column copied from an architectural treatise (fig. 44).

Also among Middleton's earliest surviving artistic efforts is a series of botanical watercolors, dating as early as 1800, that reflect the family's interest in "the delightful science" of botany. The Middleton Place gardens had been among the most distinguished in America since the 1750s, and brother Henry continued to improve them with the help of the celebrated French botanist André Michaux and others.[6] Middleton's early watercolors depicting flowering plants indigenous to South Carolina, are surprisingly well rendered for such a young man (cat. 124). Working carefully from nature in his sketchbook, he demonstrates a keen observant eye and a good command of watercolor technique.

Both Middleton's uncle William Blake (1739–1803) and his great-uncle William Middleton (1710–75) inherited estates in England thus cementing the family's close ties with England and providing ongoing reasons to return to the mother country.[7] Like other members of the Carolina oligarchy, the Middletons preferred to send their sons back to England to complete their education. Middleton's father, as well as his uncles Thomas Middleton, General Charles Cotesworth Pinckney, Charles Drayton, John Parker, Jr., and Edward Rutledge were all educated in England.[8]

Following this tradition Middleton enrolled at Trinity College, Cambridge, on 17

Figure 44 Ionic Column, *June 30, 1800, John Izard Middleton. Pen and ink with grey wash on paper. Courtesy of Middleton Place Foundation, Charleston.*

October 1803 at the age of eighteen.[9] He was, however, apparently in England as early as the summer of 1801, judging from the inscriptions on several drawings of plants in flower that he made in August of that year at Sunbury Place, Middlesex, near London. At this time he was visiting his mother's sister Anne Izard Blake and her husband William Blake at their estate on the Thames.[10] His watercolor style was unchanged from the year before.

While enrolled at Cambridge, Middleton traveled to several counties in England, visiting relatives and touring popular sights. He arrived in Britain at a time when the increasingly affluent middle and upper classes were discovering the picturesque beauty of their own country. As Jeremy Black observed, "visiting literary shrines, country houses, picturesque ruins and the natural landscape" had become fashionable.[11] In January 1804, Middleton visited Bath with "several young Americans on a party of pleasure."[12] This fashionable spa with its classical eighteenth-century Georgian architecture and fine public gardens "very much pleased" the young American. The nineteen-year-old visitor was found to be "much superior to the generality of young men of the present age, very sensible"; he was "fond of dancing," attending a ball at the Upper Assembly rooms and joining a cotillion set.[13]

By early 1806 Middleton was studying the theory and practice of landscape drawing, painting and engraving in London, attending a series of lectures by William Marshall Craig (ca. 1765–1828).[14] Later that year Middleton made a number of sketching tours. He drew several tentatively handled views of the Georgian country estate, Hamells Park, Hertfordshire, where his relative Joseph Blake was living. His *View from Hamells Park* (fig. 45) with its gnarled oak and rural setting is reminiscent of the work of Gainsborough, whom his teacher Craig admired, while *Hamlet with Steeple, Blacksmith Shop at Long Melford* in Suffolk (Botanical Sketchbook, MPF) and his etching of *Deux Chiens Mangeant un Os* (Bibliothèque Nationale, Paris), an image of two wiry wolfhounds near a rustic thatched cottage, show his awareness of the rural picturesque as expounded by Craig and others such as Gilpin and Uvedale Price.[15] Middleton's quick sketch of the facade of the dairy at Hamells designed by another champion of the picturesque, Sir John Soane (1753–1837), illustrates the Doric pediment and the tree trunks which served as columns for the portico, Soane's attempt to combine the formal and the rustic.[16]

On an excursion to the Isle of Wight in late August 1806, Middleton discovered scenery where he said "the picturesque eye is gratified instantly," and he sketched views from the castle at Carisbrook and the cliffs from Freshwater. Near Southampton he compared the "celebrated ruins" of Netley Abbey with those of Tintern Abbey on the Wye, which he had visited earlier. While explaining his reasons for preferring Tintern Abbey, he wondered—paraphrasing Richard Payne Knight—"whether the principal pleasure afforded by the sight of a grand ruin is not afforded by the *scope* it gives to an ardent *imagination*." He also sketched Stonehenge, but surprisingly described it as "a mere curiosity."

While in England Middleton developed a critical eye for architecture. During his travels he made note of the "wonderful simplicity of the architecture at Salisbury Cathedral, devoid of the tracery so inseparable from most gothic buildings." He admired its octagonal Chapter House, while finding "the most beautiful part of the

Figure 45 View from Hamells Park, *July 1806, John Izard Middleton, English-Swiss Sketchbook. Graphite on paper. Ellida Davison Rea Collection.*

cathedral" to be the later improvements by Wyatt. Middleton also sketched the portal of St. Sepulchre's Church, Cambridge, in his inscription noting his displeasure with the "beastly wooden portal totally disfiguring the original beauty of the Saxon architecture."[17]

On 6 May 1807, Middleton left England for what became a three-year tour of the Continent, the most important voyage of his young life. He sailed from Gravesend to Holland and Belgium, where he traveled for several weeks visiting art galleries, private collections and botanical gardens while sketching the coast line and local sights. He arrived in Paris on 27 May with letters of introduction from friends in England such as Joseph Allen Smith to some of the most eminent figures in Paris including General Lafayette, General Andoche Junot, General John Armstrong, and the celebrated Juliette Récamier.[18] He became acquainted with Mme. Récamier and planned to accompany her to Switzerland to see her friend Mme. de Staël. Ultimately, she preceded him, and he left Paris in mid-July. After first stopping to visit Voltaire's chateau at Ferney near Geneva, Middleton proceeded to Mme. de Staël's chateau at Coppet on the shores of Lake Geneva on 21 July. In his journal he exclaimed, "after visiting the relics of one of the greatest men, I had the satisfaction of visiting in person one of the most extraordinary women, not only of France, but of the *age, Madame de Staël.*" In the following months Middleton continued to visit the celebrated and controversial French writer Germaine Necker, Baronne de Staël, and his life was profoundly changed.[19]

Madame de Staël, political writer, novelist, playwright, literary critic, and actress, was one of the most talented women of her time. Raised on the enlightened ideas of the philosophes, and a supporter of the Revolution, she hosted a salon in Paris where much of the new French constitution of 1791 was formulated. Threatened by her brilliance, independence, and liberal political views, Napoleon repeatedly banished her from Paris. Separated from her intellectual and political salon in Paris, she traveled widely throughout Europe, often retreating to her chateau at Coppet near Geneva where she surrounded herself with admirers and friends—distinguished writers, statesmen, historians, and artists.[20]

Upon their meeting Middleton expressed to Staël his enthusiasm for her recently published novel, *Corinne, or Italy,* which had been an immediate success in Paris and which became one of the most popular books in the nineteenth century. At the time of its publication in the spring of 1807, it further angered Napoleon who again exiled the author from Paris; rebuffed, but encouraged by her book's success, Staël returned to her chateau. Fortuitously, at the age of twenty-two, Middleton found himself befriended and admired by this formidable figure, a member of Staël's intimate circle, an impressive literary and theatrical constellation actively writing and socializing at her chateau. Middleton in his journal recorded frequent "tête à têtes" with her, discussing literature, poetry, and her own work, and added that she was "good enough to open her library to me"[21] (fig. 46).

One of Staël's great passions was the theater; she frequently organized theatrical productions, directing and sometimes writing the plays that she and her friends then performed at Coppet or Geneva. Among the many performances that fall was the comedy *Deux fats, ou Le Grand Monde,* by Elzéar de Sabran who created the

Figure 46 Madame de Staël as Corinne, *after 1807, Louise Elizabeth Vigée le Brun. Oil on canvas. Courtesy of Chateau Coppet, Switzerland.*

role of a young Englishman, Mr. Sidmours, specifically for Middleton who was joined in the cast by Mme. de Staël, two of her children, and Mme. Récamier (cat. 35).[22] During the summer Middleton was increasingly captivated by Staël's beautiful friend, Juliette Récamier, whose other more serious admirers included Prince Auguste of Prussia, nephew of Frederick the Great, who had been with the group since August.[23]

In Switzerland Middleton continued to record his travels with pencil sketches. On one excursion (from 28 July to 1 August) to Chamonix and Mont Blanc with Staël and Récamier, he made a drawing of the grotto at the Mer de Glace Glacier, and late in August on a two-week tour of the Alps, he sketched cascades, glaciers, valleys and lakes, along with the Matterhorn (fig. 47)[24]

On 29 November 1807 after the last theatrical performance of the season, the Coppet group dispersed. Mme. Récamier returned to Paris, Mme. de Staël departed for Vienna where she planned to spend the winter, and Middleton set out on his "long projected journey for Italy" by way of Mont Cenis. He traveled to Turin, Genoa, Parma, Bologna, and Florence visiting churches, galleries, collectors and artists on his route, arriving in Rome 24 December 1807.[25]

Three years earlier, Staël herself had set out to explore and study Italy in preparation for her novel. With *Corinne* as his guidebook and letters of introduction to some of Staël's closest friends, Middleton could not have been better prepared for his own discovery of Italy. Staël wrote to Caroline Humboldt, the wife of Wilhelm Humboldt, Prussian ambassador to Rome and to Friederike Brun, the German-Danish poet, describing Middleton to the latter as "an intimate friend of mine"; and adding that he possessed "de l'esprit, de l'instruction, et un caractère parfaitement noble et sûr."[26] As a result Brun, her companion Charles Victor Bonstetten, and the Humboldts welcomed him to their homes and their salons which included many artists of the neoclassical movement. Within a month of arriving in Rome, Middleton had visited the studios of Antonio Canova (1757–1822), Bertel Thorvaldsen (1770–1844), and Vincenzo Camuccini (1771–1844) with Madame Brun.[27]

Brun and the Humboldts were perfectly situated to introduce Middleton not only to ancient Rome, but also to many of its leading savants. Friends of Goethe and Schiller in Germany and devotees of Weimar classicism, they became avid collectors and students of classical antiquity.[28] In Rome they surrounded themselves with archeologists and antiquarians, some of whom had guided Staël herself three years before in Rome. Among them were Giuseppe Alborghetti (1776–1846), antiquarian, poet, and member of the illustrious Arcadian academy, and Séroux d'Agincourt (1730–1814), author of *Histoire de l'art par les monuments*, both of whom Middleton came to know. Most important for Middleton was Edward Dodwell (1767–1832), the English archeologist who had returned to Rome in 1806 from his travels in Greece, and who became a friend and colleague.[29]

Middleton was quickly absorbed into this learned circle that shared the Hellenism of Johann Joachim Winckelmann (1717–68) and especially his belief that ancient Greece represented "the childhood of Europe, the foundation from which all European culture sprang."[30] The rediscovery of Greece in the late eighteenth century led to an intensive search for ancient Greek remains, as manifested in the exhibition

Figure 47 Matterhorn, *August 1807, John Izard Middleton, English-Swiss Sketchbook. Graphite on paper. Ellida Davison Rea Collection.*

of Lord Elgin's Parthenon marbles in London in 1807. These were the very years when Middleton and his compatriots were setting out to study what they believed was the evidence of early Greek civilization near Rome. Middleton dreamed of going to Greece himself and early in 1808, he wrote Staël from Rome of his plans for such a trip; however, he would not actually make this trip until much later.[31]

Middleton's two years in Rome were immensely productive ones. After a three-week visit in February and March 1808 to Naples (including Pompeii, Herculaneum, and Paestum), he embarked on an ambitious program to study and draw the picturesque scenery and ancient ruins of Rome and Latium.[32] Trained in the classics in England, he conducted in Rome what he described as "a laborious research in ancient authors" that made him well versed in the writings of Virgil, Strabo, Dionysius, Livy, Pliny, and Pausanias and with more recent historians, of which Athanasius Kircher was his favorite. Within a short time, Middleton had gained a thorough mastery of the classical and modern texts on ancient Latium.[33]

By 1808, Middleton was becoming an accomplished draftsman and watercolorist. His earlier insecurity in making plein-air sketches was overcome through the use of the camera obscura, a technical aid used by such seventeenth-century masters as Vermeer that became especially popular during the eighteenth century when it was taken up by Reynolds, Canaletto, and many others.[34] The camera obscura helped the landscape draftsman trace onto his paper the outlines of the view; however, it was only a tool, and the final quality of the resulting drawing or watercolor depended, as always, on the imagination and touch of each artist.

In Rome, Middleton benefited from the advice and instruction of the accomplished topographical watercolorist Filippo Giuntotardi (1768–1831), a friend of both Brun and Bonstetten. Giuntotardi accompanied Middleton on sketching expeditions near Rome in 1808–9; he contributed two views of Albano to Middleton's book *Grecian Remains* and also provided him with "the original sketches of most of the costume figures" that Middleton employed in making the finished watercolors in his studio. Giuntotardi himself had learned watercolor from the Swiss painter Louis Ducros (who was in Rome from 1776 to 1807); both artists specialized in large-scale watercolor views of ancient Rome, Tivoli, and the Campagna.[35] Giuntotardi's works are highly detailed and somewhat repetitively handled though his impressive foreground figures give evidence of his skill as an illustrator (fig. 48). On one occasion, Middleton credits Giuntotardi with having finished one of his drawings in watercolor (cat. 63), and apparently they collaborated on at least one other occasion as Middleton was learning watercolor technique (cat. 60).

One of Middleton's first major watercolors (cat. 61) depicts Tivoli, long a popular subject for artists on the Grand Tour. Working in the prevailing neoclassical tradition and using a narrow range of blues and greens, Middleton looked away from the nearby circular Temple of the Sybil and instead painted a panoramic view from his hotel of the waterfall on the river Aniene and a complex townscape of the medieval houses. *Capriccio of the Falls of Tivoli* (fig. 82) by Washington Allston, also looks toward the cascades and cliffs and similarly employs a planar, classicizing composition.[36] One inevitably wonders exactly when Middleton met Washington Allston. Years later, Middleton's niece wrote that the two "appeared well acquainted." The two

Figure 48 View from the Capitol of the Forum Romanum, *Filippo Giuntotardi. Courtesy the Galerie Koller, Zurich, Switzerland.*

South Carolinians, who shared many similar interests and numerous friends and contacts, must have come to know one another either in Charleston in 1800–01, in England between 1801 and 1803, or in Rome in early 1808—the three times that their paths crossed. Allston and Middleton shared an interest in classical landscape, though Allston saw himself as an heir to Poussin and his own teacher Benjamin West, while Middleton's aspirations were those of the learned antiquarian and amateur; equally important, Allston claimed he had to "paint for money," while for Middleton there was neither financial nor professional incentive.[37]

Of the many watercolors that Middleton made in 1808–9, only about a half-dozen survive; the others are known through the excellent aquatints after them made by Mathew Dubourg for Middleton's chief work, *Grecian Remains in Italy, a Description of Cyclopian Walls, and of Roman Antiquities. With Topographical and Picturesque Views of Ancient Latium.* (cat. 131). Middleton's compositions can be divided into two groups. Just over half of his views depict traditional Grand Tour subjects: in this category are Middleton's view of Tivoli (cat. 61) and the panoramas of Rome (cat. 60), as well as his views near Albano (cat. 62). These are the Roman antiquities and topographical and picturesque views of ancient Latium referred to in the second part of his title. In these compositions, he tried, as he said, to steer a course between what he called the "opposite extremes" of Gilpin and the generalized picturesque on one hand, and the danger of inartistic, literal documentation on the other.[38]

Middleton's work closely relates to that of his friend Giuntotardi as well as such contemporaries in Rome as the topographical *veduta* painters Louis Ducros (1748–1810) and Franz Kaiserman (1765–1833) (cats. 55, 56). However, his style ultimately stems from the English tradition of J. R. Cozens and Paul Sandby, and closely parallels the work of such slightly older British artists as Francis Towne, John "Warwick" Smith, and Thomas Hearne, any of whose work he might have seen earlier in London.[39] More important, both Middleton's watercolors and his book deserve special notice in the history of American art. His watercolors of 1808–9 are exactly contemporaneous with those of the British-born artists, such as Archibald Robertson and William R. Birch in Philadelphia and New York, whose work of this decade is credited with marking the start of the landscape tradition in America. Middleton's aquatints for *Grecian Remains* were conceived, and many were printed, by 1811, a decade before comparable aquatints of American scenery were published by Joshua Shaw and William Guy Wall.[40]

Albano and the Alban Hills became one of Middleton's favorite areas—as it had been for generations of artists before him—and he spent the summer of 1809 living at the convent of St. Paul and sketching in the region.[41] He made watercolors (known largely through the aquatints) of several local views, including ones of the ancient "Nymphaem" at the edge of the lake, a view from the picturesque grotto of the Convent of the Capuchins (fig. 49), another of St. Paul's convent, and one of the "Emissary" of nearby Lake Nemi for which an original watercolor exists in the collection of Middleton Place. In addition, Middleton executed a sweeping panoramic view of the whole area, *View from the Summit of Monte Cavo*, 1809 (cat. 62). For *Grecian Remains*, the watercolor became the basis of two double-page aquatints (figs. 50 and 51); in the prints, some of both the foreground and the sky as

Figure 49 View from the Grotto of the Convent of the Capuchins at Albano, *M. Dubourg after John Izard Middleton. Aquatint from Middleton's* Grecian Remains. *Courtesy of the Museum of Fine Arts, Boston.*

Figure 50 View from the Summit of Monte Cavo, *M. Dubourg after John Izard Middleton. Aquatint from Middleton's* Grecian Remains. *Courtesy of the Museum of Fine Arts, Boston.*

Figure 51 Continuation of the View from the Summit of Monte Cavo, *M. Dubourg after John Izard Middleton. Aquatint from Middleton's* Grecian Remains. *Courtesy of the Museum of Fine Arts, Boston.*

well as the single tree have been eliminated, bringing the landscape and the ruins into greater prominence.

Middleton had previously visited Albano in 1808 when the Bruns and Humboldts had summer residences there and when he courted the beautiful but very youthful Ida Brun (fig. 52). The relationship was encouraged by Staël, who doted on Ida, but in the end was frustrated by Mme. Brun. At one point Staël wrote to Brun, "If Middleton marries Ida, keep him. If he does not marry her, send him here and then home. He wastes his life doing nothing and he has talent enough to be one of the first men in America."[42]

The other half of Middleton's works in 1808–9 depicts the subjects referred to in the first part of his book title *Grecian Remains in Italy, a Description of Cyclopian Walls.* Middleton had arrived in Napoleonic Rome during a period of burgeoning interest in archeology and the antique. The official excavations in Rome of the arches of Severus and Constantine, the Colosseum, the Pantheon, and other Roman monuments had been underway since 1801 under the direction of the papal commissioner of Roman antiquities Carlo Fea.[43] At exactly the same time, an enthusiastic international group of antiquarians, led by the architect Louis Petit-Radel (1756–1836) in Paris was conducting a search for Greek ruins in Italy. As early as 1792, Petit-Radel, a member of the French National Institute in Paris had theorized that the "cyclopean walls" he found in Latium were of early Greek Pelasgic origin of Homeric times. Inspired by him, the French Institute in 1804 issued a call to scholars, artists, and travelers across Europe to discover, research, and report on all cyclopean constructions in Italy and elsewhere. Widespread activity followed, with over one hundred responses submitted by 1810.[44] In 1808 the French Institute's correspondent in Rome, Séroux d'Agincourt, commissioned the architect Giuseppe Simelli to make drawings of the monuments in the Sabine Mountains near Rome; in the same year another Italian artist, Marianna Dionigi (1756–1826) completed her series of detailed drawings of the ancient walls and gates of Latium (fig. 53).[45]

Inspired by Petit-Radel's manifesto and in full agreement with his theories, Middleton joined forces with Edward Dodwell, one of Petit-Radel's champions and correspondents in Rome, to study the ancient walls and ruins. Dodwell himself had already made three trips to Greece "with Homer and Pausanias in hand," and he had acquired there vases, coins, and other antiquities. He and the draftsman S. Pomardi had made several hundred drawings of the country, its scenery and its antiquities, some of which were published in 1819 in Dodwell's *Classical and Topographical Tour through Greece.*[46] Most important for Middleton, one of Dodwell's special interests was the "cyclopean walls," whose discovery at Tiryns and Mycenae created great excitement at this time. As Adolphe Michaelis writes, there now "appeared from the darkness of antiquity the first palpable remains of the sites hallowed by Homeric poetry and primeval legends."[47] Middleton himself enthused, "Cyclopean walls are like the infant Hercules — arrived at the full strength in infancy." Thus, Middleton's project was far from isolated or quixotic; rather, when he and Dodwell set out from Rome in 1809 they participated in one of the most exciting archeological quests of the era, albeit one based on a theory later discredited, when archeologists concluded that most of the walls were actually early Roman.[48]

Figure 52 Ida Brun, *1809, Bertel Thorvaldsen. Marble bust, modelled and exhibited at the Exhibition of the Campidoglio, 1809. Courtesy of Thorvaldsens Museum, Copenhagen.*

On excursions in March and May of 1809, Middleton traveled with Dodwell and a third companion, most likely Sir Grenville Temple, in a search for early Greek "Cyclopean" or "Pelasgic" monuments in the more remote areas of Latium, the area southeast of Rome lying between two ancient Roman roads, the Via Appia and the Via Prenestina. Here Middleton did the work that enabled Charles Eliot Norton in 1885 to conclude — with some justification — that Middleton had made "the first contribution by an American to the knowledge of classical antiquity."[49] Middleton's approach was imbued with the critical spirit of the Enlightenment, asserting the priority of observation and insisting on the material object as primary evidence, very much in the manner of his friend Bonstetten, who had published his popular *Voyage dans le Latium* in 1805.

Middleton performed many of the tasks of the modern archeologist, though like the English gentlemen who comprised the Society of Dilettanti, he would have objected to being considered a specialist. He made careful measurements and highly detailed elevations of the Saracen Gate at Segni (cat. 63), where he also dug to the original bases of four of the gates; he made both broad and minute stylistic comparisons of the ruins in Latium with those in Greece; he copied and deciphered ancient inscriptions; he visited excavations at Cora; and he collected samples of the stone used in each area. He even bought (and later illustrated) one of the original bronze nails from the ancient vessel that had been discovered at Lake Nemi. Middleton's command of the field and his confidence in his abilities were such that he did not hesitate to disagree with the classic texts when, as he said, "the local evidence is in contradiction with the testimony of ancient authors."[50] Attacking those who mixed knowledge with conjecture, he challenged Dionysius and Livy on the origins of Segni, disagreed with his favorite historian Kircher on the original plan of the temple at Prenestina, and frequently debated the theories of other ancient and modern authorities.

Figure 53 Ingresso della Cittadella di Alatri, *V. Feoli after Marianna Candidi Dionigi. Engraving from Dionigi's* Viaggi in Alcune Città del Lazio, *1809.*

Figure 54 Remains of the Temple of Hercules at Cora, *M. Dubourg after John Izard Middleton. Aquatint from Middleton's* Grecian Remains. *Courtesy of the Museum of Fine Arts, Boston.*

Figure 55 Exterior of the Great Cyclopean Gate at Norba, *M. Dubourg after John Izard Middleton. Aquatint from Middleton's* Grecian Remains. *Courtesy of the Museum of Fine Arts, Boston.*

In March Middleton and Dodwell journeyed out the Via Appia past Nemi to the hill-top villages of the Lepini Mountains. His aquatint of the *Remains of the Temple of Hercules at Cora* (fig. 54) pictures the charming prostyle Doric temple, a well-preserved republican structure from the first century B.C., while his panoramic view of the town of Cora in *Grecian Remains* emphasizes the massing of buildings on the hills, though it also includes a cyclopean wall and tower in the foreground. In nearby Norba, Middleton begins his more intense exploration of the ancient material. His panoramic view of the site of Norba—where an Italian team of archeologists is digging today—includes some of the huge polygonal boulders, then considered to be of crucial importance in proving the age of the structure. He depicted the Great Cyclopean Gate at Norba (fig. 55) in a detailed view, nearly identical in composition to one Dodwell made and reproduced in his later book on the same subject (fig. 56). Middleton explains how this happened, writing that he and Dodwell "often used our camera obscuras at the same moment, and on the same spot" as can be seen in similar views of the walls at Alatri (cat. 131) and Ferentino, where both artists drew the interior of Porta San Giovanni with the Lepini Mountains in the background (fig. 57). The two were working closely and collaboratively, and authorship as such meant less to them at this time than accuracy. Middleton wrote that "landscapes drawn by an experienced amateur will, perhaps, be frequently found more accurate than the productions, in the same line, of a professional artist" due to the professional's emphasis on "general effect." He reports making "upwards of a hundred views, either sketches or finished drawings on ancient Latium." Middleton said, "In no instance have I falsified the form, color, height, or breadth of any monument; nor in any way sought to increase the beauty of the picture, at the expense of the accuracy of the outline." His purpose was to provide documentary evidence for Petit-Radel's theories; Petit-Radel himself later praised such works made with the use of the camera obscura, "which could not deceive like the imprecise brush of a landscapist."[51]

By 8 October 1809, Middleton left Rome, apparently to return to Charleston, for he had his belongings shipped home from Naples in November of 1809 on the brig *Sophia*. He traveled by land, crossing the Alps and arriving in Coppet by October 24 where he visited Mme. de Staël for several weeks. By late November, Middleton was in Paris where he planned to wait until the spring for a frigate to take him to New York, before going on to Charleston.[52]

In Paris, with new confidence in his draftsmanship, Middleton gave drawing lessons to Auguste de Staël, age twenty, whom he befriended; almost every evening they visited their friend, Mme. Récamier. In a letter to his mother, Auguste praised Mme. Récamier: "il n'est pas possible d'etre aussi bonne et aussi aimable qu'elle l'est pour Mr. Middleton et pour moi."[53] While waiting for passage home and with thoughts still of Italy, Middleton wrote "The Confessional: A Tale," a melancholy and sentimental Gothic tale of love situated in Italy, in the manner of the widely read British author Ann Radcliffe (1764–1823), complete with a brooding romantic hero, mystery, and monasticism.[54]

More important for his work on the antiquities and cyclopean ruins in Italy, he finally made the acquaintance of Petit-Radel himself. Middleton reported that he decided to publish his drawings in 1810 only at the suggestion of Petit-Radel, who he said, greatly admired his work and who believed his drawings and watercolors would "serve as documents to prove his [cyclopean] theories."[55]

Middleton's plans to return to America in the spring changed abruptly. In April 1810 he precipitously announced his wedding engagement to the beautiful seventeen-year-old Eliza Augusta Falconnet (1793–1831), daughter of Jean-Louis Théodore Palézieux Falconnet, a Swiss banker living in Naples, and Anne Hunter, an American from Newport, Rhode Island. Middleton was married on 7 June 1810 at the Protestant Reform Church, Temple Protestant de l'Oratoire du Louvre, by the Swiss minister Jean Monod.[56]

By early July the young couple arrived in London where Middleton's mother, Mrs. Arthur Middleton, had prepared an apartment for them in her house at Cadogan Place. In London, Middleton immediately set to work on his book, printed the introduction, left forty drawings with an engraver and gave supervision of the text to a friend. By early November 1810, he sailed for Charleston from the Isle of Wight with his mother and his pregnant young wife, Eliza.[57]

In the first years after returning to Charleston, Middleton seemed to adapt to the privileged life of a prosperous and knowledgeable Charleston rice planter.[58] He worked at his art the first year after his return, adding several botanical watercolors to his sketchbook while summering in 1811 at nearby Sullivan's Island (fig. 58), finishing in watercolor a drawing of Ferentino (fig. 57), and corresponding with Dodwell in Rome and others in London about his book. He and Eliza divided their time between Charleston and the family's country seats at Middleton Place and Cedar Grove, where in April of 1812, Middleton was said to be "making great alterations and improvements" at both estates. Following the example of fellow Charlestonians such as Gabriel Manigault and his brother-in-law Henry Izard, both accomplished amateur architects, Middleton made competently rendered plans and elevations for several houses and villas in the years 1811–13. It is not known whether any were built (cats. 64, 65). In his travels as a student in England, and later in Italy and France, he had developed a knowledge of architecture, as evidenced by his comments in *Grecian Remains* on the architectural treatises of Piranesi and Antolini and his critical remarks on buildings he saw. For example, on one occasion he likened the travertine material of the Temple of Hercules at Cora to that of the Doric temples at Paestum while criticizing its "eight columns of the Doric order, of very bad proportion." Middleton returned to Charleston with firsthand knowledge of designs of French and British neoclassical architects, as we know from his sketch of Soane's dairy at Hamells. His innovative neoclassical designs reflect an assimilation of the work he had seen in Europe, his knowledge of architectural pattern books, and his awareness of recently constructed neoclassical buildings in Charleston.[59]

Charleston in the early decades of the nineteenth century ranked with New York, Boston, and Philadelphia as a sophisticated, urban center. However, by March of 1812 Middleton was beginning to show signs of unhappiness with life as a Carolina planter. Nostalgic for Europe and unable to return because of the War of 1812, he complained in an unusually caustic tone in a letter to Madame Récamier that he lived

Figure 56 Great Gate at Norba, *C. Hullmundel after Edward Dodwell. Lithograph from Dodwell's* Cyclopean, or Pelasgic Remains in Greece and Italy, *1833. Courtesy of the Museum of Fine Arts, Boston.*

Figure 57 Porta S. Giovanni, Interior, Ferentino, *1809–11, John Izard Middleton. Watercolor on paper. Courtesy of the Middleton Place Foundation, Charleston.*

Figure 58 Shells and Sea Urchin, *1811, John Izard Middleton,*
Sullivans' Island, Botanical Sketchbook. Watercolor and graphite
on paper. Courtesy of Middleton Place Foundation, Charleston.

Figure 59 Eliza Falconnet
Middleton, *1816, Thomas Sully.*
Oil on canvas. Courtesy of private
collection.

in a "vilain petit coin du monde," where he said, "we have none of the consolations of life except those of affection." One of his important "affections" lay in his baby daughter Anna, born in 1811; in the same letter he spoke of having a little girl who "can't yet speak in any language, but understands only French."[60]

Despite his isolation, Middleton kept up with the latest books, ordering volumes from England and France and borrowing others including a life of Edmund Burke, Robert Wilson's *History of the British Expedition to Egypt,* Moleville's *Histoire de la revolution de France,* Boswell's *Johnson,* Charles Rollin's *Antient History,* the *Edinburgh Review,* and *Le Journal du duc de Gramont* from the excellent collection at the Charleston Library Society.[61] He also maintained his interest in both nature and landscape, as evidenced by a sketching and "botanizing" excursion made with his cousin Henrietta Drayton and her father, Charles, in the summer of 1814 to the mountains near Greenville, South Carolina, where he and Eliza were visiting his brother Henry's family. Mrs. Henry Middleton wrote to Margaret Izard Manigault at the time, speaking of "Izard" as Middleton was often called, "I hope that he will be able to show us when he returns how the range of mountains look on paper."[62] Middleton made a few cursory plein-air pencil sketches of the mountains on this trip and recorded a number of compass bearings of local landmarks, but he never carried any farther his interest in the American landscape.

Middleton's mother, Mary Izard Middleton, had given him her estate at Cedar Grove in 1813, a year before her death, surely hoping that he and Eliza would spend the rest of their lives there. However, Middleton became increasingly critical of life in America, on one occasion pointing out to his cousin Henrietta Drayton the "deficiency in curiosity and perfect indifference" that he observed in Carolina society. Then in June 1815, little Anna died of a fever. Eliza was said to take it well, but Izard was "the picture of grief." The saddened couple planned a summer trip to the "northern states" but were delayed because of Eliza's health.[63]

The Middletons eventually arrived in Philadelphia in September of 1815 where they remained until June 1816, surrounded by numerous friends and relatives from Charleston, including Mrs. Gabriel (Margaret Izard) Manigault (daughter of Ralph and Alice Izard), her brothers Colonel George Izard and Ralph Izard, Jr., and her sister Mrs. Anne Deas. The Carolinians all lived near one another on Spruce Street which became known as "Carolina Row" and much time was spent at balls, dinners, and musical evenings.[64] Eliza Middleton was greatly admired during these months for her musical skills and her beauty, which was recorded by Thomas Sully when she sat for him, her hair and dress in Grecian mode, during the fall or winter of 1816 (fig. 59). Yet, on various occasions she was said not to be "in spirits," an allusion perhaps to the early stages of Eliza's periodical episodes of nervous depression and fatigue that ultimately developed into a serious and debilitating illness.[65]

The Middletons spent much time in Philadelphia with fellow-Charlestonians Joseph Allen Smith and his wife Charlotte Georgiana Izard. Smith is best remembered as a traveler (who spent the years 1793 to 1807 in Europe and is thought to be the earliest American to travel to Greece), as well as "the first American to form an art collection from Italian sources"; and "the first to give it to an American museum." Smith and Middleton had been in touch in England by 1806, for Smith provided him with letters to artists along his route to Rome in early 1807. Smith may well have also influenced Middleton in his own collecting activities.[66]

Like Smith, whom George Rogers described as "never to feel at home in America after his European travels," Middleton also became discontented with American life. Turning his back on his American roots, in June 1816 Middleton and Eliza sailed for Naples, where her parents lived, without returning to Charleston, for Middleton's relatives there were asked to collect and forward his "books and drawing apparatus," especially his camera obscura.[67]

Naples was experiencing stability after the defeat of Napoleon and the meeting of the Congress of Vienna. The popular Bourbon King Ferdinand had returned to the throne and the city was alive with foreign travelers and artists who after more than a decade were free to explore the Continent again.[68] The Middletons were swept up by life in the colorful city that Goethe had called a "Paradise," noting that "while Rome is conducive to study," in Naples, "one just wants to live."[69] Eliza's mother and her father, Jean-Louis Théodore Falconnet, formerly banker for the Kingdom of Naples under Murat, were frequent hosts to distinguished visitors in Naples. In 1805 Mme. de Staël had been "pleased by Mme. Falconnet," and that same year, Washington Irving attended a "conversazione" at Mrs. Falconnet's, "an American lady of Boston." There he met "handsome ladies of the nobility, . . . Russian and Prussian ambassadors," and noted that "French was the language chiefly spoken."[70]

Naples was filled with entertainments and social events, dinners, balls, and excursions; according to Eliza, Middleton had "entered so completely into all the gaieties . . . that he cannot stay at home one evening." Living at the Falconnets' summer residence at Capodimonte near the Royal Palace, the Middletons were "constantly invited" to dinners at the British minister's residence, the Casino Carascosa, which Middleton painted overlooking the Albergo dei Poveri (1751) and the Royal Botanic Garden, with the bay of Naples in the background (fig. 60). In April 1819, they attended the elaborate party at the Royal Palace honoring the Emperor and Empress of Austria, who were visiting Naples with Metternich (whom Eliza found to have "mild and gentlemanly manners"). That same summer, when the portraitist Sir Thomas Lawrence visited Naples, Eliza was impressed with the artist's ability "to seize the expression so that you can guess the character of the person whom he paints."[71]

In Naples, Middleton also set about improving his skills as a landscape artist, making many sketching excursions to the countryside, often accompanied by Eliza and other friends. In 1817 he executed a dozen or more small, accomplished plein-air pencil and wash sketches of the major attractions in the area: the ruins at Pompeii, with views of the theater and amphitheater, the Baths of Nero at Baia, the Temple of Serapis at Pozzuoli, as well as rocky coastal views of Capri and Ischia, and fishing boats in the bay of Naples with a still-smoking Vesuvius in the background. He made two views of the picturesque Monastery of Santa Maria dei Monti located on a ridge between Capodimonte and Capodichino (fig. 61). Hallowed ground for artists on the Grand Tour, the road to "S'a M'a de Monti" was described by Thomas Jones as the "scenery that Salvator Rosa formed himself upon."[72]

Middleton inscribed several of his wash drawings "d'après Huber" or "d'après Pitloo," referring to two artist-teachers in Naples. Jakob Wilhelm Huber (1781–1871),

Figure 60 Casino Carascosa, *1819, John Izard Middleton. Watercolor and graphite on paper. Courtesy of the Carolina Art Association/Gibbes Museum of Art.*

Figure 61 Monastery of Santa Maria dei Monti Near Naples, *1817, John Izard Middleton. Watercolor, brown ink and graphite on paper. Courtesy of Sotheby's Inc.*

Figure 62 View of Naples and the Bay, *ca. 1816–17, John Izard Middleton. Brown ink drawing on tracing paper. Courtesy of Middleton Place Foundation, Charleston.*

Figure 63 The Olympion or Temple of Olympian Zeus, Athens, *1821, John Izard Middleton. Pen and ink on paper. Courtesy of the Historical Society of Pennsylvania, Philadelphia.*

a German-Swiss painter in the classical and picturesque landscape tradition, taught both oil and watercolor and the use of the camera lucida, a new apparatus that was more sophisticated and portable than the camera obscura. Influenced by Huber, Middleton used the camera lucida to make a number of highly detailed brown ink drawings on tracing paper depicting views of Naples (fig. 62). Several of Middleton's drawings are direct copies of ones by Huber; while others are close variants and may well have been made under Huber's direction on sketching excursions. Huber's colleague, the Dutch painter Anton Sminck Pitloo (1791–1837) worked outdoors with his students making small plein-air studies emphasizing light and color.[73] Middleton's work shows a new concern for natural light and interest in atmospheric effects as can be seen both in his small-scale outdoor sketches and in his finished watercolors including the *Temple of Neptune* (cat. 67) executed at nearby Paestum and *View of Aetna from Greek Theater at Taormina* (cat. 66), from his trip to Sicily in June of 1818. In the Taormina view, he infused the scene with the warm glow of the early sunrise, balancing his accurate observation of topography with a more romantic concern for mood and light.

Patrick Brydone's widely read *Tour through Sicily and Malta* (1773) was influential in extending the route of the Grand Tour beyond Paestum, and by the time of Middleton's trip in 1818, numerous English travelers had visited Sicily, though it was still considered a primitive and bandit-ridden island.[74] Few Americans had visited the island and Middleton himself, writing from Sicily to his wife in Naples, complained of the numerous inconveniences including difficult lodging, fear of bandits, and extreme weather variations. Nevertheless, he affirmed that "the beauty of the country . . . and the interest of its history" amply compensated for "the trouble this tour has given us." Middleton's itinerary is known only in part; after visiting Taormina, he planned, and probably made, a tour of the island before arriving in Palermo in time for the much-celebrated festival of the city's patron, Saint Rosalia. He departed for Messina on 20 July and "exhausted by fatigue and heat," decided against his intended tour of Calabria and the former Greek colony of Tarentium, returning instead to Naples by early August.[75]

Middleton planned to leave Naples for Paris after the winter of 1819–20, but instead he and Eliza moved to Rome where they remained until April of 1823. During the spring and summer of 1821, Middleton traveled to Constantinople and to Athens, finally fulfilling his long-held dream of visiting Greece. In that year, the Reign of Terror between Greece and Turkey had begun, leading to the Greek War of Independence, and travel would have been extremely dangerous. Nevertheless, in a letter of 1867, Middleton's nephew Edward mentions having shipped to Charleston a box containing "the original acquarelles by Uncle J. I. M. of two scenes in Greece," which as yet are unlocated. However, his surviving drawing of the magnificent Corinthian columns of the Temple of Olympus Zeus, Athens (fig. 63), and a small Greek sketchbook serve to document his trip.[76]

Upon his return from Constantinople in August 1821, Middleton rejoined Eliza and her mother at Lucca where they were spending the summer. His drawing style had changed markedly in two years' time; the plein-air Naples drawings of 1817–19 are loosely sketched in pencil and wash, while the ones made in Lucca and Rome in the years 1821–23 are highly detailed, skilled works. Some forty-nine drawings from these years have been recently rediscovered and published.[77] Apparently using a camera obscura or camera lucida to set the major outlines, but working primarily in pencil—the favored drawing medium of nineteenth-century landscapists—he made painstaking studies of the scenes before him, recording buildings, hills, foliage, and figures with great care and accuracy. *Bagni di Lucca* (fig. 64) reveals his process, with only the underlying outline in the unfinished foreground, and an effective, subtle delineation of the receding building and landscape in the background. In *Grecian Remains,* Middleton depicted Rome from a distance; now more than a decade later, he describes with care the ancient monuments of the city including the Colosseum (cat. 68), the Forum (cat. 71), the Arch of Drusus, and the famous Tomb of Cecelia Metella among others. In these sketches Middleton's compositions have improved, as he learns to frame his scenes effectively and to employ convincing perspective. A few of the drawings, such as *Court of the Museum Capitolium* (fig. 65), are essentially classical outlines in the manner of John Flaxman, but most, like the ones of the Forum, demonstrate a new interest in depth and shading, accomplished with a subtle and varied use of pencil, with occasional darker lines drawn in ink.

In Rome, Middleton made a number of drawings at the Borghesi Gardens, the vast park that was so popular with landscape artists.[78] He also ventured back to the Albano and Arricia area where he had spent so much time in 1808–9. He demonstrates greater interest in the broader landscape, as is evident in comparing the 1809 aquatint of the *Ancient Tomb in the Garden at Pallazuola* (fig. 66) and the new drawing of the same subject (fig. 67). The print has the planar composition and schematic treatment typical of neoclassical style, while the later pencil drawing is a more fully realized landscape, with the tomb now seen from an angle and reduced in importance. Moreover, Middleton's technique has become more accomplished, with a variety of pencil strokes ranging from calligraphic in the foreground to the hatching and shading above the tomb in the background. At the same time, Middleton remains a classicist. Though there are hints in these works of a nascent romanticism—as in his view of the Colosseum—they never express the kind of personal and emotional response to nature that would become a hallmark of nineteenth-century style.

Middleton had begun collecting as a young man in London as early as 1806; on his first trip to Rome he began to collect more seriously, shipping back from Italy "five cases of books and pictures in 1809."[79] He was doubtlessly influenced by Joseph Allen Smith in London and in Rome by Dodwell, the Humboldts, Mme. Brun and Thorvaldsen who were active collectors of both antiquities and paintings. Then in 1816, having sold his Hobonny plantation to his brother Henry, and in 1820 his Cedar Grove plantation to his Uncle John Parker, he was financially able to become a more active buyer. In 1823 a letter from Rome, published in the *London Literary Gazette,* reported, "A Mr. Middleton from Charlestown, himself an excellent landscape-painter, has purchased in Italy, in a few years, a collection of Pictures which would do honor to the palace of a Prince even in the old World."[80]

When Middleton left Rome for Paris in the spring of 1823, he sent sixty-three paintings from his collection to the Pennsylvania Academy of the Fine Arts, where many were exhibited at the annual exhibition of 1824, some in 1825 and 1826, and a

Figure 64 Bagni di Lucca, *1821, John Izard Middleton. Graphite on paper. South Caroliniana Library, University of South Carolina, Columbia.*

Figure 65 Court of the Museum Capitolium, *1822, John Izard Middleton. Graphite on paper. South Caroliniana Library, University of South Carolina, Columbia.*

large group again in 1827. Some idea of Middleton's holdings can be gained from the Pennsylvania Academy registrar's list of 1823, the academy's exhibition catalogues, a list compiled by Pietro Palmaroli (a Roman painter and restorer), as well as from Middleton's will and inventories. The "crown of his collection" was said to be "a Portrait of a Female, by Lionardo da Vinci, admirably restored by Palmaroli."[81]

As one would expect, given his own work, the majority of Middleton's paintings were landscapes ranging from works attributed to seventeenth- and eighteenth-century artists working in Italy such as Claude, Orrizonte, Lucatelli, Panini, Poelenburgh, and Vernet. He also owned works by a number of his contemporaries working in Rome including François Granet, Pierre Chauvin, and Franz Ludwig Catel. On Middleton's death in 1849, the collection was left to his nephew Williams Middleton "to be kept at Middleton Place as an heirloom." As late as 1862, a visitor of Williams's at Middleton Place reported, "we looked first at the pictures, with which the walls of the house are literally covered—some of them are exquisite and very rare. He has the only Claude Lorrain in America." Unfortunately almost all of the collection was lost when Middleton Place was pillaged and burned by Union troops in 1865.[82]

In late April 1823, Middleton left Rome for Paris to seek medical help for his wife. Judging from family correspondence, Eliza's precarious health—long a cause for concern—had declined to a "deplorable state" with periodic episodes when she was "very much deranged." It was hoped that with the "best medical advice in Paris" she might recover.[83] The Middletons proceeded first to Switzerland for the wedding of Eliza's sister Caroline Anne Falconnet (1801–72) to Jacques-Philippe d'Arcambal. Along the route Middleton recorded parts of their journey, first with a detailed drawing of the Arch of Augustus at Susa, near the Mont Cenis pass, then with two views of les Charmettes, the country house near Chambery where Rousseau lived from 1736 to 1742, and finally a view of Voltaire's chateau near Geneva, where the philosopher spent his last years.[84]

After the d'Arcambal wedding, the Middletons proceeded to Paris, arriving in the summer of 1823. Unfortunately, the Parisian doctors were not able to effect a cure for Eliza and by the spring of 1824 her family decided she "ought not to reside with her husband in her present situation."[85] Thereafter she remained an invalid cared for at first by her sister and brother-in-law, the James de Pourtales, and subsequently by her aunt, the Countess Charles de Cadignan until her death in Paris, on 3 February 1831. At her funeral, the same Rev. Monod who had performed her marriage ceremony officiated, and her funeral and gravestone were paid for by M. le Comte de Pourtales.[86]

It would be interesting to know how modern medicine would have diagnosed Eliza's illness—whether an unresolved depression due to the loss of her child or a depressive personality with the complication of an unhappy marriage contributing to her symptoms. As early as 1820 a crisis in the marriage had obviously occurred, for mention was made of Eliza's "resolution of separating herself from him entirely." In Philadelphia, both Middleton and Joseph Allen Smith were referred to as "despot," and Thomas Hunter, Eliza's young nephew, later charged in Paris that Middleton's "tyranny and devilish temper" had caused "one of the most beautiful creatures in the world to run mad," implicating him as a possible contributor to her affliction.[87]

Figure 66 Ancient Tomb in the Garden at Pallazuola, *1812, M. Dubourg after John Izard Middleton. Aquatint from Middleton's* Grecian Remains. *Courtesy of the Museum of Fine Arts, Boston.*

Middleton's life seems to have been deeply affected by the dissolution of the marriage, for in Paris where he remained until his death, he withdrew from his earlier life of travel and work. Except for his nephews and niece, with whom he remained close and who were in Paris at various periods, he reportedly lived "quite secluded from company, seldom leaving home except to go to a play or opera." He occasionally saw visiting Charlestonians, though he told his niece in 1840 that he had "but little communication with society, and least of all American society." He remained strongly critical of America, causing his nephew to exclaim to his sister, "if you knew how manfully I fought the battles of America in repelling the accusations of uncle J I M . . . made against her."[88]

Middleton does not seem to have been active as an artist after his sojourn in Italy. The only known work from his years in Paris is a watercolor of a sultan and harem girl, inscribed "après Decamps" (Middleton Place Foundation), referring to Alexandre-Gabriel Descamps (1803–60) whose paintings of oriental subjects became popular after being exhibited at the Paris Salon of 1831. Middleton's nephew Henry reported "Uncle Izard . . . notwithstanding his familiarity with the pictures of the L[ouvre], still seems to enjoy them intensely," and he "makes an admirable interpreter and guide." Secluded in Paris, he must have spent many hours in his library, for his inventory at his death listed an extraordinary collection of over 1,600 books, several dozen engravings and paintings, and interestingly a daguerreotype apparatus.[89]

Figure 67 Ancient Tomb within Rock at Pallazuola Site of Alba Longa, 1822, John Izard Middleton. Graphite on paper. South Caroliniana Library, University of South Carolina, Columbia.

Middleton was part of a generation that came to maturity in the early nineteenth century assuming that "the Founding Fathers had won the great struggle for American liberty." Unlike his older brother Henry, he apparently felt no need to distinguish himself through public service and "civil duties."[90] The expanding economy between 1793 and 1807 had created a prosperous and mobile society, and with his inherited wealth, Middleton had both the time and money for travel and intellectual pursuits. Nor did he aspire to a professional career, choosing instead to pursue his artistic and intellectual interests as a gentleman artist and antiquarian.

His work seems scarcely to have been noticed in his own lifetime except for an occasional remark in family correspondence, and there was no known exhibition of his drawings and watercolors. Middleton often struck a modest, self-effacing posture, preferring the author's anonymity typical of the period, when "the prefix of one's name to an essay was a form of self-aggrandizement." On one occasion he denied having written an article in the *Review* while "blushing up to the eyes," yet finally made a "full confession to his wife."[91] Regarding his work for *Grecian Remains* Middleton denied any need for public acknowledgment claiming that the "daily delight experienced in the pursuit proved, in itself . . . a sufficient inducement to continue it, and an ample reward for my labors." His purpose he said, using Goethe's words, was to be able in his solitude, "to travel at my ease, over the road which I had before trodden."[92] And yet, with the slightest urging from Petit-Radel in Paris, he had quickly readied his work for publication in London.

Middleton represents a new kind of American—a pioneer in his own way. A half century before Henry James, he abandoned the young nation of Jefferson and Jackson, and instead "found solace in a purely aesthetic Italy," and in France as well.[93] His beginnings were auspicious. By the time he was twenty-five, he had prepared the text and illustrations for his extraordinary book *Grecian Remains* and was admired by such figures as Mme. de Staël and her friend the Baron de Voght, who described him as "un très joli garcon, qui a de l'esprit, quelque chose de noble dans l'âme."[94] He was one of the few Americans of his time who was completely at home in Europe and who came to know the intelligentsia of Rome, Paris, and London. He contributed to the study of classical antiquities in Rome and Latium, adding to the heated debate begun by Winckelmann and Piranesi about the relative merits of Rome and Greece. An aesthete and connoisseur, he built what was reputedly one of the great art collections in America. Finally, and perhaps most significantly, he ranks as one of the first American landscape watercolorists and draftsmen. Many of his interests and subjects prefigure those of the Hudson River School. As E. P. Richardson said, Middleton "introduced another note that was to be important in American romantic landscape, the elegiac landscape of Italy."[95] In the last twenty-five years of his life he became a solitary figure whose creative energies had faded, but his unique earlier accomplishments have won him a place in the cultural and artistic history of the nation.

NOTES

For his invaluable assistance throughout this project, I am deeply indebted to Theodore E. Stebbins, Jr.; I am also grateful to Barbara Doyle (Middleton Place) and Barbara Toscano for their assistance and support, and to Fred Burchsted and staff at Widener Library, Harvard University.

1. Mme. de Staël, *Corinne, or Italy,* trans. and intro. Avriel H. Goldberger (New Brunswick, N.J.: Rutgers University Press, 1987), p. 5.

2. For Middleton genealogy see Langdon Cheves, "Middleton of South Carolina," *SCHM* 1, no. 3 (1900): 228–62.

3. Cheves, "Middleton," p. 244; Henry A. M. Smith, "The Ashley River: Its Seats and Settlements," *SCHM* 20, no. 1 (1919): 40, 119.

4. Arthur Middleton inherited from his father "the Family Pictures now in my house in town," Cheves, "Middleton," p. 242; see also Sarah Lytle, "Thomas Middleton: At Ease with the Arts in Charleston," *Art in the Lives of South Carolinians,* ed. David Moltke-Hansen (Charleston: Carolina Art Association, 1979), pp. 1–11.

5. Henry Middleton's tutor was a Mr. Fariau, possibly Fr. J. Fariau, librarian of the Charleston Library Society in 1780. See *Catalogue of the Books Belonging to the Charleston Library Society, 1826* (Charleston: A. E. Miller, 1826), preface. See "Correspondence of Hon. Arthur Middleton," *SCHM* 26, no. 4 (1925): 204, and *SCHM* 27, no. 2 (1926): 66.

6. David Ramsay, *History of South Carolina: From Its First Settlement in 1670 to the Year 1808* (1858; reprint, Spartanburg, S.C.: Reprint Co., 1959), 2:195; Smith, "The Ashley River," p. 120. Henry Middleton regularly read the popular English *Botanical Magazine.* Mrs. Julines Hering to Mary Helen Hering Middleton, 17 August 1800 and 17 March 1804, Hering-Middleton Papers, SCHS.

7. Langdon Cheves, "Blake of South Carolina," *SCHM* 1, no. 2 (1900): 161–62. William Middleton moved from Charleston to his Suffolk estate, Crowfield Hall, in 1754; Cheves, "Middleton," pp. 233, 239.

8. See "'To Blend Pleasure with Knowledge': The Cultural Odyssey of Charlestonians Abroad" in this volume. See also Frederick P. Bowes, *The Culture of Early Charleston* (Chapel Hill: University of North Carolina Press, 1942), chap. 3, and E. Alfred Jones, *American Members of the Inns of Court* (London: St. Catherine Press, 1924).

9. *Trinity College Admissions, 1801–1850,* eds. W. W. Rouse Ball and J. A. Venn (London: Macmillan, 1911), 4:20.

10. In 1799 William and Ann Blake bought Sunbury Place. Kenneth Heselton, *A History of Sunbury Court* (Sunbury-on-Thames, Middlesex: Sunbury and Shepperton Local History Society, 1981), pp.3–16.

11. As quoted in Jeremy Black, *The British Abroad: The Grand Tour in the Eighteenth Century* (New York: St. Martin's Press, 1992), p. 5.

12. *The Bath Chronicle,* 11 January 1804, reports the arrival in Bath of Mr. J. J. Middleton, Mr. H. J. R. Pringle, and Mr. J. J. Pringle (a Charlestonian), as well as Mr. Byfield and Mr. Surtees, apparently Cambridge classmates. John Izard Middleton is sometimes identified as "J.J." Middleton.

13. Mrs. Julines Hering to Mary Helen Hering Middleton, 10 January 1804, Hering-Middleton Papers, SCHS.

14. Middleton's lecture notes closely follow the text of lectures Craig delivered at the Royal Institution and later published as *Lectures on Drawing, Painting, and Engraving* (London, 1821). Craig, drawing-master to the Princess of Wales and Painter in Watercolours to the Queen, also published *The Complete Instructor in Drawing* (London, 1806). Middleton's Lecture Notes, Ellida Davison Rea Collection.

15. Cheves, "Blake," pp. 162–63; Middleton was probably in Long Melford, Suffolk, for the wedding of his relative John Middleton (1784–1826), on 14 June 1806. Cheves, "Middleton," p. 237, n. 2.

16. Cheves, "Blake," pp. 162–63; John Soane designed the lodges (1781) and dairy (1783) for Philip Yorke's country estate, Hamells Park, in Hertfordshire. Dorothy Stroud, *Sir John Soane Architect* (London: Giles de la Mare, 1996), pp. 51–53, 119, 239; and Pierre de la Ruffinière du Prey, *John Soane: The Making of an Architect* (Chicago: University of Chicago Press, 1982), pp. 245–65.

17. John Izard Middleton, "A Fortnight's Journal of a Tour thro' the Isle of Wight . . .," 1806, Ellida Davison Rea Collection and Botanical Sketchbook, MPF.

18. In preparation for his trip, in Holland Middleton read J. J. Barthelemy's *Voyage en Italie.* Middleton had letters to Junot, Napoleon's military governor in Paris; James Bowdoin III (1752–1811) American minister to Spain; Armstrong (1758–1843) American minister to Paris; J. G. Legrand (1743–1807) architect and writer; Ennio Visconti (1751–1818) director of the Musée Napoléon; the Duponts; and others. Journal of John Izard Middleton, 1807–8, Ellida Davison Rea Collection.

19. In Middleton's own family there was considerable precedent for his Grand Tour. His parents spent the winter of 1770 in the south of France, later traveling to Rome during a three-year tour between 1768–71. Henry Middleton to William Middleton, 8 February 1770, De Saumarez Papers, SCHS. His relatives, Ralph and Alice Izard, visited the classical sites in southern Italy in 1775 with John Singleton Copley.

20. Staël's father was Jacques Necker, a wealthy banker from Geneva who became finance minister to Louis XVI before the Revolution. Staël was first banished by Napoleon from Paris in December 1802 after the publication of *Delphine.* Simone Balayé, *Lumieres et liberté* (Paris: Klincksieck, 1979), pp. 101, 246; see also Madelyn Gutwirth, *Madame de Staël, Novelist: The Emergence of the Artist as Woman* (Urbana: University of Illinois Press, 1978).

21. Journal of John Izard Middleton, 1807–8. Staël, *Corinne, or Italy,* p. xv. Staël returned to Coppet, 10 May 1807, where she remained until late November of the same year. *Correspondance Generale* 6, ed. Beatrice Jasinski (Paris: Klincksieck, 1993), p. xviii. The celebrated artist Mme. Elizabeth Vigée-LeBrun (1776–1842) visited Coppet in September and began a portrait of Mme. de Staël as Corinne. For Vigée-LeBrun see *Correspondance,* ed. Jasinski, pp. 289, 300.

22. In the summer and fall of 1807 there were also performances of Jean Racine's *Andromaque* and *Phèdre* and Staël's *Geneviève de Brabant.* Staël's companion Benjamin Constant was working on *Wallstein,* a tragedy in five acts adapted from Schiller. Pierre Kohler, *Mme. de Staël et la Suisse* (Lausanne: Payot, 1916), pp. 469–75. Danielle Johnson-Cousin, "La Société Dramatique de Madame de Staël de 1802 à 1816," *Studies on Voltaire and the Eighteenth Century* (Oxford: Voltaire Foundation, Univeristy of Oxford, 1992).

23. Prince Auguste of Prussia visited Coppet until 28 October 1807. Jasinski, pp. 239, 336–37. At Coppet, Middleton also met August Von Schlegel (1767–1845), the German translator, critic, and tutor for Staël's children, the historian baron Prosper de Barante (1782–1866), as well as François Gaudot (1756–1836), the erudite friend of Staël, and James-Alexandre de Pourtales (1776–1842), Middleton's future brother-in-law, both of whom he later saw in Rome.

24. John Izard Middleton, English-Swiss Sketchbook, 1806–7, Ellida Davison Rea Collection.

25. A performance of *Deux Fats, ou le Grand Monde* with Middleton in the role of Mr. Sidmours on 26 November 1807 was the last of the season. Jasinski, pp. 336 n. 2, 337; Journal of John Izard Middleton, 1807–8.

26. Simone Balayé, *Les Carnets de Voyage* (Geneve: Librarie Droz, 1971), p. 107. Mme. de Staël to Mme. Friederike Brun, 26 November 1807, in *Correspondance,* ed. Jasinski, p. 336. Journal of John Izard Middleton, 1807–8.

27. The painters Johann Christian Reinhart, (1761–1847) Gottlieb Schick (1776–1812) J. L. Lund (1777–1867) and Joseph Anton Koch (1769–1839) also frequented their Roman salons. For Karl Viktor von Bonstetten see *Italiam! Italiam! Charles-Victor de Bonstetten redécouvert,* ed. Doris Walser-Wilhelm and Peter Walser-Wilhelm (Bern: Peter Lang, 1996), p. 260. For Caroline von Humboldt and Friederike Brun see *Frauen zur Goethezeit, Briefwechsel,* ed. Ilse Foerst-Crato (Dusseldorf: privately published, 1975), pp. 4–6. Journal of John Izard Middleton, 1807–8.

28. *Frauen zur Goethezeit,* ed. Foerst-Crato, p. 3, 4; Louis Bobé, *Frederikke Brun* (Kobenhavn: H. Hagerup, 1910), pp. 120–42.

29. For Giuseppi Alborghetti (1776–1846) see Balayé, *Les Carnets de voyage,* p. 213. For Séroux d'Agincourt (1730–1814) see *Correspondance,* ed. Jasinski, p. 577. For Dodwell see *Italiam! Italiam!* ed. Walser-Wilhelm and Walser-Wilhelm, p. 336.

30. Michael Shanks, *Classical Archaeology of Greece* (London: Routledge, 1996), pp. 56, 65.

31. *Correspondance,* ed. Jasinski, p. 386.

32. Middleton also climbed Vesuvius which he said "cannot be described," and with the sixth book of Virgil's *Aeneid* as his guide he visited Pozzuoli, Baia, Cumae and Lake Avernus. Journal of John Izard Middleton, 1807–9.

33. One of Middleton's sources for his classical itinerary may have been Ellis Knight, *Description of Latium; or, La Campagna di Roma* (London: Longman, Hurst, Rees, and Orme, 1805). It is most likely his copy that survives at Middleton Place. J. J. Middleton, *Grecian Remains in Italy . . .* (London: Edward Orme, 1812), p. 1.

34. I am grateful to Kathleen H. Foster for her helpful suggestions regarding the camera obscura.

35. Middleton, *Grecian Remains,* pp. 3–4. Bonstetten introduced F. Giuntotardi to Mme. de Staël in Rome in 1805, and she had one of his views of the Forum at her chateau at Coppet. Balayé, *Les Carnets de voyage,* p. 192, n. 117. See Gerhard Bott, "Rom–und Tivoli–Ansichten von Filippo Giuntotardi," *Jahrbuch der Staatlichen Kunstsamlung in Badden-Wurttenberg* 21 (1984):143–50.

36. Diana Strazdes, "Washington Allston's Early Career 1796–1811" (Ph.D. diss., Yale University, 1982), pp. 120–21.

37. Eliza Middleton Fisher to Mary Helen Hering Middleton, 18 September 1839, private collection. Allston is quoted by John R. Welsh in "Washington Allston: Expatriate South Carolinian," *SCHM* 67, no. 2 (April 1966): 91.

38. J. J. Middleton, *Letter to a Member of the National Institute at Paris* (Charleston: Printed for the Author, 1814), p. 19.

39. The first exhibition of the Society of Painters in Water-Coulours took place in London in 1805; it included many landscapes by the artists mentioned. For Ducros and Kaisermann see *Images of the Grand Tour: Louis Ducros, 1748–1810* (Geneva: Editions du Tricorne, 1985), and Georg Schaefer, *Klassizismus und Romantik in Deutschland, Gemälde und Zeichnungen aus der Sammlung Georg Schafer, Schweinfurt.* Ausstellung im Germanischen Nationalmuseum Nurnberg (Schweinfurt: Sammlung Georg Schaefer, 1996).

40. Joshua Shaw, *Picturesque Views of American Scenery* (Philadelphia: M. Carey and Son, 1820–21), and William Guy Wall, *The Hudson River Portfolio* (New York: Henry I. Megarey, 1821–25).

41. Middleton, *Grecian Remains,* p. 20.

42. Mme. Brun's precocious daughter Ida Brun (b. 1792) was celebrated for her musical talent as well as her display of "attitudes," a new performance art of dance and pantomime in the style of Lady Emma Hamilton. See *Correspondance,* ed. Jasinski, p. 588; Bobé, pp. 215–16; and K. G. Holmström, *Monodrama, Attitudes, Tableaux Vivants* (Stockholm: Almqvist and Wiksell, 1967). Elena di Majo et al., *Bertel Thorvaldsen: Scultore Danese a Roma* (Roma: De Luca, Galleria Nazionale d'Arte Moderna, 1989), pp. 6–10.

43. Carlo Fea (1753–1836) was one of Staël's guides to the antiquities of Rome and a friend of Mme. Brun. For excavations in Rome before 1810 see Ronald T. Ridley, *The Eagle and the Spade* (Cambridge: Cambridge University Press, 1992).

44. On 19 March 1801 Petit-Radel introduced his ideas to the French Institute. On 28 January 1804 the French Institute printed and distributed 1,500 copies of *Eclaircissements sur les constructions de plusieurs monuments militaires de l'antiquité* (Paris: Baudouin, 1804). See Louis-Charles-François Petit-Radel, *Recherches sur les monuments cyclopéens ou pélasgiques* (Paris: l'Imprimerie Royale, 1841), pp. 63, 69. By 1810 reports of 177 cities with ancient cyclopean walls had been received from Greece, Italy, Spain, and Asia Minor. Sylvanus Urban, *Gentleman's Magazine and Historical Chronicle* 93 (February 1823): 110–12.

45. Giuseppe Simelli submitted fifty-two drawings of cyclopean constructions in 1809 to the French Institute. Petit-Radel, *Recherches,* pp. 82–83. In December 1808, M. Dionigi, a colleague of Dodwell and d'Agincourt, announced to the institute her forthcoming work, *Viaggi in alcune città del Lazio,* published in 1809. *Proces-verbaux de l'institut,* ed. Marcel Bonnaire (Paris: Librairie Colin, 1940): 3:211–12. Middleton reported seeing her book before he left Rome. Middleton, *Letter to a Member,* p. 23. Dionigi's painting *Apollo presso l'Anfrizio* was sent to the South Carolina Academy of Art at Charleston, where she was an honorary member. Nicola Marcone, *M. Dionigi e le sue opere* (Rome, 1896).

46. Charles Victor de Bonstetten to Christian Gottlob Heyne, 1808, cited by Heyne in Druckvorlage: *Gottingische gelehrte Anzeigen* 1808, S. 910–11 (91 Stuck, 6 June). I am grateful to Dr. Doris and Peter Walser-Wilhelm for bringing this letter to my attention. See also Edward Dodwell, *Views and Descriptions of Cyclopian or Pelasgic Remains in Greece and Italy* (London: Treuttel, Wurtz and Richter, 1833).

47. Adolf Michaelis, *A Century of Archaeological Discoveries* (London: John Murray, 1908), p. 32.

48. John Izard Middleton, Roman Sketchbook, June 1808. Ellida Davison Rea Collection. See Giuseppe Lugli, "Le fortificazioni delle antiche città italiche," *Atti della accademia nazionale dei Lincei, Rendiconti* 2 (June 1947):294–307. However, some scholars believe that the walls may be of early Italic or even Etruscan design.

49. Middleton, *Letter to a Member,* p. 10. Soon after his arrival, Middleton records exploring Rome's ancient ruins with Dodwell and Temple (b. 1764), son of Sir John Temple, British consul-general in New York (1785–1798). Journal of John Izard Middleton, 1807–8. Charles Eliot Norton, "The First American Classical Archaeologist," *American Journal of Archaeology* 1 (January 1885): 4.

50. Middleton, *Grecian Remains,* p. 2.

51. Middleton, *Grecian Remains,* p. 3; Middleton, *Letter to a Member,* pp. 16, 21; Petit-Radel, *Recherches,* p. 41.

52. J. I. Middleton to Fulwer Skipworth, 1 January 1811, HSP. John Izard Middleton, Roman Journal, December 1808–October 1809, Ellida Davison Rea Collection. Auguste de Staël to Mme. de Staël, 1810, private collection.

53. Auguste de Staël to Mme. de Staël, 4 January 1810, private collection.

54. J. J. Middleton, "The Confessional: A Tale," 1810. Edward Middleton Collection, SHC-UNC.

55. Middleton, *Letter to a Member,* p. 21.

56. Auguste de Staël mentions to Mme. de Staël Middleton's engagement in a letter of 10 April 1810, private collection. Société Historique du Protestantisme, Paris; Acte de Mariage, Préfecture du Département de Seine. Eliza Falconnet had been in Paris with her family since the wedding in June 1809 of her sister Anna to James Pourtales. After the Middletons' wedding they visited the Chateau de Bandeville, the Pourtales' country seat near Paris (see n. 23 above). Eliza Hunter to Mrs. Robert Mackay, 1 January and 14 June 1810, Hunter Papers, Newport Historical Society.

57. Eliza Hunter to Mrs. Mackay, 21 July, 30 August, and 4 November 1810, Hunter Papers, Newport Historical Society. Middleton, *Letter to a Member,* p. 13.

58. J. I. Middleton, letter to a friend of Mr. Falconnet of Naples, 12 March 1812, MPF.

59. Charlotte Manigault, letter to Henrietta Drayton, 17 April 1812, Drayton Papers, MPF. Middleton, *Grecian Remains,* p. 31.

60. J. I. M., to Madame Récamier, 10 March 1812, Bibliothèque Nationale, Paris.

61. Circulation records, 1811–14, CLS.

62. Charlotte Drayton Manigault, to Henrietta Drayton, 25 July 1814, Drayton Papers, MPF; Mary Helen H. Middleton to Margaret I. Manigault, 3 September 1814, HSP.

63. Mary Pringle to Henrietta Drayton, 8 September 1814, Drayton Papers, MPF; Mary Helen H. Middleton to Margaret I. Manigault, begun 31 May 1815, Cadwalader Collection, HSP.

64. Harriet Manigault, *The Diary of Harriet Manigault, 1813–1816* (Rockland, Maine: Colonial Dames of America, Chapter II, 1976), pp. 101–35; "Excerpts from a Memoir of Joshua Francis Fisher," in *Diary,* p. 42.

65. Charlotte Manigault to Mrs. Lewis Morris, 11 April 1816; Alice Izard to Margaret Izard Manigault, 26 October 1815, Manigault Family Papers, SCL.

66. Despite his Carolina roots Smith "deemed Philadelphia more central than Charleston" as a home for his collection. See "'Picture Mania': Collectors and Collecting in Charleston" in this volume; see also E. P. Richardson, "Allen Smith, Collector and Benefactor," *American Art Journal* 1 (Fall 1969): 5–19, and R. A. McNeal, "Joseph Allen Smith, 'American Grand Tourist,'" *International Journal of the Classical Tradition* 4, no. 1 (Summer 1997): 72. Smith referred Middleton to artists such as François-Xavier Fabre in Florence and Friedrich Rehberg. John Izard Middleton, Roman Sketchbook, June 1808, Ellida Davison Rea Collection.

67. George C. Rogers, Jr., "Preliminary Thoughts on Joseph Allen Smith as the United States' First Art Collector," in Moltke-Hansen, p. 8. When the Middletons left Philadelphia, they left the Sully portrait of Eliza with Mrs. Smith. Mary Helen H. Middleton to Margaret I. Manigault, 25 June 1816, Cadwalader Collection, HSP.

68. Naples had long been a favorite southern resort of the English, and the British minister at Naples and friend of the Middletons Sir William A'Court complained, "We have now nearly three hundred English here. I mean presentable people who expect to be received and entertained at my house. If this continues I shall be ruined." Harold Acton, *The Bourbons of Naples* (1956; reprint, London: Methuen, 1974), p. 208.

69. Johann Wolfgang von Goethe, *Italian Journey,* trans. Robert Heitner (New York: Suhrkamp Publishers, 1989), p. 170.

70. Falconnet had the confidence of King Joachim Murat, Napoleon's puppet ruler in Naples (1808–15), and his bank held certificates of public debt for the Kingdom of Naples. "Généalogie de la famille de Palézieux dit Falconnet," Archives Cantonales Vaudoises. *Correspondance,* ed. Jasinski, p. 599; Washington Irving, *Journals and Notebooks, 1803–1806,* ed. Nathalia Wright (Madison: University of Wisconsin Press, 1969), pp. 234–35.

71. Eliza F. Middleton to Mary Helen H. Middleton, 1 February 1818 and 12 September 1819, Hering-Middleton Collection, SCHS. Fig. 60 is inscribed on verso: "Casino Carracosa [*sic*]; occupied October 1819 by Sir William A'Court." See Vanna Fraticelli, *Il giardino napoletano, settecento e ottocento* (Napoli: Electa, 1993). I am grateful to Dr. Giancarlo C. Alisio for this reference.

72. Eliza described a sketching excursion in the spring of 1818 to the valley of la Cava and the Amalfi coast and another to Monte Cassino. Eliza F. Middleton to Mary Helen H. Middleton, 27 June 1818, Hering-Middleton Collection, SCHS. Thomas Jones, "Memoirs of Thomas Jones," *The Thirty-Second Volume of the Walpole Society* (London: Oliver Buridge, 1951), p. 104.

73. For Huber and Pitloo see Vincenzo Bindi, *La scuola di Posillipo* (Torino: Gruppo Editoriale Forma, 1983); Giuliano Briganti, et al., *In the Shadow of Vesuvius* (Naples: Electa Napoli, 1990); and *Civiltà dell'ottocento: Le arti figurative* (Napoli: Electa Napoli, 1997), pp. 393–98.

74. Andrew Wilton and Ilaria Bignamini, eds., *Grand Tour: The Lure of Italy in the 18th Century* (London: Tate Gallery, 1996), p. 96. Also influential were Jean Pierre Houel, *Voyage pittoresque à Naples et en Sicile* (1783–87), and Abbé Saint Non, *Voyage pittoresque* (1781–86).

75. Eliza F. Middleton to Mary Helen Hering, 1 August 1818, Hering-Middleton Collection, SCHS.

76. Mary Helen H. Middleton to Septima Sexta Middleton Rutledge, 25 August and 12 October 1821, HSP; Edward Middleton to Williams Middleton, 6 June 1867, MPF.

77. These drawings are now owned by the South Caroliniana Library, University of South Carolina, Columbia. See Charles R. Mack and Lynn Robertson, eds., *The Roman Remains: John Izard Middleton's Visual Souvenirs of 1820–1823 with Additional Views in Italy, France, and Switzerland* (Columbia: University of South Carolina Press, 1997).

78. Friederike Brun recorded the popularity of the Villa Borghese, as quoted in Peter Galassi, *Corot in Italy* (New Haven: Yale University Press, 1991), p. 108.

79. J. I. Middleton to Fulwar Skipworth, 1 January 1811, HSP. Included in Middleton's shipment home were works by Fabre, Bronzino, Kaiserman and Panini. Also included were nearly three dozen paintings and drawings he shipped for Smith, including works by Friedrich Rehberg, Jan Both and copies after Claude. Over 150 of Middleton's own drawings and watercolors, were forwarded on to Paris at this time. John Izard Middleton, Roman Journal, December 1808–October 1809, Ellida Davison Rea collection.

80. For transfer of Hobonny plantation in April 1816 see document from John Izard Middleton, 5 August 1839, Paris, MPF. For transfer of Cedar Grove to Parker see Smith, "The Ashley River," p. 40. "Letters from Rome," 22 February 1823, published in *The London Literary Gazette, and Journal of Belles Lettres, Arts, Sciences,* 31 May 1823, and reprinted in the *Philadelphia National Gazette,* 28 July 1823, and *CM,* 6 August 1823.

81. Register of works received, 1823–24, PAFA; Palmaroli's list, Cheves papers, SCHS; Charleston County Probate, vol. C, 1850–54, p. 230; inventaire, 8 April 1850, Archives de Paris. "Letters from Rome," *The London Literary Gazette,* 1823. P. Palmaroli (d. 1818, Rome) M. Berthelot, et al., *Grande Encyclopédie* (Paris: Larousse, 1886–1902) 25: 898.

82. *The Diary of Miss Emma Holmes, 1861–1866,* ed., John F. Marszalek (Baton Rouge: Louisiana State University Press, 1979), p. 148. Smith, "The Ashley River," p. 120.

83. Mary Helen H. Middleton to Septima Sexta M. Rutledge, 12 October 1821 and 1 May 1823, Cadwalader Collection, HSP.

84. These drawings are part of the group at the South Caroliniana Library. (See n. 77 above).

85. Mary Helen H. Middleton, letter to Septima Sexta M. Rutledge, 18 September 1825, Cadwalader Collection, HSP. Thomas R. Hunter to William and Mary Hunter, 4 July 1828, Hunter Papers, Newport Historical Society.

86. Administration Centrale des Pompe Funèbres, Arrondissement 11, private collection.

87. Mary Helen H. Middleton to Septima Sexta M. Rutledge, 1 March 1820, Cadwalader Collection, HSP. Manigault, *Diary,* p. 134. Thomas Hunter to William and Mary Hunter, 4 July 1828, Hunter Papers, Newport Historical Society.

88. Charles Izard Manigault to Col. Oliver Middleton, 10 November 1828, Cheves-Middleton Papers, SCHS. J. I. Middleton to Eliza Middleton Fisher, 26 December 1840, HSP. Henry Middleton, Jr. to Eliza Middleton Fisher, 3 March 1837, Cadwalader Collection, HSP.

89. Henry Middleton, Jr., to Eliza Middleton Fisher, August 1835, Cadwalader Collection, HSP. Inventaire, 1850, Archives de Paris.

90. Bernard Bailyn et al., *The Great Republic: A History of the American People* (Boston: Little Brown, 1977), p. 465.

91. Michael O'Brien, *Rethinking the South: Essays in Intellectual History* (Baltimore: Johns Hopkins University Press, 1988), pp. 22, 46. Mary Helen H. Middleton to Margaret I. Manigault, December/January 1812 or 1813, Cadwalader Collection, HSP.

92. Middleton, *Letter to a Member,* p. 22n; Middleton quoted Goethe's *Die Walverwandtschaften* (Oxford: Basil Blackwell, 1971), p. 220.

93. O'Brien, *Rethinking the South,* p. 109

94. Baron de Voght to Mme. Récamier, 12 November 1809, Bibliothèque Nationale, Paris. I am grateful to Mme. Beatrice Jasinski for bringing this letter to my attention.

95. E. P. Richardson, *Painting in America, from 1502 to the Present* (New York: Thomas Y. Crowell Co., 1965), p. 157.

Contributors

Angela D. Mack (ADM)
Gibbes Museum of Art

Maurie D. McInnis (MDM)
University of Virginia

J. Thomas Savage (JTS)
Historic Charleston Foundation

Robert A. Leath (RAL)
Historic Charleston Foundation

Susan Ricci Stebbins (SRS)
Museum of Fine Arts, Boston

Carmen C. Bambach
Metropolitan Museum of Art

Hugh Belsey
Gainsborough's House, Suffolk, England

John W. Coffey
North Carolina Museum of Art

Lance Humphries
Baltimore, Maryland

Michelle L. Kloss
University of Maryland

Chris Loeblein
The Charleston Museum

Ellen G. Miles
National Portrait Gallery, Smithsonian Institution

Jane Munro
Fitzwilliam Museum, Cambridge, England

Jonathan H. Poston
Historic Charleston Foundation

Wendy Wassyng Roworth
University of Rhode Island

Theodore E. Stebbins, Jr.
Museum of Fine Arts, Boston

Paintings

1. *Crokatt, William Keable and Peter Darnal Muilman in a Landscape,* ca. 1748

THOMAS GAINSBOROUGH (British, 1727–88)
Oil on canvas, 29 ½ × 24 ½ in.

Trustees of Gainsborough's House, Sudbury, and the Tate Gallery, London

Provenance: Perhaps commissioned by Henry and Peter Muilman; by descent to Peter Muilman's daughter Anne Crokatt; by descent to her younger daughter Emilia Boucherett; by descent to her son Ayscoghe Boucherett (1792–1857); by descent to his daughter Mary Barne (d. 1861); by descent to her great-great-great-grandson Miles Barne; his [anonymous sale], Sotheby's, 14 July 1993, lot 49, bought by Hazlitt, Gooden, and Fox for Gainsborough's House and the Tate Gallery

The portrait shows on the left, Charles Crokatt (1730–69), the son of the London agent of South Carolina James Crokatt (d. 1776), and his wife Esther Gaillard, and on the right, Peter Darnal Muilman (d. 1766). In the center playing a flute is William Keable (?1714–74).[1] The relationship between Crokatt and Muilman is explained by the young Peter Manigault to his mother in South Carolina in a letter from London dated 20 February 1750: "I was about a Month or six Week ago in the Country with Mr. Crokatt, at a fine Seat he has lately purchased in Essex, called Luxborough,[2] it cost him Nineteen Thousand five hundred pounds at first, and tis said, he has laid out Ten thousand pound more upon it, in Repairs & Furniture; I think he has Grandour enough for his Money. . . . Tis said that Charles Crokatt is to marry the only daughter of one Mr. Muilman a rich Hamburgh Merchant; and that Mr. Muilman's Son is to have Miss Crokatt, Charles Crokatt is a very pretty young Fellow. But young Muilman . . . is not quite so agreeable as could be wished."[3]

Manigault makes one or two minor errors. For instance, Henry Muilman, the father of the haughty young man on the right, came from Amsterdam rather than Hamburg,[4] and his son died in 1766 before Muilman married Miss Crokatt. However, the rumor that this marriage was to take place and the fact that Charles Crokatt did marry Anna Muilman on 16 April 1752 at St. George's Hanover Square, London,

suggest that both households considered that marriages were best governed by financial expediency rather than affairs of the heart.

In later correspondence, Manigault commented about the qualities of Keable's portraiture and mentioned that he had a particularly close association with visiting Americans, which may provide the motive for including his likeness in the triple portrait.[5] Keable's role as flautist implies that he served Crokatt and Muilman as music master and he may well have demonstrated his versatility by offering a few drawing lessons too. Perhaps Keable's task resembled that of a "bear-leader" on the Grand Tour, attempting, like the teachers in Hogarth's *Rake's Progress,* to help Muilman and Crokatt overcome their status as parvenus.

Keable's links with Gainsborough are more difficult to establish. A manuscript note fixed to the back of the stretcher, which was written shortly after 1789, attributes the figures to "Mr Keables" and the landscape to Gainsborough. Judging by the delineation of the features and the purple tonality of Keable's head, this statement should be seriously considered; Keable may well have contributed his own self-portrait to the group.[6]

Hugh Belsey

1. A label on the stretcher names the figures in the portrait though it fails to identify them individually. The portrait of Keable is established by the self-portrait signed and dated 1748 in the Yale Center for British Art, New Haven (B1976, 7, 47), and the other two figures are identified by their relative ages.

2. Luxborough Hall near Chigwell in Essex was a baroque villa built for Robert Knight between 1716 and 1720. It was destroyed by James Hatch shortly after he bought the house in 1800. Luxborough is low lying and liable to flood which may partly account for Crokatt's spending so much on the property. See J. Kenworthy-Brown et al., *Burke's and Savill's Guide to Country Houses,* vol. 3, *East Anglia* (London: Burke's Peerage, 1981).

3. "Peter Manigault's Letters," ed. Mabel L. Webber, *SCHM* 31 (October 1930): 272–73.

4. See the obituary of the sitter's uncle Peter Muilman in *Gentleman's Magazine* 60 (1790): 183. Henry Muilman, the father of Gainsborough's sitter, lived at Dagnam near Romford in Essex and had connections with Gainsborough through Henry Bate and Sir Richard Neave. See E. K. Waterhouse, *Gainsborough* (London: E. Hulton, 1958), nos. 45 and 513; and William Thomas Whitley, *Thomas Gainsborough* (New York: Scribner's, 1915), pp. 127–40.

5. Peter Manigault to his mother, London, 15 April 1751, quoted in "Peter Manigault's Letters," Webber, p. 278.

6. I am grateful to Andrew Wilton for discussing this point with me.

2. *Mrs. Benjamin Smith* (Anne Loughton), 1749

WILLIAM KEABLE (British, ?1714–74)
Oil on canvas, 29 ⅞ × 25 in.

Signed lower left: W Keable pinxit 1749
Carolina Art Association/Gibbes Museum of Art
Provenance: Purchased in 1883 from Mrs. Thomas Osborne Lowndes, daughter of William Loughton Smith

3. *Thomas Smith, Jr.,* 1749

WILLIAM KEABLE (British, ?1714–74)
Oil on canvas, 29 ¾ × 24 ¼ in.

Signed on a canvas label attached to the upper stretcher bar: William Keable pinxit
Inscribed on a canvas label attached to the lower stretcher bar: "Done at Richmond in Surry June 1749 in the 30th yr. of my age Thos Smith Esq."
Mr. and Mrs. Robert Goodwyn Rhett
Provenance: By family descent

British portraitist William Keable painted these portraits of Thomas Smith, Jr. (1719–90), and his sister-in-law Anne Loughton Smith (1722–60) in England in 1749.[1] A portrait of Anne Loughton Smith's husband, Benjamin Smith (1718–70; Albrecht-Kemper Museum of Art, Saint Joseph, Mo.), now attributed to John Wollaston, could also be the work of Keable (fig. 68). Peter Manigault commented on Keable's patronage by several South Carolinians in 1751. Discussing his portrait, just completed by Allan Ramsay (fig. 9; unlocated), he explained why he had commissioned it from Ramsay rather than Keable: "I was advised to have it drawn by one Keble, that drew Tom Smith, & several others that went over to Carolina, but upon seeing his Paintings, I found that though his Likenesses, (which is the easiest Part in doing a Picture,) were some of them very good, yet his Paint seemed to be laid on

with a Trowel, and looked more like Plaistering than Painting, you may guess at the Difference between Ramsay, & Keble Painting, by the Difference of their Prices, What Ramsay demands Four & Twenty Guineas for, T'other humbly hopes, you'll allow him Seven."[2]

Manigault's description of Keable's style as "laid on with a Trowel" and "more like Plaistering than Painting" characterizes Keable's use of thickly applied pigment. This is in contrast to the thin glazes of color and delicate touches of detail that Ramsay adopted after studying painting in Italy in 1736–38. Ramsay's higher prices are clear evidence of his popularity in London at this time. William Keable's work is not well known today. His earliest recorded painting may be a self-portrait (1748; Yale Center for British Art, New Haven). In the 1750s Keable was associated with the St. Martin's Lane Academy, an important London artists' organization.[3] His portrait of Sir Crisp Gascoyne, lord mayor of London in 1753 (Collection of the Marquess of Salisbury, Hatfield House, Hertfordshire), and two of Dr. Francis Douce were engraved by James McArdell.[4] His work also includes small full-length portraits.[5] By 1761 Keable was in Naples, Italy, where he continued to work as a portrait painter. Settling in Bologna in 1765, he was elected to the Accademia Clementina in 1770. He was also an accomplished violinist and several of his Italian portraits are of musicians. He died in Bologna.

Ellen G. Miles

1. The portrait of Thomas Smith, Jr., was first mentioned in a footnote to "Peter Manigault's Letters," ed. Mabel L. Webber, *SCHM* 31 (October 1930): 278, n. 14. The portrait of Anne Loughton Smith had been attributed at times to John Wollaston, Jeremiah Theus, and an unidentified artist before cleaning revealed Keable's signature. It was correctly attributed to Keable in *South Carolina Portraits: A Collection of Portraits of South Carolinians and Portraits in South Carolina* (Columbia: National Society of the Colonial Dames of America in the State of South Carolina, 1996), p. 355.
2. "Peter Manigault's Letters," Webber, pp. 276–78.
3. On Keable see Edward Edwards, *Anecdotes of Painters Who Have Resided or Been Born in England; with Critical Remarks on Their Productions* (London, 1808), p. 4; Ellis K. Waterhouse, *The Dictionary of British 18th-Century Painters in Oils and Crayons* (Woodbridge, Suffolk: Baron Publishing, 1981), p. 203; and John Ingamells, *A Dictionary of British and Irish Travelers in Italy, 1701–1800,* compiled from the Brinsley Ford Archive (New Haven: Yale University Press, 1997), p. 565.
4. Erna Auerbach and C. Kingsley Adams, *Paintings and Sculpture at Hatfield House* (London: Constable, 1971), p. 205, no. 248, illustration p. 287; John Chaloner Smith, *British Mezzotinto Portraits* (London: Henry Sotheran, 1883), 2:856–57, 864. The portraits of Dr. Douce are unlocated.
5. Waterhouse, *Dictionary,* p. 203, reproduces a signed portrait of an unknown gentleman, sold at Christie's in 1967. The Witt Library, Courtauld Institute, London, has a photograph of a double portrait by Keable of Ayscoghe Boucherett (d. 1788) and his steward, owned by Col. M. Barne in 1956.

Figure 68 Benjamin Smith, *attributed to John Wollaston. Courtesy of the Albrecht-Kemper Museum of Art, St. Joseph, Mo.*

4. *Miles Brewton,* 1756

Sir Joshua Reynolds (British, 1723–92)
Oil on canvas, 30 ⅛ × 25 in.

Signed verso: J. Reynolds, 1756
Miles Brewton House collection
Provenance: By family descent

Son of Robert (1697–1759) and Mary Griffith Brewton (1697–1761), Miles Brewton (1731–75) became one of the wealthiest men in Charleston. He was a partner of Benjamin Smith (cat. 2) and Thomas Loughton Smith in the firm of Smith, Brewton and Smith, a leading mercantile house and one of the largest slave importers on the eve of the American Revolution. Brewton's ascendancy in the city's mercantile elite was fostered by Charleston's growing wealth based on rice, indigo, slaves, and the shipping trade. His marriage in 1759 to Mary Izard, daughter of Joseph and Ann Bull Izard, brought him into the sphere of South Carolina's leading planter families and aristocratic British officials. Lord William Campbell, South Carolina's last royal governor and a son of the fourth duke of Argyll, had married Mrs. Brewton's first cousin Sarah Izard in 1763. While their rented house was being readied for what proved to be a brief occupancy, Lord and Lady Campbell (cats. 9 and 10) were guests in the Brewtons' splendid new town house (completed 1769).[1]

Active in colonial politics, Brewton served in six Royal Assemblies and the First Provincial Assembly. In 1774, the Brewtons and their two children set sail for Philadelphia where Brewton was to serve in the first Continental Congress. Tragically, they all perished at sea. Brewton's magnificent town house and all its possessions (cat. 88) passed to his sister Rebecca Brewton Motte.

During the Civil War the painting was taken to France and remained with family members abroad to preserve it from confiscation by northern troops. The portrait survived Nazi occupation of France and Allied invasions in Beritz. In 1945, Charleston family members located the painting and secured permission from their European relations to have it returned to Charleston. It was placed in the drawing room of the Miles Brewton House, where it was most likely displayed originally.[2]

ADM

1. Walter B. Edgar and N. Louise Bailey, eds., *Biographical Directory of the South Carolina House of Representatives,* vol. 2, *The Commons House of Assembly, 1692–1775* (Columbia: University of South Carolina Press, 1977), p. 96.
2. Conversations with the present owners, 24 April 1998.

5. *Sir Matthew White Ridley and Mr. Pinckney,* ca. 1764

JOHN HAMILTON MORTIMER (British, 1740–79)
Oil on canvas, 41 ½ × 29 in.

Collection of Viscount Ridley, Newcastle upon Tyne, England
Provenance: By family descent

Born in Charleston, Charles Coteworth Pinckney (1746–1825) was the son of Charles Pinckney (1699–1758) and Eliza Lucas (1722–93). He was taken to England by his father in 1753, when the latter was appointed an agent of the colony. Educated at Christ Church, Oxford, and the Middle Temple, London, Pinckney entered the English bar in 1769. He returned later that year to South Carolina, where he embarked on a career of public service. His first wife was Sarah Middleton (1756–84) whom he married in 1773; they had four children. He married his second wife Mary Stead (d. 1812) in 1786.

During the American Revolution, Pinckney was a member of the Provincial Congress and an officer in the Regiment of South Carolina troops, eventually being promoted to colonel. He took part in the defense of the fort on Sullivan's Island in June 1776 and was in command there during the siege of Charleston in 1780, when he was taken prisoner. In 1783, he was promoted to Brigadier General.[1]

After the Revolution, Pinckney resumed his law practice and held various public posts in which he staunchly defended the new system of government. In 1787, he was one of South Carolina's four delegates to the Constitutional Convention.[2] Although he was frequently offered positions in George Washington's administration, he declined all except the mission to France, which involved him in the XYZ Affair. In 1804 and 1808, he was the unsuccessful

Federalist candidate for president. The first president of the South Carolina Society of the Cincinnati, he was also instrumental in the founding of South Carolina College.

Originally thought to be by Johann Zoffany, the painting recently has been identified as an early painting by John Hamilton Mortimer, whose works include history paintings, portraits, decorative interiors, and book illustrations.[3] By 1757, Mortimer was in London studying in the studio of Thomas Hudson and later with Robert Edge Pine. In 1759, he won the first of many awards at the St. Martin's Lane Academy. Mortimer was elected a fellow of the Society of Artists of Great Britain in 1765 and was a regular contributor to their annual exhibitions. He became president of the society in 1774.

Characterized as flamboyant and reckless, Mortimer was nonetheless very much a part of the art establishment of his day. He supported the prevailing academic doctrine that elevated history painting to be the most prestigious of artistic genres. However, his radical politics and indifference toward classical subject matter set him apart from his contemporaries. Mortimer never went to Italy to study and rarely depicted scenes from classical history or mythology, preferring instead to draw upon the Anglo-Saxon past.[4]

Pinckney and Matthew Ridley (1745–1813) were fellow students at Westminster and Christ Church, Oxford. Anna Wells Rutledge stated that the two friends are shown "arguing vehemently upon that arbitrary Act (the Stamp Act)."[5] Yet their common, classical education appears to be at the heart of this portrait, as both men evaluate the virtues of the antique female bust on top of a pedestal.

ADM

1. George C. Rogers, Jr., *Charleston in the Age of the Pinckneys* (Norman: University of Oklahoma Press, 1969), pp. 122–23.

2. Rogers, *Charleston,* pp. 125–26.

3. Victoria Manners and G. C. Williamson, *John Zoffany, R.A.: His Life and Works, 1735–1810* (London: John Lane, Bodley Head, 1920), pp. 27–28. Experts at Sotheby's in London have recently reattributed the painting to John Hamilton Mortimer.

4. Jane Turner, ed., *The Dictionary of Art* (New York: Grove, 1996), 2:152.

5. Anna Wells Rutledge, "Portraits of American Interest in British Collections," *Connoisseur* 161 (May 1958): 269.

6. *The Cricketers* (also known as *Ralph Izard and His Friends),* 1764

BENJAMIN WEST (American, 1738–1820)

Oil on canvas, 40 × 50 in.

Signed bottom right: B. West London / 1764
Private collection
Provenance: By family descent; purchase from Ehrich Galleries, New York
Not exhibited

Ralph Izard commissioned this painting which is thought to be the second of two versions executed by Benjamin West. The first version, which is not signed or dated, is thought to have been commissioned by the Allen family of Philadelphia.[1]

The first four sitters, from left to right, are identified as James Allen (1742–78), Ralph Wormeley (1745–1806), Andrew Allen (1740–1825), and Ralph Izard (1741/42–1804).[2] James and Andrew Allen were the sons of Chief Justice William Allen of Pennsylvania, an early patron of Benjamin West.[3] Ralph Wormeley and Ralph Izard were sons of wealthy planters in Virginia and South Carolina respectively. All were abroad completing their education in the early 1760s.

The fifth sitter has been identified as either Arthur Middleton (1742–87) or "Mr. Beckford, a Jamaica planter."[4] While both identities are plausible, the inclusion of Arthur Middleton is complicated by the fact that West arrived in England in August 1763 and Arthur left England four months later in December.[5] For Arthur to have been portrayed, the undated version must have been painted during these few months. The second version, dated 1764, was painted after Arthur's departure. However, this does not explain the various minor discrepancies between the two paintings that center around this figure, such as the slight change in hair style and the omission of Arthur's sword.[6]

The name of Mr. Beckford is put forth by Izard and Middleton family tradition.[7] He may be Peter Beckford (?1739–1811), son of Julines Beckford of Steepleton, Dorset, who received his education at Westminister and New College, Oxford, by 1757.[8] The Beckford family was one of the oldest and most powerful in Jamaica, connected to a prominent English branch. An earlier Peter Beckford was a wealthy planter, speaker of the Jamaican House of Assembly, and brother to William Beckford, lord mayor of London. William Beckford (1760–1844) was a famous novelist, travel writer, art patron, and builder of Fonthill Abbey. He was a friend and patron of West in the 1790s.[9]

Wormeley and Izard both attended Cambridge but their friendship may have begun in English public school. Both were from families of long-standing influence in their respective colonies who had a tradition of educating their sons in England. At young ages (Wormeley and Izard were twelve), they were sent away; Izard was enrolled at both Hackney and Eton. Both were students at Eton, where they probably met, and continued at Cambridge, where Wormeley attended Trinity Hall and Izard "finished" his education at Christ College. Izard's holding the cricket bat is probably significant since he was described as having excelled in "all the manly exercises then in vogue," including cricket, while Wormeley admitted late in life to his son with regret that he never learned to fence.[10]

Ralph Izard returned to Charleston with Ralph Wormeley on 2 December 1764.[11] Presumably the painting came to Charleston at this time along with Izard's other possessions from England. Wormeley spent several months in Charleston visiting Izard both in town and at the family plantation at Goose Creek. Wormeley apparently became friendly with a number of Charlestonians because he came back to visit the next year without Izard.[12] The relationship between the Allens, Ralph Izard, and Ralph Wormeley is summed up in a letter from Peter Manigault addressed to Andrew Allen in Philadelphia, dated 13 April 1765, in which he mentions that "Mr. Izard and Mr. Wormeley set out from hence (Charleston) about a month ago for Virginia, on their way to Philadelphia," and concludes: "I most heartily wish you a happy meeting with your friends."[13] Izard and Wormeley stopped in New Bern and visited Governor Tryon before traveling to Rosegill Plantation, the Wormeley seat in Middlesex County, Virginia. Wormeley's father apparently made him stay home, and Izard set out for Philadelphia alone.[14] Wormeley, Izard, and Andrew Allen were all painted separately in England at almost the same time as *The Cricketers,* and it is useful to compare the conversation piece with the individual portraits.[15]

In 1771, Izard returned to England with his family and purchased a house on Berners Street. He must have brought the painting back with him because a letter, dated 8 August 1774, from Ralph Izard in Geneva to George Dempster in London states: "You mention nothing about my two pictures. The conversation piece, over the chimney, in the parlor, and Mrs. Izard's portrait, in the middle drawing room. Will you be so good as to have them sent to Mr. West's, in Newman-street, and beg the favor of him to take care of them for me. Mr. Howard cannot, I think, have any objection. If he objects to parting with the former, take the latter only."[16]

After the Revolution, the Izards returned to Charleston and lived in an exceptional town house on the corner of Meeting and South Battery, designed by James Hoban, later architect of the White House. They also spent much time at the Elms, their Goose Creek plantation, where Izard made extensive landscape improvements.[17] After Ralph Izard's death in 1804, Alice DeLancey Izard seems to have divided her time between the Elms and a house in Philadelphia.

An intriguing letter survives that hearkens to the relationship of two of the sitters and the location of the picture. In January 1805, Margaret Izard Manigault wrote from town to her mother at the Elms about the visit to Charleston of Ralph Wormeley, Jr., son of the subject of the painting, Ralph Wormeley: "He called at South Bay to see the picture of his Father. Nobody there could tell him which it was but he said he saw no likeness in any. Mr. M. intends paying him a visit soon—And I am sure it will give me the greatest pleasure to pay any attention to him. 'Your own Friend, & your Father's friend, never forget.'"[18] The letter seems fairly convincing evidence that Ralph Wormeley the elder knew *The Cricketers* painting and its whereabouts and told his son about

it. Also, the letter indicates that the painting was not in the Izards' town house and was probably at the Elms.

Eventually the painting moved to Alice DeLancey Izard's home on Spruce Street in Philadelphia. An undated newspaper article by an unknown author captured the scene in her drawing room: "The lovely old lady, seated on a sofa opposite the fireplace, was just under the picture of her husband, painted by Sir Benjamin West, while Mr. Izard was at Cambridge University, England. He with four friends, prepared to play cricket, formed the group with the river Cam, spanned by a bridge for background. She always sat under that picture when she received."[19]

A copy of the single figure of Ralph Izard was painted by Thomas Sully (1783–1872) in 1818 (fig. 69). It was probably commissioned by Ralph Izard's second surviving son George, who after an illustrious military career retired to Philadelphia and was later appointed by President Monroe as governor of Arkansas Territory.[20] In this painting Ralph is no longer surrounded by his friends, but stands opposite a plinth carved in bas relief with mythological scenes.

In her 1831 will, Alice DeLancey Izard bequeathed *The Cricketers* to her grandson Walter Izard,[21] who later willed the painting to his sister Mrs. Joseph Heyward (Alice Izard). At her death it became the property of the younger Walter Izard (b. 1828) of Goode, Bedford County, Virginia (the sitter's great-grandson). According to family tradition it was sold to "carpetbaggers" after the Civil War in 1867. The painting was then sold to Ehrich Galleries in New York from which it was purchased in 1907.[22]

ADM and Jonathan H. Poston

Figure 69 Ralph Izard, *1818, copy by Thomas Sully after Benjamin West. Oil on canvas. Courtesy of Dr. & Mrs. Price Cameron.*

1. Helmut von Erffa and Allen Staley, *The Paintings of Benjamin West* (New Haven: Yale University Press, 1986), p. 571, nos. 726 and 727.

2. Alan Simpson, "Colonial Cricketers in London," *Colonial Williamsburg,* Spring 1993, p. 35.

3. Chief Justice William Allen was the richest man in Philadelphia and was educated at Cambridge as well. He sent West along with his son John Allen and Edward and Joseph Shippen on the Grand Tour to Italy. Robert C. Alberts, *Benjamin West: A Biography* (Boston: Houghton Mifflin, 1978), pp. 23–27.

4. Von Erffa and Staley, *The Paintings of Benjamin West,* p. 571, no. 726.

5. Von Erffa and Staley, *The Paintings of Benjamin West,* p. 571, no. 726.

6. Barbara Doyle, "Swordsmanship; or, It May Be Art . . . But Is It Cricket?" *The Middleton Family Letter,* Summer 1993, p. 1; see also "West's Cricketers," *Colonial Williamsburg,* Summer 1993, p. 11.

7. Clarence Winthrop Bowen, ed., *The History of the Centennial Celebration of the Inauguration of George Washington as First President of the United States* (New York: D. Appleton, 1892), pp. 476–77. The painting is reproduced on page 181, but close examination of the illustration suggests it may be a copy.

8. John Ingamells, *The Dictionary of British and Irish Travelers in Italy, 1701–1800* (New Haven: Yale University Press, 1997), pp. 70–71.

9. Alberts, *Benjamin West,* 244–50; Lesley Lewis, "English Commemorative Art in Jamaica," *Commemorative Art* (April 1966), p. 131.

10. Anne Izard Deas, ed., *Correspondence of Mr. Ralph Izard of South Carolina* (New York: Charles Francis, 1844), pp. i–iv; Jonathan H. Poston, "A Deposed Virginia Aristocrat: Ralph Wormeley V of Rosegill, 1744–1788" (M.A. thesis, College of William and Mary, 1979), pp. 14–16.

11. "Extracts from the Journal of Mrs. Ann Manigault," ed. Mabel L. Webber, *SCHM* 20 (1919): 128–41; *SCG,* 3 December 1764.

12. See the letterbook of Peter Manigault, 1763–1773, SCHS, especially the letters from Peter Manigault to Ralph Izard, 13 January 1765 and 19 April 1765.

Manigault openly describes liaisons between Wormeley and Izard with several slave women at the Elms as well as describing their sociability and preparations for their trip north. Wormeley returned to Charleston the next year because of a friendship with a prominent young woman called "Becky." See also "The Letterbook of Peter Manigault," ed. Maurice Crouse, *SCHM* 70 (April 1969): 84–85. Late in life Wormeley corresponded on a seemingly intimate basis with John Rutledge; see Poston, "Virginia Aristocrat," p. 58.

13. Peter Manigault to Andrew Allen, 13 April 1765, letterbook of Peter Manigault.

14. Peter Manigault to Ralph Izard, 13 April 1765, 19 April 1765, 12 January 1765, letterbook of Peter Manigault.

15. Robert Edge Pine painted Wormeley in 1763 in his gown, with Trinity Hall in the background; see Virginia Hall, *Portraits in the Virginia Historical Society* (Richmond: University Press of Virginia, 1981), pp. 264–65. Andrew Allen was painted by West; see Von Erffa and Staley, *The Paintings of Benjamin West,* p. 486, private collection. Ralph Izard was painted by Johann Zoffany, unlocated; see Bowen, *History of the Centennial Celebration*, p. 101.

16. Ralph Izard to George Dempster, 8 August 1774, quoted in Deas, *Correspondence of Mr. Ralph Izard,* p. 10.

17. Jonathan Poston, *The Buildings of Charleston* (Columbia: University of South Carolina Press, 1997), p. 251; George Rogers, Jr., "Changes in Taste in the Eighteenth Century," *Journal of Early Southern Decorative Arts* 8 (May 1982): 13–14.

18. Margaret Izard Manigault to Alice DeLancey Izard, 27 January 1805, Izard Papers, LC. The way in which she describes young Wormeley not seeing his father's likeness in any of the pictures suggests there may have been other conversation pieces hanging in the drawing room at South Bay.

19. "Salon of Mrs. Izard," newspaper clipping, n.d., Izard Papers, SCL.

20. Edward Biddle and Mantle Fielding, *The Life and Works of Thomas Sully (1783–1872)* (Philadelphia: Wickersham Press, 1921), p. 186, no. 873.

21. Will of Alice DeLancey Izard, Charleston County Wills, Book G (1826–34), 39:605.

22. Von Erffa and Staley, p. 571, no. 727. Bowen, ed., *History of the Centennial Celebration,* p. 477.

7. *Thomas Middleton of The Oaks,* 1770

BENJAMIN WEST (American, 1738–1820)
Oil on canvas, 51 ¾ × 39 ½ in.

Signed lower left: B. West 1770
Carolina Art Association/Gibbes Museum of Art, gift of Miss Alicia Hopton Middleton
Provenance: By family descent

Figure 70 Thomas Middleton of Crowfield (?), *ca. 1770, Benjamin West. Oil on canvas. Courtesy of Middleton Place Foundation, Charleston.*

The son of Henry Middleton of Middleton Place and younger brother of Arthur Middleton (cat. 8), Thomas (1753–97) inherited The Oaks in Berkeley County, South Carolina, which had been in the Middleton family since 1678. He was sent to England to continue his education, but returned at the approach of hostilities in January 1774. He was elected to the second Provincial Congress and the General Assembly (1774–76). He later married Ann Manigault.

The portrait of *Thomas Middleton of The Oaks* by Benjamin West has been compared to the portrait thought to be Thomas's first cousin *Thomas Middleton of Crowfield (?)* (fig. 70). While the latter is not dated, the similarity in size, the use of "Vandyke" costume and drapery, and the positioning of the figures suggest that they were painted as companion pictures.[1]

Stylistically the Thomas Middleton portrait is among those works by West that demonstrate the influence of Anton Raphael Mengs (1728–79), whom the artist met and copied during his travels in Rome.[2] A clear precursor is the portrait of *John Allen,* ca. 1760 (private collection), which resembles in stance the portrait of Lord Grey painted by Mengs in the same year.[3] The portrait of John Allen has the added similarity of the sitter being dressed in "Vandyke" costume. Comparisons have also been drawn between the Thomas Middleton portrait and the near-contemporaneous painting by

Thomas Gainsborough known as *The Blue Boy* (Henry E. Huntington Library and Art Gallery, San Marino, California).[4]

The portrait of Thomas Middleton by West is the only identifiable image in the 1827 wash drawing titled *Friends and Amateurs in Musick* by the sitter's son of the same name (fig. 29).

ADM

1. Helmut von Erffa and Allen Staley, *The Paintings of Benjamin West* (New Haven: Yale University Press, 1986), p. 530, no. 660.
2. Von Erffa and Staley, *The Paintings of Benjamin West,* p. 17.
3. John Allen was the son of West's early patron Pennsylvania Chief Justice William Allen, whom West painted while still in Italy. Von Erffa and Staley, *The Paintings of Benjamin West,* p. 17, no. 582.
4. Estill Pennington, *Look Away: Reality and Sentiment in Southern Art* (Atlanta: Saraland Press, 1989), pp. 8–9.

8. *Arthur Middleton, His Wife Mary Izard, and Their Son Henry Middleton,* 1772

BENJAMIN WEST (American, 1738–1820)
Oil on canvas, 60 × 71 ½ in.

Signed lower left: Benj. West./London 1772
Middleton Place Foundation, Charleston
Provenance: Middleton family, by descent

Arthur Middleton (1742–87) was the eldest son of Henry Middleton (1717–84) of Middleton Place and Mary Williams Middleton (1725–61). He succeeded his father as a member of the Continental Congress in 1776 and was one of the signers of the Declaration of Independence. Arthur was educated in England, at the Westminster School; Trinity Hall, Cambridge; and the Inner Temple, London.

Returning to Charleston in 1763, Arthur wed Mary Izard (1747–1814), daughter of Walter Izard and cousin of Ralph Izard (cat. 6 and 12). He was elected to the Commons House of Assembly from St. Helena's Parish, serving until 1768 when he and his wife sailed for London. They spent three years traveling in England and southern Europe. After the birth of their first son, Henry (1770–1846), in London on 28 September 1770, they had their group portrait painted by Benjamin West.

The influence of Raphael in the Middleton family portrait is undeniably evident and accords with West's reverence for the Renaissance master, as expressed to John Singleton Copley: "What they [the ancients] have done in Statuary, Raphael, seems to have acquiered in painting. In him you see the fine fancey in the arraignment of his figures into groops, and those groops into a whole with that propriety and fitness to his subject Joynd to a trouth of charector and expression, that was never surpass'd before nor sence."[1]

Figure 71 Niccolini-Cowper Madonna, *1508, Raphael. Courtesy of the National Gallery of Art.*

Sarah Lytle, a past director of Middleton Place, suggests that the Middleton family portrait is most closely associated with the *Niccolini-Cowper Madonna* (fig. 71), by Raphael, a painting known to hold a prominent place in eighteenth-century English connoisseurship. Lytle argues that West, perhaps with Middleton's approbation, "would turn to the image of Raphael's Holy Family as inspiration."[2] Arthur Middleton is known to have studied the "fine arts at Rome and perfected his taste in literature, music and painting."[3] The comparison between the Middleton family portrait and the

Niccolini-Cowper Madonna is most evident in the profile of Mary Middleton's face, in the child's grasp of his mother's bodice, and in the intimacy created by focusing on the family unit.[4]

A copy of the head of Arthur Middleton by amateur artist Thomas Middleton (1791–1863), is in the collection of the South Carolina Historical Society.

ADM

1. Guernsey Jones, ed., *Letters and Papers of John Singleton Copley and Henry Pelham, 1739–1776* (Boston: Massachusetts Historical Society, 1914), pp. 194–97.
2. Sarah Lytle, "From Urbino to Middleton Place: The Pervasive Influence of Raphael," *Middleton Place Notebook* 5, no. 4 (Winter 1983), pp. 2–5.
3. Langdon Cheves, "Middleton of South Carolina," SCHM 1 (July 1900): 243–44.
4. Lytle, "From Urbino to Middleton Place," pp. 2–3.

9. *Lady William Campbell* (Sarah Izard), before 1776

NATHANIEL HONE (Irish, 1718–84)
Oil on canvas, 30 × 25 in.

The Campbell-Johnston Family, care of Historical Portraits Limited,
London, England.
Provenance: By family descent

The daughter of Ralph Izard (1717–61) and Rebecca Blake Izard, Sarah Izard (174?–84) was born in South Carolina and married Lord William Campbell (cat. 10) on 17 April 1763: "On Sunday last the right hon. Lord William Campbell, 4th son to his present Grace the duke of Argyle, and commander of his majesty's ship the Nightingale, was married to Miss Sarah Izard, daughter of the late Ralph Izard, Esq; a young lady esteemed one of the most considerable fortunes in the province."[1] Sarah had three children: William, an officer in the Royal Navy, who later resided in Carolina on an Izard family estate; Louisa, born in 1766, who wed Right Honorable Sir Alexander Johnstone in 1799; and Caroline, who died unmarried in 1789.[2]

Sarah and her husband lived in Charleston for one year before they were forced to flee the city in 1776 in the first wave of revolutionary action. They were guests of her cousin Miles Brewton (cat. 4) before they moved into 34 Meeting Street, a house which they leased from Sarah's cousin, Mrs. Elizabeth Blake. An inventory of the contents of their house prepared after 1777 provides wonderful insight into life at the last royal governor's residence in South Carolina. It was prepared as a schedule for losses sustained by the family as a result of the outbreak of the Revolutionary War.[3]

The portrait of Lady Sarah Campbell by Nathaniel Hone and that of her husband are the only paintings listed in the inventory. They apparently hung in the library and are described as follows: "3 Portraits of Ld & Ly Willm & Mrs. Campbell in Oil, by Hone." The third portrait of Mrs. Campbell is presumed to be that of Lady Sarah's sister Rebecca, the youngest daughter of Ralph Izard, who married Colin Campbell in 1768.[4]

Hone's portraits of Lord and Lady Campbell returned to England and descended through the Campbell family. However, their return could not have been before the Charleston-born miniature portrait painter Charles Fraser (1782–1860), who became a professional artist in 1818, copied the portrait of Lady Campbell on ivory (fig. 72). Listed in his account book under the year 1834, the miniature was purchased by the Carolina Art Association in 1973.[5] The two portraits are identical in color and presentation and thus suggest that Fraser was working from the original. Fraser mistakenly identified the portraitist as Joshua Reynolds.[6]

Nathaniel Hone was born into a merchant-class family in Dublin. After marrying well, he settled in London where he had a successful practice painting mainly miniature portraits in watercolor on ivory as well as enamels. Only later in his career did he gain a reputation for painting in oils. Active in artists' associations, he was a founding member of the Royal Academy and exhibited there from 1769 to 1784. In 1774, he directly opposed Joshua Reynolds by proposing Thomas Gainsborough for the presidency of the Royal Academy. A feud ensued that led to Hone's rejection by the Royal Academy.[7]

ADM

Figure 72 Lady William Campbell, *Charles Fraser. Watercolor on ivory. Courtesy of the Carolina Art Association/Gibbes Museum of Art.*

10. *Lord William Campbell,* before 1776

NATHANIEL HONE (Irish, 1718–84)
Oil on canvas, 30 × 25 in.

The Campbell-Johnston Family, care of Historical Portraits Limited,
London, England.
Provenance: By family descent

1. *SCG,* 23 April 1763, quoted in Langdon Cheves, "Izard of South Carolina," *SCHM* 2 (1901): 234–35. Sarah was a second cousin to Ralph Izard (cat. 6 and 12).
2. *Burke's Peerage,* cited in Cheves, "Izard of South Carolina," p. 235
3. T. 1/541, Public Record Office, London, microfilm, transcribed as appendix 7 in Graham Hood, *The Governor's Palace in Williamsburg: A Cultural History* (Williamsburg, Va.: Colonial Williamsburg Foundation, 1991), pp. 307–13.
4. *SCG,* 26 June 1768.
5. Object file, Gibbes Museum of Art. The miniature of Lady Sarah Campbell by Fraser was purchased from a dealer in London who had recently acquired it through auction at Sotheby's. In the auction catalogue the miniature is listed as the property of Lady Nicholas Gordon Lennox.
6. Charles Fraser, account book, 1818–39, collection of the Carolina Art Association/Gibbes Museum of Art. The description reads, "Copy of Sr Joshua's portrait of Lady Campbell ——— So." The inscription on the verso of the miniature reads, "Copy from Sir Joshua ——— by Chs Fraser So Carolina."
7. Brian Stewart and Mervyn Cutten, *The Dictionary of Portrait Painters in Britain up to 1920* (Suffolk: Antique Collectors' Club, 1997), p. 259.

The last colonial governor of South Carolina, Lord William Campbell (d. 1778) was the fourth son of John, fourth duke of Argyll (d. 1770), and his wife the Honorable Mary Bellenden (d. 1736), a celebrated beauty and wit. Campbell entered the Royal Navy and rose rapidly to the rank of captain in 1762, when he was appointed to the 20–gun *Nightingale.* He was sent to stations in the West Indies and South Carolina where he appears to have stayed until 1763, when he married Sarah Izard.[1]

By December 1764, he received his first important appointment as governor of Nova Scotia, a position he held until 1773. He was evidently dissatisfied in Halifax, for he petitioned twice for transfer, once in 1771 and again in 1773. His final plea was granted and on 18 June 1775, he arrived in Charleston as governor of South Carolina, where he was received in "sullen silence" on the portico of the recently completed Exchange Building.[2]

Within a year Campbell was forced to flee his home. He joined forces with Admiral Sir Peter Parker, who had been given instructions to form a squadron and sail to America to launch an attack on Charleston. Parker arrived at Cape Fear in May 1776, where Campbell joined him as a volunteer. The unsuccessful attack of the British on 28 June 1776 against the defenses at Sullivan's Island and Haddrell's Point was a major victory for Carolinians.[3] Campbell returned to England to his wife and children and died on 5 September 1778, probably from the wounds he sustained during the unsuccessful attack.[4]

Two other portraits of Campbell are known to exist, one by Francis Cotes (duke of Argyll, Inveraray) and another by Thomas Gainsborough (private collection, England). According to Ellis Waterhouse, a companion portrait by Gainsborough of Lady Sarah Campbell belonged to Mrs. E. J. Adams of Baltimore in 1893.[5] At present it remains unlocated. Anna Wells Rutledge recorded other portraits of Lord William and Lady Sarah by John Singleton Copley, but these, too, have never been located.[6]

ADM

1. Allen Johnson and Dumas Malone, *Dictionary of American Biography* (New York: Scribner's, 1937), 3:464.
2. George C. Rogers, Jr., *Charleston in the Age of the Pinckneys* (Norman: University of Oklahoma Press, 1969), p. xiii.
3. Johnson and Malone, *Dictionary of American Biography,* 3:464.
4. Mrs. D. Blake to Mrs. Horry, 5 January 1779, quoted in Langdon Cheves, "Izard of South Carolina," *SCHM* 2 (1901): 235–36.
5. Ellis Waterhouse, *Gainsborough* (London: Edward Hulton, 1958), p. 58.
6. Anna Wells Rutledge, "Portraits of American Interest in British Collections," *Connoisseur* 161 (May 1958): 267.

11. *Mrs. Ralph Izard* (Alice DeLancey), 1772

THOMAS GAINSBOROUGH (British, 1727–88)

Oil on canvas, 30 ¼ × 25 ⅛ in.

Signed verso: Mrs. Alice Izard/ formerly Alice DeLancey/ painted in London/
by / Gainsborough/ 1772
Lent by the Metropolitan Museum of Art, bequest of Jeanne King De Rham,
in memory of her father, David H. King, Jr., 1966
Provenance: By family descent; sold to David H. King, Jr., of New York

Born in rural Westchester, New York, Alice DeLancey (ca. 1746–1832) was the daughter of Peter DeLancey (1705–70) and Elizabeth Colden (1719–84), the niece of James DeLancey, and the granddaughter of Dr. Cadwallader Colden, both of whom served as lieutenant governors of New York. Most of the DeLancey family were militant loyalists.[1]

As a young woman Alice was admired for her great personal beauty and intelligence. On a visit to relatives in New York City she met Ralph Izard (cat. 6) from Charleston, who was a friend to her cousin Captain James DeLancey. On 1 May 1767, she wed Izard in New York and returned with him to live at the Elms plantation near Charleston until their departure for England in 1771. Alice DeLancey Izard spent the next twelve years abroad. In London the Izards lived in a fashionable house on Berners Street, where they lived "genteely without any pomp," although Alice was presented at court.[2] In 1774 and 1775 she and Ralph traveled on the Continent, and in 1777 the family moved to Paris for the duration of the Revolutionary War.

After her husband returned to America in 1780, Alice DeLancey Izard remained in Paris for three years with her children. Returning to the Elms in 1784, Alice gave birth to the last of her fourteen children, seven of whom lived to maturity and through marriage forged ties with members of the Manigault, Smith, Middleton, and Deas families.

After her husband's death in 1804, she spent much of her time in Philadelphia at a house on Spruce Street between Ninth and Tenth streets, where her daughter Margaret Izard Manigault and two sons also established residences. There she became noted for her salons and card parties.[3]

At Alice Izard's death, the portrait was inherited by her daughter Anne Izard Deas. It remained in the family until it was sold by the sitter's great-grandson Dr. Robert Watts of New York.[4] Alice Izard was one of only two Americans Gainsborough is known to have painted.[5]

There are at least three copies known to exist. In 1936, M. Knoedler and Company organized an exhibition titled "Masterpieces of American Historical Portraiture," in which a portrait identified as Mrs. Ralph Izard and attributed to John Singleton Copley was displayed (fig. 73). The accompanying catalogue documents that the painting had been exhibited in *Portraits of Ladies of Old New York, XVIII and XIX Centuries,* Museum of the City of New York, 1936, and passed by direct inheritance to Mrs. Frederick Wombwell, whose great-grandmother was a sister of Mrs. Ralph Izard.[6] The painting, now unlocated, was never in Knoedler's inventory, but was borrowed for their exhibition. While the attribution to Copley is doubtful, the portrait is clearly after the Gainsborough original.

113

Another version was painted by Charles Fraser (fig. 74), and it is discussed in Charles Manigault's "Description of Paintings" (cat. 128): "My Grand Mother [Izard] Painted by Chs Fraser of this City. This Copy I believe was made from one belonging to 'Aunt Deas' My Mothers Sister & was one of Fraser's Earliest works, & very inferior. but the only Portrait that My Mother had of Her Mother. . . ."[7] This copy is identical to the Gainsborough in coloration. While Gainsborough made the portrait oval, Fraser's copy is rectangular with a painted oval in the background.

In 1816, Ralph Izard, Jr., took up residence in the Charleston house on South Bay built by his parents, Alice and Ralph Izard, in the 1790s. In a letter, he explained to his mother, "My father's picture occupies the wall on the left of the drawing room as you enter, opposite the piazza door; yours is over the sopha opposite the fire place in the same room."[8] This is probably the Gainsborough portrait. Fraser was twenty-four when Izard moved to South Bay, and he would have had an opportunity to see the painting early in his career. However, when he actually copied it is still unknown.

A late-nineteenth-century pastel copy of the Gainsborough portrait by an unknown artist is held privately by family descendants. Besides a letter between family members dated 1895 describing this work as a copy after the Gainsborough, nothing else is known. Finely executed and very similar to the Gainsborough, the colors are slightly lighter, which may be a result of the medium used.[9]

An engraving of the Gainsborough portrait was done in the 1850s for a series titled *The Ladies of the Republican Court* (fig. 75). In the engraving the painting is extended at the bottom to include a ledge upon which Alice DeLancey Izard rests her arm and hand which holds a basket of flowers.

ADM

Figure 73 Alice DeLancey Izard, *artist unknown. Oil on canvas. Currently unlocated. Courtesy of the Knoedler Gallery, New York. At one time thought to be by John Singleton Copley.*

Figure 74 Alice DeLancey Izard, *Charles Fraser. Oil on canvas. Courtesy of private collection.*

1. George DeLancey Hanger, "The Izards: Ralph, His Lovable Alice and Their Fourteen Children," *Transactions of the Huguenot Society of South Carolina* 89 (1984): 72–73.

2. John Watts, Jr., to Alice's mother from "Reminiscenses," DeLancey Papers, Museum of the City of New York, quoted in Hanger, "The Izards," p. 74.

3. Will of Alice DeLancey Izard, Charleston County Wills, Book G (1826–34), 39:605.

4. Object file, accession page, Metropolitan Museum of Art, New York. A question remains as to whether Gainsborough painted more than one portrait of Alice Izard. Another version of Alice Izard with an identical inscription on the verso is discussed and illustrated in Clarence W. Bowen, ed., *The History of the Centennial Celebration of the Inauguration of George Washington as First President of the United States* (New York: D. Appleton, 1892), p. 478, illustration opposite p. 59. It is documented as belonging to Mrs. Henry Fulton of New York, a great-granddaughter of the sitter. The information on Charleston portraits illustrated in the volume was supplied by Dr. Gabriel Manigault, an Izard family descendant. However, in a paper Manigault prepared but never delivered for the Chicago Exposition of 1893 (Manigault Papers, SCHS) he states that the portrait of Alice Izard belonged to Dr. Robert Watts, the sitter's great-grandson from whom the Metropolitan Museum portrait descends. Ellis K. Waterhouse, *Gainsborough* (London: Edward Hulton, 1958), p. 75, reiterates the Fulton provenance and states that the portrait was in that collection in 1875, but was destroyed by fire in California. The latter information was supplied to Waterhouse by Anna Wells Rutledge (letter to Martha Severens from Frick Art Reference Library dated 24 August 1981, Gibbes Museum of Art archival files). In a letter of January 1967 in the Paintings Department Archives of the Metropolitan Museum, Waterhouse states that the Metropolitan portrait is the "missing Gainsborough." He suggests, however, that there may have been two versions.

5. Ellis K. Waterhouse, January 1967, Metropolitan Museum of Art, Paintings Department Archives.

6. *Masterpieces of American Historical Portraiture* (New York: M. Knoedler and Company, 1936), p. 21. Photocopy of catalogue and photograph provided by M. Knoedler Gallery, New York. Reviewed in Alfred M. Frankfurter, "Portraits of American History," *Art News* 7 (November 1936): 11–12.

7. MDP.

8. Ralph Izard to Mrs. Alice Izard, Charleston, 9 June 1816, Ralph Izard Papers, LC, reel 2, container 3.

9. Exhibition files, Gibbes Museum of Art. The author would like to thank Henry Burke for sharing this information.

Figure 75 Alice DeLancey Izard. *Engraving from* The Ladies of the Republican Court. *Courtesy of Jonathan H. Poston.*

12. *Mr. and Mrs. Ralph Izard,* 1775

JOHN SINGLETON COPLEY (American, 1738–1815)
Oil on canvas, 69 × 88 ½ in.

Museum of Fine Arts, Boston, Edward Ingersoll Brown Fund
Provenance: Purchased by Charles Izard Manigault in 1831, by family descent
until 1907 sale

In 1771, Ralph Izard returned from Charleston to London with his wife, Alice DeLancey (cat. 11).[1] During his residence Izard was involved, unofficially, as a representative of the American cause. Despite his preference for living in cosmopolitan London, he was deeply committed to the American cause and vehemently opposed to the recent British actions. He was a frequent visitor to Parliament where he made many friends, but little progress in arguing for the rights of the colonies.[2]

In July 1774, political frustrations led Izard to seek respite by traveling on the Continent. John Singleton Copley left America at the same time, fleeing the obsession with politics and perhaps the difficulties he sensed were to come. He sailed first for England before setting off for Europe, arriving in Rome in October 1774. During the next four months, he produced two paintings, the *Ascension* (Museum of Fine Arts, Boston) and the portrait of the Izards.[3]

By November, the Izards were also in Rome; the first mention of their contact with Copley, however, occurred in Naples in January 1775. Together they traveled to Paestum (probably becoming the first Americans to see these Greek temples), and by mid-March, when they were back in Rome, Copley's portrait of the Izards was described as nearly finished.

This was Copley's third double portrait, the two previous ones completed just prior to his departure from America. While similar in composition, many other elements of the Izards' portrait stand in vivid contrast to the earlier portraits. The canvas reveals a dramatically different aesthetic, as if Copley could not choose between the many luxuries of Rome, packing his image with material objects rendered with lustrous coloring. Copley's letters echo the enthusiasm revealed on his canvas: "There is a kind of luxury in seeing, as in eating and drinking, and the more we indulge our senses in either, the less they are to be restrained."[4]

The objects in the painting almost overwhelm the Izards; they include the Colosseum in the background, a Greek krater vase on the ledge above Ralph's head, a sculptural group on the table between them, and a drawing of that sculptural group. On one level, the painting serves as a telling document about the self-fashioning of the Izards. Highlighted are the cultural affiliations, most noticeably their participation in the English tradition of the Grand Tour, defining them as wealthy English colonials. Yet this painting is distinctive. Instead of following tradition and depicting the Izards in the insouciant standing pose perfected by Pompeo Batoni, the leading practitioner of Grand Tour portraiture, Copley has shown the Izards in the active pose of practicing their connoisseurship, of managing ideas and exercising judgment over the lessons posed by the antiquity surrounding them. In this act of considera-

tion, the painting becomes more than a document of wealth and social class, for there is a strong political subtext imbedded in the unusual collection of objects assembled for this painting. This subtext points to the divergent choices faced by Americans during the political crisis with Great Britain.

According to Izard's grandson, Charles Izard Manigault, the painting depicts his grandparents, "sitting at a table, she having just copied on paper these statues, & is shewing it to her husband, who (judging from his countinance) is evidently going to give her his candid opinion of her sketch." Scholars have also proposed that the sketch might represent another of the Izards' purchases.[5] Copley has presented a complex image of two contemplative individuals: Mrs. Izard looks at her husband, as he gazes out toward the viewer, formulating his response. Their left forearms establish a strong horizontal line that draws our attention to the midpoint— the drawing in his hand—a drawing of the sculptural group seated on the table between them, that, by its double inclusion, carries weighted significance.

In contrast to the practice established by Batoni, the sculptural group that occupies center stage was not one of the most celebrated works in Rome, nor was it in one of the most celebrated collections. Despite the widely agreed-upon importance of material objects in Copley's paintings, the iconography of the sculptural group has been variously interpreted over the last three centuries. While other scholars have noted the numerous identities, most have adhered to the modern reading of the sculptural group as Orestes and Electra.[6] That identification, however, gained popularity only in the nineteenth century and was not the preferred one when the Izards and Copley encountered it. Since 1704, the more commonly accepted identification was Papirius and his Mother, an identification supported by its prevalence in the eighteenth century and corroborated by family history in Charles Izard Manigault's lengthy discussion of the sculpture group in his account of the painting.[7]

The Papirius story relates a choice of personal loyalties—Papirius had to decide between loyalty to his mother and loyalty to his country. A common rhetorical device employed in the American crisis was that Britain was the mother and the American colonies were her children. Izard himself used the terms "Mother Country" and "children" when discussing the situation.[8] To be a good child, America was expected to obey her parent, but to do so she must sacrifice the right to be represented in matters of taxation. To be a good parent, Britain must recognize the child's liberty, but to do so she would have to sacrifice the sovereignty of parliamentary authority. Thus at the heart of this somewhat obscure sculptural group is the question of conflicting loyalties between mother and child, with the child, Papirius, being hailed as a hero for siding with country rather than his mother.[9]

The Greek volute krater on the ledge above Izard's head also functions on two levels. First, it reinforces the central theme of the Izards as connoisseurs, for Greek vases were thought at the time to offer a new paradigm for the beauty of ancient art.[10] Second, it reinforces the theme of divided loyalties as it presents an alternative choice to the one posed by the Papirius sculpture. The figures on the vase have been identified as Apollo, Artemis, and their mother, Leto. When shown together, they usually refer to the story of Niobe, mother of seven sons and seven daughters, who boasted to Leto that her happiness exceeded that of Leto for she had more children. In anger Leto summoned her children who slew all of Niobe's fourteen children.

The Papirius sculpture and the Greek krater vase suggest different courses of action for both America and Britain. The Papirius sculpture suggests loyalty to country before mother, while the Greek krater vase suggests loyalty to mother. By placing the vase behind Izard, nearly obscured by darkness, and by placing the sculptural group in a central position, doubly included, Izard's inclination towards loyalty to country seems clear. Before the painting was completed, Izard did just that. He returned to London and advocated the American cause. After the Declaration of Independence was announced, he moved his family to Paris, hoping to secure passage for them and for his belongings to America. Unable to do so, he began diplomatic service to the American nation as commissioner to the Court of Tuscany.[11]

While the sculptural group and the Greek krater vase are unusual emblems in a Grand Tour portrait, the image of the Colosseum is certainly more frequently encountered. But its use here, especially in the context of the other emblematic elements is significant as it suggests the likely outcome of the child's disobedience. The Colosseum served as an evocative reminder of the decadence of empire that led to the fall of Rome.[12] Both Izard and Copley were deeply concerned with the bloodshed in the colonies in the early months of 1775 and the certainty of

continued violence. Copley wrote to his wife, "Your situation must be very unpleasant; the daily expectation of bloodshed must render every thoughtful person unhappy."[13] Thus for Copley and Izard, in March 1775 when the painting was nearing completion, did they see a parallel between the ruined remains of the Roman Empire and the future course of the British Empire?

Above the entire scene is a richly painted gathering sky. Even that detail seems to hold the possibility for greater meaning as Izard commented, "The melancholy prospects of American politics, has thrown a continual cloud on all my amusements, and has lessened them exceedingly."[14] Copley would have known Izard's anxiety and concern, and the portrait he created conveys the serious and thoughtful countenance of the Izards in sharp contrast to the gaiety of the typical Grand Tour portrait. Ultimately, Copley's portrait of Mr. and Mrs. Izard is a revealing portrait of eighteenth-century colonial Americans, pondering the lessons of antiquity: civic virtues and the course of empire.

Remarkably, though, Ralph and Alice Izard never took possession of their painting. They had agreed upon a price of 200 guineas, but the Revolutionary War ruined Izard's finances and he never felt able to afford it. Charles Izard Manigault explains that Ralph Izard's son George contacted Copley in 1812, but that Copley still demanded a price greater than he could afford. When Charles Izard Manigault made his first trip to England in 1824, he met with Copley's widow and they agreed upon a price of 150 guineas. The painting arrived in Charleston in 1831 where it became one of Manigault's most prized possessions, remaining with him during the shelling of Charleston in the Civil War.[15]

MDM

1. For more on the biography of Ralph and Alice Izard see cat. 6 and 11, and "Reflections of Refinement: Portraits of Charlestonians at Home and Abroad" in this volume.

2. George DeLancey Hanger, "The Izards: Ralph, His Lovable Alice and Their Fourteen Children," *Transactions of the Huguenot Society of South Carolina* 89 (1984): 95.

3. John Singleton Copley to Henry Pelham, 14 March 1775, quoted in Guernsey Jones, ed., *Letters and Papers of John Singleton Copley and Henry Pelham, 1739–1776,* (1914; reprint, New York: DeCapo Press, 1970), p. 295.

4. John Singleton Copley to John Greenwood, Rome, 7 May 1775, quoted in Martha Babcock Amory, ed., *The Domestic Life of John Singleton Copley, R.A.* (Boston: Houghton, Mifflin, 1882), p. 51.

5. MDP.

6. For a fuller discussion of the interpretation of this sculptural group see Maurie D. McInnis, "Lessons from Antiquity: John Singleton Copley's Portrait of Mr. and Mrs. Izard," *Winterthur Portfolio* (in submission). For a recent interpretation of the sculptural group as Orestes and Electra see Eleanor Jones, catalogue no. 4, *The Lure of Italy: American Artists and the Italian Experience,* Theodore E. Stebbins, Jr., et. al. (Boston: Museum of Fine Arts, 1992), pp. 156–58.

7. Francis Haskell and Nicolas Penny, *Taste and the Antique: The Lure of Classical Sculpture, 1500–1900* (New Haven: Yale University Press, 1981), pp. 288–91; MDP.

8. For Ralph Izard's use of "Mother Country" see Anne Izard Deas, ed., *Correspondence of Mr. Ralph Izard of South Carolina* (New York: Charles Francis, 1844), p. 19; for his use of "children" see Deas, *Correspondence,* p. 40.

9. References to the mother and child relationship between Britain and America were ubiquitous during the period. See Lester C. Olsen, *Emblems of American Community in the Revolutionary Era: A Study in Rhetorical Iconology* (Washington, D.C.: Smithsonian Institution Press, 1991), pp. 125–99.

10. Copley painted the Greek vase with such specificity that many have assumed it must have been based on an actual vase. The Greek vase scholar Sir John Beazley accepted it as such and included it in his list of works by the Niobid painter; unfortunately, such a vase remains unlocated. Sir John Beazley, *Attic Red-Figure Vase Painters,* 2d ed. (Oxford: Clarendon Press, 1963), p. 608.

11. Izard remained in Paris until 1780 where he was involved with the negotiations for an alliance with France. In 1782, he was chosen as a representative to the Confederation Congress. He served the South Carolina legislature in the 1780s, refusing to stand for governor, and in 1789 was elected to the United States Senate where he was a leader of the strong federalist faction in national politics from South Carolina. In 1797, he suffered a debilitating stroke; he died in 1804.

12. William L. Vance, *America's Rome* (New Haven: Yale University Press, 1989), pp. 43–67, and Meyer Reinhold, *Classica Americana: The Greek and Roman Heritage in the United States* (Detroit: Wayne State University Press, 1984), chap. 3.

13. John Singleton Copley to his wife, Rome, 4 December 1774, quoted in Amory, *Domestic Life,* 40–41.

14. Ralph Izard to George Dempster, Naples, 21 January 1775, quoted in Deas, *Correspondence,* p. 42.

15. Manigault, "Description of Paintings," cat. 128.

13. *George Boone Roupell,* 1779–80

JOHN SINGLETON COPLEY (American, 1738–1815)

Oil on canvas, 84 × 54 in.

The Detroit Institute of Arts, Founders Society purchase, Robert H. Tannahill Foundation

Provenance: Lord Lyndhurst to Roupell family in England

George Boone Roupell (1762–1838) was the son of George Roupell (1726–94) and Elizabeth Prioleau (1726–1811).[1] The elder Roupell became searcher of His Majesty's Customs at Charles Town in 1746 and was deputy post-master general for the Southern District of America.[2] A loyalist, he left the colony in 1777 after refusing to take an oath abjuring allegiance to George III.[3] Leaving his wife and daughter behind, he took his son, George Boone, with him to England "as well for his education as to prevent his being persecuted by the rebels."[4]

George Roupell returned to his position in the post office during the British occupation of Charleston from 1780 to 1782, but was forced to move to St. Augustine in East Florida to discharge the duties of his office when the British evacuated.[5] He owned a house on the corner of Friend and Tradd and a plantation near Beaufort, South Carolina, which he called Rupelmonde, and where he died in 1794.[6]

George Roupell illustrated the botanical papers that Dr. Alexander Garden sent to the Royal Society.[7] Two other works are a small full-length profile drawing of Charlestonian Isaac Mazyck dated 1756, in the collection at the Gibbes Museum of Art, and a wash drawing entitled *Mr. Peter Manigault and His Friends* (fig. 76).[8]

After traveling with his father to London in 1777, George Boone remained in London the rest of his life, entering the bar around 1791. Frustrated in his attempts to secure an appointment to the post office in the West Indies, he declined an offer to go to Jamaica.[9] Boone married into the McCulloch family.[10] After his mother's death, he and his sister Mary Magdelan Roupell inherited Rupelmonde and the house on Tradd Street.[11]

The portrait of George Boone Roupell by John Singleton Copley was completed in 1780 probably after the sitter's father had returned to Charleston to resume his office. It was exhibited at the Royal Academy along with three other portraits in 1780.[12] However, neither father nor son ever took possession of the painting. It remained with Copley and was inherited by his

Figure 76 Mr. Peter Manigault and His Friends, *George Roupell. Courtesy of the Henry Francis du Pont Winterthur Museum.*

son Lord Lyndhurst. Anna Wells Rutledge suggests that the financial difficulties experienced by many loyalists whose funds were cut off by the new state governments may have been the cause. She also states that Lord Lyndhurst, who was a friend of George Boone, eventually gave the portrait to the subject's family.[13]

ADM

1. Artist files, Gibbes Museum of Art, "Notes prepared for Brig. General George Roupell at request of Anna Wells Rutledge," Spring 1970.

2. According to Bryding McAdams a portrait of George Roupell by an unidentified artist is in the collection of family descendants in England. Another likeness is the Wedgwood profile in the collection of the Birmingham Museum of Art. A portrait of George Boone Roupell's mother, Elizabeth Prioleau Roupell, is illustrated in Anna Wells Rutledge, "Portraits of American Interest in British Collections," *Connoisseur* 161 (May 1958) p. 269.

3. Governor Bull's Certificate, 3 January 1778, Roupell Correspondence, SCHS.

4. Memorial to the Lords Commissioners of the Treasury, 1 October 1777, Roupell Correspondence, SCHS.

5. Memorial on behalf of George Roupell by George Boone Roupell to the Commissioners, 22 March 1784, Roupell Correspondence, SCHS.

6. Will of George Roupell, Roupell Correspondence, SCHS.

7. Edmund Berkeley and Dorothy Smith Berkeley, *Dr. Alexander Garden of Charles Town* (Chapel Hill: University of North Carolina Press, 1969), pp. 127–29.

8. These drawings are discussed at length in Anna Wells Rutledge, "After the Cloth Was Removed," *Winterthur Portfolio* 4 (1969), pp. 59–62. An 1854 copy of *Mr. Peter Manigault and His Friends* was drawn by Louis Manigault, great-grandson of the subject (Carolina Art Association/Gibbes Museum of Art). An inscription on the copy states that the original was done between 1754 and 1760.

9. George Boone Roupell to General Tonyn, 29 January 1791, Roupell Correspondence, SCHS.

10. George Boone Roupell married Fanny McCulloch around 1793. Mary Magdelan Roupell to George Boone Roupell, 7 May 1794, Roupell Correspondence, SCHS.

11. Will of Elizabeth Roupell, 9 December 1811, Roupell Correspondence, SCHS.

12. Jules David Prown, *John Singleton Copley* (Cambridge: Harvard University Press, 1966), 2: 275.

13. Rutledge, "Portraits of American Importance," pp. 269–70.

14. *Henry Laurens,* 1782

JOHN SINGLETON COPLEY (American, 1737–1815)

Oil on canvas, 54 1/8 × 40 5/8 in.

Signed lower right: J. S. Copley. R.A. Pinx 1782
National Portrait Gallery, Smithsonian Institution, Washington, D.C.

Provenance: Richard Bagwell (1840–1918), Clonmel, Ireland; his widow, Harriet Bagwell; Lewis and Simmons, London; sold 29 March 1920 to Thomas B. Clarke (1848–1931); his estate; sold as part of the Clarke collection on 29 January 1936 (through M. Knoedler and Company, New York) to the A. W. Mellon Charitable Trust, Pittsburgh; given to the National Gallery of Art in 1942; transferred to the National Portrait Gallery in 1965

Henry Laurens (1724–92) was a wealthy Charleston merchant-planter who played a major role in many events of the American Revolution. Active first in the Provincial Congress of South Carolina, Laurens was a member of the Continental Congress from 1777 to 1779. He was on fourteen different committees in the Continental Congress before serving as its president from November 1777 to December 1778. In 1780, the Congress dispatched Laurens to negotiate a loan from Holland. Captured by the British en route, he was charged with treason for his involvement in the Revolution and imprisoned for fifteen months in the Tower of London. He was released in late 1781. Physically weakened by his ordeal, Laurens briefly remained in London to recover. There John Singleton Copley created this likeness.

Copley depicts Laurens in a grand setting, framed by massive columns, a swag of drapery, and a table covered with documents relating to his work as president of the congress. One document bears the inscription "Ratification Treaties May 1778." On a letter signed by Louis XVI, king of France, is written, "We Pray God very dear Friends and Allies to take you into his Holy Keeping." Both are references to the colonies' alliance with France, which Laurens had helped to secure.

Although it has been assumed that Laurens commissioned the portrait, evidence suggests this was not the case. First, the portrait remained in the British Isles after Laurens left London. Second, Valentine Green, who engraved Copley's famous *Watson and the Shark* (National Gallery of Art, Washington, D.C.) in 1779, made a mezzotint of the portrait in 1782. This print was offered for sale as a companion to Green's 1781 mezzotint of a full-length portrait of George Washington painted by John Trumbull in 1780.[1] As a pair, the engravings seem intended to represent the leadership of both military and legislative interests in the American Revolution. Thus, Copley may have painted his portrait of Laurens with the specific plan of an engraving in mind. This might explain why a canvas of a size typically used to represent a three-quarter–length figure was used here for a full-length portrait. Third, Laurens, writing from France to Edward Bridgen in England, requested two copies of the mezzotint for his daughter: "the young lady is exceedingly anxious to have two of the engravings of her father's likeness . . . you know I mean the engravings which were to be made after Mr. Copley's painting."[2] This suggests that Laurens's family did not anticipate owning the painting itself.

A disputed family account maintained that a larger version of the Copley portrait hung in the Laurens's South Carolina mansion and was destroyed by fire in 1861. If this were the case, the National Portrait Gallery version would be a study for, or perhaps a replica of, this larger painting. However, there is no documentation to confirm that a larger version ever existed.

A painting by South Carolina artist Charles Fraser (fig. 77) owned by Laurens's descendants may be the one indicated by family history. The Fraser copy does not have the same colors as the original painting, and when it was exhibited in Charleston in 1822, it was described as "copied from an engraving."[3]

Michelle L. Kloss

Figure 77 Henry Laurens, *copy by Charles Fraser after Valentine Green engraving of Henry Laurens by John Singleton Copley. Oil on canvas. Courtesy of private collection.*

1. An unattributed, undated press clipping from an English newspaper, in *Press Clippings from English Newspapers on Matters of Artistic Interest, 1686–1835,* 3 vols. (London: National Art Library, Victoria and Albert Museum, n.d.), 1:219, reads, "This Day is published, Price 15s. A Whole Length Portrait in Mezzotinto of Henry Laurens, Esq; President of the American Congress, in 1778; From a capital Picture, painted from the Life by Mr. J. S. Copley, R.A. elect. and engraved by Mr. V. Green, Mezzotinto Engraver to his Majesty . . . Published, and sold by the Proprietor, J. Stockdale, Bookseller . . . of whom may be had, the Whole Length Portrait of General Washington, Price 15s, engraved also by Mr. V. Green, and to which that of Mr. Laurens is intended as a Companion. N.B. The Purchasers of either of those Prints will have the liberty of seeing the original Picture of Mr. Laurens, at Mr. Stockdale's."
2. Henry Laurens to Edward Bridgen, 10 July 1782, Brooklyn Historical Society.
3. *CC,* 5 April 1822.

15. *Dr. John Moultrie, Jr.,* ca. 1784–98

PHILIP REINAGLE (British, ?1749–1833)

Oil on canvas, 30 ¼ × 25 ½ in.

Carolina Art Association/Gibbes Museum of Art, purchased with funds contributed by the American descendants of Dr. John Moultrie, Jr.
Provenance: By family descent; Christie's, London, England

The son of Dr. John Moultrie (1702–71), who emigrated to Charleston from Scotland in 1728, Dr. John Moultrie, Jr. (1729–98), followed in his father's footsteps and returned to Edinburgh for his medical education. Known as the first native South Carolinian to practice medicine, his thesis on yellow fever gained him an international reputation.[1]

In the early 1760s, Dr. Moultrie, Jr., was appointed lieutenant governor of East Florida, where he acquired substantial acreage south of St. Augustine. In 1762, he married Eleanor Austin (1738–1826), only daughter of Captain George Austin and Ann Ball of Charleston. Austin, a wealthy merchant and business associate of Henry Laurens, owned plantations on the Ashepoo and Pee Dee rivers and an estate called Aston Hall near Shifnal Parish Church in Shropshire, England, his principal residence.[2]

There is a local tradition that the couple eloped because Captain Austin was opposed to the marriage. However, after a lapse of years, Henry Laurens interceded by taking a portrait of Austin's daughter and her two sons with him while on a visit to England. Laurens took the portrait to Aston Hall, and while Austin was away, asked the servants to hang it in the dining room. At first, Austin objected to the portrait, but eventually he and his daughter were reconciled.[3]

Dr. Moultrie, Jr., became the governor for East Florida in 1771, and during the Revolution remained a loyalist. His younger brother General William Moultrie (1730–1805) com-

manded the American forces in the battle of Fort Sullivan, 28 June 1776, and was later the governor of the state of South Carolina. After the war, England ceded the Florida region back to Spain and in 1783 Dr. Moultrie was forced to leave the country with his family. He spent the remainder of his life in England.

Reinagle's modest, frank portrayal of Dr. Moultrie, Jr., was painted in England between 1784 and 1798.[4] The son of a Hungarian musician, Reinagle was apprenticed to Allan Ramsay for seven years and later became his assistant. He often painted small full-length portraits in the tradition of Johann Zoffany, as well as sporting pictures, exhibiting at the Royal Academy and the British Institute from 1773 to 1829.

ADM

1. See Eleanor Winthrop Townsend, "John Moultrie, Jr., M.D., 1729–1798," *Annals of Medical History,* 3d ser., 2, no. 2 (New York: Paul B. Hoeber, 1940): 98–109.
2. Josiah Smith, Jr., letterbook, 1771–84, SHC-UNC, pp. 14–24, 63–74, 153–60, 452–55, 266–72.
3. Anne Simons Deas, *Recollections of the Ball Family of South Carolina and the Comingtee Plantation* (1909; reprint, Charleston: South Carolina Historical Society, 1978), pp. 54–55.
4. Martha Severens, *Selections from the Collection* (Charleston: Carolina Art Association, 1977), p. 70.

16. *John Moultrie III and Family,* ca. 1782

JOHN FRANCIS RIGAUD (British, 1742–1810)

Oil on canvas, 77 ½ × 60 ⅛ in.

Carolina Art Association/Gibbes Museum of Art, purchased from Colnaghi's with funds from the Moultrie and Ball families

Provenance: By family descent until 1984; Colnaghi, London, England

Born in Charleston, John Moultrie III (1764–1823) went to England with his father, Dr. John Moultrie, Jr. (cat. 15), in 1783 when the latter left British Florida because of his loyalist affiliations. Upon the death of his grandfather, George Austin, Moultrie III inherited the estate at Aston Hall in Shropshire, England.[1] He married Catherine Gaillard Ball (1766–1828), daughter of Charleston loyalist Elias Ball of Wambaw Plantation and later of Frenchay, Gloucestershire.

The artist, John Francis Rigaud, a French Huguenot by descent, received his early training in Italy and was made a member of the Accademia Clementina in 1765. After a brief stay in Paris, Rigaud arrived in London in 1771 and found success as a portraitist and architectural painter. He exhibited at the Royal Academy from 1772 through 1810 and posthumously in 1812, 1813, and 1815.[2] Most of Rigaud's architectural paintings are now lost, but several of his portraits are still extant, including a wonderful depiction of three fellow academicians, Sir William Chambers, Joseph Wilton, and Sir Joshua Reynolds.[3]

The portrait of John Moultrie with his wife and son George Austin Moultrie (1787–1866) is an example of late-eighteenth-century high-style English portrait painting. The opulent setting and costumes confirm the status of this Charleston-born couple who lived in England on the family estate. Yet even though John Moultrie III remained in England, his brother James returned to Charleston and inherited the

Austin plantation on the Ashepoo River. James Moultrie followed in his father's footsteps and became a physician, perpetuating a family tradition that is continued today.

ADM

1. Charleston artist John Blake White described life at Aston Hall. He visited the estate while studying with Benjamin West in England from 1800 to 1803. John Blake White Journal, SCHS (cat. 122).
2. See Stephen Francis Dutilh Rigaud, "Facts and Recollections of the XVIIIth Century in a Memoir of John Francis Rigaud Esq., R.A.," ed. William L. Pressly, in *The Fifth Volume of the Walpole Society* (Great Britain: W. S. Maney and Son, 1984), 5:1–164.
3. Ellis Waterhouse, *The Dictionary of British Eighteenth Century Painters in Oils and Crayons* (Woodbridge: Antique Collectors' Club, 1981), p. 311.

17. *Joseph Manigault*, 1785

GILBERT STUART (American, 1755–1828)
Oil on canvas, 27 ½ × 22 ½ in.

Mr. and Mrs. Edward Lining Manigault
Provenance: By family descent

Joseph Manigault (1763–1843) was the eldest son of Peter Manigault (1731–73) and Elizabeth Wragg (1736–72). Orphaned at an early age, Joseph, his brother Gabriel, and two sisters were raised by their grandparents, Gabriel Manigault and Ann Ashby. In 1781, Joseph embarked for Europe to complete his education. He studied law at the Middle Temple, London, at which time Gilbert Stuart painted his portrait. He traveled to Geneva to continue his studies (cat. 41) and returned to England in 1783. He resumed his law studies but had to abandon them because of poor health.

Manigault returned to South Carolina in 1785 and established himself as a planter. He inherited more than 22,000 acres and hundreds of slaves from his father and paternal grandfather. He was first married to Maria Henrietta Middleton (1772–91), the daughter of Arthur and Mary Izard Middleton (cat. 8), and then to Charlotte Drayton (1781–1855) of Drayton Hall, with whom he had eight children.

Manigault represented Christ Church Parish in several General Assemblies. He was also active in local institutions, serving as commissioner of the Charleston Orphan House, vice president of the South Carolina Association, and trustee of the College of Charleston.[1]

Painted early in Stuart's career, the portrait of Joseph Manigault displays many of the stylistic attributes for which the artist would become noted, particularly his emphasis on bust-length character studies. Influenced by the simplified linearity of George Romney, the portrait demonstrates the loose, visible brushwork, in the manner of Reynolds and Gainsborough, that was high fashion.[2]

ADM

1. N. Louise Bailey and Elizabeth Ivey Cooper, eds., *Biographical Directory of the South Carolina House of Representatives, 1775–90* (Columbia: University of South Carolina Press, 1981), 3:473–74.
2. Dorinda Evans, *Benjamin West and His American Students* (Washington, D.C.: Smithsonian Institution Press, 1980), p. 54.

18. *Mrs. Roger Smith (Mary Rutledge) and her son Edward Nutt Smith,* 1786

GEORGE ROMNEY (British, 1734–1802)
Oil on canvas, 91 × 58 in.

Historic Charleston Foundation/Nathaniel Russell House, purchased from Christie's, London, in 1975 with funds from anonymous donors
Provenance: By family descent until 1889

Mary Rutledge (1785–1837) was the daughter of John Rutledge (d. 1750) and Sarah Hext (1724–92) and a sister of Edward Rutledge, signer of the Declaration of Independence, and John Rutledge, president and first governor of the state of South Carolina. In 1768, she married Roger Moore Smith (1745–1805), son of Thomas Smith (cat. 3) of Charleston, and Sarah Moore.

Roger Moore Smith and his first cousin Thomas Loughton Smith (1741–73) reached a level of financial success during the colonial period that had few equals among Charleston's elite. With plantations on the Charleston Neck, they became part of the Carolina aristocracy. Roger's marriage to Mary Rutledge cemented an alliance between a leading merchant family and a preeminent family of attorneys and public servants.[1]

Although Smith was a lieutenant colonel in the South Carolina militia, he was not known as a Revolutionary patriot. In May 1784, Henry Laurens described him in a letter to the countess of Huntington as one who had "lagged at home in the day of calamity." Smith had "halted" when others continued to march forward.[2] A merchant with considerable holdings on both sides of the Atlantic, Smith might well have hesitated in the face of revolution and warfare.

To ensure a proper education for her children after the war, Mary Rutledge Smith and her seven children left for London around 1785. She may have traveled without her husband since Roger Smith was still in Charleston in June 1786. However, at some point he met his wife and children in England and escorted them home in 1788.[3]

Mary Rutledge Smith was not without friends and relations abroad. Her London circle included John Adams and his wife Abigail, a distant relation of her husband, and Thomas Jefferson. In 1786, John Adams introduced Thomas Rhett Smith, Mary's eldest child, to Jefferson in Paris: "Mr. Smith, a Son of the Lady you Saw here, who is a Sister of our old Acquaintances the Rutledges, will deliver you this Letter. He goes to reside Sometime in France."[4] While there, Thomas Rhett Smith dined with General Lafayette.[5]

From 4 January to 4 May 1786, Mary Rutledge sat for the artist George Romney.[6] After an early career as an itinerant artist, Romney arrived in London in 1762. He traveled to Italy in 1773, and by 1776 was a competitor of Joshua Reynolds. Romney exhibits a greater concern for a reserved statuesque quality that distinguishes his work from the work of Reynolds.[7] In 1781, Romney met the sitter with whom his career was thereafter linked—Emma Hart, later wife of Sir William Hamilton and lover of Horatio Nelson. Romney used her as a model and painted her numerous times.[8]

In 1822, the portrait of Mary Rutledge Smith was exhibited in the first exhibition of the South Carolina Academy of Fine Arts along with a Romney portrait of Lady Hamilton (Emma Hart).[9] The Smith portrait was a favorite of Charlestonians. It made several appearances at the academy and was included in an early exhibition of the Carolina Art Association after its founding in 1858.[10]

ADM

1. George C. Rogers, Jr., *Evolution of a Federalist: William Loughton Smith of Charleston (1758–1812)* (Columbia: University of South Carolina Press, 1962), p. 29.
2. George C. Rogers, Jr., "The World of Mary Rutledge Smith," unpublished article, p. 8, HCF files.
3. Rogers, "Mary Rutledge Smith," p. 10.
4. John Adams to Thomas Jefferson, 16 May 1786, Jefferson having returned to Paris from a brief stay in London, quoted in Rogers, "Mary Rutledge Smith," p. 13.
5. Rogers, "Mary Rutledge Smith," p.13. Invitation at SCL.
6. Rogers, "Mary Rutledge Smith," p. 10.
7. Sir Roy Strong, *The British Portrait, 1660–1960* (Woodbridge, Suffolk: Antique Collectors' Club, 1991), p. 226.
8. Strong, *The British Portrait,* p. 227.
9. *CC,* 29 March 1822.
10. *CM,* 19 March 1824; Gabriel E. Manigault, "History of the Carolina Art Association, Prepared for the City Year Book of the Hon. John F. Ficken for 1895," *Year Book, City of Charleston, S.C. 1894* (Charleston, 1895), and *Catalogue of the Carolina Art Association* (Charleston: Walker, Evans, and Co., 1858).

19. *Allen Smith, Seated above the Arno, Contemplating Florence,* 1797

FRANÇOIS-XAVIER FABRE (French, 1766–1837)

Oil on canvas, 27 ¼ × 35 ⅛ in.

Signed and dated lower right: F.X.Fabri/Florentiae 1797
Lent by the syndics of the Fitzwilliam Museum, Cambridge, England

Provenance: Lord Holland, . . . Henry Sinclair of Dalkey Lodge, Dublin; his sale (anon.), Christie's 1 December 1916, lot 101, bought Agnew's for Charles B. O. Clarke; by descent to the late J. P. S. Clarke and Mrs. K. A. J. L. Clarke

Joseph Allen Smith (1769–1828) was one of America's most ambitious Grand Tourists. Born in Charleston, the youngest child of Benjamin Smith (1717–70) and his second wife, Mary Wragg, he spent almost fifteen years in Europe, traveling across the Continent from Portugal to Russia, visiting Spain, Britain, France, Italy, Denmark, Persia, Ireland, and Greece. This trip—initially undertaken for health reasons—led to extensive and frequently adventurous travels that furnished him with introductions to many of the leading aristocratic families in Europe; he famously dined en famille with the Czar. It was, perhaps, the ease with which he moved through European society (not least among members of the opposite sex) that may have encouraged him to aspire to a diplomatic posting around 1804.[1]

This portrait was painted on Smith's first trip to Italy, made between 1793 and the beginning of 1797, partly in the company of John Henry Petty, Earl of Wycombe (1765–1809), himself a seasoned Grand Tourist. It depicts Smith seated above Florence, overlooking the Arno and three of its most distinctive landmarks, the Ponte Alla Carraia, Ponte Santa Trinità, and Ponte Vecchio. In the distance, at the end of a long avenue of cypresses, are San Francesco e Salvatore al Monte (1489) and San Miniato al Monte.

Smith is shown in profile—an allusion to the antique portrait gems and cameos that he collected—wearing a fashionable high-collared blue coat and brown knee-britches. Positioned around him are references to Italy's classical

heritage: an ornate Corinthian capital at his feet, a pedestal supporting his left arm, and a stone block with artistically conceived Egyptian hieroglyphs behind him.

The composition owes much to Tischbein's full-length, recumbent portrait *Goethe in the Roman Campagna* (1786, Frankfurt, Städelsches Kunstinstitut), a drawing after which Fabre owned.[2] In both paintings, the sitters wear a large white mantle, draped around the body. As Aileen Ribeiro has pointed out, this may be the type of cloak that Hester Lynch Piozzi observed in Milan in 1785 and described as "an odd sort of white riding coat, not buttoned together, but folded round their body after the fashion of the old Roman dress that one has seen in statues."[3] In fact, as Fabre later acknowledged, Smith himself determined the composition of the portrait;[4] it presents a precise record of the images of elegance and refinement that this Grand Tourist wished to project.

Exactly how artist and sitter met is uncertain. But they may have been introduced by Lord Holland (1766–1837), who with his mistress Lady Webster (1771–1845; later his wife), was an intimate of the circle of the countess of Albany (1752–1824) and the poet Vittorio Alfieri (1749–1803), with whom Fabre formed a ménage à trois. Fabre sent the portrait to Lord Holland with a number of other paintings sometime in 1798; by mid-1799 the consignment had arrived in London.[5] Smith commissioned four further works from Fabre around this time: another portrait of himself life-size

among the ruins of Rome (cat. 20), and three history paintings, preliminary sketches for two of which are exhibited here (cat. 51 and 52).[6]

François-Xavier Fabre was born in Montpellier and began his studies there under Jean Coustou. In Paris he worked under Joseph-Marie Vien, and, from 1783, under Jacques-Louis David. In 1787, he won the Premier Grand Prix de Rome and left for Italy the following year. His studies at the French Academy in Rome were interrupted by the outbreak of the French Revolution and the consequent severing of relations with the Holy See, which created hostility toward the French population in Rome. In 1793, Fabre left for Florence, where he remained until 1824, supporting himself as a teacher, copyist, and portraitist. Like Smith, Fabre was a collector, who inherited the countess of Albany's possessions on her death in 1824. These formed the basis of the Musée Fabre, which the artist established in 1828 in his home town of Montpellier.

Jane Munro

1. R. A. McNeal, "Joseph Allen Smith, 'American Grand Tourist,'" *International Journal of the Classical Tradition* 4, no. 1 (Summer 1997): 72. See also "'Picture Mania': Collectors and Collecting in Charleston" in this volume.

2. Musée Fabre, Montpellier (inv. no. 837–1–991). Allen Smith may have met Tischbein in Naples, where he was director in the Academy from 1789 until his departure for Germany in 1799.

3. H. L. Piozzi, *Observations and Reflections Made in the Course of a Journey through France, Italy and Germany* (London, 1789), 1:93, quoted in Aileen Ribeiro, *The Art of Dress: Fashion in England and France, 1750–1820* (New Haven: Yale University Press, 1995), p. 222.

4. Fabre to Lord Holland, Florence, 24 August 1799, Holland House Papers, vol. 51637, fol. 97, British Library, Department of Manuscripts: "Quant à la composition du portrait de Mr Smith vous avez deviné parfaitement juste: l'honneur de la composition est tout à lui. J'ai tout au plus le mérite de l'execution."

5. Fabre to Lord Holland, 30 June 1798, Holland House Papers, vol. 51637, fol. 86.

6. Philippe Bordes, "Francois-Xavier Fabre: Peintre d'histoire," *Burlington Magazine* 2 (March 1975): 159. Bordes quotes a letter from the countess of Albany, 12 July 1797, in which she writes that Smith was making several "large purchases," including three paintings and two portraits. Fabre's letter to Lord Holland, quoted cat. 51, n. 1, confirms that two of these were *Ajax dragging Cassandra from the Altar of Minerva* and *Menelaus and Helen.* The third appears to have been *Hector's Farewell,* two drawings which are in the Musée Fabre (inv. nos. 837–1–384 and 837–1–385). According to manuscript extracts of Smith's accounts, kept by his son (private collection), the latter was the most expensive of the paintings he commissioned at 220 pounds. The same source suggests that he also commissioned two further "small pictures," one of which appears to have depicted Hector reproached by Paris; the title of the second is unclear from the manuscript.

20. *Allen Smith Overlooking the Roman Campagna,*
ca. 1797

François-Xavier Fabre (French, 1766–1837)

Oil on canvas, 7 × 8 ½ in.

Musée Fabre, Montpellier, France
Provenance: From the artist

Joseph Allen Smith ordered a second portrait from Fabre; this one shows him seated among the ruins of ancient Rome. The portrait was apparently never completed, but the surviving oil sketch reveals its similarity both to the portrait of Smith overlooking the Arno and to Wilhelm Tischbein's portrait *Goethe in the Roman Campagna* (Frankfurt, Städelsches Kunstinstitut). The relationship to Tischbein's portrait is particularly striking, as Smith is shown in a pose and costume virtually identical to Goethe's and similarly surrounded by antiquarian Grand Tour props. Smith's location is likely Monte Milvio with the Ponte Milvio crossing the Tiber seen in the background.

MDM

21. *Charles Izard Manigault and His Family,* 1829–31

Ferdinando Cavalleri (Italian, 1794–1861)
Oil on canvas, 58 ¼ × 49 ½ in.

Signed lower left: Ferd. Cavalleri. Pinx. Roma. 1831
Anne Jenkins Sawyers, courtesy of The Charleston Museum, Joseph
Manigault House
Provenance: Charles Izard Manigault, by family descent

In 1829, Charles Izard Manigault (1795–1874), his wife Elizabeth Heyward (1808–77), and their children Charles and Louis resided in Rome as part of their extended Grand Tour.[1] They decided to continue a Charleston tradition of having a family portrait painted while abroad and chose the Italian painter Ferdinando Cavalleri. When Manigault's family portrait arrived in Charleston in 1831, it was one of two important new additions to his painting collection. The other was the John Singleton Copley portrait of his grandparents, *Mr. and Mrs. Ralph Izard* (cat. 12). In his travel journal (cat. 125), Manigault recorded his intent that the Cavalleri portrait be a companion to the Copley: "In adopting the idea of my Grandfather's, & Grandmother's Portraits by Copley when they upwards 50 years previously were painted in Rome, we wished our portraits also to be a memento of our visit to the 'Eternal City.'"[2]

The view chosen by Manigault, however, differs greatly from the one chosen by the Izards. The Izard portrait emphasizes ancient Rome, while the portrait of the Manigault family emphasizes Papal Rome, a view chosen by Manigault. "The back ground is to be a view comprising the Castle & bridge of St. Angelo with St. Peters which we think one of the most interesting in Rome."[3] The other major element of the painting is the fountain on the loggia. This fountain is clearly adapted from the base of Gian Lorenzo Bernini's Triton Fountain (1642–43) in the Piazza Barbarini. Manigault

was generally pleased with the likenesses in the painting. As he commented at the time, "It is thought that he has succeeded admirably with us even in catching the likeness of our two little boys Charles not yet 4 years, Louis 12 months." He paid Cavalleri $220 for the painting and $50 for the frame and packing.[4]

After these paintings arrived in Charleston, Manigault entertained frequently, proudly displaying his new additions. In May 1832, John Berkley Grimball visited the Manigaults:

At 5 o'clock went to dine with Mr. C[harles] Manigault. . . . [He] is a great lover of paintings and show[e]d us some excellent pieces—amongst them were three lately rec[eive]d from Europe—One a family piece-representing Mr. & Mrs. Manigault and their children. . . . Another—a family piece representing Mrs. Pringle & her son Julius—taken also at Rome [cat. 22]. . . . The third is also a family piece—representing Mr. & Mrs. Izard—[Manigault's] Grandfather & Mo[ther]—this is pronounced a good painting done by a celebrated artist . . . done long ago, but it seems it was not in the power of Mr. Izard to pay for it—it has remained in England therefore until the last year when Mr. C[harles] Manigault bought it.[5]

The portrait by Cavalleri was a major addition to Manigault's painting collection, and it was the grandest portrait commissioned during his life. There were certain aspects about it, how-

ever, that disappointed him. He commented, "The Interior of the picture is also good. The Paint excellent, & applied with judgment. . . . Our likenesses having been taken while we remained at Rome, & thus secured, we had to leave the finishing of it to the Painter's leisure. . . . It was evident that Cavaleri the painter had put the finishing touches to it rather carelessly, ignorant of what treasures of the Portrait Art I possess. The gilt frame which came with this picture (made also in Rome) is a very handsome one."[6] The portrait is thinly painted in certain areas, revealing some of the alterations made by the artist as he worked. These may be the careless touches to which Manigault referred.

MDM

1. Elizabeth Heyward was the daughter of Nathaniel Heyward and Henrietta Manigault, daughter of Peter Manigault and Elizabeth Wragg; thus, she and Charles were first cousins. They were married in 1825 when Elizabeth was only seventeen years old. "The Heyward Family of South Carolina," ed. James B. Heyward, *SCHM* 59 (1958): 156–57.
2. MDP.
3. Charles Izard Manigault, travel journal, 6 and 10 February 1830, CLS.
4. Manigault, travel journal, 10 February 1830, CLS.
5. John Berkley Grimball, diary, 9 May 1832, SHC-UNC.
6. MDP.

22. *Mrs. John Julius Pringle (Mary Izard) and John Julius Izard Pringle,* 1829–31

FERDINANDO CAVALLERI (Italian, 1794–1861)
Oil on canvas, 37 ¾ × 29 ½ in.

Signed lower left: Ferd. Cavalleri. Pinx. Rom. 1831
Mr. and Mrs. John Julius Pringle
Provenance: Mrs. John Julius Izard Pringle, by family descent

In 1829 Mary Izard Pringle (1780–1858) and her son John Julius Izard Pringle (1808–62) resided in Rome.[1] While there they followed the lead of their cousins the Manigaults in commissioning a family portrait from the Italian painter Ferdinando Cavalleri. The view chosen by the Pringles not only emphasizes ancient Rome, but also creates a visual essay on the experience of the Grand Tour. Mary Pringle and her son Julius are shown in an indoor space (one that could not have been in as close proximity to the Forum as the painting suggests). She is seated on a chaise longue, examining a book open to a print of the Arch of Titus, which is also visible behind them and to which Julius Pringle points, almost as if he is lecturing on particular details to his mother.

As was common with overseas commissions, this portrait and that of the Manigault family took longer to complete than Cavalleri had originally promised. Julius Pringle reported in November 1831 why the paintings had been delayed: "Cavalleri also wrote to excuse his negligence for not having finished them, as he said his Sovereign had called him to Turin to paint the family of his Majesty, therefore our noble selves had been in consequence put aside."[2] When the painting arrived in Charleston in 1832, it was displayed in the Manigault residence along with the other Cavalleri portrait (cat. 21), and the portrait of the Izards by John Singleton Copley (cat. 12).

MDM

1. In 1806, Mary Izard married John Julius Pringle in England. He died the next year. John Julius Izard Pringle was their only child. In 1833 she married Joel Roberts Poinsett. Her son spent much of his life in Europe, dying in Rome in 1862. Mary Pringle Fenhagen, "Descendants of Judge Robert Pringle," *SCHM* 62 (1961): 156.
2. Julius Pringle to Charles Izard Manigault, Paris, 8 November 1831, Manigault Family Papers, SCHS.

23. *Rocky Landscape with Figures in Recession,* ca. 1650

Purchased as SALVATOR ROSA (Italian, 1615–73)

Oil on canvas, 20 ⅛ × 26 in.

Art Gallery of Nova Scotia, Halifax

Provenance: Purchased by Joseph Allen Smith in Italy in 1797; Pennsylvania Academy of the Fine Arts, gift of the United States of America in recognition of the historic 1813 decision by the Hon. Sir Alexander Croke, Justice of the Court of Vice-Admiralty, Halifax, respecting prizes of war. Presented by the United States Consul-General of Halifax, 1952

Salvator Rosa was one of the most popular painters among British collectors in the late eighteenth century. He was perceived to be a romantic figure who remained true to his artistic principles without bending to patrons or tradition, and his art was thought to reflect that. While his subject matter was greatly varied, his landscapes were most highly prized by English collectors. In contrast to the pastoral scenes of Claude Lorrain, Rosa's landscapes were thought to be wild and rugged—the very embodiment of the sublime.[1] Characteristic of Rosa's paintings were the *banditti,* figures of wandering mercenaries and bandits who appear singly or in groups.[2]

This painting and cat. 24 reveal many of the elements valued in Rosa's paintings, especially the wild and unkempt landscape characterized by dark waters, blasted trees, and mountainous settings.[3] They are two of three Salvator Rosas that Joseph Allen Smith gave to the Pennsylvania Academy; the third is *Mercury, Argus and Io* (cat. 25). They were first exhibited at the academy in 1814 and then almost annually until 1870.[4]

Purchased by Smith in 1797 in Italy, these paintings were part of the collection that he was assembling for a public institution in the United States and that ultimately formed the core collection of the Pennsylvania Academy. His goal was to collect "those objects which were most admired, in the hopes that they might possibly be of some service to his coun-trymen when they should turn their thoughts to the study of Painting & Sculpture."[5]

Most of the plaster casts, gems, engravings, and books Smith acquired were released from embargo for shipment in 1800, but many paintings remained in storage in Italy for more than a decade because of the Napoleonic Wars. When finally released in 1812, Britain and the United States were at war, and the ships carrying Smith's paintings were seized by a British ship off the coast of Nova Scotia and the ships and paintings were taken there as prizes to be condemned and sold. The Halifax Admiralty Court ruled that because the paintings belonged to a public institution, they were not subject to prize court suits. The twenty-one paintings and fifty-two prints were delivered to the academy, although apparently only after severe water damage. In 1952 the Pennsylvania Academy of the Fine Arts gave these two landscapes to the Art Gallery of Nova Scotia, Halifax, in gratitude for the 1812 Halifax Admiralty Court ruling.[6]

MDM

1. John Sunderland, "The Legend and Influence of Salvator Rosa in England in the Eighteenth Century," *Burlington Magazine* 115 (December 1973): 785–86.
2. Andrew Wilton and Ilaria Bignamini, eds., *Grand Tour: The Lure of Italy in the Eighteenth Century* (London: Tate Gallery, 1997), p. 42.
3. Jonathan Scott, *Salvator Rosa: His Life and Times* (New Haven: Yale University Press, 1995), pp. 206–7.
4. Anna Wells Rutledge, *Cumulative Record of Exhibition Catalogues: The Pennsylvania Academy of the Fine Arts 1807–1870* (Philadelphia: American Philosophical Society, 1955), p. 186.
5. Joseph Allen Smith papers, PAFA, quoted in E. P. Richardson, "Allen Smith, Collector and Benefactor," *American Art Journal* 1, no. 2 (Fall 1969): p. 10.
6. The saga of the pictures is recounted in greater detail in Richardson, "Allen Smith," pp. 8–16.

24. *Landscape with Two Soldiers and Ruins,* ca. 1650

Purchased as SALVATOR ROSA (Italian, 1615–73)

Oil on canvas, 19 × 25 in.

Art Gallery of Nova Scotia, Halifax

Provenance: Purchased by Joseph Allen Smith in Italy in 1797; Pennsylvania Academy of the Fine Arts, gift of the United States of America in recognition of the historic 1813 decision by the Hon. Sir Alexander Croke, Justice of the Court of Vice-Admiralty, Halifax, respecting prizes of war. Presented by the United States Consul-General of Halifax, 1952

25. *Mercury, Argus and Io,* ca. 1653–54

SALVATOR ROSA (Italian, 1615–73)

Oil on canvas, 48 ⁹⁄₁₆ × 74 ³⁄₁₆ in.

Private collection

Provenance: Joseph Allen Smith gift to the Pennsylvania Academy of the Fine Arts; sold Christie's, New York, 11 January 1989, lot 78

One of the most important acquisitions made by Joseph Allen Smith in Italy for the Pennsylvania Academy of the Fine Arts was this large landscape believed to be by Salvator Rosa. Smith acquired this painting in Italy no later than 1797. The composition exists in other versions, notably in the Nelson-Atkins Museum, Kansas City, and in the Lyndon Harris Collection, United Kingdom. The Nelson-Atkins picture has a provenance from the Chigi Collection, Rome, and, like the other two versions, was purchased in Italy in the 1790s.

The 1658 inventory of the Chigi collection, Rome, listed *Mercury, Argus and Io* as a pendant painting to Claude Lorrain's *David at the Cave of Adullam* (National Gallery, London). Very different in theme and composition, these paintings were considered perfect pendants because both painters were reputed the greatest landscape painters of their day. Hanging together, the artists' paintings served as paragons of the two different schools: the serenity of Claude Lorrain contrasting with the sublimity of Rosa.[2]

The subject matter of the painting is drawn from Ovid's *Metamorphoses,* which recounts the tale of Jupiter's many loves, among them, Io, daughter of the king of Argos. When news of their liaison reached Jupiter's wife, Juno, Jupiter disguised Io as a white heifer, but even in this form she was beautiful. Seeing through the disguise, Juno asked her husband for the gift of the cow, a request Jupiter could not refuse. She asked the hundred-eyed Argus to watch over Io. Jupiter then sent his son Mercury to lull Argus to sleep with his reed pipe, and when Argus slept, Mercury severed his head.[3]

Mercury, Argus and Io was frequently exhibited at the Pennsylvania Academy. It was first listed in the 1811 catalogue, again in 1814, and then almost annually thereafter.[4]

MDM

1. Jonathan Scott, *Salvator Rosa: His Life and Times* (New Haven: Yale University Press, 1995), pp. 191–94. Another version of *Mercury, Argus and Io* is illustrated on p. 126.
2. Eliot W. Rowlands, *The Collections of the Nelson-Atkins Museum of Art: Italian Paintings, 1300–1800* (Kansas City, Missouri: Nelson-Atkins Museum of Art, 1996), p. 312. Rowlands identified this work as a copy after the Nelson-Atkins painting. Other Rosa scholars believe it an original work. Letters in the files of Simon Dickinson Inc., New York.
3. Rowlands, p. 309.
4. Anna Wells Rutledge, *Cumulative Record of Exhibition Catalogues: The Pennsylvania Academy of the Fine Arts 1807–1870* (Philadelphia: American Philosophical Society, 1955), p. 186.

26. *Dying Magdalen*

Purchased as CORREGGIO (Antonio Allegri, Italian, 1489–1534)
Oil on canvas, 48 ¾ × 41 ½ in.

Dr. and Mrs. Price Cameron, Charleston
Provenance: Joseph Allen Smith, by family descent
Not exhibited

Correggio was one of the most admired painters of the sixteenth century, with a reputation that rivaled even that of Raphael. His reputation remained strong throughout the nineteenth century. English collector William Hamilton's most prized painting, *Venus Disarming Cupid,* was believed to be a Correggio (fig. 30). Joseph Allen Smith was pleased to purchase *Dying Magdalen,* a painting that he also believed was by Correggio.[1]

Most of the works of art acquired by Smith in Italy were intended for a public institution, but others, such as this one, were kept in his private collection. The painting was lent by Smith to the Pennsylvania Academy in 1823 where it was exhibited as "The Dying Magdalen, an exquisite and invaluable original picture."[2] In 1824 this painting was included in the South Carolina Academy's annual exhibition; it was described in two newspaper editorials: "The first painting which is presented to the visitor . . . is the 'Dying Magdalen,' or 'Mary of Magdala,' said to be the work of the great Correggio. . . . [She] is described by Luke as being a woman who was a great sinner, and some commentators have concluded thence that she was an improper character . . . at the same time, [we see] her humility and her devotion to her Lord, with whom she found favor, and by whom her sins were forgiven. Correggio has managed the subject so perfectly, as to convey to the beholder the idea, that Mary is in a full and perfect reliance on her God."[3]

The author of the newspaper editorial was amateur artist John S. Cogdell. His comments reveal that aspect of the painting most valued by nineteenth-century audiences—its moral content. While Cogdell encouraged the public to attend the exhibition, he did not admire the painting. In a letter to Samuel F. B. Morse he wrote, "We have a Correggio as it is called— A Dying Magdalene—I have written two numbers to bring it into the notice of our visitors— as far as I was able to write about a painting . . . that had never laid hold of my own admiration . . . but it belongs to Mr. Joseph Allen Smith— a travelled Gentleman of our State—& therefore you know must be genuine original & beautiful."[4]

After Smith's death in 1828, the painting was lent to the Pennsylvania Academy again for exhibition from 1832 to 1838.[5] At that time, this painting and fourteen other works were released to an attorney acting, presumably, on behalf of Smith's son Joseph Allen Smith, who later changed his name to Allen Smith Izard.[6]

MDM

1. Ian Jenkins and Kim Sloan, *Vases and Volcanoes: Sir William Hamilton and His Collection* (London: British Museum Press, 1996), pp. 82–84.
2. Anna Wells Rutledge, *Cumulative Record of Exhibition Catalogues: The Pennsylvania Academy of Fine Arts, 1807–1870* (Philadelphia: American Philosophical Society, 1955), p. 14.
3. *CM,* 2 February 1824.
4. John S. Cogdell to Samuel F. B. Morse, Charleston, 3 April 1824, Samuel F. B. Morse Papers, reel 5, container 9, LC.
5. Rutledge, *Cumulative Record of Exhibition Catalogues,* p. 14.
6. E. P. Richardson, "Allen Smith, Collector and Benefactor," *American Art Journal* 1, no. 2 (Fall 1969): 16.

147

27. *Madonna della seggiola*

Copy after RAPHAEL (Italian 1483–1520)
Oil on board, 29 ⅜ × 28 ¾ in.

Middleton Place Foundation, Charleston
Provenance: Middleton family, by descent

By the middle of the nineteenth century, Raphael's *Madonna della seggiola (Madonna of the Chair)* became "without exception, the best known of Raphael's Madonnas. . . . It is, therefore, incontestably the favorite with the public, if not with artists and amateurs."[1] Its immense popularity began at the beginning of the century as focus shifted from Raphael's fresco paintings to his easel paintings and his Madonnas in particular. By the middle of the nineteenth century, artists had to wait as long as two years to copy it.[2] Numerous versions existed in America, the earliest probably the one John Smibert brought with him to Boston in 1729.

The earliest known copy in Charleston was the one purchased by Joseph Allen Smith. Copies after important Old Master paintings played an important role in educating Americans about famous works of art, and it is clear that they heightened interest in the originals. In 1830, Smith's nephew Charles Izard Manigault first saw the original *Madonna della seggiola.* His comments reflect the fame this painting had achieved by the time of his visit: "It is in this Palace that we behold one of the most valuable collections of pictures in the world—originals of the most celebrated masters—amongst them was most delighted with the Madonna painted by Rafael which we often see in the United States where we call it 'the Madonna' as if there was but one Madonna as a

painting known. . . . This American 'Madonna' is called the Madonna della Segulo for the mother sitting in a chair. —Uncle Smith Had this copied when in Italy 25 years ago & it is a most charming copy of this most enchanting picture."[3]

Indeed, the *Madonna della seggiola* was a cultural icon, a painting familiar to all and enjoyed by connoisseurs and tourists. Young Ralph Izard Middleton lacked enthusiasm for the standard objects of admiration on the Grand Tour, but even he was enthusiastic about Raphael's *Madonna della seggiola.* Of his visit to the Pitti Palace, the residence of the grand duke, he wrote: "its splendid gallery of pictures holds the first place. There is the Madonna della Sedia [*sic*] of Raphael commonly called the Madonna and oh, how shall I tell you of its beauties . . . even my untutored eye gazed upon it with delight."[4] Its popularity was due, in part, to the fact that it was thought to combine moral and artistic virtues. By owning a copy, the patron reinforced his or her own commitment to such values.

This copy descended in the Middleton family and was most likely the copy owned by John Izard Middleton and included in the list of paintings at the time of his death.[5]

MDM

1. James P. Walker, *Book of Raphael's Madonnas* (New York, 1860), p. 39, quoted in David Alan Brown, *Raphael and America* (Washington, D.C.: National Gallery of Art, 1983), p. 22.
2. Brown, *Raphael and America,* p. 23.
3. Charles Izard Manigault, travel journal, 7 November 1830, CLS.
4. Ralph Izard Middleton to Nathaniel Russell Middleton, Florence, ca. 1835–36, Middleton Family Papers, SCHS.
5. Earlier it was believed that this might have been the copy owned by Smith, but it is now known that both Smith and Middleton owned copies.

28. *The Cumaean Sibyl*

Copy after DOMENICHINO (DOMENICO ZAMPIERI, Italian, 1581–1641)
Oil on canvas, 48 ½ × 35 ¾ in.

Middleton Place Foundation, Charleston
Provenance: Middleton family, by descent

Domenichino was one of the most famous and influential Bolognese artists working in the seventeenth-century classical style. Renowned for his fresco cycles, he was best known to American and British collectors through copies of his most famous easel paintings.[1]

Domenichino painted the original "Cumaean" sibyl in 1616–17 for Cardinal Scipione Borghese, a collector of antique statuary and an important patron of contemporary artists, including Bernini, Caravaggio, and Guido Reni. Domenichino's *Cumaean Sibyl* was an extremely popular figure; at least seventeen contemporary copies of the Borghese picture are known. Domenichino's sibyl is heavily influenced by Raphael's *St. Cecilia with Saints* in Bologna and stands at the front of a long line of female figures with large, pure eyes and a distant look popular in Domenichino's work. In fact, his image of *St. Cecilia* (Musée du Louvre, Paris) employs a virtually identical female figure.[2]

The Cumaean sibyl is historically Apollo's priestess at Delphi. It was her prophesy that Christ would be born of a virgin in a stable at Bethlehem that made her an important Christian symbol. There are several allusions to this sibyl in classical literature, including Ovid's *Metamorphoses* and Virgil's *Aeneid,* and she seems to have been the most popular of the sibyls to be represented in Italian painting.[3]

Of all of the representations of the Cumaean sibyl, Domenichino's seems to have been a favorite with nineteenth-century collectors. When Charles Izard Manigault was presented to Prince Borghese, he wrote, "The 'Sibyl' [was] the original Painting which made the greatest impression on me of which we often see copies." An 1858 *Charleston Courier* article outlined the history of the sibyls and called Domenichino's *Cumaean Sibyl* the "most celebrated."[4] This copy was probably purchased by a member of the Middleton family in the late eighteenth or early nineteenth century.

MDM

1. Robert Erich Wolf et al., *The Age of Correggio and the Carracci: Emilian Painting in the Sixteenth and Seventeenth Centuries* (Washington, D.C.: National Gallery of Art, 1986), pp. 430–31, and Jane Turner, ed., *The Dictionary of Art* (New York: Grove, 1996), 9:88–93.
2. Richard E. Spear, *Domenichino* (New Haven: Yale University Press, 1982), pp. 191–97.
3. Michael Helston and Francis Russell, *Guercino in Britain: Paintings from British Collections* (London: National Gallery, 1991), p. 58.
4. *CC,* 10 April 1858.

29. *Group of Cherubs*

ITALIAN SCHOOL

Oil on canvas, 30 × 36 ⅛ in.

Carolina Art Association/Gibbes Museum of Art,
gift of Miss Alicia Hopton Middleton
Provenance: Middleton family, by family descent

This work is typical of the playful and decorative images popular with many nineteenth-century collectors. When exhibited by Nathaniel Russell Middleton at the 1858 Carolina Art Association exhibition, the artist was listed as unknown. At a later date, the painting acquired an association with Francesco Albani (1578–1660), a leading proponent of the classical Bolognese school.

Nathaniel Russell Middleton (1738–1820) was the son of Alicia Hopton Russell and Arthur Middleton. He was an officer of the Carolina Art Association and contributed his *Group of Cherubs,* along with Benjamin West's portrait of *Thomas Middleton* (cat. 7), Angelica Kauffman's *Cymon and Iphigenia* (cat. 33), and two Dutch landscapes by Andreas Schelfhout to the 1858 exhibition.[1]

MDM

1. *Catalogue of the Carolina Art Association*
(Charleston: Walker, Evans, 1858).

30. *Interior of a Church,* 1628

ANTONI SMETS (active early seventeenth century)
Oil on copper, 4 ⅛ × 5 ⅞ in.

Signed verso: A. Smets 1628
Carolina Art Association/Gibbes Museum of Art, gift of Henry Cheves
Provenance: Probably purchased by Thomas Middleton, by family descent

31. *Interior of a Church,* 1628

ANTONI SMETS (active early seventeenth century)
Oil on copper, 4 ⅛ × 5 ⅞ in.

Signed verso: A. Smets 1628
Carolina Art Association/Gibbes Museum of Art, gift of Henry Cheves
Provenance: Probably purchased by Thomas Middleton, by family descent

These two small paintings showing the interior of churches are the only examples of Dutch painting in the exhibition. Unfortunately, this underrepresents the craze for Dutch landscapes and interiors in nineteenth-century Charleston. These are probably the "Two Interiors (Very Small) painted on Copper," included on a list of amateur artist Thomas Middleton's paintings. On that list they were ascribed to Peter Neef (Pieter Neeffs, 1605–56), who was well known for his interior views of churches. They are instead the work of Antoni Smets, a painter active in The Hague in the seventeenth century.[1]

The value placed on Dutch landscape, interior, and genre scenes is perhaps best documented in the collection of amateur artist John S. Cogdell. His painting collection is particularly important because it is one of the few in Charleston to be inventoried in probate court and thus provides some sense of relative merit as viewed by the executors. In his collection of forty paintings, many of which were by him and other American artists, the three most valuable paintings, according to the court, were Dutch scenes: *A Landscape with Cattle* by Bergheim ($100); *Card Players* by Teniers ($50); and *A Man Lighting His Pipe with Other Figures,* an old painting ($150)[2] (fig. 78).

MDM

1. Cheves-Middleton Papers, SCHS.
2. Inventory of John S. Cogdell, Charleston County Inventories, Book B (1844–50), pp. 286–91.

Figure 78 A Man Lighting His Pipe, *artist unknown. Originally in the collection of John S. Cogdell.*

In Pursuit of Refinement 153

32. *Madonna of the Apple*

Purchased as CARLO CIGNANI (Italian, 1628–1719)

Oil on canvas, 37 × 28 in.

Private collection

Provenance: Charles Izard Manigault, by family descent

This painting was one of four of religious subject matter owned by Charles Izard Manigault (cat. 21). While most Charleston collections had a broad sampling of religious works in the seventeenth-century Italian and Flemish styles, Manigault's collection was dominated by portraiture. The additions he made to his collection of Biblical and historical subjects were carefully considered and seem generally to have been works of high quality, though not considered masterpieces today. In the catalogue of his painting collection, he recorded that he purchased the painting in Rome on 4 March 1848 as an original work by Carlo Cignani, describing it as a "charming picture, perfect in every respect."[1]

While not a familiar name today, in the last decades of the seventeenth century, Cignani was the leading master working in Bologna and director for life of the local academy. A distinguished pupil of Francesco Albani, Cignani is particularly noted for his gentle manner, a stylistic break from the more energetic style of Albani's classicism. This quality resonated with collectors in the nineteenth century. Evidence suggests that Cignani used assistants extensively in carrying out the many commissions that he received. Thus, while many pictures were produced by his studio, many fewer were done by Cignani himself.[2]

Manigault's other religious works included a copy after the *Marriage of St. Catherine* from the Louvre, a copy of the *Little Spanish Madonna* by Murillo (both unlocated), and a fragment of a painting that he believed to be from an original by Correggio,[3] which is unfortunately in poor condition today.

MDM

1. MDP.
2. Robert Erich Wolf et al., *The Age of Correggio and the Caracci: Emilian Painting in the Sixteenth and Seventeenth Centuries* (Washington, D.C.: National Gallery of Art, 1986), p. 412.
3. MDP.

33. *Cymon and Iphigenia,* ca. 1780

ANGELICA KAUFFMAN (Swiss, 1741–1807)

Oil on canvas, 24 ⅜ in. (diam.)

Carolina Art Association/Gibbes Museum of Art, gift of Miss Alicia Hopton Middleton

Provenance: Collection of Nathaniel Russell Middleton, by family descent

The Swiss-born Angelica Kauffman enjoyed international success as a painter of portraits and mythological, historical, and literary subjects. She was especially admired in England, where she was one of the founding members of the Royal Academy of Arts. Her neoclassical compositions became extremely popular through engravings and reproductions on ceramics, textiles, and furniture. After 1781 Kauffman settled in Rome and developed a fashionable clientele that included many Grand Tour visitors and European aristocrats.[1]

Cymon and Iphigenia is a good example of Kauffman's sentimental subjects and appealing style. The story comes from Boccaccio's *Decameron* as retold in English verse by John Dryden.[2] Cymon, a handsome youth of noble birth, was so boorish and dull that he was sent to live with peasants. When he spied the sleeping Iphigenia, he fell in love, and the sight of her beauty transformed him into an intelligent gentleman. The painting was engraved and published by William Wynne Ryland in London, 1782. Ryland's stipple engraving—the last of many he produced after Kauffman's work[3]—includes Dryden's lines:

The fool of nature stood with stupid eyes,
And gaping mouth, that testified surprise,
Fix'd on her face, nor could remove her
   sight.
New as he was to love and novice to delight.

Kauffman sometimes painted replicas of her own work, but it is possible that the Charleston painting is the original owned by Ryland himself, as indicated by an inscription on the print. Ryland was in financial trouble and was forced to sell his paintings in 1782.[4] A member of the Middleton family acquired the picture in London in the 1780s or later. Nathaniel Russell Middleton exhibited it at the Carolina Art Association in 1858.[5]

Wendy Wassyng Roworth

1. Wendy W. Roworth, ed., *Angelica Kauffman: A Continental Artist in Georgian England* (London: Reaktion Books, 1992). Victoria Manners and G. C. Williamson, *Angelica Kauffmann, R.A., Her Life and Her Works* (1924; reprint, New York: Hacker Art Books, 1976), includes an illustration of Ryland's stipple engraving of *Cymon and Iphigenia.* Before she arrived in England in 1766, Kauffman met Benjamin West and several Americans on tour in Italy. See A. S. Marks, "Angelica Kauffman and Some Americans on the Grand Tour," *American Art Journal* 12 (1980): 5–24.

2. This subject was very popular. Benjamin West painted several versions in the 1760s, and Joshua Reynolds exhibited one at the Royal Academy in 1789. The actor David Garrick produced an operetta called *Cymon and Iphigenia* in 1768 at Drury Lane. See Helmut von Erffa and Allen Staley, *The Paintings of Benjamin West* (New Haven: Yale University Press, 1986), pp. 264–66; Martin Postle, *Sir Joshua Reynolds: The Subject Pictures* (Cambridge: Cambridge University Press, 1995), p.229; Peter Walch, "Angelica Kauffman" (Ph.D. diss., Princeton University, 1968), pp. 321–22.

3. The engraving differs slightly from the painting in the background foliage, especially at the far right above the sleeping woman, where a mountain can be seen in the print. Ryland exhibited a proof of *Cymon and Iphigenia* in 1780 and published the completed engraving as a pendant to Thomas Burke's engraving after Kauffman's painting *Death of Eloisa* (from Alexander Pope's poem), owned by the earl of Exeter. D. Alexander, "Kauffman and the Print Market in Eighteenth-Century England," in Roworth, *Angelica Kauffman,* pp. 168, 183. See also *Angelika Kauffmann und ihre Zeit: Graphik und Zeichnungen von 1760–1810* (Düsseldorf: C. G. Boerner, 1979), pp. 65, 67.

4. Soon after this, Ryland was tried and convicted of forgery, declared bankrupt, and executed in August 1783. Alexander, "Print Market," pp. 172–74.

5. *Catalogue of the Carolina Art Association* (Charleston: Walker, Evans, 1858), no. 13: "Scene from Boccaccio's Cimon and Iphigenia. Circular, 2' 1 in diameter. N.R. Middleton." No. 44 in this exhibition was also by Kauffman: *The Inspiration of Shakespeare* from the collection of N. R. Paine. A note states that it had previously been owned by the late Mr. Peter Smith, who brought it from England and exhibited it with others at the Academy of Fine Arts in Broad Street.

34. *Italian Landscape,* ca. 1805–6

WASHINGTON ALLSTON (American, 1799–1843)

Oil on canvas, 40 × 50 ¾ in.

Signed lower left: W. Allston

Addison Gallery of American Art, Phillips Academy, Andover, Mass.

Provenance: Edmund Dwight, Boston, Mass., by 1837; by family descent to
Mrs. William P. Homans (Edith W. Parkman), Canton, Mass.; with Vose
Galleries of Boston, Inc., Boston, Mass., January 1943

Washington Allston, born in South Carolina in 1779, became the most sophisticated American painter of his generation, a master of classical landscape before becoming the first great American romantic painter. The Allstons (or Alstons) were a prominent landholding family who had settled on the Waccamaw River. As a boy, Allston went to Charleston to study at Mrs. Colcott's school;[1] as a young man he was sent north to Newport, Rhode Island, before entering Harvard College, from which he graduated in 1800. Returning to Charleston, already an aspiring painter, he counted fellow artists Charles Fraser and Edward Malbone among his companions. He then "sold his patrimonial estate" in South Carolina and determined to study abroad, aiming to become, as he put it, "the first painter, at least, from America."[2]

Allston was fortunate to study with Benjamin West in London for about three years; then in late 1803 he traveled with the painter John Vanderlyn to Paris, where he executed his first mature work, *Rising of a Thunderstorm at Sea,* 1804 (Museum of Fine Arts, Boston). In Rome from late 1804 to 1808, he came into contact with the innovative group of German classicists then working in the city, including Joseph Anton Koch and Gottlieb Schick, among others.

In her excellent study of Allston's early work, Diana Strazdes argues that *Italian Landscape* was likely painted in Paris in 1804, because its effective lighting on the lake and mountain and the fine rendering of an ancient city in the middle distance were clearly inspired by such works as Poussin's *Landscape with Orpheus and Eurydice,* about 1650 (Musée du Louvre, Paris).[3] Nonetheless, it seems unlikely that Allston could have executed such a completely realized, rigorous classical scene without having experienced Rome firsthand and without seeing for himself the classicizing landscapes being made there at just this time by the Germans, especially by Koch. Thus a date of about 1805–6 seems most likely.

Allston returned to America in 1808, settling in Cambridgeport, near Boston. He was back in England from 1811 to 1818, then spent the rest of his life in Boston producing works such as *Moonlit Landscape* (Museum of Fine Arts, Boston), a romantic memory of Italy, and his unfinished masterpiece, *Belshazzar's Feast* (Detroit Institute of Arts). While no longer a resident of Charleston, he remained a frequent correspondent with friends and family, especially amateur artist John S. Cogdell.[4]

Theodore E. Stebbins, Jr.

1. William H. Gerdts, "The Paintings of Washington Allston," in William H. Gerdts and Theodore E. Stebbins, *A Man of Genius: The Art of Washington Allston (1779–1843)* (Boston: Museum of Fine Arts, 1979), remains the best source on the painter.
2. As quoted in Gerdts, "The Paintings of Washington Allston," p. 25.
3. Diana J. Strazdes, "Washington Allston's Early Career" (Ph.D. diss., Yale University, 1982), pp. 99–101. See also the essay on "Italian Landscape" by Allison Kemmerer in Susan Faxon et al., *Addison Gallery of American Art: Sixty-five Years* (Andover, Mass.: Addison Gallery of American Art, 1996), pp. 311–12.
4. For Allston's voluminous correspondence with Cogdell see *The Correspondence of Washington Allston,* ed. Nathalia Wright (Lexington: University Press of Kentucky, 1993).

35. *Madame Récamier, 1808*

PIERRE GUÉRIN (French, 1774–1833), after François Gérard
Oil on porcelain, 14 ⅜ × 9 ¾ in.

Middleton Place Foundation, Charleston
Provenance: Middleton family, by descent

This portrait of Madame Récamier is a reduced-scale copy by Pierre Guérin, after one executed by François Gérard in 1805 and given in 1808 to Prince Auguste of Prussia. Gérard was a pupil of Jacques-Louis David and was commissioned to paint the celebrated Récamier after David failed to complete his portrait.[1]

Juliette Récamier was a leading Parisian socialite—beautiful, coquettish, and brilliant—who was famous for her frequent salons for politicians, writers, and artists. Gérard has presented Madame Récamier in an informal pose, dressed in a fashionable Empire-style high-waisted dress—a style derived from classical drapery. Draped around her is a golden shawl, probably a much-desired Indian silk import. The clinging material and the cut of the dress accentuate the physical beauty for which Madame Récamier was famous.[2]

John Izard Middleton and Madame Récamier first met in the fall of 1807 when they were cast in a play written by Madame de Staël.[3] He likely commissioned this smaller copy of Gérard's portrait to commemorate his esteem for her. It was painted by Pierre Guérin, best known for his classical history paintings of the 1790s. Guérin was a renowned teacher of many notable French artists of the next generation including Géricault and Delacroix.

MDM

1. Arts Council of Great Britain, *The Age of Neo-Classicism* (London: Arts Council of Great Britain, 1972), p. 68.
2. David Irwin, *Neoclassicism* (London: Phaidon, 1997), p. 324.
3. For more on Middleton's relationship with Récamier see Susan Ricci Stebbins, "John Izard Middleton: 'Talent Enough to Be One of the First Men in America'" in this volume.

36. *Battle between the Turks and the Greeks,* 1822

FRANZ LUDWIG CATEL (German, 1778–1856)

Oil on canvas, 15 ⅝ × 21 ½ in.

Carolina Art Association/Gibbes Museum of Art, gift of Sally Middleton
Provenance: Purchased by John Izard Middleton, by family descent

37. *The Acropolis and the Areopagus,* 1822

FRANZ LUDWIG CATEL (German, 1778–1856)

Oil on canvas, 16 ½ × 22 inches

Signed lower left: F. Cat—Roma/1822
Carolina Art Association/Gibbes Museum of Art, gift of Sally Middleton
Provenance: Purchased by John Izard Middleton, by family descent

Born in Germany, Catel first studied art at the Berlin Kunstakademie before enrolling in the Académie des Beaux-Arts in Paris in 1807. In 1811, he moved to Italy where he remained for the rest of his life. There he specialized in Italian landscape painting and in Neapolitan folk scenes popular with the flood of tourists after the Napoleonic Wars.[1] These paintings depict scenes from the Greek War of Independence, which began in March 1821, as the Greek subjects of the Ottoman Empire vowed to free their country of four centuries of Turkish rule. The revolution inspired many Europeans because of its dual ideals of Christianity against Islam and civilization against barbarism.[2]

Living in Rome in 1823, John Izard Middleton lent these two paintings (along with sixty others) to the Pennsylvania Academy of the Fine Arts where they were exhibited in 1824.[3] Prompted by his trip to Constantinople (and perhaps Greece) in 1821, Middleton may have commissioned these paintings from Catel. Painted in 1822, the works are among the earliest to depict the Greek War of Independence and were probably the first images of the war exhibited in America.

Middleton's collection on loan to the Pennsylvania Academy was split. Some of the paintings were returned to Middleton, then resident in Paris. Others, including the Catels, were sent to Middleton family members in Charleston.[4] Paintings of the Greek War of Independence would have been welcome in Charleston. Citizens embraced the Greek struggle, raising funds and holding public rallies. In 1824 a committee for the "Cause of the Greeks" resolved to take contributions privately and in the churches. The committee proclaimed, "liberty, may shriek over the desolate plains of Thessaly and Greece; but at last it shall be said; that the Citizens of South-Carolina essayed with the means that they possessed to impede progress of such horrors." To raise money they hosted a "Greek Ball" at the Broad Street Theater.[5]

MDM

1. Jane Turner, ed., *The Dictionary of Art* (New York: Grove, 1996), 8:84–85.

2. Nina Athanassaglou-Kallmyer, *French Images from the Greek War of Independence, 1821–1830* (New Haven: Yale University Press, 1989), pp. 8–16.

3. "Register of Works Received for Exhibition," PAFA, 1823–24. The author would like to thank Lance Humphries for bringing this list to her attention. See also Anna Wells Rutledge, *Cumulative Record of Exhibition Catalogues: The Pennsylvania Academy of the Fine Arts, 1807–1870* (Philadelphia: American Philosophical Society, 1955), p. 49.

4. Gabriel E. Manigault, "Paper to Be Delivered before the Congress on Art of the Chicago Exposition," ca. 1893, Gabriel Manigault Papers, SCHS.

5. *CM,* 9 January, 20 January, 13 February, and 6 April 1824.

38. *Two Figures on a Country Road next to a Cottage,* ca. 1850

LOUIS RÉMY MIGNOT (American, 1831–70)
Oil on canvas, 30 × 41 ¾ in.

Signed lower right: Louis R. Mignot f./[5?]0
Mr. and Mrs. Edward Crawford, Charleston
Provenance: Frank S. Schwarz and Son, Philadelphia

Unquestionably the most accomplished southern-born landscape painter of the nineteenth century, Louis R. Mignot was equally celebrated for his radiant winter scenes and his poetic interpretations of the tropics. The latter were inspired by an 1857 expedition to Ecuador in the company of his fellow painter Frederic E. Church. Mignot enjoyed a brilliant career in New York before the Civil War compelled his emigration to England where he died in 1870 at the age of thirty-nine.

Mignot was born in Charleston to a French Catholic family.[1] His father, Rémy Mignot, owned a prosperous confectionery business in fashionable King Street. There is no reason to doubt one posthumous biographer's assertion that "from his childhood [the boy] showed an overpowering bent to the study of landscape and the use of the pencil."[2] Unfortunately, Charleston, with no professional art academy and a small, provincial artist community, offered scant opportunity for an aspiring painter. In 1848 Mignot left the city to pursue art studies in Europe. That he was only seventeen years old suggests the high degree of his ambition and independence.

Instead of going to Rome, Paris, or London—the usual destinations for American artists abroad—Mignot made straight for The Hague in the Netherlands where he reportedly had family connections.[3] He soon entered the studio of Andreas Schelfhout (1787–1870), the preeminent Dutch landscape painter of his generation. The few extant paintings from Mignot's four years at The Hague show him conscientiously rehearsing the subjects, compositions, and techniques of his master. *Two Figures on a Country Road next to a Cottage,* apparently dated 1850, is a respectful rendition of a traditional type of rustic scene practiced and taught by Schelfhout, but pioneered two centuries earlier by such painters of the Dutch Golden Age as Jacob van Ruisdael and Meindert Hobbema. Artfully composed from nature sketches, the picture balances the enfolding gloom of the forest with the open meadow and sky. The thatched cottage, rutted road, and conversing couple add the requisite picturesque touches to the scene. In the nearly five years that Mignot studied in the Netherlands, he not only mastered the grand style of Dutch landscape painting, he also acquired a superb technical proficiency matched by few American contemporaries. These would serve him well when, by early 1855, he left Europe to commence his career in New York.

John W. Coffey

1. For more on Mignot's Carolina childhood and adolescence see David Moltke-Hansen, "Roots and Influences: Mignot and Charleston," in Katherine E. Manthorne with John W. Coffey, *The Landscapes of Louis Rémy Mignot: A Southern Painter Abroad* (Washington, D.C.: Smithsonian Institution Press, 1996), pp. 23–33.
2. Tom Taylor, *Catalogue of the Mignot Pictures with Sketch of the Artist's Life* (London, 1876), p. 1.
3. Taylor, *Catalogue of the Mignot Pictures,* p. 2.

39. *Sir Thomas More Taking Leave of His Daughter, Margaret Roper,* ca. 1857

JOHN BEAUFAIN IRVING, JR. (American, 1825–77)

Oil on canvas, 49 ½ × 39 ½ in.

Provenance: by family descent
Mr. and Mrs. Daniel Ravenel, Charleston
Not exhibited

Born to a prominent Charleston family, John Beaufain Irving left his position at the Charleston Customs House in order to pursue his interest in art. His year of study in New York was followed by an extended stay (1851–57?) in Düsseldorf, a city that rivaled Rome, Paris, and London during the mid-nineteenth century as a center of artistic interest and training, especially for young Americans. There he studied with the German-American artist, Emanuel Leutze. After the Civil War, Irving moved to New York where he specialized in genre painting.[1]

While in Düsseldorf, Irving concentrated on history painting, particularly scenes of the English Tudor and Stuart periods. There he completed this painting representing Sir Thomas More (1478–1535) on the way to his execution. Irving's painting was displayed in the Carolina Art Association's 1858 exhibition as the first work purchased by the organization. In 1861 a fire destroyed the building where the association's collection was housed. Only a few pictures were saved, including Irving's *Sir Thomas More.*

MDM

1. William H. Gerdts and Mark Thistlethwaite, *Grand Illusions: History Painting in America* (Fort Worth, Tex.: Amon Carter Museum, 1988), pp. 125–27, 159–60.

40. *A View of the Roman Forum,* 1858

FAURE

Oil on canvas, 26 ½ × 37 in.

Carolina Art Association/Gibbes Museum of Art, gift of Mrs. Wilmot D.
Porcher
Provenance: Francis James Porcher, by family descent

Francis James Porcher (1821–70), son of Francis Yonge Porcher and Sarah Julia Pelot, was a prominent cotton factor in Charleston and representative to the 1860 Secession Convention.[1] In 1858 Porcher made a Grand Tour and purchased many paintings, most likely including this view of the Roman Forum. Porcher identified the painting as "an original by Faure at Rome" in his collection catalogue, but there were many artists by that name at work in the nineteenth century.

Porcher's view of the Roman Forum is characteristic of the eighteenth-century *veduta* tradition, although by 1858 this topographical style had generally been eclipsed by more romantic and evocative interpretations of ruins. Views of ancient Roman ruins were popular with Charlestonians and appear in many inventories. Porcher's description of the painting emphasizes the topographical and archeological accuracy of this image. Interestingly, he identifies some of the monuments by names in use in the eighteenth century: "This view is taken from the southern base of the Capitoline Hill. The three columns in the center of the foreground are the remains of the Temple of Jupiter Tonans—on the left stands the arch of Septimus Severus—on the right are the seven columns of the Temple of Concord—near to the center of the Forum is seen an isolated column erected in the seventh century in honor of the Emperor Phocas—to the right of this are three columns the remains of the Temple of Castor and Pollux."[2]

During Porcher's 1858 tour, he significantly increased the size of his collection. He acquired seven paintings in Florence and two in Rome in July 1858, five in the Netherlands in August 1858, and three at the Liverpool Art Exhibition in September 1858.

MDM

1. Curtis Carrol Davis, "That Elusive Mr. Legaré: Author and Artist," *Transactions of the Huguenot Society of South Carolina* 78 (1973): 60, and Catherine Cordes Porcher Porcher, "A Huguenot Family of Ancient Lineage," *Transactions of the Huguenot Society of South Carolina* 81 (1976): 110.
2. "F. J. Porcher Catalogue of Paintings," Carolina Art Association/Gibbes Museum of Art. By the nineteenth century the Temple of Jupiter Tonans was known as the Temple of Vespasian, the Temple of Concord as the Temple of Saturn.

41. *The Fairies and the Peasant Child,* 1860

EDOUARD STEINBRUCK (German, 1802–82)

Oil on canvas, 28 ¾ × 36 ⅛ in.

Signed bottom center, verso, respectively: Steinbruck; Steinbruck 1860
Carolina Art Association/Gibbes Museum of Art, gift of Miss Louisa Porcher
Provenance: Francis James Porcher, by family descent

Edouard Steinbruck was a German painter who studied in Düsseldorf and later was a professor at the Berlin Academy from 1854 to 1876. He was best known for his works of romantic or poetical subject matter executed in a crisp linear style.

Francis J. Porcher (see cat. 40) contacted Steinbruck in 1860 about the commission. In reply Steinbruck assured Porcher that he would put "immediately into action the commission which you have given me," hoping to "satisfy as well you as myself in this work."[1] Porcher received his painting in October 1860. In his collection catalogue he commented: "In the realms of fancy, this beautiful painting holds the same relation to art that the poem of the German, Teich, does to literature. The artist evidently held brotherhood with the poet for he has told the story of the little girl's adventure over the stream into fairy-land quite as well as the poet."[2]

The poet to whom Porcher referred was probably Ludwig Tieck (1773–1853), a romantic fairy-tale writer.[3] Porcher acquired only one more painting before the Civil War brought an end to his collecting activities. By then he owned fifty-two paintings, nearly all European.

MDM

1. Ed[ouard] Steinbruck to F. J. Porcher, Berlin, 4 March 18[6]o, object file, Carolina Art Association/Gibbes Museum of Art.
2. "F. J. Porcher Catalogue of Paintings," Carolina Art Association/Gibbes Museum of Art.
3. Martha R. Severens, *Selections from the Collection of the Carolina Art Association* (Charleston: Carolina Art Association, 1977), p. 80.

Works on Paper

42. *Joseph Manigault,* 1782

Ink on paper, 2 $^{15}/_{16}$ × 2 $^{7}/_{16}$ in.

Inscribed verso: "Joseph Manigault de Charlestown, South-Carolina, déssené
à Génève 1782"
Mr. & Mrs. Peter Manigault, Charleston
Provenance: Joseph Manigault, by family descent

In 1781, Joseph Manigault (cat. 17) was sent to Geneva, Switzerland, to complete his education. As the son of Peter Manigault, who traveled in the 1750s, Joseph was an heir to Charleston's Grand Tour tradition. Shortly after his arrival in Europe, he informed his brother Gabriel that his general plan was "to learn french, Fencing, Dancing, and if I can a little of Musick" in Geneva, and then "to return to England at farthest in a Year and a half to go on with the Law."[1] Geneva was a fashionable center for education in the late-eighteenth century as the British aristocracy began to view London as too debauched for proper academic training. Geneva's clean Alpine air and Huguenot

clergymen-tutors were considered a more sober alternative. Charlestonians educated in Geneva included William Loughton Smith, John Laurens, Henry Laurens, Jr., Francis Kinloch, and John Petrie, as well as Joseph and Gabriel Manigault. In 1773 John Laurens assured his family they had made the right decision by sending him to Geneva: "you will think *Geneve* greatly in vogue, when I tell you that we count sixty English at present—among whom are the Duke of Hamilton, Lords Stanhope, Mahon, Chesterfield, Lumley, etc. & so far are they from being an impediment to each other's Study by herding together and forming a variety of Parties of Pleasure, that it is become quite the Fashion to take a great number of Lessons, and to make no visits but in the afternoon."[2] This sketch of Joseph Manigault is by an unknown amateur artist, perhaps one of his fellow students.

RAL

1. Joseph Manigault to Gabriel Manigault, London, 1 October 1781, Louis Manigault Papers, Duke University.
2. John Laurens to James Laurens, Geneva, 19 December 1773, quoted in George C. Rogers, Jr., *Evolution of a Federalist: William Loughton Smith of Charleston (1758–1812)* (Columbia: University of South Carolina Press, 1962), pp. 66–67.

43. *Governor William Bull II* and *Mrs. Bull,* ca. 1780

Attributed to DUPAN (Swiss?, active late eighteenth century)
Paper; *Mrs. Bull,* 3 ⅛ × 2 ½ in.; *Governor Bull,* 3 × 2 ⅜ in.

South Carolina Historical Society, Charleston, gift of Francis Kinloch Bull, Jr.
Provenance: Governor and Mrs. William Bull II, by family descent

After their removal to London in 1778, Governor William Bull II and his wife, Hannah Beale, became the leaders of Charleston's Tory exile community. Their house in Surry Street was a gathering place for Charleston loyalists and traveling Charlestonians who came to pay their respects to the former lieutenant governor. Despite suffering losses of more than £50,000, Governor Bull and his wife maintained a sociable household. In 1781, he sent the following invitation to Gabriel Manigault: "It is but fair previously to apprize Mr. M. of the hardships he must encounter on this Expedition. He will have his Feelings of humanity hurt by scenes of desolation (the unhappy consequences of war) in a poor old but always hospitable house, to sit down in bottomless chairs, at disjointed Tables covered with plain & scanty viands, nothing to excite a languid, but enough to satisfy an healthy appetite, no glittering sideboard that dazzles the sight, no jellies that cloy, nor frothy syllabubs that tantalize with emptiness while they flatter the Taste, where no varied Dessert will crown the frugal Meal, but the choicest flowers of hearty welcome will be scattered throughout to invite content & satisfaction."[1]

These paper cutout silhouettes are the only known images of Governor and Mrs. Bull. They are attributed to an artist named Dupan who was probably the son of Bartholemy Dupan, a noted Swiss artist. Dupan and Charlestonian William Loughton Smith became friends and traveling companions during Smith's student years in Geneva in the late 1770s.[2] In 1780,

Smith noted that Dupan could "cut out likenesses without looking at the card."[3] Cutting out silhouettes was a fashionable eighteenth-century parlor game, and one can easily imagine the scene during an evening in the Bulls' depleted drawing room in Surry Street.

RAL

1. William Bull II to Gabriel Manigault, London, 17 June 1781, Manigault Family Papers, SCL.
2. George C. Rogers, Jr., *Evolution of a Federalist: William Loughton Smith of Charleston (1758–1812)* (Columbia: University of South Carolina Press, 1962), pp. 90, 92.
3. William Loughton Smith to Gabriel Manigault, 30 September 1780, London, Manigault Papers, SCL.

44. *Design for a Monument to William Wragg, Esq.*

Attributed to RICHARD HAYWARD (British, 1728–1800)
Pen and ink with wash on paper, 8 ¾ × 6 ¼ in.

Historic Charleston Foundation, gift of Francis Kinloch Bull, Jr.
Provenance: Governor William Bull II, by family descent

In South Carolina's revolutionary age, perhaps no individual represented the loyalist cause better than William Wragg (1714–77). His surviving monument in Westminster Abbey is unique as a memorial to a native colonial American and South Carolinian. Wragg, son of the Charleston and London merchant Samuel Wragg (d. 1750) and Huguenot heiress Marie DuBose, attended Westminster School and entered the Middle Temple, London. Thereafter he practiced law in England before returning to South Carolina. At his father's death he assumed ownership of Ashley Barony and became one of the colony's wealthiest men.[1] He was appointed to the Royal Council but by 1756, he became embroiled in a power struggle between the council and Commons House over control of the tax office. When Governor William Henry Lyttleton arrived in the province, he deemed Wragg the "Chief Incendiary" of the tax dispute and suspended him from the council on 26 November 1756. [2]

William Wragg entered the Commons House of Assembly where he voted against the Stamp Act resolutions and opposed placing a statue of William Pitt (cat. 72) in Charleston. Wragg became a leading foe of nonimportation acts, including, ironically, attempts to enforce simplicity in funerals and mourning. His letters against Christopher Gadsden led that patriot to vilify Wragg publicly.[3]

By 1774, South Carolina's Whig leadership confined Wragg to his plantation on the Ashley for refusing to sign the association for nonimportation. The revolutionary council banished him from South Carolina in 1777 for his refusal to take the oath of abjuration. Leaving his much younger second wife (and first cousin) Henrietta Wragg and their three daughters, William Wragg set sail with his seven-year-old son on the *Commerce* for Amsterdam. On 22 September, just off the coast of Holland, his ship was struck by a storm, and he drowned attempting to save his son, who was ultimately saved by his slave Tom.[4] Carolinians in London went into mourning. Among them was Wragg's old neighbor, Lieutenant Governor William Bull II, who wrote Manigault that Wragg's sister had arranged with the dean of Westminster for the monument in the abbey.[5]

William Wragg's memorialization in the abbey was unusual. Burial within any parish church in a vault or grave and with a monument placed on the wall denoted high status.[6] Even more, Westminster Abbey represented arrival at an "English Valhalla." Yet by the mid-eighteenth century, this burial place of monarchs and national figures had become cluttered. Alexander Pope had first suggested the use of nonroyal parts of the abbey as "a Pantheon to great men," and the dean, dependent on monument fees for building repairs, became more liberal about selling monument space in the nave. By 1760, Horace Walpole remarked on

the "crowds and clusters of tombs." Still, as the throngs came to admire these sculptural spectacles, it was "a fashionable place to see and be seen."[7]

Wragg's sister selected Richard Hayward (1728–1800), a mason of "statuary" with a large shop in Piccadilly, as sculptor for the monument.[8] An apprentice to the great Henry Cheere of Hyde Park Corner, he became independent in the mason-sculptor craft in the mid-1740s and later studied in Rome. His career advanced with mantels and other carvings for such notable country houses as Woburn, Blenheim, and Kedelston, as well as London's Somerset House.[9] Hayward's only other known American commission was the 1769 statue of Norborne Berkeley, Baron de Botetourt, governor of Virginia, still preserved in Williamsburg.[10] Hayward had already completed at least five memorials in the abbey by the time of the Wragg commission. An unsigned drawing for the approval of the patron depicts salient characteristics of the work, including dimensions, details, and the proposed inscription. The surviving monument reveals some deviations from the drawing.[11]

Richard Hayward's design incorporates traditional elements from memorial sculptures but also boasts features of newer taste and particular details relating to the death of Wragg by drowning. The flat obelisk and bordered tablet were found in high-style work since the early eighteenth century and in pattern books such as James Gibbs's *Book of Architecture.* Hayward's female allegorical figure, draped in classical garb and holding a bough (of laurel?), followed a popular convention. Nonetheless, the sculptor employed the Greco-Roman altar, or cenotaph, seen more in later romantic art. In his original design, a hairy paw supported the altar, yet in the actual sculpture a dolphin-like creature provided support. Shells, dolphins, and water serpents decorate the cenotaph, which frames a scene of a shipwreck with the coast of Holland in the background. The design and the resulting sculpture exemplify the highly decorative style of all of Hayward's work including his characteristic use of contrasting marble.[12]

Jonathan H. Poston

1. Walter B. Edgar and N. Louise Bailey, eds., *Biographical Directory of the South Carolina House of Representatives,* vol. 2, *The Commons House of Assembly 1692–1775* (Columbia: University of South Carolina Press, 1977), pp. 731–33. Wragg's wealth at his death included 7,100 acres of land, 256 slaves, a large brick house on (East) Bay, overall valued at £36,359. Inventory of William Wragg, Esq., 1779, Charleston County Wills and Inventories, Book 100 (1776–84), pp. 87–94.

2. Eugene Sirmans, "The South Carolina Royal Council," *William and Mary Quarterly,* 3d. ser., 18 (July 1961): 388–89.

3. E. Stanly Goldbold, Jr., and Robert H. Woody, *Christopher Gadsden and the American Revolution* (Knoxville: University of Tennessee Press, 1982), pp. 89–95.

4. *SCG,* 6 December 1780; Gabriel Manigault to his grandmother, 8 October 1777, Manigault Family Papers, SCL.

5. Mary Wragg is mentioned in his will and was the "remaining afflicted sister in England." Will of William Wragg, Esq., 9 June 1777, Charleston County Will Book 19 (1780–83), pp. 3–4.; Kinloch Bull, *The Oligarchs in Colonial and Revolutionary Charleston: Governor William Bull II and His Family* (Columbia: University of South Carolina Press, 1991), p. 26.

6. Julian Litten, *The English Way of Death* (London: Robert Hale, 1991), pp. 195–200.

7. Judi Culbertson and Tom Randall, *Permanent Londoners* (London: Robson Books, 1991), pp. 5–103; David Bindman and Malcolm Baker, *Roubillac and the Eighteenth-Century Monument* (New Haven: Yale University Press, 1995), pp. 9–23.

8. Carolinians had patronized English artists for the sculpture that adorned the interior pillars of old St. Philip's Church. "Sketch of the History of Charleston," *Year Book, City of Charleston, S.C., 1880* (Charleston: R. L. Bryan, 1881), p. 267.

9. Margaret Whinney, *Sculpture in Britain 1530–1830* (Middlesex: Penguin Books, 1964), pp. 143–44; Rupert Gunnis, *Dictionary of British Sculpture 1660–1881* (London: Abbey, 1960), pp. 194–95.

10. Frances Norton Mason, ed., *John Norton and Sons* (Richmond: Dietz Press, 1937), pp. 224–26, 265, 295, 313, 335; Graham S. Hood, *The Governor's Palace in Williamsburg* (Chapel Hill: University of North Carolina Press for Colonial Williamsburg Foundation), pp. 273–78.

11. The drawing was once folded and addressed on the back: "Lady Caroline Dun ____ ____ Street." Further research may provide a name and connection.

12. See James Gibbs, *Book of Architecture,* plate 122; Nicholas Penny, *Church Monuments in Romantic England* (New Haven: Yale University Press, 1977), pp. 6–8, 65–168. Katherine Esdaile, *English Church Monuments* (London: Batsford, 1946), p. 105; Hood, *Governor's Palace,* pp. 275–77.

45. *Mrs. Barnard Elliott* (Juliet Georgianna Gibbes), 1803

JOHN RUSSELL (British, 1745–1806)
Pastel on paper, 24 × 18 in.

Signed upper right: J. Russell, R.A. pinxit 1803
Carolina Art Association/Gibbes Museum of Art,
bequest of Mrs. Alexina I. C. Holmes
Provenance: By family descent

46. *Mrs. Jonathan R. Wilmer* (Sarah Reeves Gibbes), 1803

JOHN RUSSELL (British, 1745–1806)
Pastel on paper, 24 × 18 in.

Signed upper right: J. Russell, R.A. pinxit 1803
Carolina Art Association/Gibbes Museum of Art,
bequest of Mrs. Alexina I. C. Holmes
Provenance: By family descent

Through marriage the daughters of Robert Gibbes (1732–94) and his second wife Sarah Reeves (1764–1825) forged connections with many of the aristocratic families of Charleston and vicinity. The pastels of Juliet Elliott (1778–1850) and her sister Sarah Wilmer (1775–1804) were executed in London in 1803 while they were on the Grand Tour.[1]

John Russell was apprenticed to portraitist Francis Cotes. Primarily a pastellist, he exhibited yearly at the Royal Academy from 1769 to 1806 and published a practical instruction manual on painting with crayons. In 1788 he was elected to the Royal Academy and enjoyed royal patronage as painter to the king and the prince of Wales. Russell was an amateur astronomer and made detailed watercolor and pencil studies of the moon with the use of a telescope. To deter fading and deterioration of his pastels, he studied chemistry and made his own medium with no oil or resin.[2]

The pastels of the Gibbes sisters are on characteristic steely blue paper and exhibit Russell's masterful ability to render the filmy fabrics of the Empire-style dresses and the soft billowing hair styles of the period. In contrast, the facial features are crisply delineated, particularly emphasizing the eyes.

ADM

1. Martha Severens, *Selections from the Collection* (Charleston: Carolina Art Association, 1977), p. 73.
2. Patrick J. Noon, *English Portrait Drawings and Miniatures* (New Haven: Yale Center for British Art, 1979), p. 73.

47. *Charles Manigault,* 1829

Drawing, 7 ⅞ × 5 ⅜ in.

Private collection
Provenance: Charles Izard Manigault, by family descent

This sketch is preserved in the journals of Louis Manigault, son of Charles Izard Manigault (cat. 21). In the journal he notes, "'Saulini' who made our Likeness's in Cameo at Rome in 1829, sent a Painter to take these Likenesses of us, to assist him in his Work. Portrait of Charles Manigault." The likeness of Mrs. Charles Manigault (Elizabeth Heyward) is included later in the volume (fig. 79).[1]

Cameos, an item of adornment that first became popular during the Hellenistic period, achieved their greatest popularity under the Roman Empire and were revived in the nineteenth century as a popular form of ornament. The first set Charles Izard Manigault purchased featured the likeness of his wife, Elizabeth. Their traveling companion, Mrs. John Julius Pringle (cat. 22), also commissioned a set for herself. Manigault described the process: "In effecting this a painter first comes to one's lodgings & takes a little profile likeness in colored crayons which in about an hour he does with great exactness. . . . With the little drawing before him the artist setting at . . . [a] machine which all engravers on stone have, he . . . cuts away at this stone shaping the white part of the

stone after the likeness & cutting down to the red surface — this is very tedious & this is called a Cameo."[2] Manigault also purchased a set of "real cameos," perhaps meaning an antique set, that were highly valued by Grand Tour travelers in the eighteenth and nineteenth centuries. Unfortunately, none of Manigault's cameos are known to survive.

MDM

1. Journals of Louis Manigault, 2:220, private collection.
2. Charles Izard Manigault, travel journal, Rome, February 1830, CLS.

Portrait of Mrs Charles Manigault, née Elizabeth Heyward, taken at Rome (Italy) 1829 to assist in making a stone Cameo likeness of her, executed there by Saulini; and which with a shell Cameo likeness of Charles Manigault, are, in 1879, still preserved in our family.

Figure 79 Mrs. Charles Manigault *(Elizabeth Heyward), 1829. Courtesy of private collection. This sketch was made by an unknown artist for the cameo maker Saulini to aid him in his work.*

"Saulini" who made our Likeness's in Cameo
at Rome in 1829, sent a Painter to take
these Likenesses of US, to assist him in his Work
— Portrait of Charles Manigault. —

48. Page in the *"Album Amicorum"* style dedicated to Joseph
Allen Smith and originally containing a double-sided drawing by
Leonardo da Vinci and a small drawn copy by a follower of Leonardo

Jacques-Guillaume Legrand (French, 1743–1807/8)
Pen and medium-brown ink on blue-gray laid paper, 10 ¹⁄₁₆ × 8 ¹⁵⁄₁₆ in.
(25.6 × 22.8 cm) maximum sheet, irregular borders

Watermark along left border of recto too cropped for identification

Inscribed:

[Recto:] Souvenir d'amitié / a j. allen Smith /
par j. G. Legrand [paraph] en floréal an 9 [i.e.,
21 April to 20 May of the year 1801 in the
republican calendar]. / Leonardo né au chateau
de Vinci près de florence vers 1443 / ou / 1445 /
mort a fontainebleau agé de 75 ans. [*cancelled*,
dans les bras de . . .] en 1518 / ou / 1520 / il fut
eleve d'andré verrochio [*sic*, Andrea
Verrocchio] et devint chef de / l'ecole floren-
tine [.] Michel ange et raphael etudierent/ sur
ses cartons. il cultiva la poesie, la Musique,
l'architecture, / la sculpture, l'anatomie etc.a. /
fut savant dans les Mathematiques qu'il appli-
qua comme / ingenieur à la Mechanique à
lhydraulique. fit un excellent/ traité sur la
peinture. / il porta au plus haut degré le dessin,
la grace et l'expression. / ses eleves les plus
connus sont / andré salaino ou salai / antonio
bottrafio [*sic*, Boltraffio] / marco uggioni [*sic*,
Marco d'Oggiono] / caesar sisto [*sic*, Cesare da
Sesto] / paul lomazzo [Gian Paolo Lomazzo].

[Verso:] de la main de Leonardo da vinci /
notice./ l'ecriture est a / gauche, et doit se / lire
dans une glace / Parmegianino.[1]

Lent by the Metropolitan Museum of Art; Rogers
Fund, 1917, 17.142.2
Provenance: Jacques-Guillaume Legrand; Joseph
Allen Smith, Thomas Sully,[2] Francis T. S. Darley
(grandson of Thomas Sully); Thomas Nash (by
inheritance), New York; purchased from Nash in
New York in 1917

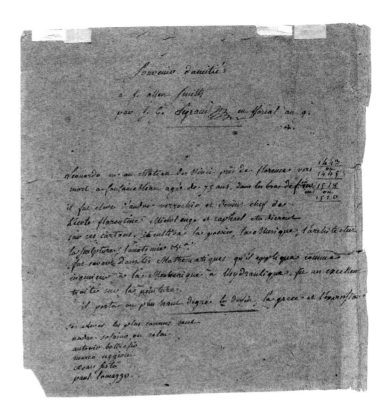

49. Allegorical Design: *The Lizard and the Sleeping Man*

(recto) Notation and Designs for the Staging of *"La Danae,"* Seen in Plan and Perspectival Elevation (verso)

LEONARDO DA VINCI (Italian, 1452–1519)
Pen and medium-brown ink on off-white laid paper, 7 ¹⁵⁄₁₆ × 5 ⅝ in. (20.2 × 13.7 cm), recto upright

Text is retranscribed by author with original orthography.

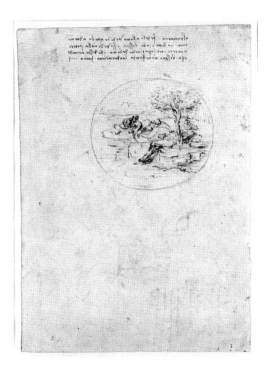

Recto inscribed toward the center of the upper border in pen and medium brown ink by Leonardo, script reading from right to left:

ilramarro • fedele allomo vedēdo quello adormē / tato • cō batte • cholla bisscia esse vede nōlla potere/ vincere core sopra ilvolto dello mo • ello dessta accioche / essa • bisscia nonoffenda loadormētato • homo [paraph] (The lizard faithful to man, seeing him asleep, fights with the snake, and as he [the lizard] sees that [he] cannot conquer her [the snake], he [the lizard] runs over the face of the man to wake him so that the snake may not harm the sleeping man).

Verso inscribed on the upper left quadrant in pen and medium brown ink by Leonardo, script reading from right to left, but with numbered fractions reading left to right:

6 ¾ _____ • 2 • 4 ¾ acrissio giācristofano / 13 ¼ _____ acrisio _____ 1 • 1 ¼ • 3 • 2 • ¾ [reworked and fraction separated with a long line from numbers below] • 1• 2 siro tachō / 15 _____ 2 ⅓ • 1 • 8 • 3 ¼ danae francº romano / 14 _____ 1 • 1 • 4 • 3 • 2 • 1 • 2 merchurio • gian-batista da osimo [*or,* daossmo] / 8 _____ 2 • 1 • 2 • 2 giove giāfrancº tantio / ⅓ servo [*cancelled,* piac]• / anūtiatore [annuntiatore]• dellafesta / + [*or possibly, a faded* 4] i quali si miar-avigliano / della nova stella essinginochiano / e quella adorano essingino / chiano e cō musicha finisscha / no la festa _____ / annv[tia]tore 3

Not exhibited
The Metropolitan Museum of Art; Rogers Fund, 1917, 17.142.2
Provenance: Jacques-Guillaume Legrand; Joseph Allen Smith, Thomas Sully,[2] Francis T. S. Darley (grandson of Thomas Sully); Thomas Nash (by inheritance), New York; purchased from Nash in New York in 1917

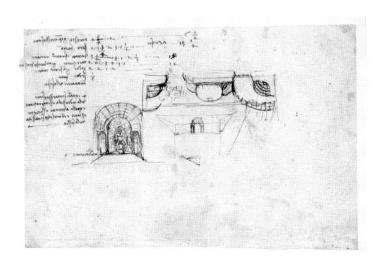

This thin blue paper mount was a page from an album (now dispersed), which apparently contained an array of pasted-on drawings, among them Leonardo's double-sided sheet with the allegorical design and stage set notations here illustrated. At the time that Leonardo's sheet was purchased by the Metropolitan Museum of Art in October 1917, another small pen and brown-ink sketch, a grotesque head of a man in profile, was discovered glued underneath (fig. 80).[3] This is the drawing referred to in Jacques-Guillaume Legrand's inscription on the verso of the mount, at the bottom center, as being by Francesco Parmigianino (Italian, 1503–40).[4] This grotesque head is now rightly considered to be a copy after Leonardo.[5] Archival photographs taken before the removal of both sheets of drawings from the blue paper mount document that Legrand had attached Leonardo's large double-sided sheet in a vertical orientation, showing the side that portrays the small, circular allegorical scene of the man sleeping; underneath, the small sketch of the

grotesque man was centered in the upper half of the mount.[6] Some of this evidence is still clear today from both the glue residues and the disposition of Legrand's inscriptions on the mount's verso. On the upper left, Legrand's explanation about Leonardo's "mirror-handwriting" (which we now know to have resulted from left-handedness and possibly mild dyslexia) would have been exactly aligned with the artist's own lines of text above the circular image of the allegorical design.

The verso of Leonardo's sheet, containing his notations and sketches for various staging elements, may or may not have been glued down along all four borders. It is therefore possible that it was not always viewable. Another drawing that was also part of the Metropolitan Museum of Art's purchase from Thomas Nash in October 1917 was similarly pasted onto a page of blue paper from the same album that Legrand gave to Joseph Allen Smith. This is Leonardo's important sheet of sketches in metalpoint and pen and brown ink for a Nativity (fig. 81), which includes an early idea for the famous *Virgin of the Rocks* (Musée du Louvre, Paris; and National Gallery, London), drawings which share the identical provenance as the pieces here exhibited.[7] The blue paper mount for the sketches of the Nativity and the Virgin at the Rock, however, bears only Legrand's succinct inscription "De la main de Leonardo da Vinci" along the top. It is therefore Joseph Allen Smith's enormous distinction to have owned as early as 1801 two of the most significant works by Leonardo in American collections today.

Leonardo's small circular sketch on the recto of no. 49, possibly intended for a medal,[8] is rendered with the quick, reinforced outlines, full of movement, and the delicate horizontal parallel hatching that are typical of his drawings from the first half of the 1490s. As Leonardo tells us, the sketch portrays a man sleeping by a tree, while to his right, a green lizard ("ramarro") loyally attempts to overcome a grass snake

("biscia") that threatens him. This fable, or moralizing story, on the lizard and the sleeping man is probably to be interpreted as an allegory on the virtues of fidelity, alertness, and protectiveness. It derives from the tradition of medieval bestiaries and Leonardo's close reading of Pliny the Elder's *Naturalis historia* (first century A.D.). For Legrand, who presented Leonardo's sheet as a gift to Joseph Allen Smith, the small sketch and fable may have had personal meaning, summing up the spirit of a great friendship.

The famous verso of Leonardo's sheet (no. 49) relates to the staging on 31 January 1496 of a musical comedy in rhyme, titled *La Danae,* composed by Baldassare Taccone, chancellor to Lodovico Sforza, "Il Moro," the ruler of Milan. This piece in five acts was performed in Milan at the house of Gian Francesco Sanseverino, who was captain of the Sforza army and count of Carazzo. The list of names on the upper left quadrant of the sheet neatly identifies, in right to left columns, the actors for the roles in the performance: Acrisius, king of Argos and the father of Danae, was to be played by Gian Cristofano (presumably, the sculptor Gian Cristoforo Romano),[9] the gardener Sirus by Taccone (the playwright himself), while Danae, the headstrong princess and main character, was to be acted by a man (not unusual for the time), a certain Francesco Romano. The god Mercury, who was to descend from Olympus cleverly hoisted from a rope and pulley, was to be played by Gian Battista da Osimo (Ossma?). The lecherous god Jupiter, who shrewdly transformed himself into a rain of gold to impregnate Danae, was to be portrayed by Gian Francesco Tantio, a well-known literary figure of the day and editor of Bernardo Bellincione's *Rime* in 1493. The piece also included roles for a servant and for at least one "heavenly messenger" (*annunziatore*). A floor plan and two perspectival elevation sketches of the stage setting are seen in the center of the sheet. In the per-

Figure 80 Grotesque head, *copy after Leonardo da Vinci. Pen and brown ink on beige paper. Shown on original mount. Courtesy of the Metropolitan Museum of Art. All rights reserved.*

spectival elevation sketch on the left, the figure seen seated on a throne surrounded by an aureole of flames can be identified with Jupiter,[10] the seducer of Danae, and the flanking figures represent other gods, for according to the play, "beautiful sky became visible, with Jupiter and the other gods, lit by an infinite number of lamps like stars," and indeed the barrel vault of the theatrical space was transformed to accommodate ingenious lighting machinery.[11] The meaning of Leonardo's numbers and fractions reains unclear. The dated text of Taccone's masque helps establish generally the date for Leonardo's drawings on the sheet.

Carmen C. Bambach

1. I am indebted to Emilie de Thonel d'Orgeix for checking my transcription. Compare Jean Paul Richter, *The Literary Works of Leonardo da Vinci* (Oxford: Oxford University Press, 1939), 1:392–93, no. 705A (verso), and 2:276, no. 1264A (recto); and Carlo Pedretti, *The Literary Works of Leonardo da Vinci: Commentary* (Berkeley and Los Angeles: University of California Press, 1977), 1:402, no. 705A (verso) and 2:265, no. 1264A (recto).

2. A letter by Bryson Burroughs to Bernard Berenson on 26 April 1918 (that is, a year and a half after the acquisition of the drawings) states that the drawings (as well as another by Leonardo discussed later in the text) were bought from Thomas Nash, Esquire, and that they belonged to Thomas Sully, the portrait painter (Archive of the Department of Drawings and Prints, the Metropolitan Museum of Art). For earlier versions of the provenance, corrected here, see Bryson Burroughs, "Drawings by Leonardo da Vinci on Exhibition," *Metropolitan Museum of Art Bulletin* 13 (1918): 214–17 and Jacob Bean (with the assistance of Lawrence Turčić), *15th and 16th Century Italian Drawings in the Metropolitan Museum of Art* (New York: Metropolitan Museum of Art, 1982), pp. 116–18, no. 108.

3. See Metropolitan Museum of Art 17.142.3; pen and dark-brown ink, 3 ⅝ × 2 in. (9.2 × 5.2 cm) As stated in a letter by Bryson Burroughs to Thomas Nash, Esquire (the owner), on 19 October 1917, just four days after the acquisition of the drawings (Archive of the Metropolitan Museum of Art).

4. This drawing was still thought to be by Parmigianino at the time it was mentioned by Bryson Burroughs in his letter to Thomas Nash, cited above.

5. Compare Bean, *15th and 16th Century Italian Drawings,* pp. 120–21, no. 111.

6. See Archive of the Department of Drawings and Prints, negative nos. 37135 and 37139, the Metropolitan Museum of Art.

7. See Metropolitan Museum of Art 17.142.1; metalpoint partly reworked with pen and dark-brown ink on pink prepared paper; lines ruled with metalpoint, 7 ⅝ × 6 ⅜ in. (19.4 × 16.3 cm). For the archival photograph recording this drawing on Legrand's original blue paper mount, see Archive of the Metropolitan Museum of Art, negative no. 37134. Compare Bean, *15th and 16th Century Italian Drawings,* pp. 114–15, no. 107.

8. Patricia Trutty-Coohill, *The Drawings of Leonardo da Vinci and His Circle in America,* ed. Carlo Pedretti (Florence: Giunti, 1993), pp. 42–44, no. 9.

9. Kate T. Steinitz, "Le Dessin de Léonard de Vinci pour la représentation de la *Danae* de Baldassare Taccone," *Le Lieu théâtral à la renaissance* (Paris: Éditions du Centre National de la Recherche Scientifique, 1968), pp. 35–40; Pedretti, *The Literary Works of Leonardo da Vinci,* 1:402 (verso) and 2:265 (recto); Carlo Pedretti, *Leonardo architetto* (Milan: Electra, 1981), pp. 111–12, 291–93; and Eugene Winternitz, *Leonardo da Vinci as a Musician* (New Haven: Yale University Press, 1982), pp. 77–79.

10. Both the subject of the musical piece and the format of the illustration support this identification of the figure as Jupiter, for the tiny figure is similar to the motif on the lower left of the related sheet of sketches in the *Arundel Codex,* fol. 231ᵛ (British Museum, London). The latter sheet contains preparatory designs for the staging of the festival play *Paradiso,* performed to celebrate the marriage of Duke Gian Galeazzo Sforza to Isabella of Aragon.

11. Compare Marialuisa Angiolillo, *Leonardo feste e teatri* (Naples: Società Editrice Napoletana, 1979), pp. 57–58; Winternitz, *Leonardo da Vinci as a Musician,* pp. 77–79; Mariangela Mazzocchi Doglio and Giampiero Tintori, *Leonardo e gli spettacoli del suo tempo,* exhibition cat. (Milan: Rotonda di Via Besana, 1983), pp. 58–62; Trutty-Coohill, *The Drawings of Leonardo da Vinci,* pp. 42–44, no. 9.

Figure 81 Studies for a Nativity, *Leonardo da Vinci. Pen and brown ink, preliminary sketches in metal point, on pink prepared paper. Courtesy of the Metropolitan Museum of Art. All rights reserved.*

Although it was probably common for American collectors to acquire drawings while traveling in Europe in the late eighteenth century, few survive to document this interest.[1] Among other art acquisitions made by Joseph Allen Smith during his European travels was a group of drawings he acquired in Italy in 1797[2] and two drawings by Leonardo, including this one, that were given to him in 1801 by the French architect, scholar, and collector Jacques-Guillaume Legrand.[3] Smith's connections with Legrand remain elusive, but he was perhaps drawn to him by their mutual interest in classical antiquity. Legrand would publish a number of treatises on ancient and modern architecture,[4] and at the time he gave this drawing to Smith, he was at work on his biography of Giovanni Battista Piranesi, whom Legrand described as "always in the middle of ruins."[5]

Smith's associates in the Parisian artistic community also included Ennio Quirino Visconti, the important classical archeologist and historian, and Dominique Vivant-Denon, who would subsequently be named the director of the Musée du Louvre.[6] Both Visconti and Denon played key roles in assembling and arranging objects at the Louvre, including those treasures brought to Paris after the French invasion of Italy.[7] In addition to the wide-ranging acquisitions Denon made for the museum, he was himself a voracious collector, owning an important collection of drawings by the great masters.[8] Although little can be determined at this time regarding the scope of Legrand's drawing collection,[9] it apparently contained works of some consequence if he was in the position to present authentic drawings by Leonardo as "souvenirs of friendship," as he did with this drawing. Its previous provenance remains unknown, but in the turmoil of the French Revolution and the Napoleonic Wars, art objects were coming on the market, many of which were certainly known to those such as Denon and Visconti, and probably Legrand.

Smith therefore knew those who had access to drawings of the finest quality.

Legrand may have been attracted to this drawing for several reasons. First, as an example of the work of an important Renaissance artist, architect, and engineer, it might have had special appeal to Legrand, himself an architect. Its rapid execution and unfinished appearance may have particularly appealed to him as well. Writing of Piranesi, Legrand observed that he never did any finished drawings, and quoted the artist as stating: "I realize that the complete drawing isn't on my drawing paper. However, it is very much in my head."[10] Increasingly, in the closing years of the eighteenth century, the sketch was thought to reveal the most direct and immediate impression of artistic genius.[11] Whether these particulars were appreciated by Smith is not known, but when he returned to the United States in 1807 with both of his Leonardo drawings, he undoubtedly brought with him the earliest authentic works by this Renaissance master to reach this country.[12] Their subsequent ownership by the artist Thomas Sully, who from his youth had strong ties to Charleston, adds yet a further dimension to the history of collecting in South Carolina.[13]

Lance Humphries

1. One of the earliest surviving drawing collections in this country, that owned by James Bowdoin III of Maine, was probably largely acquired by him from the studio of John Smibert in Boston and thus was not acquired by Bowdoin abroad. Over one hundred drawings from Bowdoin's collection were included in his 1811 bequest to Bowdoin College and remain there today. On this collection see David P. Becker, *Old Master Drawings at Bowdoin College* (Brunswick, Maine: Bowdoin College Museum of Art, 1985), pp. xiv-xvi. At nearly the same time that Smith acquired his drawing by Leonardo, his future nephew-in-law, Robert Gilmor, Jr. (1774–1848), of Baltimore, was in Europe and acquired drawings on his Grand Tour. His earliest documented drawing acquisition, a *Cameo Portrait of a Man in a Medallion* attributed to the Dutch artist Willem van Mieris (1662–1747), was purchased in Amsterdam in 1800 and is now among other drawings from Gilmor's collection on deposit at the Baltimore Museum of Art. On this drawing see Lance Humphries, "Robert Gilmor, Jr. (1774–1848): Baltimore Collector and American Art Patron" (Ph.D. diss., University of Virginia, 1998), 2:260.

2. See Thomas Gely to Lady Webster (later Lady Holland), 28 January 1797, Holland House Papers, British Library, Department of Manuscripts, where he mentions that Smith is in Florence and that he has acquired paintings by Correggio and by Guido Reni, as well as "de trés beaux dessins." I would like to thank Jane Munro for this reference.

3. The gift is documented by Legrand's inscription on the mount transcribed here. A third drawing of a grotesque head, found under the present work when it was acquired by the Metropolitan Museum of Art, was also given to Smith at this time. This drawing is now believed to be a copy after Leonardo. See Jacob Bean (with the assistance of Lawrence Turčić), *15th and 16th Century Italian Drawings in the Metropolitan Museum of Art* (New York: Metropolitan Museum of Art, 1982), pp. 120–21.

4. For a list of Legrand's publications see his entry in Thieme-Becker, *Allgemeines Lexikon der Bildenden Künstler* (Leipzig: Verlag von E. A. Seemann, 1928), 22:572.

5. See gallery catalog of R. S. Johnson International, with an essay on Piranesi by R. Stanley Johnson, *Giovanni Battista Piranesi, 1720–1778* (Chicago: R. S.

Johnson, 1980), p. 75. Legrand's manuscript biography of Piranesi (Bibliothèque Nationale, Paris, manuscript n.a.f. 5968) remains an important source on the artist because Legrand knew Piranesi's sons and coworkers and thus had access to direct testimony of Piranesi's artistic practice.

6. Smith's friendship with Legrand, Denon, and Visconti was apparently of some consequence. In 1808 he wrote letters of introduction to all three for Rembrandt Peale, who was traveling to Paris to study. This is mentioned in Charles Willson Peale to Thomas Jefferson, 21 February 1808, in Lillian B. Miller et al., eds., *The Selected Papers of Charles Willson Peale and His Family,* vol. 2, pt. 2, *Charles Willson Peale: The Artist as Museum Keeper, 1791–1810* (New Haven: Yale University Press, 1988), pp. 1063–65. The editors have not identified the "Ennis Visconte" mentioned in Peale's letter, but he was surely Visconti.

7. On Visconti and Denon's role in the larger world of collecting during this period see Francis Henry Taylor, *The Taste of Angels: A History of Art Collecting from Rameses to Napoleon* (Boston: Little, Brown, 1948), in particular the chapter "Vivant-Denon and the Musée Napoléon," pp. 548–64. Visconti's important role as an historian of classical antiquities and museum organizer is discussed extensively in Francis Haskell and Nicholas Penny, *Taste and the Antique: The Lure of Classical Sculpture, 1500–1900* (New Haven: Yale University Press, 1981), p. 50ff.

8. Francis Haskell, *Rediscoveries in Art: Some Aspects of Taste, Fashion and Collecting in England and France* (Oxford: Phaidon Press, 1976), p. 82. In light of Smith's connections to Legrand and Denon it is interesting that the grotesque head found beneath the present drawing has been identified as relating to a similar grotesque head on a sheet of Leonardesque studies from Denon's collection now in the collection of the British Museum. On these two drawings see Bean, *15th and 16th Century Italian Drawings,* pp. 120–21.

9. At least part of Legrand's drawing collection was sold in Paris in 1808. See Frits Lugt, *Répetoire des catalogues de ventes publiques* (The Hague: Martinus Nijhof, 1938), vol. 1, no. 7336.

10. Johnson, *Giovanni Battista Piranesi,* p. 77.

11. On this see Wendelin A. Guentner, "British Aesthetic Discourse, 1780–1830: The Sketch, the *Non Finito,* and the Imagination," *Art Journal* 52, no. 2 (Summer 1993): 40–47.

12. The very early presence of these drawings in the United States has not been recognized heretofore. When they were first published by the museum, the identities of Smith and Legrand were unknown, and it was assumed that Thomas Sully had acquired the works in London during one of his painting trips to England. See Bryson Burroughs, "Drawings by Leonardo da Vinci on Exhibition," *Bulletin of the Metropolitan Museum of Art* 13, no. 10 (October 1918): 214–15. Smith's identity was unknown to more recent scholars as well, including Jacob Bean. Apparently believing that Sully acquired the drawings in London, Bean assumed that they had been in London for some time and thus believed Smith was in London as well. See Bean, *15th and 16th Century Italian Drawings,* p. 117. The two other drawings by Leonardo at the Metropolitan were not acquired until the twentieth century and were purchased from European collections. See Bean, *15th and 16th Century Italian Drawings,* pp. 118, 119–20.

13. Although archival documents at the Metropolitan Museum of Art establish that the drawings were owned by Thomas Sully, their presence in his collection cannot be documented. It seems unlikely, although not impossible, that Sully acquired the drawings directly from Smith, but he could have obtained them from Smith's connections in either Philadelphia or Charleston. They were probably among a number of drawings and prints that comprised Sully's artistic portfolio. On Sully's death, the contents of his studio were sold, but drawings were not included. See *Executor's Sale. Estate of Thomas Sully, Dec'd. Catalogue of Valuable Oil Paintings and Engravings, Being the Private Collection of the Late Thomas Sully, Artist, to Be Sold on Friday, December 20, 1872* (Philadelphia: M. Thomas and Son, 1872). A copy of this catalogue is in the library of the American Philosophical Society, Philadelphia. By his will, Sully left his daughter Jane Sully Darley a number of portfolios and boxes that contained drawings. In addition to his own work, these portfolios surely contained drawings by other artists. See newspaper clipping "Sully the Artist: The Will of the Celebrated Painter—His Disposal of His Pictures, Objects of Art, and Relics," from the *Philadelphia Telegraph,* 16 November 1872, tipped into Sully's "Register of Paintings," New York Public Library, New York (AAA roll N18). Jane Sully Darley's son, Francis T. S. Darley, who is known to have owned the present drawings, probably acquired them from his mother, but this cannot be documented.

50. *The Lame Man Healed by Peter and John,* 1719

NICOLAS DORIGNY, after Raphael (Italian, 1483–1520)
Etching, 20 ½ × 30 in.

Dr. and Mrs. Price Cameron, Charleston
Provenance: Joseph Allen Smith, by family descent

In 1711 Nicolas Dorigny, an engraver working in Rome, was persuaded by a group of English enthusiasts to come to England and engrave the Raphael cartoons at Hampton Court. The seven Raphael cartoons were designs for tapestries of the Acts of Apostles. Brought to England around 1623, they were considered the greatest works of art in that country and were thought second in importance only to the Raphael frescoes in the Vatican apartments. They were "universally allowed" to be "the most valuable Set of portable Pictures in the World."[1]

Dorigny was not the first to engrave the cartoons; earlier versions exist from 1707, 1710, and 1712. What distinguishes Dorigny's set is their superior quality. His aim was to produce accurate transcriptions of the cartoons and thus the print size varies in accordance with the proportions of the cartoons. The original intent was for these engravings to be made at Queen Anne's expense as gifts for visiting dignitaries, but the £4,000–5000 sterling demanded by Dorigny was thought exorbitant, and ultimately he undertook the project as a commercial venture at his own expense.[2]

Although later sets after the Hampton Court cartoons were issued, the Dorigny prints still fetched a high price at auction in the late-eighteenth century.[3] This set was purchased by Joseph Allen Smith, presumably in England. Prints formed an important component of a well-rounded art collection in the nineteenth century. Valuable prints such as these, pur-chased in complete sets and illustrating the most important works of art in the world, were usually kept in portfolios and brought out to share with other connoisseurs.

MDM

1. *Spectator,* 25 October 1711, quoted in Timothy Clayton, *The English Print, 1688–1802* (New Haven: Yale University Press, 1997), p. 49.
2. Clayton, *The English Print,* pp. 49–51.
3. Clayton, *The English Print,* p. 26.

51. *Ajax Dragging Cassandra from the Altar of Minerva,* ca. 1796

FRANÇOIS-XAVIER FABRE (French, 1766–1837)
Pen and ink with wash on blue paper, 13 × 18 ⅞ in.

Musée Fabre, Montpellier, France

In addition to the two portraits mentioned in cat. 19 and 20, Joseph Allen Smith commissioned three paintings on classical themes by Fabre in the late 1790s. This and the following drawing are preliminary studies for two of these paintings commissioned in 1796, the sizes of which at that date remained to be established.[1] Whether the themes were chosen by Smith or Fabre is unclear, although Fabre's comment that he found the subjects very beautiful, if rather similar, lead one to suspect that the choice was Smith's. In 1797–98, Fabre wrote to Lord Holland that he was working "without a break"[2] on Smith's paintings, although he does not specify the subjects. Certainly, by 1799 he felt that his work had benefited from turning his attention to history painting and away from portraiture.[3] None of the finished paintings has survived, if indeed they were ever completed. Another drawing for this composition is in the Musée Fabre (no. 412) and the Uffizi, Florence (no. 235).

The subject of this drawing, *Ajax Dragging Cassandra from the Altar of Minerva,* tells the story of the sack of Troy, when the priestess and prophetess Cassandra sought refuge near the altar of Athena (Minerva). Ajax of Locri attempted to drag her from the temple, and in doing so, removed both the girl and the statue. The Acheans later wanted to stone him for this sacrilegious act, but Ajax sought sanctuary at the altar of the goddess whom he had just insulted, and was saved.

Jane Munro

1. Fabre to Lord Holland, 11 October 1796, British Library, Department of Manuscripts, Holland House Papers, vol. 51637, fol. 69: "il m'a chargé tout récemment de deux tableaux pour lui, il n'en a pas encore fixé la grandeur, les sujets seront Ajax qui enlève Cassandre du temple de Minèrve, et Ménélas qui retrouve Hélène réfugiée au pied de la statue de Venus." See also fols. 53, 69, 70,75, 77, 79.
2. Fabre to Lord Holland, 25 October 1797, British Library, Department of Manuscripts, Holland House Papers, vol. 51637, fol. 80.
3. Fabre to Lord Holland, 24 August 1799, British Library, Department of Manuscripts, Holland House Papers, vol. 51637, fol. 97: "Depuis que je m'occupe beaucoup plus de tableaux d'histoire que de portraits il me semble que j'ai fait quelques pas vers le mieux."

52. *Menelaus and Helen,* ca. 1796

Fʀᴀɴçᴏɪѕ-Xᴀᴠɪᴇʀ Fᴀʙʀᴇ (French, 1766–1837)
Graphite on paper, squared up, 15 ⅛ × 11 ⅝ in.

Musée Fabre, Montpellier, France

Laure Pellicier has suggested that the composition of this drawing is a simplified version of one Fabre used in two other, more finished drawings depicting Cleombrotus and Leonidas, both in the Musée Fabre.[1] Like cat. 51, the subject of this drawing is taken from the *Iliad.* Helen, wife of Menelaus, was carried off by Paris to Troy, thus instigating the ten-year war between the Greeks and Trojans. She lived with Paris as his wife, and on his death married Deiphobus. There are several accounts of the reunion of Menelaus and Helen after the Greeks captured Troy. Fabre depicts a version in which Helen made peace with her husband from the temple of Aphrodite. Menelaus's anger was dispelled at the sight of her beauty, and he again fell deeply in love with his wife.

Jane Munro

1. See Laure Pellicier, *Le Peintre François-Xavier Fabre (1766–1837)* (Université de Paris, Thèse de doctorat de l' État, 4 vols., 1982), 4:884. Nos. 248 and 249.

53. *History of Proserpine,* ca. 1795

PLATE FROM *Collection of Engravings from Ancient Vases Mostly of Pure Greek Workmanship Discovered in Sepulchres in the Kingdom of the Two Sicilies, 1791–95*
WILHELM TISCHBEIN (German, 1751–1829) engraving, 15 × 21 in.

Inscribed in pencil on the bottom: "Vase presented to Prince Coruloski by the Queen of Naples, explained at Rome, & representing the History of Perserpine"
Dr. and Mrs. Price Cameron, Charleston
Provenance: Joseph Allen Smith, by family descent

54. *Birth of Dionysus,* ca. 1795

PLATE FROM *Collection of Engravings from Ancient Vases Mostly of Pure Greek Workmanship Discovered in Sepulchres in the Kingdom of the Two Sicilies, 1791–95*
WILHELM TISCHBEIN (German, 1751–1829) engraving, 9 ¼ × 15 in.

Inscribed in pencil on the bottom: "Birth of Bacchus"
Dr. and Mrs. Price Cameron, Charleston
Provenance: Joseph Allen Smith, by family descent

William Hamilton was undeniably one of the most important antiquarians of the late eighteenth century. Appointed minister plenipotentiary to Naples in 1764, he was thus resident in Naples during a period of extraordinary archeological discovery and research. As the resident representative of the British government, one of Hamilton's duties was to assist his countrymen in gaining access to the jealously guarded excavations of antiquity. In doing so, he often had access to material, sites, and excavations that allowed him to become one of England's most important collectors of antiquity.

One of Hamilton's many collecting passions was for Greek (then commonly called Etruscan) vases. Hamilton's collection of vases was acquired from other collections, the art market, and excavations, and they were at this time in plentiful supply. Beginning in 1766, his first collection was published in a sumptuous collection of colored engravings: *The Collection of Etruscan, Greek and Roman Antiquities from the Cabinet of the Honble Wm Hamilton.* In 1772, the first collection of Greek vases was sold to the British Museum, thus fulfilling Hamilton's desire that these objects reside in a public collection.[1]

By the time the first book was issued, Greek vases were becoming rare on the market. Hamilton commented in a letter to Josiah Wedgwood: "You cannot conceive how very scarce the true ancient Etruscan vases are now."

In 1789 the situation was unexpectedly changed when a new cache of vases was discovered. Hamilton's collecting bug was awakened, and "he declared that he could resist no longer." He once again amassed a collection of more than seventy vases. With the accumulated evidence of the new discoveries, Hamilton became convinced that the vases were of Greek, not Etruscan, origin.[2]

The German painter Wilhelm Tischbein arrived in Naples in the spring of 1787 accompanying Johann Wolfgang Goethe. Primarily known as a neoclassical portrait painter, Tischbein was so taken with Naples that he decided to remain rather than accompany Goethe on the rest of his journey. He was appointed director of the Neapolitan Academy of Fine Arts and supervised the publication of Hamilton's second collection of vases. Hamilton engaged Tischbein to oversee the drawings and engravings for the publication. The first volume was advertised in 1791, but it was not received until 1794; the third volume was received in 1800.[3]

The choice of simple outline instead of the elaborately colored engravings of the first publication was a matter of economy and it happened to coincide with the taste of the day. As Hamilton explained in the introduction to the first volume, "There are no monuments of Antiquity, that should excite the attention of modern artists more than the slight drawings on the most excellent of vases, they may from

them form a just idea of the spirit of the ancient Greek artists, of the conceptions, and of their facility in the execution of them."[4] The images in Hamilton's second collection of vases were particularly valued for what they represented in terms of mythology, such as these two views, both of which are annotated by Joseph Allen Smith indicating the mythological scenes that they represent. Smith's notation on the "History of Proserpine" also suggests that he was present at a ceremony when the vase was presented as a gift and the story explained.

MDM

1. Ian Jenkins and Kim Sloan, *Vases and Volcanoes: Sir William Hamilton and His Collection* (London: British Museum Press, 1996), pp. 42–50.
2. Jenkins and Sloan, *Vases and Volcanoes,* p. 52.
3. Jenkins and Sloan, *Vases and Volcanoes,* pp. 52–54.
4. William Hamilton and Wilhelm Tischbein, *Collection of Engravings from Ancient Vases Mostly of Pure Greek Workmanship Discovered in Sepulchres in the Kingdom of the Two Sicilies* (Naples, 1791) 1:32.

55. *The Colosseum,* 1796

FRANZ KAISERMAN (Swiss, 1765–1833)
Watercolor on paper, 38 ½ × 25 ½ in.

Signed lower left: Keiserman fecit Roma 1796
Private collection
Provenance: Purchased by Joseph Allen Smith, by family descent

56. *The Arch of Constantine,* ca. 1800

FRANZ KAISERMAN (Swiss, 1765–1833)
Watercolor on paper, 20 ½ × 24 ½ in.

Inscribed verso: "arco di trionfo cretti dal—a costantino in memoria della battaglia da lui guadagnata contro Maxenzio a Ponte Molle / detta / Milvio / Kaiserman fece"
Private collection
Provenance: By family descent

Born in Switzerland, Kaiserman went to Rome in 1789 where he was an assistant in the workshop of Louis Ducros, who is best known for his large-scale watercolors of Roman views. After leaving Ducros's workshop, Kaiserman was patronized by Princess Borghese (née Pauline Bonaparte) and her husband Camillo Borghese who commissioned from him large, accurately drawn views of well-known Roman sites. By 1800 his reputation was firmly established and his work was popular with both Roman clients and tourists.[1]

Like his teacher, Louis Ducros, Kaiserman's images of Roman ruins heightened the grandeur of ancient Rome by employing deceptions of scale exaggerating the proportions of ancient monuments.[2] His works are characterized by finely drawn minutiae and exquisite coloring that made his works particularly popular with British and German tourists.[3]

It is not known how many pictures Joseph Allen Smith purchased from Kaiserman, but three are known to survive. Two feature views of Roman ruins, and the other is set on the river in Tivoli with the Temple of Sibyl on the hillside above. *The Colosseum* and *The Temple of Castor and Pollux* (fig. 34) demonstrate the transformation in this pictorial type in the nineteenth century. This image is part of the *veduta* tradition, a composition that represents a landscape or town view that is largely topographical in conception. While Kaiserman's rendition of these monuments is accurate, it evokes romantic sentiments as well. Kaiserman's composi-

tional format emphasizes the majesty of the ruins by using dramatic scale oppositions, the enormity of the Colosseum versus the small cart in the foreground, while at the same time alluding to the struggle between man and nature as vegetation has already begun its conquest of the man-made structure.

Kaiserman's *The Arch of Constantine,* perhaps from the collection of John Izard Middleton, features the arch erected in honor of Emperor Constantine to commemorate his victory over Maxentius in A.D. 312 with the Colosseum in the background. The base of the arch was still partly buried when this watercolor was executed. It was not until 1804–5 that Pope Pius VII had the arch excavated down to the ancient pavement. Kaiserman's rendition of this monument is virtually identical to Louis Ducros's watercolor executed for Sir Richard Colt Hoare of Stourhead (Hoare Collection, National Trust), who purchased thirteen landscapes from Ducros between 1786 and 1793.[3] In Kaiserman's image, the triumph of nature is less evident, and the staffage figures in the foreground have been altered.

MDM

1. Jane Turner, ed., *The Dictionary of Art* (New York: Grove, 1996), 17:731–32.

2. *Images of the Grand Tour: Louis Ducros, 1748–1810* (Geneva: Edition du Tricone, 1985), p. 7.

3. *Images of the Grand Tour,* pp. 26–27, 46, 70.

57. *Fickle Love,* ca. 1790s

Italian

Gouache on paper, 13 ⅓ × 16 ¼ in.

Inscribed lower center: "Amor Volubile"
Dr. and Mrs. Price Cameron, Charleston
Provenance: Joseph Allen Smith, by family descent

While a large oil painting would have been destined for a public reception room, small gouache views such as this were more likely destined for a gentleman's cabinet and were popular with those on the Grand Tour. William Hamilton's villa in Naples had a cabinet room that featured small drawings, gouache views of Vesuvius erupting, and other small works.[1] Joseph Allen Smith's collection contained a number of these whimsical images inspired by recent excavations at Pompeii, providing further evidence of his interest in antiquity. There intact fresco paintings featuring a black background and delicate decoration with Cupids engaged in a wide variety of tasks stimulated the production of such playful images as this one derived from decoration at the House of the Vettii.

MDM

1. Ian Jenkins and Kim Sloan, *Vases and Volcanoes: Sir William Hamilton and His Collection* (London: British Museum Press, 1996), p. 86.

58. *Vesuvius Erupting,* ca. 1820

Italian
Gouache on paper, 11 ¾ × 16 ⅝ in.

Inscribed lower center: "Eruzione dell' Anno 1820"
Private collection
Provenance: Charles Izard Manigault, by family descent

59. *Temple of Jove at Pompeii,* ca. mid-nineteenth century

Italian
Gouache on paper, 10 ¹⁵⁄₁₆ × 16 ⁷⁄₁₆ in.

Inscribed lower center: "Temple de Giove a Pompeii"
Private collection
Provenance: Charles Izard Manigault, by family descent

Views featuring the Bay of Naples, Pompeii, and Vesuvius, especially in eruption, were favorites with those on the Grand Tour. Charles Izard Manigault purchased at least five gouache views of the region, including the two pictured here.

Vesuvius held special fascination for travelers not only because it had buried the towns of Pompeii and Herculaneum in A.D. 79, but because small eruptions continued to occur, giving artists ample opportunity to observe the scientific phenomenon.[1] An 1855 Neapolitan guidebook owned by fellow Charlestonians William and Harriett Aiken listed the fifty-four known eruptions of Mount Vesuvius. This spectacular image, according to the inscription, is based on the eruption of 1820, highlighting the burst of fiery lava with vivid oranges and reds that contrast with the cool blues of the Bay of Naples. The artist has composed the image in order to highlight the still-smoldering Vesuvius in the background.

South of Mount Vesuvius lay the town of Pompeii which was buried by the A.D. 79 eruption. Rediscovered in 1748, the town became a leading destination on the Grand Tour in the nineteenth century. This gouache view represents the building known now as the Temple of Jupiter, which was excavated in 1816–17. The Aikens' 1855 guidebook described it as "an imposing building on an elevated basement at the North end of the Forum, occupying the finest site in the city."[2]

MDM

1. Ian Jenkins and Kim Sloan, *Vases and Volcanoes: Sir William Hamilton and His Collection* (London: British Museum Press, 1996), pp. 165–74.
2. John Murray, *A Handbook for Travellers in Southern Italy,* 2nd ed. (London, 1855), p. 196.

60. *View of Rome and the Ponte Molle,* 1808

John Izard Middleton (American, 1785–1849),
with Filippo Giuntotardi (Italian, 1768–1831)
Watercolor on paper, 20 ½ × 26 ¼ in.

Inscribed on reverse, lower right: "Veduta dale Monte Mario—si veggano
Ponte Molle torre quinto Tivoli Monte Gennaro—Giuntotardi 1808"
Middleton Place Foundation, Charleston
Provenance: Middleton family, by descent

In a highly successful watercolor, Middleton depicted one of the best known of all views of Rome, one that had been painted by generations of artists. Middleton's inscription, in Italian, mentions Filippo Giuntotardi, though without specifying Giuntotardi's role in the creation of this work. The view includes the Ponte Milvio, also called the Ponte Molle, and beyond it the Tor di Quinto area, Tivoli, and Mount Gennaro. At the upper left of the composition, one sees the ancient Ponte Milvio crossing the Tiber. Many historical events were associated with this site. It was here in A.D. 312 that the Emperor Maxentius was thrown from the bridge to his death after being defeated in battle by Constantine, an event that marked the triumph of Christianity. Poussin sketched the bridge and the surrounding area on several occasions, and Claude Lorrain incorporated it into more than one of his capriccios. Both Richard Wilson in 1753 (Yale Center for British Art, New Haven) and Jan Van Bloemen, called Orizzonte, in 1736 (Delegazione Montedison, Rome) painted views similar to Middleton's.

After crossing the Ponte Milvio, a traveler would enter Rome on the Via Flaminia which led towards the Porta del Popolo and the center of the city. Looking northeast across the Tiber and the rural Flaminio area of Rome, towards the Sabine Mountains, artists often took their view from the slopes of Monte Mario, named after Marius (186–57 B.C.), the legendary Roman general.

Middleton in 1808 was just beginning to work in large landscape watercolors. This work is probably number 10 from Middleton's list, "Finished Colored Views" recorded in his Roman journal.[1] (However, it seems likely that the composition was a joint effort, though the nature of his collaboration with Giuntotardi— with whom he often worked in watercolor—is uncertain. Guintotardi probably contributed the figures and tree in the foreground, while the underlying drawing and handling of the washes may well be credited to Middleton.) He treats the broad expanse of the river with a markedly luminous and picturesque effect and makes a carefully finished and accurate panoramic view of the outskirts of Rome. Aside from the two peasant women in the foreground, the emptiness and stillness of the middle ground and the uniform tonal values of the palette lend a peaceful and serene effect to the composition.

SRS

1. John Izard Middleton, Roman Journal, December 1808–October 1809, Ellida Davison Rea Collection.

61. *View from My Window at the Hotel Sibella, Tivoli,* 1808

JOHN IZARD MIDDLETON (American, 1785–1849)

Watercolor on paper, 22 ⅝ × 17 ⅝ in.

Inscribed on reverse, lower right: "Veduta dalla ma finestra all albergo della Sibella—
Tivoli—1808."
Middleton Place Foundation, Charleston
Provenance: Middleton family, by descent

Dramatically situated on the lower slopes of the Sabine Hills, Tivoli was one of the most historic and picturesque sites on the Roman Campagna and thus a necessary stop for every Grand Tourist. Founded four centuries before the birth of Rome, much visited by Augustus and Horace, and a holiday resort for wealthy Romans since ancient times, its ruins, famous gardens at the Villa d'Este, and spectacular views of the cascades attracted generations of tourists and artists from the time of Claude, Dughet, and Vanvitelli. Painters sometimes combined the three most popular sights there —the famous Temple of Vesta, the natural cascades on the hillside, and the broad view of the distant Campagna—while on other occasions isolating only one or two of these elements.

Middleton's view of Tivoli looks south, away from the popular picturesque view of the Temple of the Sybil, now known as Vesta, and concentrates on the medieval town and the waterfall. The Aniene river has since been diverted from this spot, though at the time this was the view from Middleton's hotel, as he notes on the watercolor itself. A very similar view, from a closer vantage point, was made by the English painter Thomas Patch, ca. 1750–54 (Mellon Collection, Yale Center for British Art, New Haven). In addition, Middleton might have been in contact at this time with fellow South Carolinian, Washington Allston, who was in Rome for part of 1808. Allston's *Capriccio of the Falls at Tivoli,* ca. 1808 (fig. 82), a study of the cliffs and falls from a lower perspective, emphasizes the area's rugged terrain in a manner similar to views of Tivoli by Joseph Anton Koch (1769–1839).[1] Also notable is the closely related, asymmetrical *View of Tivoli,* 1813 (Collection Georg Schaefer, Obbach), by Johann Christian Reinhart (1761–1847), a member of the German artistic community in Rome and a friend of Allston's.

SRS

Figure 82 Capriccio of the Falls at Tivoli, *ca. 1808, Washington Allston. Oil on canvas. Courtesy of the Baltimore Museum of Art.*

1. Diana Strazdes, "Washington Allston's Early Career 1796–1811" (Ph.D. diss., Yale University, 1982), pp. 120–21.

62. *View from the Summit of Monte Cavo,* ca. 1809

JOHN IZARD MIDDLETON (American, 1785–1849)
Watercolor on paper, 25 × 48 ½ in.

Private collection
Provenance: By family descent

This work, the most accomplished and largest of Middleton's panoramic compositions, presents an intriguing combination of ancient and modern elements. Monte Cavo itself—once revered as the sacred mountain Mons Albanus of the Latins, and now rarely visited—is the second-highest point in the Alban Hills, which bound the Roman Campagna to the east and south, and stands more than 3,000 feet above sea level. Looking west as Middleton does, in the distance on the right, one sees Lake Albano, bisected by a tall tree, with the towns of Albano and Castel Gandolfo on its shores and Arricia and Genzano amidst the hills, and finally the small, circular Lake Nemi, while on the distant horizon one makes out the Mediterranean Sea. This view was much recommended by the guidebooks of the day and was one of Middleton's favorites. He thought it "one of the most interesting, perhaps, as relates to antiquity: it embraces the whole scene of the Aeneid, from the promontory of Circe to the mouths of the Tiber."[1]

On the summit of Monte Cavo had stood the huge and celebrated Temple of Jupiter Latialis, the sanctuary of the Latin League, said to have been built by Tarquinius Superbus in the late sixth century B.C. Middleton, however, would have seen almost nothing of the temple, as its remains had been completely destroyed in 1783 when Cardinal York used the site and all the ancient materials to rebuild the church of the Passionist Convent—an act described as vandalism by many contemporary antiquarians. Middleton, in the foreground of his watercolor, nonetheless, includes a large broken cornice along with remains of columns, bases, and plinths from an early Doric temple. These oversized antique elements apparently were inspired by his imagination rather than observation, though he claims to have found "in a field adjoining the Convent, part of a small fluted column of white marble";[2] in this case his antiquarian interests prevailed over his realism. In the foreground stand two figures, a traveling gentleman and a monk, perhaps one from the Passionist Convent, who may be arguing the merits of the temple's removal. Finally, in the middle ground, we see the figure of an artist under his umbrella at work in the landscape, perhaps a self-portrait of Middleton himself.

SRS

1. John Izard Middleton, *Grecian Remains in Italy* (London: Edward Orme, 1812), p. 24.
2. Middleton, *Grecian Remains in Italy,* pp. 23–24.

63. *View outside the Saracen Gate at Segni,* May 1809

JOHN IZARD MIDDLETON (American, 1785–1849)
Watercolor on paper, 17 ½ × 23 ¼ in.

Inscribed on label formerly attached to verso: "Veduta exteriore della porta detta Sarracena a Segni—Maggio, 1809. J I M cam osc Giuntotardi, colorì"
Private collection

Middleton traveled with the English archeologist Edward Dodwell in May of 1809 to Segni, a remote town of Latium in the Hernici Valley southeast of Rome. Traveling on horseback from the Via Latina, Middleton wound his way up the barren sides of a craggy mountain to reach Segni, with its cyclopean ruins, which he thought were of "the highest antiquity." In his text for *Grecian Remains,* he wrote that "Greece cannot boast a town of which there are more singular ruins." Segni has a well-preserved stretch of polygonal city walls with many ancient gates that Middleton studied with care, digging to the original bases of four of them. His favorite was the first and largest gate, the Porta Saracena, of which he wrote, "nothing can be more grand than this very ancient gate." This gate is depicted in the present watercolor but was not illustrated in his book, *Grecian Remains.* However, the book does include elevations of the gate, which Middleton measured as "about ten feet high and eight feet wide . . . composed of five enormous blocks" and whose pyramidal form he likened to the "most ancient gates in Greece."[1]

In the watercolor a winding footpath leads to the Porta Saracena, while in the middle ground, two curious antiquarians, possibly Middleton and Dodwell, study the gate. One holds a guidebook, while gesturing to his companion who has climbed to the top of the architrave to explore the cyclopean structure.

According to the old label in Middleton's writing, he collaborated on this work with the Italian watercolorist Filippo Giuntotardi (1768–1831) with whom he often sketched and worked and whom he credited with making most of the original sketches for the "costume figures," which he then used in the watercolors for *Grecian Remains.* Here, Middleton, using a camera obscura for accuracy of outline, made the original sketch of the ancient walls and mountainous landscape, while Giuntotardi finished it in watercolor.

SRS

1. John Izard Middleton, *Grecian Remains in Italy* (London: Edward Orme, 1812), p. 38.

64. *Elevation, East Front of a House for South Carolina, No. 1,* 1811

JOHN IZARD MIDDLETON (American, 1785–1849)
Pen and ink with colored washes on paper, 7 1/16 × 10 1/4 in.

Signed lower right: J I M 1811 no. 1
Special Collections, Robert Scott Small Library, College of Charleston

65. *Elevation, House No. 2,* 1811

JOHN IZARD MIDDLETON (American, 1785–1849)
Pen and ink with colored washes on paper, 6 7/8 × 10 1/4 in.

Signed lower left: J I M. 1811 no. 2
Special Collections, Robert Scott Small Library, College of Charleston

In December 1810, Middleton returned to Charleston from a lengthy Grand Tour of England and continental Europe. Beginning in 1811, he executed several floor plans and elevations for houses and villas in the neoclassical style, as well as drawings for outbuildings, including a conservatory. The handful of drawings that survive, dated as late as 1813, demonstrate his skill as a draftsman and his promise as an architect, though it is not known whether any of his designs were ever executed. Middleton apparently acquired his architectural knowledge from his travels in Europe and from architectural pattern books in the manner of the gentleman-amateur of the period. Many of the latest English architectural source books were available for study at the Charleston Library Society such as William Chambers's *Treatise on the Decorative Part of Civil Architecture* (London, 1791). Middleton would also have had access to architectural libraries of Charlestonians such as that of his brother-in-law Henry Izard (1771–1826), another amateur architect.[1]

In Charleston, Middleton would have known the work of Gabriel Manigault (1758–1809), an accomplished amateur architect who visited Charles Bulfinch in Boston in 1793 and who had introduced aspects of Robert Adam's neoclassicism to Charleston. Middleton would have known Manigault's Joseph Manigault House, ca. 1803, as well as other recently constructed houses such as the Middleton-Pinckney House, ca. 1797, and the Nathaniel Russell House of 1808, all of which made use of semicircular bays and oval rooms.

Middleton's *House No. 2* of two stories over a raised basement, features a central projecting rounded bay that contains a colonnaded semicircular entrance porch on the first level and a circular room above it on the second floor. This design is reminiscent of the Hôtel de Salm in Paris, ca. 1786, with its rounded central bay, and—closer to home—of Bulfinch's use of the same element in the James Swan house of ca. 1796. Middleton might also have known Montebello, ca. 1799, General Samuel Smith's house near Baltimore. Its distinctive plan with three semicircular bays is remarkably similar to *House No. 2.* Middleton's bold design also reflects his knowledge of the innovative work of Sir John Soane (1753–1837) in England. The elegant, symmetrical facade for *House No. 2* recalls Soane's often repeated motif of a central swelling curve as seen in his country houses such as Tendring Hall, Suffolk, 1784–86, or his design for a hunting casino, 1783. Middleton's severely geometric plan with its central round room and identical semicircular bays (fig. 83) reflects a building that he knew well, Soane's neoclassical rustic dairy at Hamells.

Middleton's adventurous neoclassical design for *House No. 1* suggests his familiarity with the abstract, geometrical work of Claude-Nicholas Ledoux (1736–1806) in France. Middleton's house has the appearance of a single-story pavilion, set on a raised basement, following the example of such French hôtels as Ledoux's Pavilion at Louvenciennes, which Jefferson had admired in Paris, as well as Jefferson's expanded Monticello of 1793–1809. However, unlike Monticello it is asymmetrical in plan and in all elevations but the south. The east front, illustrated here, shows the massive entrance stairs on the north and south sides, the long side portico with its Tuscan columns, and at the left a projecting circular bay. The Doric frieze on the entablature, with its triglyphs and undecorated metopes, adds a simple and elegant unifying element to the structure.

SRS

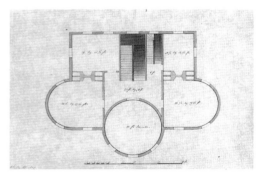

Figure 83 Plan of Interior, Second Floor, House No. 2, *1811, John Izard Middleton. Pen and ink with colored washes on paper. Courtesy of Special Collections, Robert Scott Small Library, College of Charleston.*

1. See Maurie McInnis, "The Politics of Taste: Classicism in Charleston, South Carolina, 1815–1840" (Ph.D. diss., Yale University, 1996), p. 98. Owner of the Elms at Goose Creek, Henry Izard was also the brother-in-law of the architect Gabriel Manigault.
2. I am most grateful to Professors Keith Morgan, Harold Kirker, and Maurie McInnis for their invaluable suggestions regarding Middleton's architecture.

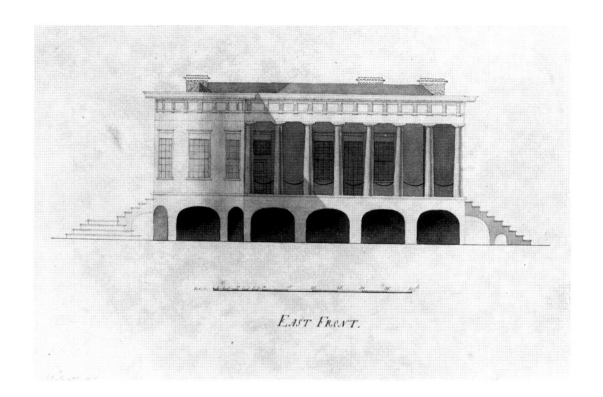

EAST FRONT.

66. *View of Aetna from Greek Theater at Taormina,*
ca. 1818

JOHN IZARD MIDDLETON (American, 1785–1849)
Watercolor on paper, 25 $\frac{7}{16}$ × 39 $\frac{3}{8}$ in.

Private collection

On 10 June 1818, Middleton set out from Naples for a two-month tour of Sicily, in the company of several traveling companions. Having waited too late in the season for a journey to Greece, Middleton chose instead to visit Sicily, the "Greece of Theocritus." Disliking the sea, he traveled south by horseback and mule through Calabria, then across the straits to Messina and Catania, before fulfilling his aim of reaching the summit of Mount Aetna by late June. Aetna, one of the world's most active volcanoes and Europe's tallest at almost 11,000 feet, was a difficult ascent, and after braving below-freezing weather, Middleton wrote that he was "amply compensated on his arrival at the summit."[1]

Middleton's grand composition, with its sweeping view of the ruins of the Greek theater at Taormina overlooking the Sicilian sea, depicts the very sight that Goethe described in 1787. From the uppermost section of the theater, he wrote, "one looks past the entire long mountainous range of Etna, to the left is the sea shore up to Catania, even to Syracuse; then the enormous, smoking volcano concludes the broad, wide ranging picture, but not in a frightening manner, because the atmosphere has a softening effect that makes Etna look more distant and gentler than it is."[2] This watercolor of the famous view predates Thomas Cole's painting of the same subject (Wadsworth Atheneum, Hartford) by some quarter century.[3] Middleton

took his view at sunrise (as Cole later did), as one observes from the long shadows being cast by the ancient ruins. Middleton's work is more topographically accurate than Cole's. He includes the hills to the right and places the snowcapped volcano in proper perspective, while Cole, the romantic, takes liberties in dramatizing and simplifying the scene.

SRS

1. Eliza Falconnet Middleton to Mary Helen Hering Middleton, 27 June and 1 August 1818, SCHS.
2. Johann Wolfgang von Goethe, *Italian Journey,* ed. Thomas P. Saine and Jeffrey L. Sammons (New York: Surhkamp, 1989), p. 236. The Greek theater dates from the third century B.C. but was rebuilt by the Romans.
3. See Theodore E. Stebbins, Jr., et al., *The Lure of Italy: American Artists and the Italian Experience* (Boston: Museum of Fine Arts, 1992), p. 262.

67. *Temple of Neptune,* ca. 1818–19

JOHN IZARD MIDDLETON (American, 1785–1849)
Watercolor on paper, 10 × 17 ⅞ in.

Carolina Art Association/Gibbes Museum of Art, gift of the estate of
Sally Middleton
Provenance: By family descent

A favorite subject of Grand Tour artists was Paestum, the ancient Greek colony of Poseidonia, founded around 600 B.C. and situated fifty miles southeast of Naples. Isolated and forgotten from the ninth to the eighteenth centuries, its temples were rediscovered in 1746 by the architect Mario Gioffredi; from the 1760s on there was an outpouring of views of Paestum and its Doric temples, from those by Antonio Jolli in 1758 and Hubert Robert in 1760 to the series of etchings by Piranesi, *Differentes vues . . . de Pesto* (published posthumously in 1778), that emphasized their monumental quality.

Paestum was the most accessible and closest image of ancient Greece, and by the 1770s it had become an important site for Grand Tourists.[1] John Singleton Copley and the Ralph Izards visited Paestum together as early as January 1775, and Rembrandt Peale used the Piranesi etchings of the temple as a background in his 1806 portrait of William Short (Muscareele Museum of Art, College of William and Mary). In later years, numerous American painters depicted Paestum, including many members of the Hudson River School.[2]

In his journal Middleton recorded an excursion he made to Paestum from Naples in the winter of 1808.[3] In his brief visit he studied the architecture of the "three immense temples," which he described as "perhaps the most remarkable in the world" and stated that "their architecture proves them to be of the highest antiquity."

Middleton made frequent sketching excursions during his years in Naples (1816–20), and on one to Paestum he depicted the Temple of Neptune. Of the three temples, he found the proportion of its columns and its architecture "much more perfect." The austere Temple of Neptune, now known as the Temple of Hera II, dates from the mid-fifth century B.C., and with its external shell still practically intact, it is considered to be one of the most beautifully proportioned Doric temples of antiquity. It is often compared to the Temple of Zeus at Olympia, and the use of Doric refinements in the construction suggests the involvement of an architect trained in Greece.

Middleton recorded the frontal view of the main entrance, with its massive fluted columns, and accurately illustrates the strong, simple frieze, with its triglyphs and undecorated metopes. He emphasizes the colossal size of the temple, which measures nearly 200 feet long by 80 feet wide, by placing a small figure to scale in top hat and walking stick, walking toward the temple at the left. Though its colors are somewhat faded, this work provides evidence of Middleton's increasing interest in sunlight and light effects. Here the foreground of the pastoral scene lies in the shade, while the first rays of morning sunlight dramatically illuminate the temple's facade.

SRS

1. See Andrew Wilton and Ilaria Bignamini, eds., *Grand Tour: The Lure of Italy in the 18th Century* (London: Tate Gallery, 1996), pp. 107, 144.
2. For American artists at Paestum see Kathleen Hohlstein, catalogue no. 50 in Theodore E. Stebbins, Jr., et al., *The Lure of Italy: American Artists and the Italian Experience* (Boston: Museum of Fine Arts, 1992), p. 269, n. 2.
3. Journal of John Izard Middleton, 1807–08, Ellida Davison Rea Collection.

68. *Interior of the Colosseum,* 1821

John Izard Middleton (American, 1785–1849)
Graphite, brown and blue washes, and white gouache on paper,
13 × 9 ½ in.

Signed lower right: J I M Roma 1821
South Caroliniana Library, Columbia, gift of David and Margaret Rembert

69. *Landscape with Trees and Aqueduct,* 1822

John Izard Middleton (American, 1785–1849)
Graphite with white chalk on blue paper, 9 ½ × 13 ¼ in.

Signed lower right: J I M 1822
South Caroliniana Library, Columbia, gift of David and Margaret Rembert

Begun in the early years of the reign of the Emperor Vespasian (from A.D. 72) and finished by his son Titus, the Colosseum is the most beautiful amphitheater of the Roman world and one of the great sights of antiquity. Seating nearly 70,000 spectators, it was used for bloody gladiatorial contests and wild animal hunts. The Colosseum became a popular subject for artists beginning in the eighteenth century. It was the subject of several prints by Piranesi and came to be one of the best-known symbols of ancient Rome. The first American to paint the Colosseum was John Singleton Copley, who included a distant view of it in his portrait *Mr. and Mrs. Ralph Izard,* 1775 (cat. 12).

Middleton's *Interior of the Colosseum* shows a close-up view of the crumbling arch that forms the main entry to the structure on the southwest side. One looks past a top-hatted tourist into the center to see the cross, erected in 1744 in memory of the Christian martyrs thought to have died there, along with several of the stations of the cross placed around the perimeter of the floor. In its dark colors and its bold composition, and with the ruined arch looming above while framing the far side, this is one of Middleton's most romantic views.

Landscape with Trees and Aqueduct also represents an experiment for Middleton in its handling, as it shows him taking up a manner akin to the traditional medium of French draftsmen of the seventeenth and eighteenth centuries, substituting pencil for the traditional black chalk used with white chalk on blue paper. His style here is reminiscent of that of the great French master Claude Lorrain and is even closer to that of J. B. Oudry (1686–1755). In making this careful, elegant view of a wooded landscape with a winding stream to the right and the Claudian Aqueduct (built in the first century A.D.) to the left, Middleton added white gouache to the recesses and shadows of the aqueduct, demonstrating an interest in the play of reflected lights and shadows, while the absence of figures increases the feeling of solitude. Construction of the aqueducts, which carried water from the nearby mountains to Rome, was one of the engineering achievements of the ancient Romans, and generations of artists drew and painted the aqueducts both for their historical associations and their picturesque charm. They became particularly popular with the American artists who flocked to Rome later in the nineteenth century.

SRS

70. *Distant View of the Vatican, Rome,* 1822

JOHN IZARD MIDDLETON (American, 1785–1849)
Graphite on paper, 9 ¾ × 7 ⅛ in.

Inscribed lower right: "J I M 1822"
South Caroliniana Library, Columbia, gift of David and Margaret Rembert

71. *Forum romanum,* 1822

JOHN IZARD MIDDLETON (American, 1785–1849)
Graphite and ink on paper, 9 ½ × 13 ½ in.

Inscribed lower right: "J I M 1822"
South Caroliniana Library, Columbia, gift of David and Margaret Rembert

In the *Forum romanum* Middleton depicted the central site of ancient Rome for Grand Tourists, one hallowed by history and painted by generations of artists from the sixteenth century on. Here Roman civilization had been forged and the popular assemblies of the republic had met; here the empire was born in 27 B.C., and it was here that Gibbon in 1764 conceived his landmark history, *The Decline and Fall of the Roman Empire.*

Middleton's view looks northwest toward the Capitoline Hill. At left stand the three Corinthian columns of the Temple of Castor and Pollux, dating from the fifth century B.C. In the center, barely visible, is the Arch of Septimus Severus (A.D. 202), while to the right over the trees one sees the fine seventeenth-century dome of the Church of San Luca and Santa Martina. As an archeologist and architect, Middleton was interested in the excavations of the Forum, which had begun in 1788 and continued in the early part of the nineteenth century under the direction of Carlo Fea.[1] In Middleton's composition, parts of the columns of the temple at the left remain buried, while only the upper half of the Arch of Septimus Severus is visible above ground. He indicates piles of dirt and the workers' wagons in the middle ground, while in the right foreground of the drawing one is able to observe the artist's work in progress where two oversized figures have been erased but are still visible.

In *Distant View of the Vatican,* Middleton portrays another one of the great sights of Italy: the first view of St. Peter's and the Vatican from the road approaching the city from the north. Middleton has taken his view from just above the Arco Oscuro between the hillsides of the Monte Parione near the Villa Giulia, just outside the Porta del Popolo. This view became popular in the late eighteenth and nineteenth centuries and was painted by many European artists including Francis Towne, Jean-Auguste-Dominique Ingres, André Giroux, George von Dillis, and another American, George Inness.[2]

Employing a camera obscura or a camera lucida to establish the major elements of his scene, Middleton then used graphite with skill and confidence to make these drawings. In the *Distant View of the Vatican,* spare, calligraphic strokes over the white paper on the right give a sense of sunlight on the hillside, while vertical and horizontal hatching suggests the shaded road and wall on the left. The figure descending the path is subordinated to Middleton's interest in rendering the play of light and shadow in the foliage and trees. At the upper right, the trees are drawn quickly and schematically, contrasting with the more precise delineation of the Vatican in the background.

SRS

1. Margaret R. Scherer, *Marvels of Ancient Rome* (New York: Phaidon, Metropolitan Museum of Art, 1955), p. 33.
2. See Janet Comey, catalogue no. 27 in Theodore E. Stebbins, Jr., et al., *The Lure of Italy: American Artists and the Italian Experience* (Boston: Museum of Fine Arts, 1992), pp. 211–12.

Sculpture

72. *Statue of William Pitt, Earl of Chatham,* 1770

JOSEPH WILTON, R.A. (British, 1722–1803)

Marble (Carrara), 7 ft., 6 in.

City of Charleston, on loan to The Charleston Museum

Fewer than half a dozen public statues were brought to the original thirteen colonies, and of these only two have survived: Richard Hayward's rendering of Norborne Berkeley, baron De Botetourt, governor of Virginia, and Joseph Wilton's slightly earlier sculpture of William Pitt, defender of American liberties in Parliament at the time of the Stamp Act, long a treasure of the city of Charleston.

In early May 1766, when the news reached South Carolina that the hated Stamp Act had been repealed, the Commons House of Assembly sitting in Charleston took numerous tangible steps to celebrate. Among these, they voted to erect a statue honoring William Pitt, the earl of Chatham, whose persistent opposition had a great effect in the parliamentary repeal.[1] The House appropriated £7,000 for this purpose.[2]

Agent Charles Garth's surviving correspondence reveals many details about the ordering and progress of the work. He recommended "Mr. Wilton" who had just finished a statue of Pitt for Cork in Ireland that was "admired by every body." It was agreed that Pitt would appear standing as if speaking, holding the Magna Carta in one hand. By November, the committee, led by Speaker Peter Manigault, wrote Garth that they determined to place the statue "to form a Vista" at the intersection of Broad and Meeting streets, "in the most Public part of our Town, where two of the broadest

and longest of our Streets that run East and West, North and South intersect each other at right angles." The committee, though, felt that Wilton's open-space design was "rather too stiff in the attitude" but left it to Garth to consult the "best Connoisseurs."[3] The statue was near completion in November of 1769. By the time of the commission of the Pitt statue for Charleston, Joseph Wilton was the most important of the three sculptors who had become founding members of the Royal Academy. His extensive work as "Sculptor to the King" has been eclipsed, however, by later criticism of the "uneven" quality of his efforts.[4] Soon after the South Carolinians commissioned their statue, New York also ordered a sculpture of Pitt from Wilton, and a bronze statue of King George III. The New York Pitt statue was considerably "under the size" of the Charleston version.[5]

In May 1770, the *Gazette* reported that the statue was "highly finished and reckoned as complete a Piece of Sculpture as ever was done in England."[6] A celebratory crowd gathered to take the statue to the armory on 31 May where it was to remain until the foundation and pedestal were raised. William Adron, an assistant of Wilton, accompanied the statue to Charleston to see to its placement and the completion of the base with "marble tables for inscription, shields for arms, etc."[7] Work on the foundation was performed by Peter and John Horlbeck, who charged the colony of South Carolina for two prime hands to "assist Mr. Adron from June 7 to July 7."[8]

In April 1780, British artillery fired on the city and a shell "broke off the right arm of the Pitt statue and shattered the right hand that held the copy of the Magna Carta." Although damaged, the figure was pictured in the Phoenix Fire Map of Charleston in 1788 and in a watercolor sketch by Charles Fraser (probably done from memory).[9] Pitt's political reversal about the colonies during the Revolution no longer endeared him to the former patriot cause, and his monument came to be considered an obstruction and nuisance. By 1791, the legislature ordered city council to remove Pitt's statue from the intersection. The *City Gazette* reported that the statue had been removed and fell from its base causing the head to be broken from the body.[10]

By 1808, however, the statue was rescued from the ignominy of lying in the dirt against the wall of the Orphan House and was erected on a new pedestal in front of the building. There "it was surrounded daily by groups of happy children impressively reminding them of the great charter of liberties."[11] With the relandscaping of Washington Square Park in 1881, the city of Charleston embarked on a campaign to place the statue in this park on yet another base.[12] Due to conservation issues, the piece was again removed to The Charleston Museum in 1984. A current proposal would place it in the hall of the new Charleston County Judicial Center near the site where it originally stood.

Jonathan H. Poston

1. E. Stanly Godbold and Robert H. Woody, *Christopher Gadsden and the American Revolution* (Knoxville: University of Tennessee Press, 1982), p. 68; George C. Rogers, Jr., *Charleston in the Age of the Pinckneys* (Columbia: University of South Carolina Press, 1980). Pitt's maneuvering against the Stamp Act was fairly complex but after a two-year absence from the Commons, he attended and requested complete repeal due to the lack of representation of the colonies in Parliament; see Jack P. Greene and J. R. Pole, eds., *The Blackwell Encyclopedia of the American Revolution* (Cambridge, Mass., and Oxford: Basil Blackwell, 1991), pp. 119–23.

2. See details of the appropriation in D. E. Huger Smith, "Wilton's Statue of Pitt," *SCHM* 15 (1914): 21–22.

3. Derived from letters between the Honorable Charles Garth and the Committee of Correspondence of the Commons House of Assembly and documents from Wilton to Garth, published in "Correspondence of Charles Garth," ed. Joseph W. Barnwell, *SCHM* 28 (1927): 79–93.

4. Margaret Whinney, *Sculpture in Britain, 1530–1830* (London: Penguin Books, 1964), p. 137, and Rupert Gunnis, *Dictionary of British Sculptors, 1660–1851* (Cambridge: Harvard University Press, 1954), pp. 434–37.

5. The New York Pitt statue survives only in pieces today in the New-York Historical Society, but the Cork example is still extant. Charles Henry Hart, "Charles Willson Peale's Allegory of William Pitt, earl of Chatham, and Pitt Statues in Cork Ireland and Charleston, South Carolina" (Boston: Presented to the Massachusetts Historical Society, 1915). A satiric cartoon appeared in England portraying, among other events, the shipment of the Pitt statue to Charleston; see Joan D. Dolmetsch, *Rebellion and Reconciliation: Satirical Prints on the Revolution at Williamsburg* (Charlottesville: University Press of Virginia, 1976), p. 39.

6. *SCG,* 17 and 24 May 1770.

7. "Correspondence of Charles Garth," ed. Barnwell, p. 93. Adron remained in Charleston briefly and took orders for tombstones and other carvings to be sent back to Carolina patrons from London. *SCG,* 12 July 1770.

8. Peter Horlbeck and John Horlbeck, invoice, 14 June 1770, HCF archival files, courtesy of a private collection.

9. See Charles Fraser, "View of Broad Street, 1796," sketchbook, SCHS.

10. Smith, "Wilton's Statue," pp. 31–32.

11. Smith, "Wilton's Statue," p. 33. Charles Fraser, *Reminiscences of Charleston* (Charleston: Garnier Company, 1854), p. 36.

12. Smith, "Wilton's Statue," pp. 34–35. See *Year Book, City of Charleston, S.C. 1881* (Charleston: 1882).

73. *The Wreck of the Rose in Bloom,* 1809

JOHN DEVAERE (Belgian, 1754–1830)
Marble, 59 × 42 ⅞ in.

Signed lower right on capital base: John Devaere/Native of Ghent/sculpsit 1809
Carolina Art Association/Gibbes Museum of Art, Victor Morawetz Fund purchase
Provenance: By family descent

The marble relief was commissioned as a
memorial to General John McPherson who died
in the shipwreck of the "Rose in Bloom." He was
accompanied by his daughter, Elizabeth (later
Mrs. James R. Pringle), who, according to legend, had dreamed of the impending disaster on
three previous nights. General McPherson, a
member of the South Carolina militia during
the American Revolution, is shown drowning
while his daughter is rescued by a sailor.[1]

Devaere who had trained in Paris, Rome, and
London was employed to make designs for
Wedgwood. The relief was to be installed in
what is now the First Scots Presbyterian
Church, but was rejected due to the partial
nudity of the figure of Elizabeth. It remained in
the McPherson family until it was purchased by
the Carolina Art Association/Gibbes Museum
of Art in 1937.[2]

ADM

1. Francis W. Bilodeau, ed., *Art in South Carolina,*
1670–1970 (Charleston: Carolina Art Association,
1970), p. 119.
2. Bob Raynor, "The Sinking of the 'Rose in Bloom,'
1806" *Carologue* 2, no. 1 (Spring 1995): 8–17.

74. *George Washington,* ca. 1790s

Giuseppe Ceracchi (Italian, 1760–1801)
Marble, 23 ¾ × 20 × 11 in.

Carolina Art Association/Gibbes Museum of Art, gift of Mrs. Julius Heyward
Provenance: John Izard Middleton, by family descent

Italian sculptor Giuseppe Ceracchi made two trips to the United States (1791–92 and 1794–95) hoping to receive a congressional commission for a monument to George Washington (1732–99). To solicit support for the monument, he modeled a series of portrait busts of prominent Americans, including Washington. Ceracchi's terra cotta bust of Washington (Musée des Beaux-Arts, Nantes) was one of only two portraits in sculpture of the first president known to have been taken from life. When completed, Ceracchi's bust of Washington was displayed and admired by many as a true likeness.[1]

Ceracchi's monument design was more elaborate than Congress had originally envisioned, and they delayed funding the project. Accordingly, the artist returned to Italy in 1792, taking with him the terra cotta busts of Americans that he had executed, with hopes that he could continue working on the American project. Many of these terra cotta busts were carved in marble while he was in Italy. Because of political patronage difficulties in Italy he continued to pursue American commissions, especially the George Washington monument, and returned to Philadelphia in 1794, leaving his collection of busts in Florence.[2]

Unfortunately for Ceracchi, the federal government was struggling with revenue problems and was not interested in allocating the estimated $30,000 cost for Ceracchi's monument. After a failed attempt to raise sufficient private funding through a subscription program, Ceracchi left America for Paris. His unsteady career in Paris ended at the guillotine in 1801 when he was implicated in an anti-Bonaparte conspiracy.[3]

This colossal marble bust was purchased, according to family history, by John Izard Middleton around 1820. At that time the bust was in the studio of Antonio Canova, who used it as a model for his statue of George Washington for the North Carolina Capitol. Middleton may have purchased this bust in 1822 from the estate of Canova as many things in the studio were sold after the sculptor's death. With the rest of his art collection, the bust was given to Middleton's nephew, Williams Middleton, and remained at Middleton Place until given to the Gibbes Museum of Art. Family history records that it was one of the objects buried by Williams Middleton in 1864–65 and thus survived the 1865 arson at Middleton Place that tragically destroyed most of the Middleton art collection.[4]

Scholars disagree on whether this is a sculpture from the hand of Ceracchi or an Italian work made from one of his busts left in Italy.[5] Whether by Ceracchi or not, this marble bust presents one of the most forceful and classical portraits of George Washington. Wearing Roman military uniform, his hair is closely cropped and bound by a fillet in the ancient manner. The strong jaw line and the aquiline nose make this an image not generally considered an accurate likeness of Washington, but instead an image that captures the firm resolve that many attributed to his character. It is colossal in size, and with the deeply cut curls, incised irises, and drilled pupils, it possesses a powerful countenance.

MDM

1. Ulysse Desportes, "Giuseppe Ceracchi in America and His Busts of George Washington," *Art Quarterly* 26, no. 2 (Summer 1963): 141–42. The other sculpture from a life sitting is by Jean Baptiste Houdon.
2. Desportes, "Giuseppe Ceracchi in America," pp. 152–61.
3. Jane Turner, ed., *The Dictionary of Art* (New York: Grove, 1996), 6:323–24.
4. Object file, Carolina Art Association/Gibbes Museum of Art.
5. See Desportes, "Giuseppe Ceracchi in America," p. 169, who argues that it is a copy from another hand made from Ceracchi's terra cotta. For the opposite view see Elizabeth Bryant Johnston, *Original Portraits of Washington* (Boston, 1882), p. 170; Frances Davis Whittemore, *George Washington in Sculpture* (Boston: Marshall Jones, 1933), pp. 37–38; and Gustavus A. Eisen, *Portraits of Washington* (New York: Robert Hamilton, 1932), pp. 844–45, all of whom argue that the Middleton bust is by Ceracchi.

75. *Trust in God,* ca. 1836

Lorenzo Bartolini (Italian, 1777–1850)
Marble, 18 ⅞ × 13 × 8 ⅝ in.

Carolina Art Association/Gibbes Museum of Art, gift of Mrs. Julius Heyward
Provenance: John Izard Middleton, by family descent

Lorenzo Bartolini's early training was in Florence, but in 1799 he went to Paris and entered the studio of Jacques-Louis David. There he struck up a friendship with Jean-Auguste-Dominique Ingres. The Napoleonic government favored Bartolini with many commissions and an appointment to the school of sculpture in the Accademia di Carrara. In the years following Napoleon's defeat, Bartolini, working in Florence, was patronized mostly by foreigners and by those formerly loyal to Napoleon.[1]

Bartolini's most famous work was *Trust in God,* a crouching, adolescent female nude originally commissioned by a private patron in 1834. The plaster model was completed that year, but the marble version was not ready until 1836, when it was received with great enthusiasm as the public saw the work as an expression of high moral content.[2]

By the 1830s, Bartolini was one of the most famous sculptors at work in Florence. When in Florence, it was popular to visit the studios of sculptors, many of them American. In 1829, American sculptor Horatio Greenough was working in the studio of Bartolini. Charles Izard Manigault records his visit:

We all visited Mr. Greenhough an American sculptor who is studying under the famous Bartolini whose studio we afterwards repaired to & examined with great pleasure several interesting specimens of his art consisting of full sized statues & some interesting busts. . . . Before leaving Bartolini's we walked thro' several rooms in the 2d story where on shelves under shelves & all over the floor we beheld a forest of busts in plaster of various distinguished individuals but 9/10ths of them of English Ladies & Gentlemen who have passed thro' this city in their travels. Here many an empty headed fop & dandy & many a silly female who display their insipped countenance have gone home with an idea of immortalizing themselves in marble—We found Bartolini in his costume di travaille chissling away at a statue in his own private room where we were introduced to him—he is near sixty but scarcely appears 50 & has a fine intelligent countenance.[3]

Many copies of *Trust in God* are known to exist, both in plaster and marble, clothed and unclothed. John Izard Middleton's is likely a reduced-scale version of this popular work.[4] It is not known when this statue entered Middleton's collection.

MDM

1. Jane Turner, ed., *The Dictionary of Art* (New York: Grove, 1996), 3:294–97.
2. Turner, ed., *The Dictionary of Art,* 3:296–97.
3. Charles Izard Manigault, travel journal, Florence, 30 October 1829, CLS.
4. Bartolini's career is discussed more fully in Douglas K. S. Hyland, *Lorenzo Bartolini and Italian Influences on American Sculptors in Florence, 1825–1850* (New York: Garland Publishing, 1985).

76. *Venus Italica,* mid-nineteenth century

Copy after Antonio Canova (Italian, 1757–1822)
Marble, 42 × 14 × 14 in.

Historic Charleston Foundation, Aiken-Rhett House, gift to The Charleston
Museum, transferred to Historic Charleston Foundation
Provenance: Purchased by William Aiken, Jr., by family descent

Antonio Canova was one of the most famous artists of his generation. Visitors to Florence in the early nineteenth century flocked to his studio, and in Italy his most famous work was *Venus Italica.* Originally commissioned by the grand duke of Tuscany, it was intended to replace the celebrated *Venus de' Medici* (fig. 84), taken from Florence by the French. When the baron ordered a copy of the original Venus, Canova asked if he might introduce a few variations. The result was a sculpture that had little to do with the original and was in actuality Canova's challenge to that most famous work of antiquity. Canova introduced the idea of modesty, not present in the original, with the drapery and the turn of the head. Canova's Venus was seen by contemporaries as a rival to the antique Greek sculpture, and it quickly gained patriotic and political associations that increased its fame and popularity.[1]

After the end of the Napoleonic Wars, the *Venus de' Medici* was eventually returned to Florence. Visitors to that city invariably made comparisons between the two works of art. In fact, more comments exist in Charlestonians' diaries and journals about the two Venuses than any others. Charles Izard Manigault found Canova's statue "beautiful," but he did not think that it compared favorably to the Greek original. He wrote:

the celebrated Venus of Canova which while the French had possession of the celebrated Venus de Medici . . . occupied the pedestal in the Tribune. . . . But this Queen of Statues having been restored to Florence . . . the Venus of Canova has sculked off to hide her diminished head under the protection of the grand duke—This Venus of Canova is certainly very beautiful & blends female modesty with a display of the most perfect symmetry of forms gracefulness & beauty & is apparently just from a bath & is endeavoring to screen with a garment a part of her nudity—But the Venus de Medici is an undisguised display of all there is beautiful in the human form has an exalted mien & an unconscious air of any improper thought connected with this full display of all that is admirable & enchanting in the female form.[2]

When Alicia Hopton Russell Middleton first saw Canova's statue, she was well aware of the comparison frequently made, but she thought, "it can scarcely exceed in beauty Canova's—I never thought I could admire statues, but this is exquisitely beautiful." When she finally did go to see the *Venus de' Medici,* however, Canova's statue fell from favor. Middleton commented, "I am just beginning to see some beauty in statuary in spite of naked truth. I prefer the Venus di Medici to Canova's, tho' (you know every one must criticize) notwithstanding the beauty of the head we think it too small—it seems there are some doubts whether it really belongs to the

Figure 84 Venus de' Medici, *ca. 100 B.C. Marble. Uffizi Gallery, Florence.*

statue tho' it is acknowledged that it must be by the same artist."[3] Her son Ralph Izard Middleton was even more harsh in his criticism of Canova, writing:

Here also is the Venus of Canova. In this I was disappointed, and upon expressing my opinion to Mr. Kinloch I was glad to find that I had not committed treason. Indeed he says that the statue never had the celebrity among artists which it so undeservedly enjoys with the public, and that C[anov]a himself is by no means looked upon as having excelled in his art . . . in all the loveliness of her charms as if to challenge comparison stands the Venus de Medici . . . the finest statue existing that is to say the original parts of it, for both the arms are modern and some say even the head. Now the arms may be detected at first glance, but the head is exquisitely beautiful and does honor to the artist, whatever age he may have lived.[4]

Such comments reflected a decline in Canova's reputation that began almost immediately after his death, perhaps in reaction to his extraordinary popularity during his lifetime. Despite such sentiments, this sculpture remained one of the most popular, and many Grand Tourists purchased small-scale replicas in plaster. Sculptors made copies in marble, such as this one, which William Aiken likely purchased on his 1857–58 Grand Tour.[5] While he and his wife were traveling, an art gallery was added to their house (fig. 28), for which they acquired a substantial collection of statues and pictures. A small notebook kept by Mrs. Aiken records the hotels where they stayed, persons with whom they dined and traveled, and tantalizing comments such as "ordered a statue from Hiram Powers & one from [left blank]. Bought a mosaic table . . . bought some pictures."[6]

MDM

1. For more on Canova's *Venus Italica* see Fred Licht, *Canova* (New York: Abbeville Press, 1983), pp. 191–93; *Antonio Canova* (Venice, Italy: Marsilio Editori, 1992), pp. 282–91; Hugh Honour, "Canova's Statues of Venus," *Burlington Magazine* 111 (October 1972): 658–70; and Douglas Lewis, "The Clark Copy of Antonio Canova's *Hope Venus*," in *The William A. Clark Collection* (Washington, D.C.: Corcoran Gallery of Art, 1978), pp. 105–15.

2. Charles Izard Manigault, travel journal, 7 November 1829, Florence, CLS.

3. Alicia Hopton Russell Middleton to Nathaniel Russell Middleton, Florence, 7 November 1835, and Alicia Hopton Russell Middleton to Charles Izard Manigault, Florence, 1 December 1835, Middleton Family Papers, SCHS.

4. Ralph Izard Middleton to Nathaniel Russell Middleton, Florence, ca. 1835–36, Middleton Family Papers, SCHS.

5. I would like to thank Christopher M. S. Johns and David Steel for their information on Canova and mid-nineteenth-century copyists.

6. Mrs. William Aiken, travel notebook, 18 November 1857, Charleston Museum.

Miniatures

77. *John Hopton,* 1771

YOUNG (British, active 1770s)
Watercolor on ivory, 1 ⅜ × 1 ⅛ in.

Signed lower right: Young 1771
Historic Charleston Foundation, Nathaniel Russell House,
gift of Mrs. Henry M. Abbot
Provenance: By family descent

The son of William Hopton (d. 1786) and Sarah Ward, John Hopton (1748–1831) served as a clerk in Henry Laurens's mercantile firm from 1765 until 1769. Upon completion of his apprenticeship, Hopton traveled extensively in order to establish business relations with merchants trading in Carolina,[1] as revealed by this letter of introduction from Henry Laurens to Stephenson, Holford and Company in Lisbon:

> This Letter will be delivered to you by Mr. John Hopton a Young Gentleman who served an Apprenticeship in my Counting House and was freed from that Engagement about a Year ago, since which he has been informing himself in a particular manner in some necessary Branches in the West India Trade and the Trade in the interior parts of this, his own Country, and now in prosecution of a plan which I recommended to him he is going to Europe, intends to visit Oporto, Lisbon, Cadiz, & c., Amsterdam, Rotterdam, & Hamburgh, London, Bristol, Liverpoole, & many of the Trading and manufacturing Cities & Towns in Great Brittain. He will be supported with Money to live genteely in the Character of a Young Merchant, by his Father, William Hopton, Esquire who has been Some years past retired from Trade and who will also give him a handsome Capital Sum at his first setting down to Business.[2]

Hopton later became one of Charleston's most successful merchants.[3] During the Revolution, however, his wavering political affiliations did not hold him in good stead on either side of the Atlantic. Eventually Hopton's properties were confiscated by the Whigs, and he left South Carolina with the British in 1782. He settled in England where he died a wealthy retired merchant in the suburbs of London.

Little is known about the artist Young. He is thought to have worked in London and exhibited at the Society of Artists from 1767 to 1775. He may be identical with an artist of this same name who exhibited at the Free Society of Artists from Bristol in 1769 and 1783. Young may also have worked in Bath in 1803.[4]

ADM

1. N. Louise Bailey, Mary L. Morgan, and Carolyn R. Taylor, eds., *Biographical Directory of the South Carolina Senate, 1776–1985* (Columbia: University of South Carolina Press, 1986), 2:747.
2. George C. Rogers, Jr., and David R. Chesnutt, eds., *The Papers of Henry Laurens* (Columbia: University of South Carolina Press, 1979), 7:315.
3. Leila Sellers, *Charleston Business on the Eve of the American Revolution* (Chapel Hill: University of North Carolina Press, 1934), p. 52.
4. Daphne Foshett, *Miniatures Dictionary and Guide* (Woodbridge, Suffolk: Antique Collector's Club, 1987), p. 681.

78. *Alice DeLancey Izard* (Mrs. Ralph Izard), ca. 1772

GEORGE ENGLEHEART (British, 1750/3–1829)
Watercolor on ivory, 2 × 1 ½ in.

DAR Museum, Washington, D.C.
Provenance: By family descent, purchased in 1982

George Engleheart was among a number of miniature portrait painters who painted Alice DeLancey Izard.[1] Having studied for a time in the studio of Joshua Reynolds, Engleheart is considered one of the most prolific miniaturists of his time, painting over 4,800 portraits. He served as miniature painter to the king from 1790 and painted George III twenty-five times.[2]

Engleheart exhibited regularly at the Royal Academy from 1773 to 1822 and came to rival the fashionable Richard Cosway. However, in contrast to Cosway's romantic, sketchy style, Engleheart's miniatures exhibit a tight and orderly hatching technique.[3] His work is characterized by a simple directness that is evident in the unadorned features of Alice Izard.

ADM

1. See "Reflections of Refinement: Portraits of Charlestonians at Home and Abroad" in this volume.
2. Martha R. Severens, *The Miniature Portrait Collection of the Carolina Art Association* (Charleston: Carolina Art Association, 1984), p. 30.
3. John Murdoch, *The English Miniature* (New Haven: Yale University Press, 1981), pp. 19–20.

79. *Margaret Izard* (Mrs. Gabriel Manigault), ca. 1774

JEREMIAH MEYER (German-British, 1735–89)
Watercolor on ivory, 1 ⁵⁄₁₆ × 1 ⅜ in.

Carolina Art Association/Gibbes Museum of Art, purchase
Provenance: By family descent, to Berry Hill Galleries

The eldest child of Ralph and Alice DeLancey Izard (cat. 11 and 12), Margaret (1768–1824) was born in Charleston but spent much of her childhood in England and France with her parents. In 1785, Margaret married Charleston's noted gentleman-amateur architect, Gabriel Manigault (1758–1809), son of Peter and Elizabeth Wragg Manigault.[1] They lived in Charleston and at his plantation, The Oaks, in St. James, Goose Creek Parish. In 1805, they moved to Clifton, an estate near Philadelphia, where Gabriel Manigault died in 1809. After his death Margaret spent much of her time at her house in Philadelphia on Spruce Street near that of her brothers Colonel George Izard and Ralph Izard, Jr., her sister Mrs. William Allen Deas (Anne Izard), and her mother whose house was "between Ninth and Tenth streets."[2] The area was known as "Carolina Row."

Meyer, a native of Germany, studied in London and attained the position of miniature portrait painter to the queen and painter in enamel to the king in 1764. He was a founding member of the Royal Academy where he exhibited from 1764 to 1783. Meyer's miniatures are characterized by light colors and extraordinary detail.

Two other portraits of Margaret Manigault are known to exist, one by Gilbert Stuart painted in 1794 along with that of her husband (Albright-Knox Museum, Buffalo), and a miniature by Edward Malbone dated 1801 (Carolina Art Association/ Gibbes Museum of Art).[3]

ADM

1. Langdon Cheves, "Izard of South Carolina," *SCHM* (1901): 216.
2. Will of Alice DeLancey Izard, Charleston County Wills, Book G (1826–34) 39:605.
3. Ruel Parkee Tolman, *The Life and Works of Edward Greene Malbone* (New York: New-York Historical Society, 1958), p. 208.

80. *Anne* (recto) *and Elizabeth* (verso) *Izard,* ca. 1784

ATTRIBUTED TO JEREMIAH MEYER (German-British, 1735–89)
Watercolor on ivory (double-sided) 1 ⁷⁄₁₆ × 1 ¾ in.

Private collection, England
Provenance: By family descent

The daughters of Ralph and Alice DeLancey Izard, Elizabeth (1777–84) and Anne Izard (1779–1863) were born in Paris before their father returned to America in 1780 after serving as commissioner to Tuscany. Alice DeLancey Izard remained in Paris with her children during the war years before returning to America in 1783. A childhood playmate may well have been the daughter of Thomas Jefferson, who was sent to Paris to assist in concluding peace with Britain and who through a letter to John Jay in January 1783 requested that proper lodging be secured for him near Alice Izard and her children "with whom a little motherless daughter accompanying me, might sometimes be permitted to associate."[1]

Elizabeth died at the age of seven. Anne grew to maturity and married William Allen Deas (b. 1764), state senator of South Carolina from 1800 to 1804. In 1844, Anne Izard Deas published a volume of her father's correspondence which was illustrated with a drawing of Ralph Izard after the miniature portrait by Jeremiah Meyer (unlocated) drawn by her son Charles Deas.[2]

ADM

1. Julian P. Boyd, ed., *The Papers of Thomas Jefferson* (Princeton, N.J.: Princeton University Press, 1950–74), 6:217–18, 259–61, quoted in George DeLancey Hanger, "The Izards: Ralph, His Lovable Alice and Their Fourteen Children," *Transactions of the Huguenot Society of South Carolina* 89 (1984): 78.
2. Anne Izard Deas, ed., *Correspondence of Mr. Ralph Izard of South Carolina from the year 1774 to 1804; with a Short Memoir* (New York: Charles S. Francis, 1844), frontispiece.

81. *Benjamin Stead, Jr.,* 1803

GEORGE ENGLEHEART (British, 1750/3–1829)
Watercolor on ivory, 2 ⅜ in. (diam.)

Signed: E [lower right]; G. Engleheart/Pinxit 1803 [verso]
Carolina Art Association/Gibbes Museum of Art
Provenance: By family descent, purchase

Benjamin Stead, Jr., was the son of Benjamin Stead (d. 1776), London factor for Peter Manigault, and Mary Johnson, daughter of Governor Robert Johnson of South Carolina. His sister was Mary Stead Pinckney (d. 1812).[1] The miniature of Benjamin Stead, Jr., is one of five in the collection at the Gibbes Museum of Art listed in George Engleheart's account book.[2] The others are another miniature portrait of Stead himself, painted at a slightly earlier age, a miniature of Stead's wife, and two of his nephew Ralph Stead Izard. Unlike the other miniatures, that of Benjamin Stead, Jr., is set in an ivory snuff box, which gives it an added note of luxury.

ADM

1. Langdon Cheves, "Izard of South Carolina," *SCHM2* (1901): 236.
2. Martha R. Severens, *The Miniature Portrait Collection of the Carolina Art Association* (Charleston: Carolina Art Association, 1984), pp. 32–34.

82. *Mrs. Alexander Garden* (Mary Anna Gibbes), 1803

ADAM BUCK (Irish, 1759–1833)
Watercolor on ivory, 2 ¾ × 2 ¼ in.

Signed lower left: ABuck, 1803
Carolina Art Association/Gibbes Museum of Art, gift of Anna Gibbes
Provenance: By family descent

Known as the "Heroine of the Stono," as a
young girl Mary Anna Gibbes (1767–1817), the
sister of Juliet Gibbes Elliott (cat. 45) and Sarah
Gibbes Wilmer (cat. 46), rescued an infant
cousin from her family's plantation while it was
under siege by the British.[1] She was the daughter of Robert Gibbes and his second wife, Sarah
Reeves. In 1784, she married Major Alexander
Garden (1757–1829), son of the noted physician
and naturalist Dr. Alexander Garden, for whom
the gardenia is named.

   Buck was a native of Cork, Ireland, and
painted miniature portraits and watercolors
there and in Dublin until 1795 when he moved
to London. He regularly exhibited at the Royal
Academy and is best known for his work
Painting on Greek Vases drawn and engraved by
him and published in 1812. His portrait of Mrs.
Garden, depicting her as an attractive young
matron of thirty-six years, is a pleasing assem-
blage of curves and colors. The blue and white
cameo-like buckle on her dress may relate to
Buck's interest in antiquity.[1]

ADM

1. Martha R. Severens, *The Miniature Portrait
Collections of the Carolina Art Association*
(Charleston: Carolina Art Association, 1984), p. 19.

83. *Mrs. John Izard Middleton* (Eliza Augusta Falconnet), ca. 1810

NICHOLAS-FRANCOIS DUN (French, 1764–1832)
Watercolor on ivory, 2 ⅞ × 2 ⁷⁄₁₆ in.

Signed lower right: Dun
Carolina Art Association/Gibbes Museum of Art, gift of Sally Middleton
Provenance: By family descent

Thought to have been painted around the time of her marriage to John Izard Middleton, the miniature by Dun captures a youthful Eliza Middleton at the height of the beauty for which she was noted.[1] The soft coloring and careful detailing contribute to a genuinely feminine portrayal. A native of France, Dun also painted in Naples where he worked until his death. He is renowned for his exacting sense of detail and minute attention to clothes.

ADM

1. See "John Izard Middleton: 'Talent Enough to be One of the First Men in America'" in this volume.

84. *Mrs. Arthur Middleton* (Alicia Hopton Russell Middleton), 1836

ANDREW ROBERTSON (Scottish, 1777–1845)
Watercolor on ivory, 3 ¾ × 3 in.

Signed right edge: AR 1836
Carolina Art Association/Gibbes Museum of Art, gift of Alicia Hopton Russell Middleton
Provenance: By family descent

Alicia Hopton Russell (1789–1840) was the daughter of Nathaniel Russell (cat. 138) and Sarah Hopton (1753–1832). Her uncle was the wealthy merchant John Hopton (cat. 77) of Charleston and then later London. She married Arthur Middleton (1785–1837) of Stono Plantation in 1809. With her son Ralph Izard Middleton, daughter Ann Manigault Middleton, and their African-American household slave Lydia, she left for Europe on 10 May 1835 for an eighteen-month Grand Tour, visiting London, Paris, Rome, Florence, and Naples.[1]

A native of Aberdeen, Andrew Robertson began practicing art at fourteen. He studied with the portraitist Henry Raeburn and upon his arrival in London in 1801, was encouraged by Benjamin West. He exhibited extensively at the Royal Academy and was appointed miniature painter to the baron of Sussex in 1805. The large format of his miniature of Mrs. Middleton appears to imitate full-scale oil portraits, representing a trend in miniature portrait painting that emerged in the 1830s in response to the increasing popularity of photography. While demonstrating a distinct realism in depicting her face, the artist also emphasizes bright, contrasting colors and the sitter's fashionable clothing.[2]

ADM

1. Alicia Hopton Russell Middleton, letters, Middleton Family Papers, 1835–36, SCHS; and Alicia Hopton Russell Middleton, travel journal, 1835, Middleton Family Papers, SCL. Also see " 'To Blend Pleasure with Knowledge': The Cultural Odyssey of Charlestonians Abroad" in this volume.
2. Martha R. Severens, *The Miniature Portrait Collections of the Carolina Art Association* (Charleston: Carolina Art Association, 1984), pp. 102–03.

85. *Joshua Lazarus,* ca. 1840

AMELIE DAUTEL D'AUBIGNY (French, ca. 1796–1861)
Watercolor on ivory, 5 × 3 ⅞ in.

Signed lower left: D'Aubigny
Carolina Art Association/Gibbes Museum of Art, gift of
Mrs. Edgar M. Lazarus
Provenance: By family descent

Joshua Lazarus (1796–1861) was president of the congregation Kahal Kadosh Beth Elohim, the oldest Jewish synagogue in the South, from 1851 to 1861. He was instrumental in bringing natural gas to the city of Charleston. This miniature along with one of his wife, Phebe Yates (1794–1870) (Gibbes Museum of Art), a native of Liverpool, and his sister Emma Lazarus (1798–1865) (Gibbes Museum of Art) were probably painted by Amelie Dautel D'Aubigny while the family was traveling abroad after 1835.[1] The wife of the painter Pierre D'Aubigny, Mme. D'Aubigny was a student of Louis-Francois Aubry. She excelled at miniature portraits and exhibited at the Paris Salon from 1831 to 1844.

While Joshua Lazarus conveys a sense of seriousness, by contrast, his wife is given an almost wistful expression. Emma Lazarus's demeanor, however, borders on haughtiness.[2] Both women appear to be wearing the same dress; this could be a true reflection of the situation, or the artist might have used the outfit as a stock item. All three miniatures exhibit careful detailing and prominent stippling in the faces of the sitters which was also common in American miniatures from the same period.

ADM

1. According to a family letter in the Gibbes Museum archives, Joshua Lazarus and Phebe Yates were married in Liverpool in October 1835.
2. Martha R. Severens, *The Miniature Portrait Collections of the Carolina Art Association* (Charleston: Carolina Art Association, 1984), pp. 27–28.

86. *Louis Manigault,* ca. 1850

TINGQUA
Chinese
Watercolor on ivory, 6 ¾ × 5 ½ in.

Signed, in English and Chinese: Tingqua
Private collection
Provenance: By family descent

Louis Manigault (1828–99), the son of Charles Izard Manigault and Elizabeth Heyward (cat. 21), was an obvious inheritor of the Grand Tour tradition. During three and a half decades before the Civil War, Louis made no fewer than five trips abroad.[1] In 1850, he retraced his father's footsteps by departing to Asia and commemorated the event by having his miniature portrait painted by Tingqua, one of China's most important artists working in the western style. In his journal, Manigault recorded, "When my father was in Canton he had his likeness painted on the largest piece of ivory he could find. . . . Ting-hua, son of Lamqua who probably painted my father, is about 40 years old. His painting of me does not resemble me in the least, but is merely sent home as a Curiosity. In it I am leaning on my desk at Russell & Co., my boy is handing me a letter from my father, whilst the Factories are seen through the window. I am dressed exactly in Canton dress, & truly the painter tried his best to make a good likeness."[2]

Tingqua was Lamqua's younger brother, and together these artists pioneered the movement to create Chinese art in the western style for the export market. While in Canton, Manigault collected broadly in Chinese export art. In addition to the miniature, he also acquired a set of views by Tingqua depicting the garden of

Figure 85 Houqua's Garden, *1850, Tingqua. Gouache on paper. Courtesy of private collection.*

Figure 86 Scene of Pearl River, *1850, Sunqua. Oil on canvas. Courtesy of The Charleston Museum.*

Canton's leading export merchant, Houqua (fig. 85), a set of marine paintings by Namchong, and a set of genre paintings by Sunqua (fig. 86), two other Chinese artists who specialized in works for the export market.[3]

RAL

1. Anne Jenkins Batson, *Louis Manigault, Gentleman from South Carolina* (Roswell, Ga.: Wolfe Publishing, 1995).
2. Louis Manigault, travel journal, 1850, pp. 25–27, private collection (cat. 127).
3. For more on Chinese export painting see Carl L. Crossman, *The Decorative Arts of the China Trade: Paintings, Furnishings and Exotic Curiosities* (Woodbridge, England: Antique Collectors Club, 1991).

Decorative Arts

87. Settee, ca. 1750–60

BRITISH

Mahogany, beech secondary, 39 ⅛ × 56 ¾ × 27 ¼ in.

Settee: The Charleston Museum
Provenance: John and Rebecca Perry Drayton, then through the Porcher,
Blake, and Middleton families

Heralded as one of America's first great Palladian-inspired houses, Drayton Hall, constructed between 1738 and 1742, was actually one of the Carolina Lowcountry's last substantial colonial plantation houses. While the builder and carvers who worked at Drayton Hall are unrecorded, their reliance on imported design books is obvious. The chimneypiece in the great first-floor hall, for example, is derived from plate 64 of William Kent's 1727 *Designs of Inigo Jones.* That Drayton Hall stood out as something of a grand enigma among its simpler plantation neighbors is suggested by the 1758 announcement for the sale of a plantation across the Ashley River which had the selling point that "from this House you have the agreeable Prospect of the Honourable John Drayton, Esqr's Palace and Gardens."[1]

Important groups of British imported furniture were associated with Drayton Hall. Several pieces were recorded in ca. 1845 drawings done by Lewis Reeves Gibbes, a great-grandson of John Drayton, the builder. The drawings include four of furniture, three slab tables including one with Vitruvian scroll decoration (fig. 87), and a pedimented glazed cupboard with the Drayton arms in the pediment cartouche (fig. 88), which probably were ordered at the time of the house's construction.

Slightly later in date, ca. 1750–60, is a suite of highly carved early rococo mahogany seating furniture which does not appear in the Gibbes sketchbook but has a strong history of ownership at Drayton Hall. Over the years, this settee

and its matching suite of chairs have been dubbed Charleston, Philadelphia, English, Irish, and Portuguese and even dismissed as nineteenth-century Georgian revival products.

Recent research has suggested a probable origin and maker. Similarities exist between the Drayton Hall seating furniture and a number of chairs associated with Yorkshire houses, most notably the dining room chairs at Nostell Priory and chairs from the destroyed Kippax Park. These and other Yorkshire houses such as Wentworth Woodhouse and Burton Constable were supplied with furniture by the Wakefield, Yorkshire, firm of Wright and Elwick. Another related set of eight chairs was offered by Partridge of London in their 1990 summer exhibition.[2] A virtually identical set of eight chairs, differing from the Drayton Hall pieces only in their use of over-the-rail upholstery and rear cabriole legs, was illustrated in *The English Chair* by London dealer Moss Harris with the provenance "from Sir Alfred Jodrell, Bt., Bayfield Hall, Holt, Norfolk."[3]

John Drayton (1713?–79) was in step with British taste. Recent research in the papers of Governor William Henry Lyttelton suggests that Drayton was in Britain between 1756 and 1758.[4] He may have purchased the furniture at that time. A few years earlier John Drayton's nephew, William Drayton of Magnolia, left for England in 1750 to study law at the Inner Temple in London. In 1752, William Drayton, Peter Manigault, and Daniel Blake traveled together on the "northern circuit" stopping at

Figure 87 Sketch of British marble slab table with Vitruvian scroll decoration, ca. 1845, Lewis Reeves Gibbes. Gibbes sketchbook, Drayton Papers. Courtesy of Drayton Hall Plantation.

Figure 88 Sketch of British cupboard, ca. 1845, Lewis Reeves Gibbes. Gibbes sketchbook, Drayton Papers. Courtesy of Drayton Hall Plantation.

York, Durham, Newcastle, Carlisle, Westmoreland, Lancaster, and Harrowgate. They also toured the great houses and gardens of the north including those at Castle Howard.[5] John Drayton may have entrusted the selection of furniture to his twenty-year-old nephew who was visiting Yorkshire.

Alternatively, the settee and chairs may have come into the family by marriage. In 1752, John Drayton married as his third wife, Margaret Glen, sister of Governor James Glen. The English-born Margaret may have secured the furniture at the time of this union. While their provenance remains a mystery, these pieces are among the most exceptional British imports with colonial Charleston histories.

JTS

1. Quoted in Jessie Poesch, *The Art of the Old South: Painting, Sculpture, Architecture & the Products of Craftsmen 1560–1860* (New York: Alfred A. Knopf, 1983), p. 51.

2. Partridge Fine Arts, London, summer exhibition catalogue, 1990, pp. 58–59.

3. Moss Harris, *The English Chair: Its History and Evolution* (London: M. Harris and Sons, 1946), pp. 59, 117, 123.

4. Kinloch Bull, Jr., *The Oligarchs in Colonial and Revolutionary Charleston: Lieutenant Governor William Bull and his Family* (Columbia: University of South Carolina Press, 1991), pp. 40–41.

5. George C. Rogers, Jr., *Evolution of a Federalist: William Loughton Smith of Charleston (1758–1812)* (Columbia: University of South Carolina Press, 1962), p. 95.

88. Upholstered open armchair, ca. 1765–75

British

Mahogany, birch and beech secondary woods, 40 ¼ × 29 ⅞ × 28 ⅝ in.

Mr. and Mrs. Peter Manigault, Charleston
Provenance: Miles Brewton, by family descent

Among the surviving eighteenth-century furniture in the Miles Brewton House from the Brewton period of occupancy (1769–75) are eight upholstered "elbow" chairs from a suite that probably numbered twelve originally.

Miles Brewton (cat. 4) and his wife, Mary Izard Brewton, traveled in England during 1768–69 when they likely purchased or ordered furnishings for their new house. Peter Manigault placed a large order for furniture and silver with his friend London merchant Benjamin Stead in 1771. In a postscript to the order, he suggested that Brewton had imported great quantities of furniture and plate from London: "I suppose you will think either my Wife or myself very extravagant. I should almost think so myself. If I had not seen Brewton & Ln Smith's Bills for Furniture & Plate which I assure you, are twice as large."[1]

Rarely produced in American centers prior to the neoclassical period, "elbow" or "French" chairs as they were called in contemporary documents were favored in Charleston and available both as British imports and locally made products. Charleston cabinetmaker Thomas Elfe charged thirty pounds each for the form, but his account book for the period 1768–75 indicates that of nine his shop produced, eight were sold as pairs. A 1779 Charleston newspaper described "twelve handsome French chairs" at the residence of Mrs. Rowan and the 1786 inventory of Daniel Horry lists eight French armchairs in the "Long Room." Given Charleston's affinity for British taste, it is not surprising that Charleston-made examples of

this form are virtually indistinguishable from their British prototypes. The use of birch and beech as secondary woods on the Miles Brewton House examples suggests British manufacture.[2]

Conservation of the chairs was carried out in 1991–92 by upholstery conservator Elizabeth Lahikainen. During the de-upholstery process, some of the chairs were found to retain historic and probably original underupholstery that indicated the tufting pattern that has since been restored (fig. 89). All eight chairs had some evidence of late-eighteenth- or early-nineteenth-century wallpaper used to support the fabric liner of the seat-back upholstery. Nineteenth-century photographs of the great second-floor dining room, later the primary drawing room, show the chairs upholstered variously in Victorian chintz.

In his journal entry for 7 March 1773, Josiah Quincy of Massachusetts noted that he had "dined with considerable company at Miles Brewton, Esqr's. . . . The grandest hall I ever beheld, azure blue satin window curtains, rich blue paper with gilt, mashee borders, most elegant pictures, excessive grand and costly looking glasses etc."[3] Quincy's reference to "azure blue" curtains as well as the discovery of a blue silk fiber in the underupholstery of one chair guided the selection of a reproduction silk damask in a popular eighteenth-century pattern woven at the Prelle looms in France.

JTS

Figure 89 During conservation in 1991–92, each chair revealed evidence of wallpaper, a nondecorative technique used in a later reupholstery to support the fabric liner. This block print design is identical to a stamped document in the Waterhouse Archives, Boston, manufactured by Moses Grant, Jr., and Company, Boston, between 1811 and 1817.

1. Susan Lively, "Going Home: Americans in Britain 1740–1776" (Ph.D. diss, Harvard University, 1997), pp. 66–67; "The Letterbook of Peter Manigault, 1763–1773," ed. Maurice A. Crouse, *SCHM* 70 (1969): 188–89. "Ln Smith" refers to Thomas Loughton Smith, a merchant and Miles Brewton's business partner.

2. For a Charleston-made example of the elbow or French chair form see John Bivins and Forsythe Alexander, *The Regional Arts of the Early South: A Sampling from the Collection of the Museum of Early Southern Decorative Arts* (Winston-Salem, N.C.: Museum of Early Southern Decorative Arts, 1991), p. 94.

3. "Journal of Josiah Quincy, Junior, 1773," *Proceedings of the Massachusetts Historical Society* 49 (June 1916): 444–46.

89. Upholstered armchair, ca. 1790–1800

London, England

Mahogany, secondary woods unrecorded, 37 ½ × 23 × 24 in.

Stamped: P. Cubitt

Mr. and Mrs. Peter Manigault, Charleston

Provenance: By descent through Alston and/or Pringle family

In 1991, examination of chairs from a surviving suite in the Miles Brewton House revealed that two of a set of five upholstered shield-back chairs bore the incised stamp "P. Cubitt." Cubitt is most probably the cabinetmaker identified as a subscriber to Thomas Sheraton's 1791 *The Cabinet-maker's and Upholsterer's Drawing-Book.* No other examples of his work are currently recorded.

Colonel William Alston (1756–1839) (cat. 106) perhaps ordered the chairs when he redecorated the house following his 1791 marriage to Miles Brewton's niece, Mary Brewton Motte. The form of the chair, favored for drawing rooms, was known in Charleston at least as early as 1783 when a large shipment of London-made furniture shipped to Thomas Hutchinson included "12 Rich Carved Cabriole Mahogany chairs stuffed backs and seats." In 1785, a shipment recently arrived from England included "Mahogany oval stuffed Chairs for drawing rooms."[1]

JTS

1. Joseph Lewis vs. Estate of Thomas Hutchinson, judgment rolls, 1793, roll 253A, District of Charleston, Court of Common Pleas, Charleston, as cited in M. Allison Carll, "An Assessment of English Furniture Imports into Charleston, South Carolina, 1760–1800," *Journal of Early Southern Decorative Arts* 2, no. 2 (November 1985): 4; *Charleston Evening Gazette,* 24 November 1785.

90. Japanned chair, ca. 1800–15

ENGLISH

Woods unrecorded, 34 ½ × 18 × 20 in.

Private collection

Provenance: Pinckney family, by family descent

For years in Charleston, great confusion has surrounded the Pinckney family's English suite of japanned and painted seating furniture in the neoclassical style. The popular misconception is that Charles Cotesworth Pinckney ordered the *vernis Martin* furniture in Paris soon after his arrival there in 1796.[1]

By family tradition, the two sets, each with distinctive painted decoration, were owned by brothers Charles Cotesworth Pinckney (cat. 5) and General Thomas Pinckney. The set with a tradition of ownership by Charles Cotesworth Pinckney has tablets painted with cathedrals, ruined abbeys, and landscape scenes probably representing the north of England. One identifiable scene depicts Durham Cathedral. The Pinckney family had roots in Bishop Auckland in Durham County and the tablets may represent a bespoke commission alluding to the family's British origins.

The chair exhibited here is from the set traditionally belonging to Thomas Pinckney and decorated in the chinoiserie taste of the early-nineteenth century. Painted in imitation of Chinese lacquer, the chairs and their accompanying sofas feature gilt decoration and cell-pattern diapering on a black ground, although recent conservation testing suggests that the ground may have originally been blue. Within decorative gilded reserve panels on each tablet back are painted polychrome chinoiserie scenes. These chairs survive in amazingly intact condition. While the chairs and their accompanying upholstered recamier sofas are now recognized as of English manufacture, questions still exist about their date and maker. That this was a known pattern produced by an English manufacturer, perhaps Seddons, is suggested by a virtually identical japanned side chair illustrated in *The Connoisseur's Complete Period Guides.*[2]

If the suite dates from the opening years of the nineteenth century, documentation may exist in an invoice from Bird, Savage and Bird (London) to Charles Cotesworth Pinckney (Charleston) dated 2 July 1802:

> 24 Tablet top Chairs with cane seats, japanned
> Puce ground stone colour ornaments yellow trellis in the boxes 14/ £ 16.16
> 6 Chairs with scroll Elbows and caned seats japanned to match the above 26/ 7. 4[3]

The popularity of imported painted and gilded seating furniture in Charleston during the neoclassical period is confirmed in surviving inventories and invoices as well as extant examples such as the suite (ca. 1800) owned by the Allston family and a pair (ca. 1800) with a Bacot family history, all in the collection of the Historic Charleston Foundation. Advertisements such as J. Mauger's 1803 offer of "English Cain-bottom Painted Chairs—10 Dozen" suggest that this style of furniture was available in great quantity. Contemporary letters also hint at the richly colored quality of Charleston interiors. In 1808, Margaret Izard Manigault described to her mother Alice DeLancey Izard the Izard town house on South Battery: "The house at South Bay is in excellent order, & very handsomely furnished. The Drawing room with rich Chintz curtains lined with yellow, a beautiful carpet, chairs & sofas of cane of the most fashionable make handsomely painted & gilt. They are black & gold with thick yellow cushions. The dining room with green curtains & their old Drawing Room chairs."[4]

JTS

1. Samuel and Narcissa Chamberlain, *Southern Interiors of Charleston, South Carolina* (New York: Hastings House, 1956), p. 29.

2. Ralph Edwards and L. G. G. Ramsey, eds., *The Connoisseur's Complete Period Guides to the Houses, Decoration, Furnishing and Chattels of the Classic Periods* (New York: Bonanza Books, 1968), p. 1045, plate 21.

3. Pinckney-Means Papers, SCHS.

4. *CC,* 26 May 1803; Margaret Izard Manigault to Alice DeLancey Izard, Charleston, 25 November 1808, Izard Papers, LC.

91. Grecian couch, ca. 1817

English

Rosewood, secondary woods unrecorded, 31 ½ × 81 × 25 ¼ in.

Stamped: GILLOWS • LANCASTER
Private collection
Provenance: General Charles Cotesworth Pinckney, by family descent

On 12 July 1817, Isaac Coffin wrote from London to the Misses Pinckney, daughters of General Charles Cotesworth Pinckney (see cat. 5 and 90), expressing regret that they had "rejected" some furniture their father purchased, "for it's all the fashion in the Houses of the first Nobility & Gentry in England. True it is, that it was made by Mr. Gillow at Lancaster, where many pieces of his Furniture are finish'd & sent to Town, as the countemen [*sic*] are not so debauched as in the Capital, he is the first Upholsterer in the Kingdom."[1]

Coffin's use of the term "rejected" suggests that the Pinckneys had decided not to keep the Gillows furniture in the Grecian taste. It seems more than a coincidence that a June 1817 auction notice for the month prior to Coffin's letter describes the Grecian-style suite convincingly. The following advertisement appeared in four Charleston newspapers:

New and Handsome FURNITURE
By J. Simmons Bee.
On FRIDAY next, at 11 o'clock, will be sold without reserve, at the Charleston Auction Establishment, No. 99, East-Bay,
THE FOLLOWING ARTICLES OF English made FURNITURE, of the latest fashion
VIZ:
2 handsome Rosewood Grecian Couches, neatly carved and moulded, shaped feet and brass castors, cane backs and seats, 2 back cushions, round bolster and feather pillows, with handsome blue ground chintz cases, trimmed and lined.
2 Rosewood Curricle Chairs, to match,
12 Rosewood Drawing Room Chairs, with cane seats cushions and covers.
4 Rosewood Chairs, as above, with scroll elbows, cushions, &c. to match the above.
The cost and charges of the above Articles, is upwards of 1000 dollars[2]

If indeed this advertisement was for the Pinckney suite, it would appear that the family had a change of heart or the furniture failed to sell, because the exhibited Gillows furniture and related seating pieces have descended to the present day in the Pinckney family.

While not as well known as the names Chippendale, Sheraton, and Hepplewhite, Gillows of Lancaster and London was one of the most important cabinetmaking firms in late-eighteenth- and early-nineteenth-century England. Patronized by British nobility, even the Lancaster branch boasted nine dukes listed in its account books for the nineteenth century. Founded in Lancaster about 1730 by Robert Gillow the elder (1704–72), the firm established a London shop and manufactory in 1769. It remained under family supervision into the nineteenth century and still makes furniture today.[3]

JTS

1. Isaac Coffin to the Misses Pinckney, 12 July 1817, Charles Cotesworth Pinckney Papers, LC. Charles Cotesworth Pinckney's three daughters were Maria (d. 1836), Harriott (1776–1866), and Eliza Lucas (d. 1851).
2. *Charleston Southern Patriot and Commercial Advertiser,* 16 June 1817; *Charleston Times,* 19 June 1817; *CC,* 20 June 1817; *CG,* 23 June 1817.
3. For a history of the Gillow firm see Lindsay Boynton, ed., *Gillow Furniture Designs 1760–1800* (Royston: Bloomfield Press, 1995).

92. Cup and cover, 1734–35

LEWIS PANTIN I
London, England
Silver, 10 ¼ in. (height)

South Carolina State Museum, Columbia
Provenance: Governor James Glen, by family descent

James Glen (1701–77) served as royal governor of South Carolina longer than any other colonial governor. Appointed in 1738, he took up his post in 1743 and held office until 1756. During the latter part of his term, Glen rented the handsome Pinckney mansion on East Bay for 100 pounds sterling per annum from Charles and Eliza Lucas Pinckney, then resident in England. Educated at Leyden, Glen practiced law and held various public offices in Scotland before his appointment in South Carolina. Succeeded by William Henry Lyttelton in 1756, Glen retired to his plantation outside Charleston and later returned to England where he died in London on 18 July 1777.[1]

Lewis Pantin, the maker of this impressive covered cup, was likely the son of Simon Pantin II and grandson of Simon Pantin I, a distinguished Huguenot silversmith. Lewis Pantin entered his mark in 1734, the same year this piece was crafted. There is no record of his apprenticeship. The radiating applied straps of the domed cover and alternating vertical applied straps of the lower bell-shaped body are typical of Huguenot wares of the baroque period. Once thought to have been introduced into Britain by Huguenot emigré craftsmen, the two-handled cup and cover actually has its roots in mid-seventeenth-century England. It represents a synthesis of British and French baroque design elements. Such cups were intended largely for display and were perhaps used on ceremonial occasions.[2]

JTS

1. John W. Raimo, *Biographical Directory of American Colonial and Revolutionary Governors 1607–1789* (Westport, Conn.: Meckler Books, 1980), pp. 434–35.
2. Christopher Hartop, *The Huguenot Legacy: English Silver 1680–1760 from the Alan and Simone Hartman Collection* (London: Thomas Heneage, 1996), pp. 88, 356.

93. Pair of candlesticks, ca. 1753

Maker unknown (hallmarks indistinguishable)
London, England
Silver, 10 × 5 ½ in. (diam.)

Private collection
Provenance: Eliza Lucas Pinckney, by family descent

Charles (1699–1758) and Eliza Lucas Pinckney (1722–1793) were married in 1744. They departed South Carolina in April 1753 and lived in England until 1758. Charles Pinckney represented South Carolina as commissioner to the board of trade, a position that enabled him to make numerous business and social contacts in London.

Although their hallmarks are now indistinguishable, these candlesticks, engraved with the arms of Pinckney impaling Lucas, probably date to about 1753 and may have been among the Pinckneys' London purchases. Their baluster form, common in the baroque period, is enhanced with molded rocaille and the bases are highly chased with asymmetrical rococo decoration typical of the transitional-style sticks from the late 1740s and early 1750s.

JTS

94. Teapot, 1752–53

THOMAS WHIPHAM
London, England
Silver and wood, 6 × 4 ⅝ in. (diam.)

Engraved: "ELP" (for Eliza Lucas Pinckney)
The Charleston Museum
Provenance: Eliza Lucas Pinckney, by family descent

Mrs. Charles Pinckney's selection of a new-fashioned, inverted, pear-shaped teapot, sometimes called "double bellied" in contemporary parlance, reflects the mid-century rococo vogue for increasing complexity in both form and decoration. This shape displaced the simpler globular form of teapot, and decoration previously limited to engraving gave way to chased decoration in the rococo taste. This example combines both floral chasing and a handsomely engraved cartouche with the monogram "ELP." The teapot may have been purchased in London for use in the Pinckneys' rented town house on Craven Street, described by Eliza Lucas Pinckney: "'Tis however a very hansome one and gentilely furnished in a very good street and in the Center of every thing."[1]

JTS

1. Quoted in Elise Pinckney, ed., *The Letterbook of Eliza Lucas Pinckney 1739–1762* (Columbia: University of South Carolina Press, 1997), p. 80.

95. Tea canisters and matching sugar canister, 1754–55

FREDERICK VONHAM

London, England

Silver, sugar canister, 5 ⅛ × 3 ⅝ × 3 ⅛ in.; tea canister,
4 ⅞ × 3 ¼ × 2 ⅞ in.

Private collection

Provenance: Family descent through Joseph Manigault, son of Peter
Manigault

Peter Manigault (1731–73) returned to South
Carolina in December 1754 after four years of
education and travel in England and on the
continent. Although admitted to the South
Carolina bar in 1755, Manigault left the law to
enter the political arena and manage the business affairs of London firms with Carolina
interests. He also operated his and Ralph Izard's
Goose Creek plantations. On 8 June 1755,
Manigault married Elizabeth Wragg. Peter
Manigault returned to England in May 1773
where he died at the London house of his friend
Benjamin Stead, a former Carolinian who
established himself as a leading London merchant in 1759.[1]

By family tradition the canisters were originally owned by Peter's father Gabriel Manigault
(1704–81). However, the 1754–55 date letters
for Frederick Vonham's elaborately chased
bombe-form tea canisters with matching sugar
canister suggest that Peter Manigault purchased
them possibly as a present for his mother prior
to his departure from England. The family tradition may derive from the fact that Peter predeceased his father. Individual objects of silver
are not delineated in the inventory of Peter
Manigault's town house but it does list an
impressive 969 ounces of plate valued at
£1,980.[2]

Frederick Vonham's mark as a largeworker was
entered 22 December 1752. No record of his
apprenticeship or freedom survives, and it is
likely that he was of German origin.[3]

1. Walter B. Edgar and N. Louise Bailey, eds.,
*Biographical Directory of the South Carolina House
of Representatives,* vol. 2, *The Commons House of
Assembly 1692–1775* (Columbia: University of South
Carolina Press, 1977), pp. 431–33.
2. Inventory of Peter Manigault, 14 February 1774,
Charleston County Inventories (1772–76), pp. 402–14.
3. Arthur G. Grimwade, *London Goldsmiths 1697–
1837: Their Marks & Lives* (London: Faber and Faber,
1990), p. 690.

JTS

96. Covered cup, 1757–58

THOMAS WHIPHAM
London, England
Silver, 11 ½ × 4 ¾ in. (base diam.)

Engraved: "P.P." (for Philip Porcher)
The Rivers Collection Foundation, Charleston
Provenance: Philip Porcher, by family descent

Philip Porcher (1730–1800), owner of the 600–acre Oldfield Plantation in St. Stephen's Parish, was a rice and cotton planter. By purchase and grant, he extended his holdings to an additional 9,467 acres and a house on Elliott Street in Charleston. On 2 December 1756, Porcher married Mary Mazyck, daughter of Isaac Mazyck and Jeanne Marie de St. Julien. The Fourth General Assembly (1782) ordered Porcher banished and his property confiscated because he accepted a British commission following the fall of Charleston (1780). The acts were never enforced.[1]

In the eighteenth century, covered cups were the ideal gift to mark an occasion such as a christening, a military victory, or sporting event. Their function was primarily commemorative although on ceremonial occasions they might resume their original use as drinking vessels. The simple inverted bell shape was the standard form for such cups from the 1720s into the 1780s, but considerable elaboration could be achieved through applied ornament, engraving, or chasing. This severe but handsome example is typical of the plain versions of the form that also remained popular throughout the period as a restrained alternative to more elaborately decorated cups.

JTS

1. Walter B. Edgar and N. Louise Bailey, eds., *Biographical Directory of the South Carolina House of Representatives,* vol. 2, *The Commons House of Assembly 1692–1775* (Columbia: University of South Carolina Press, 1977), p. 534.

97. Salver, 1762–63

SAMUEL COURTAULD I (1720–65)
London, England
Silver, 13 ¼ in. (diam.)

Engraved with arms of Governor William Bull, Jr.
Historic Charleston Foundation
Provenance: William Bull, by family descent; Christie's sale, 18 January 1997

William Bull (1710–91) was born at Ashley Hall Plantation in St. Andrew's Parish. Educated during his early years in South Carolina, he later studied at Leyden University where in 1734 he became the first native-born American to receive the degree of doctor of medicine. After returning to Charleston, Bull entered politics and on 27 November 1759 he was appointed lieutenant governor of South Carolina. Between 1759 and 1775, he was called on five times to serve as acting governor and is best remembered for his success with Indian affairs. At the time of the Revolution and with a fortune at stake, William Bull sided with the crown. Banished from the state in 1777, he returned under the British occupation in 1780 to serve as intendant and general of police.[1]

Bull sailed with the British evacuating Charleston in December 1782 and never returned. Charleston merchant Nathaniel Russell, a close friend of Bull, acted as his attorney after 1782. Both Bull and Russell lost many of their personal possessions when the British sacked Ashley Hall.[2] On 4 July 1791, William Bull died in exile in London and was buried at St. Andrews, Holborn.

Engraved with the arms borne by Governor William Bull, this impressive salver with elaborately cast and pierced rim with putti masks and vintage is a handsome example of London rococo silver. The decorative qualities of the rim are enhanced by the wide flat-chased border of rocaille. Silversmith Samuel Courtauld was born in 1720, apprenticed to his father, Huguenot immigrant Augustine Courtauld, and entered his mark with the Goldsmiths' Company in 1746.[3]

JTS

1. Walter B. Edgar and N. Louise Bailey, eds., *Biographical Directory of the South Carolina House of Representatives,* vol. 2, *The Commons House of Assembly 1692–1775* (Columbia: University of South Carolina Press, 1977), pp. 122–25.
2. Kinloch Bull, Jr., *The Oligarchs in Colonial and Revolutionary Charleston: Lieutenant Governor William Bull and His Family* (Columbia: University of South Carolina Press, 1991), p. 274.
3. Arthur G. Grimwade, *London Goldsmiths 1697–1837: Their Marks & Lives* (London: Faber and Faber, 1990), p. 475.

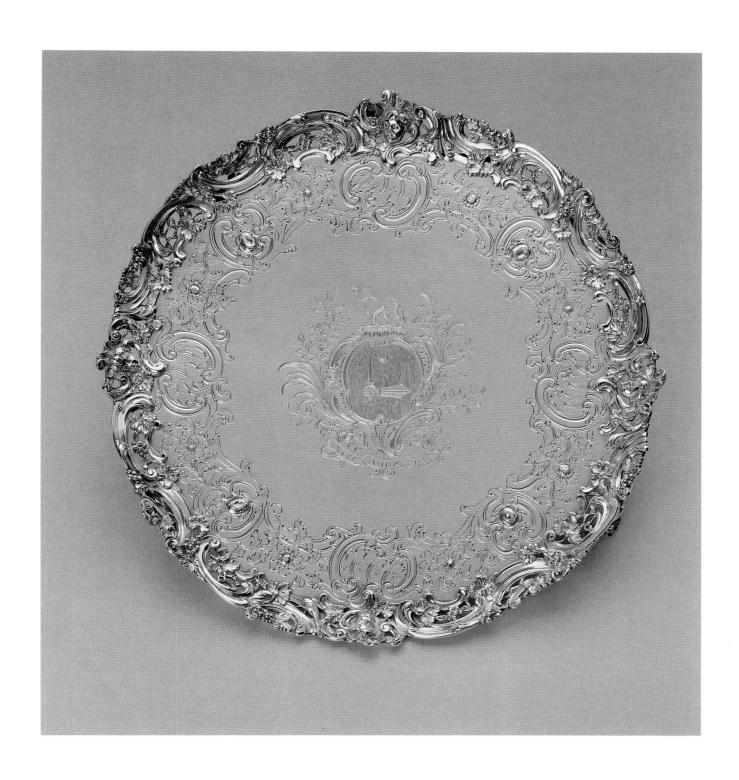

98. Covered cup, 1769–70

John Swift
Silver gilt, 15 ¾ in. (height)

Historic Charleston Foundation
Provenance: William Bull, by family descent; Sotheby's sale, London, 6 March 1997

Among the important pieces of London silver purchased by South Carolina governor William Bull (cat. 97) is a matched pair of silver covered cups. The will of Governor William Bull's widow, Hannah Beale Bull, records the bequest, "To each of my nieces Katherine Stapleton and Maria Hannah Beale one of my large Silver Cups with covers Gilt within. . . ."[1] Both cups bequeathed by Mrs. Bull have survived: the exhibited example was given to the Historic Charleston Foundation in 1997, and an identical cup is in the City of Bristol Museum and Art Gallery, Bristol, England. The Bristol cup retains its gilt-washed interior, but the body and cover were never intended for silver gilt, a later enhancement added to the Charleston cup. The engraved armorial design incorporates the Bull family motto: *Ducit amor patriae* (love of country leads).

The design of this cup and its mate is based on the celebrated Pelham gold cup made for Colonel James Pelham in 1736 by George Wickes to a design by William Kent. Wickes's London firm had been appointed goldsmiths to the prince of Wales in 1735. The design for the cup was subsequently engraved and published by John Vardy in 1744 as plate 28 in *Some Designs of Mr. Inigo Jones and Mr. William Kent.*[2]

Kent's design is basically late baroque and rather conservative given that rococo silver designs with asymmetrical decoration had appeared by the early 1730s. The Pelham cup has been seen as a stylistic bridge between the late baroque of the 1730s and the neoclassical style of the 1770s, hence its popularity. Numerous examples are known, including a version by John Jacobs in 1755 (private collection), Thomas Heming in 1763 (private collection), and Governor Bull's pair by John Swift of 1769–70.

JTS

1. Quoted in Sotheby's sale catalogue, LN7150, Silver, Portrait Miniatures and Objects of Vertu, London, 6 March 1997, lot 179, p. 68.
2. For information on the Pelham gold cup and its later versions see John Hayward, "The Pelham Gold Cup," *Connoisseur* (July 1969), pp. 162–66; and Elaine Barr, *George Wickes, 1698–1761: Royal Goldsmith* (London: StudioVista/Christie's, 1980), pp. 95–96.

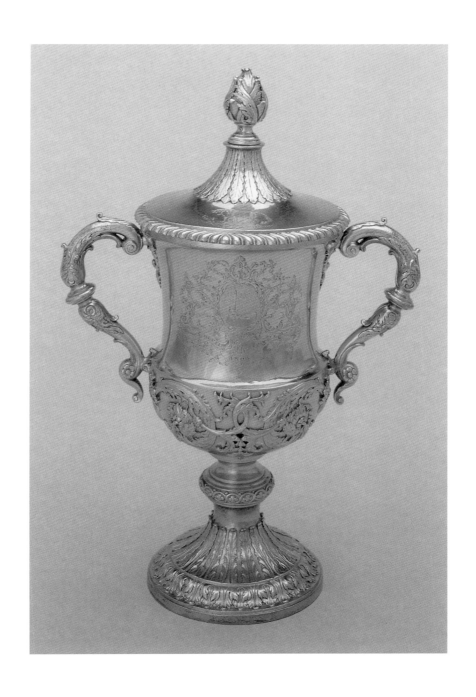

99. Tea kitchen, 1770–71

FRANCIS BUTTY AND NICHOLAS DUMEE
London, England
Silver, 20 ¼ × 7 ⅜ × 7 ⅜ in. (base)

Engraved: "Anne Branford"
Private collection

During the 1750s, a fashionable new object of tea equipage known then as a tea kitchen came into fashion replacing the tea kettle with stand and lamp as the largest and most impressive object associated with the serving of tea. This tea kitchen, exuberantly chased in the rococo taste, was owned by Anne Branford, wife of Thomas Horry and daughter of William and Elizabeth Branford.

The partnership of silversmiths Francis Butty and Nicholas Dumee spanned the years from 1758 to 1773 when the firm's bankruptcy was announced in *The Gentleman's Magazine.* Such a showy object, complicated in its design as well as its fabrication to conceal the heated cast-iron slug for keeping the water hot, had to be imported. In March 1772, DuPont, Brewton, and Company advertised this form among their cargo of fashionable tea, coffee, and table silver: "A CONSIGNMENT of elegant London made PLATE, consisting of the following Articles, viz. A large rich chased Kitchin, a Coffee Pot to match ditto, a Milk Pot to match ditto. . . ."[1]

JTS

1. *South-Carolina Gazette and Country Journal,* 17 March 1772.

100. Epergne, 1771–72

FRANCIS BUTTY AND NICHOLAS DUMEE
London, England
Silver, 18 ¾ × 17 × 17 in.

Middleton Place Foundation, Charleston
Provenance: Middleton family, by descent

On their extended European tour of 1768–71, Arthur and Mary Izard Middleton (cat. 8) observed firsthand the increasingly copious displays of consumer goods available on the London market. Surviving at Middleton Place and among descendants are numerous pieces of London hallmarked silver bearing the date letter for 1771–72. These objects represent conscious consumer choices made by Charlestonians traveling abroad.

One of the more commanding silver objects purchased by the Middletons is an epergne by the London silversmiths Francis Butty and Nicholas Dumee. The Middletons' epergne is in a late-rococo taste with the conceit of its naturalistic silver tree branches, each of which supports a pierced basket. While no single design element betrays its rococo origins, the overall airiness of the whole object foreshadows designs soon to appear in the neoclassical taste. The term epergne, which was not used in France, has two possible original meanings: "Treasury," as in bringing together in one place the pleasures and necessities of the table, is a possible noun form; as a verb, the other suggested meaning implies "sparing" or saving service.[1]

The intricate and multiple elements found in rococo epergnes placed them outside the manufacturing capabilities of colonial American silversmiths. Their use as centerpieces for the most elaborate of social dining rituals, combined with their expense, limited their presence to only the most elite American households. The inventory of the goods and chattels left in Charleston when Lord William Campbell (cat. 10), South Carolina's last royal governor, fled the city in 1775, lists among an impressive array of silver, "1 Epergne wth 2 suits of Glasses" valued at seventy pounds, as well as "1 Chest for the Epergne" at 1 pound, 5 shillings.[2]

JTS

1. Philippa Glanville, *Silver in England* (London: Unwin Hyman, 1987), pp. 80–82.
2. Public Records Office, London, document T. 1/541. For a transcript of Lord William Campbell's inventory see Graham Hood, *The Governor's Palace at Williamsburg: A Cultural Study* (Williamsburg: Colonial Williamsburg Foundation, 1991), pp. 307–13.

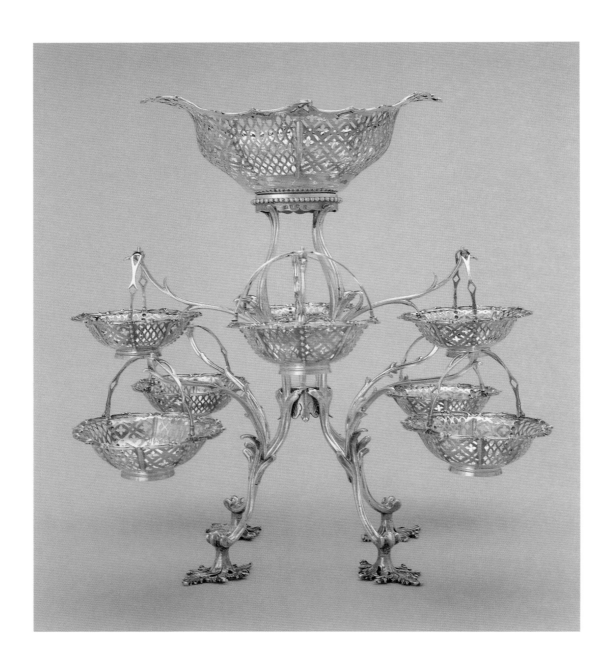

101. Candlesticks, 1771–72

JOHN CARTER
London, England
Silver, 14 ¼ × 4 ¾ × 4 ¾ in.

Middleton Place Foundation, Charleston
Provenance: Middleton family, by descent

John Carter, a leading London retailer, made a practice of purchasing Sheffield-made candlesticks in the neoclassical taste and then overstriking their provincial hallmarks with full London marks, perhaps to reassure his metropolitan customers of their quality. The silver acquired by the Middletons (cat. 100 and 102) also included a set of candlesticks marked by John Carter in the form of Corinthian columns on a plinth with neoclassical swags framing two applied oval cartouches, one with the Middleton coat of arms and the second with the monogram "A.M." The impressive scale of the sticks is enhanced by their stepped bases.

English candlesticks in a columnar form, most often in the Corinthian order, were fully developed by the late 1750s. John D. Davis, Colonial Williamsburg's curator of metals, has observed: "Candlesticks of this type are often considered solely a function of the neoclassical movement, and, indeed, their sheer quantity after 1760 and their obvious formal derivation have made them emblematic of the movement. There are, however, earlier eighteenth-century columnar candlesticks with a pretention towards architectural correctness, which are expressions of the classical strain in Palladian taste. . . . The presence of these earlier candlesticks as prototypical material, the standard renderings of the orders in many eighteenth-century design books, and the obvious and appropriate choice of such models, help explain the early incidence of fully developed columnar candlesticks in silver in the neoclassical style."[1]

JTS

1. John D. Davis, *English Silver at Williamsburg* (Williamsburg: Colonial Williamsburg Foundation, 1976), p. 32.

102. Bottle stands or bottle sliders, 1771–72

THOMAS LANGFORD

London, England

Silver, 4 ¾ in. (diam.)

Middleton Place Foundation, Charleston
Provenance: Middleton family, by descent

The form referred to today as a wine coaster was known in the eighteenth century as a bottle slider or bottle stand. Developed in the eighteenth century as a result of the widespread use of glass decanters and bottles, their purpose was to avoid marking the table or sideboard surface. At least one Charleston silversmith produced the form locally. In 1768, Charles Harris, "Working Silversmith from London," notified clients that he "makes and sells all sorts of new fashioned bottle stands."[1] The 1771–72 date letter places these among Arthur and Mary Izard Middleton's London purchases, and the cast neoclassical swags repeat the motif found on their John Carter columnar candlesticks (cat. 101) of the same date, suggesting a conscious selection of compatible as well as fashionable table equipage.

No record of the apprenticeship or freedom of Thomas Langford survives. He is recorded in 1773 as a plateworker at 26 Angel Street, St. Martin's Le Grand, London.[2]

JTS

1. Alfred Coxe Prime, ed., *The Arts and Crafts in Philadelphia, Maryland & South Carolina, 1721–1785: Gleanings from Newspapers* (Topsfield, Mass.: Walpole Society, 1929), p. 67.
2. Arthur G. Grimwade, *London Goldsmiths 1697–1837: Their Marks & Lives* (London: Faber and Faber, 1990), p. 575.

103. Candlesticks, 1774–75

JOHN CARTER
London, England
Silver, 12 × 5 × 5 in.

Private collection
Provenance: Ralph and Alice DeLancey Izard, by family descent

The industrial revolution introduced new technology to silver production. These candlesticks,
like the earlier John Carter examples (cat. 101)
of 1771–72, owned by Arthur and Mary Izard
Middleton, were not made in the traditional
manner of silversmithing with chased relief
produced by hand and hammer. Instead, they
were assembled from mass-produced parts
stamped out by steel dies. The die-stamping
industry flourished in Sheffield and made this
city a specialist in production of candlesticks.
These innovations reduced the cost of candlesticks, since parts could be stamped from relatively thin gauges of silver and weighted with a
resinous material. John Carter was a specialist
maker of candlesticks and salvers. His mark is
often found overstriking pieces made by
Sheffield or Birmingham makers. Carter was
also a subcontractor to the firm of Parker and
Wakelin, whose account books illustrate the
complexities of the London silver retail market.

Three candlesticks of this design have
descended in the Izard family, each with a
lozenge engraved with the family crest. The
importance of silver as a means of style transmission is evident in these candlesticks confirming the introduction of the neoclassical
vocabulary into colonial Charleston households
well before the American Revolution.

JTS

104. Covered sugar bowl and plate, 1784

JEAN-NICOLAS BOULANGER

Paris, France

Silver, sugar bowl, 5 × 6 ¾ × 3 ¾ in.; plate, 9 ¼ × 6 ⅛ in.

Private collection; on loan to the Historic Charleston Foundation

Provenance: By family descent

Descending through the Middleton family, the engraved "AM" monogram on this elegant sugar bowl and stand by Parisian silversmith Jean-Nicolas Boulanger was thought at first to be that of Arthur Middleton of Stono, born in 1785. Recent research by Charlotte Crabtree and Robert Leath has proposed a logical provenance. Arthur's mother was Ann Manigault whose brother Joseph Manigault was in Europe in 1784, studying in London and Geneva. Fully availing himself of the opportunity to buy European goods, Joseph Manigault commissioned a portrait in London by Gilbert Stuart (cat. 17), purchased a chariot for his brother Gabriel, and bought a fortepiano for his sister Harriett. He likely purchased for his sister Ann this French sugar bowl, still rococo in shape but with neoclassical festoon decoration by the young Boulanger, who had become a master silversmith only the year before, in 1783. The nearly microscopic marks typical of French silver include the maker's mark "JNB," the tiny numerals "84" buried within the warden Henry Clavel's mark, and a mark on the rim confirming that the piece was originally intended for export.

JTS

105. Teapot and stand, 1785

THOMAS WATSON
London, England
Silver and wood

Engraved: "JMCG" (for James and Mary Christiana Gregorie)
Private collection

James Gregorie (1740–1807) was born in Edinburgh and by 1757 had immigrated to Virginia where he was associated with a group of Scottish merchants in Urbanna, Virginia, on the Rappahannock River. In June 1780, Gregorie moved to British-occupied Charleston where he established himself as a successful merchant. Tragedy befell the Gregorie family in 1784 when the ship *Earl of Galloway* carrying his wife, Ann Ross Gregorie, her mother, Theodosia Ross, and three Gregorie children, Ann, Elizabeth, and Theodosius, was lost at sea en route from London to Charleston. On 23 February 1789, James Gregorie wed Mary Christiana Hopton, daughter of Charleston merchant William Hopton and sister of Mrs. Nathaniel Russell (nee Sarah Hopton). They had no children. Active in the business and social affairs of Charleston, Gregorie maintained close ties with his native Scotland through membership in the St. Andrew's Society.[1]

James Gregorie's teapot and stand are one of the best-documented examples of London silver imported into Charleston, appearing in the account book of London merchant James Douglas:

Thomas Watson
1 Oval Threaded Tea Pott Richly engraved with Borders & Festoons
1 Stand for do Engraved bouge & Ornamented Shield
Engraving 2 Arms & Crests on Do
1 Beaded Antique Milk Urn polished Inside & out & richly engraved with Festoons &C. Paid for Gregorie's Arms[2]

The arms and crests incorporate the Gregorie motto "Een Do And Spare Not," a distinctive element that enabled positive identification of the teapot and stand. A sizable quantity of British silver purchased by James Gregorie and his second wife, Mary Christiana Hopton Gregorie, has been recorded through recent family research (fig. 90). Dying childless in 1823, Mrs. Gregorie bequeathed her silver to her niece, Alicia Hopton Russell Middleton, elder daughter of Nathaniel and Sarah Russell and wife of Arthur Middleton of Stono. Engraved with the initials "JMCG" for James and Mary Christiana Gregorie, many pieces survive in family possession and in the collection of the Historic Charleston Foundation's Nathaniel Russell House.

JTS

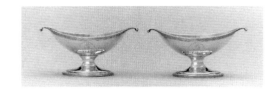

Figure 90 Pair of salt cellars, 1792–93, Duncan Urquhart and Naphtali Hart, London. Engraved "JMCG" with crest and motto "EEN DO SPARE NOT." Courtesy of the Historic Charleston Foundation.

1. Flora Belle Surles, *Anne King Gregorie* (Columbia, S.C.: R. L. Bryan Company, 1968), pp. 3–6.
2. James Douglas, account book, William L. Clements Library, University of Michigan, Ann Arbor. These items are among the recorded goods shipped to James Gregorie under the heading "London 15th, March 1785." For a discussion of the book see Elizabeth A. Fleming, "Staples for Genteel Living: The Importation of London Household Furnishings into Charleston During the 1780s," in *American Furniture*, ed. Luke Beckerdite (Hanover, N.H.: University Press of New England for Chipstone Foundation, 1997), pp. 342–57.

106. Breadbasket, 1788–89

HESTER BATEMAN
London, England
Silver, 5 ⅛ × 16 × 12 ⅛ in.

Mr. and Mrs. Peter Manigault, Charleston
Provenance: By family descent

On 24 August 1775, Miles Brewton (cat. 4) and his family sailed for Philadelphia. He had been elected a delegate to the second Provincial Congress. The ship and Brewton family were lost at sea. Brewton's splendid new town house was inherited by his sisters Rebecca Brewton Motte and Frances Brewton Pinckney. Mrs. Motte lived there during the British occupation of Charleston (1780–82) when she played unwilling hostess to British military leaders, Sir Henry Clinton and Lords Rawdon and Cornwallis. In 1791, Colonel William Alston (cat. 89) married Mary Brewton Motte and purchased the Brewton House from his mother-in-law and her sister.

William Alston, known as "King Billy," owned seven plantations and 723 slaves at the time of his death. His principal plantation seat, Clifton, in Georgetown County was visited by George Washington on 29–30 April 1791, during the president's southern tour. His son-in-law, Robert Y. Hayne, remembered Alston as "courteous in his manners, social in his disposition. . . . His house was the abode of a refined and elegant hospitality."[1]

"Refined" and "elegant" are terms applicable to Alston's silver breadbasket by the eighteenth-century silversmith Hester Bateman, whose London firm produced domestic wares from 1761 to 1790. Although it bears the London date letter for 1788–89, the breadbasket may well have been purchased in 1791 at the time of Alston's marriage to Mary Brewton Motte. The Alston crest may have been done in England or in Charleston. Thomas Coram, the Charleston artist, advertised in 1781 that he could execute "all kinds of devices, ornaments, arms, names, cyphers, etc. etc. engraved on plate."[2] The practice of sending designs for arms and crests to be engraved abroad was also known. In 1783, Charleston goldsmith and jeweler William Wightman notified customers, "from his correspondence in Europe he will be able to furnish them with all manner of seals with their cyphers, crests, or arms, engraved in an elegant manner."[3]

JTS

1. Quoted in Terry W. Lipscomb, *South Carolina in 1791: George Washington's Southern Tour* (Columbia: South Carolina Department of Archives and History, 1993), pp. 10–11.
2. *Charleston Royal Gazette*, 24 October 1781.
3. *South Carolina Gazette and General Advertiser*, 7 June 1783.

107. Breadbasket, 1815–16

MAKER'S MARK: IH
London, England
Silver, 11 ¾ × 14 ⅞ × 12 ¾ in.

Middleton Place Foundation, Charleston
Provenance: Middleton family, by descent

This breadbasket descended through the line of
Oliver Hering Middleton (1798–1892), third son
of Henry Middleton (1770–1846) of Middleton
Place and his English-born wife Mary Helen
Hering. Educated in England, Henry Middleton
was active in politics for most of his life. He
served in the South Carolina House of
Representatives (1802–8) and South Carolina
Senate (1810) and was governor of the state
(1810–12), United States congressman (1815–19),
and minister to Russia (1820–30).[1]

This basket is in the rococo revival style in
fashion during the Regency period, inspired by
the exotic tastes of the prince regent at his
Carlton House. The Middletons' selection of a
heavy breadbasket in the Regency rococo taste
placed them at the vanguard of fashion and
thoroughly in step with contemporary English
aristocratic taste.

JTS

1. N. Louise Bailey, Mary L. Morgan, Carolyn L.
Morgan, eds., *Biographical Directory of the South
Carolina Senate, 1776–1985* (Columbia: University of
South Carolina Press, 1986), 2: 1102–04.

108. Epergne, 1817–18

WILLIAM ELLIOTT
London, England
Silver and glass, 11 ¾ × 16 ¼ × 14 in.

Middleton Place Foundation, Charleston
Provenance: Middleton family, by descent

Henry Augustus Middleton (1793–1887), like his brother Arthur, was educated at Harvard and Litchfield Law School. In 1819, he married Harriott Kinloch, and this handsome neoclassical silver epergne with glasses was likely acquired at the time of the marriage.[1] Richly decorated with cast and applied bacchic masks and grapevines, the Middletons' epergne represents a later classical expression of a popular refinement for the dining table.

The epergne form enjoyed great popularity in Charleston, and by the early-nineteenth century and through technological innovation in the production of silver it was more readily available in Charleston's retail establishments. William Wightman, jeweler and goldsmith at 185 Meeting Street, advertised in 1805 among his London goods just received "Elegant Epergnes, with Cut glasses for the center of Tables."[2]

JTS

1. The epergne was exhibited and listed in the catalogue of *St. Philip's Annual Antique Exhibition*, 9 March to 15 April 1939 as "from the Middleton family" and "lent by J. J. Pringle Smith," great-grandson of Henry Augustus Middleton.
2. *CC*, 6 February 1805.

109. Race cup, 1817–18

PAUL STORR (1771–1844) for Rundell, Bridge and Rundell

London, England

Silver gilt, 13 × 8 ¼ in. (diam.)

Engraved: "Charleston Races/South Carolina/February 1818"

Around the foot of the base is the engraved inscription: "RUNDELL BRIDGE ET RUNDELL AURIFICES REGIS ET PRINCIPIS WALLIAE REGENTIS BRITANNIAS FECERUNT LONDINI" [Made in London by Rundell Bridge and Rundell, goldsmiths to the king and to the prince of Wales, regent of Britain].

The Chrysler Museum, Norfolk, Va., gift of Walter P. Chrysler, Jr., in honor of Roy B. Martin, Jr.

Race week, held annually each February, was the highlight of Charleston's social season. In 1792, the South Carolina Jockey Club built the Washington Race Course in the northern neck of Charleston. In his *Reminiscences of Charleston* of 1854, artist Charles Fraser recalled the excitement of the week: "Schools were dismissed. The judges, not unwillingly, adjourned the Courts, for they were deserted by lawyers, suitors and witnesses. Clergymen thought it no impropriety to see a well contested race; and if grave physicians played truant, they were sure to be found in the crowd on the race ground. . . . The whole week was devoted to pleasure and the interchanges of conviviality: nor were the ladies unnoticed, for the Race ball, given to them by the Jockey Club, was always the most splendid of the season."[1]

Race cups represented lucrative commissions for London's leading goldsmiths, and in true British fashion, the South Carolina Jockey Club commissioned for their 1818 races a resplendent trophy worthy of any British meet. The design of the cup is derived from the celebrated Medici Vase, published in both Piranesi's *Vasi* of 1778 and C. H. Tatham's *Etchings of Ornamental Architecture* of 1799. Between 1807 and 1819, Paul Storr worked exclusively for the royal goldsmiths Rundell, Bridge and Rundell, for whom he crafted many versions of the Medici Vase.

The South Carolina Jockey Club cup is noteworthy and unique in its distinctly American patriotic symbolism, combined with the traditional trophy imagery of laurel wreaths and grapevines. The domed cover is engraved with four panels of stars and stripes enclosed by bands of grapevines, and the finial takes the form of an American eagle clutching an olive branch and lightning bolts. The incorporation of marine decoration in the form of shells flanked by variants of hippocamps with the head and torso of a man, the forelegs of a horse, and the tail of a fish probably alludes to Charleston's coastal geography.

JTS

1. Charles Fraser, *Reminiscences of Charleston* (Charleston: Garnier, 1854), pp. 61–63.

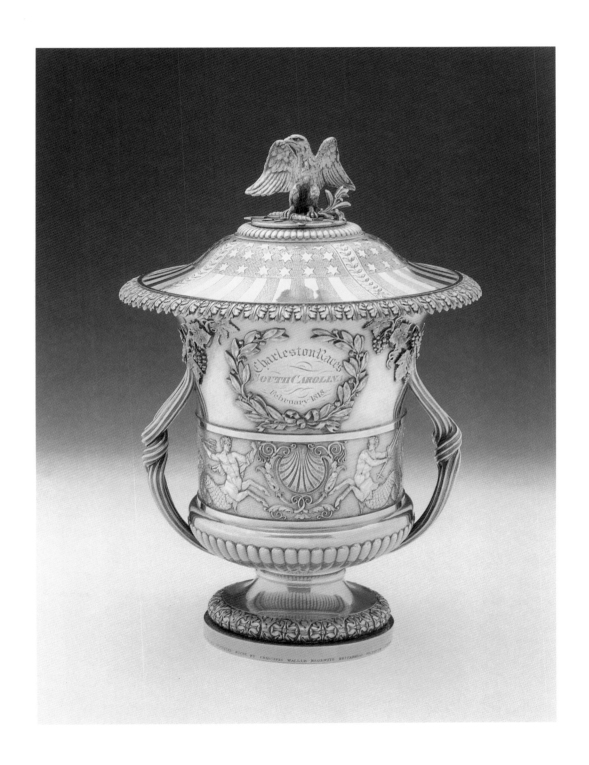

110. Handled mug, 1740–41; chased and engraved ca. 1845

RICHARD GURNEY AND THOMAS COOKE

London, England

Silver, 5 in. (height)

Engraved:
  Coll. BMV Winton apud Oxon
  D.D.
  Guliel Heyward Trapier
  Carolinensis Americ.
  In usum Jun. Sociorum
  A.S. 1845.

[Inscription expansion]: Collegio Beatae Mariae apud Oxonia Donum Dedit Gulielmus Heyward Trapier Carolinensis Americae in usum Juniorum Sociorum Anno Salvationis 1845. [William Heyward Trapier of Carolina in America gave the gift to the College of the Blessed Virgin Mary at Oxford for the use of the junior fellows in the year of grace 1845.]

New College, Oxford, England

Provenance: Purchased by Paul Trapier, ca. 1845

The 1 June tradition of Julep Day at New College, Oxford, was introduced in 1845 by South Carolina traveler William Heyward Trapier, a planter from the parish of Prince George, Winyah. Trapier owned two plantations on the Black River near Georgetown, Turkey Hill and Ingleside, and kept a Charleston town house. According to tradition, Trapier visited New College in 1845 and was asked to stay for dinner. His host offered him a drink. When he requested a mint julep, the confession was made that nobody at New College knew how to make the southern specialty. Producing the drink with such materials as he found at hand, Trapier apparently pledged to produce the family receipt, present to the college a silver cup suitable for julep drinking, and endow in perpetuity an annual julep festival for every member of the college to commemorate the anniversary of his 1 June visit. The handled mug remains at New College, and the original julep recipe is a guarded secret of the steward.[1] Already an antique when presented by Trapier, the cup was engraved at his direction.

JTS

1. Typescript, New College, Oxford, Archive 2846. The text of the typescript, written by Kentucky native Barry Bingham, apparently appeared in the *Louisville Courier-Journal*, 1 July 1942.

111. Flatware, 1856–57

GEORGE WILLIAM ADAMS OF CHAWNER AND COMPANY

London, England

Monogrammed: "RFWA" (for Robert Francis Withers Allston)

Silver, dinner fork, 8 ½ in.; tablespoon, 8 ¾ in.; dessert fork, 6 ⅝ in.; dessert spoon, 7 in.; teaspoon, 5 ⅝ in.; fish fork, 10 ⅜ in.; fish knife, 12 ⅞ in.; ladle, 13 ⅜ in.

Historic Charleston Foundation

Provenance: Governor Robert Francis Withers Allston, by family descent

In August 1857 Governor Robert Francis Withers Allston (1801–64) and his wife, Adele Petigru Allston (1810–96), purchased the Nathaniel Russell House, now 51 Meeting Street, from the estate of Russell's younger daughter, Sarah Dehon. Allston, a successful planter, businessman, and former state senator, was the owner of Chicora Wood Plantation in Georgetown County. His role as governor required that he spend significant time in the capital city of Columbia but Charleston's social and economic power base provided enticement to establish residency in that city as well. Between June and November of 1855, the year before his election as governor, Mr. and Mrs. R. F. W. Allston and daughter Adele traveled abroad and visited Paris.

The Allstons redecorated their new town house in the fashionable revival styles of the mid-nineteenth century. In January 1858, the jewelry and silverware firm of W. H. McEwan on King Street provided a silver castor, a silver waiter, and a set of fruit knives and forks for $176.00. The same firm may well have retailed this fashionable renaissance revival flatware.[1]

By the mid-nineteenth century, the firm of Chawner and Company emerged as the most important firm of silver spoon and fork manufacturers in Victorian London. William Chawner established the firm in 1815 at Hosier Lane, Smithfield. In 1838, four years after Chawner's death, George William Adams married Mary Ann Chawner and was probably

made a partner in the firm by his mother-in-law. Adams produced a wide variety of flatware patterns including Canova, Tudor, Palm, and Corinthian, all of which were exhibited by Chawner's at the Great Exhibition of 1851.[2]

JTS

1. Receipts for the Allston's purchases are in the R. F. W. Allston Papers, SCHS.
2. James Lomax, *British Silver at Temple Newsam and Lotherton Hall* (Leeds: W. S. Maney and Son, 1992), pp. 34–35.

112. Coffee pot with cup and saucer, ca. 1770

MEISSEN

Dresden, Germany

Porcelain with rose palette enamel decoration; pot, 9 ¼ × 6 ½ × 5 in.;
cup, 2 × 3 ¾ × 3 ⅛ in.

The Charleston Museum, gift of Josephine Pinckney
Provenance: Descended in the Brewton-Motte family

Before the American Revolution, the ceramics choices of colonial American consumers were severely restricted by the mercantilist system imposed by Great Britain. Generally, an American could choose among Chinese porcelains imported by the British East India Company and the wares of Britain's domestic manufactories.[1] European travel, however, provided an opportunity to escape the British monopoly.

This coffee set descended in the family of Rebecca Brewton Motte (1737–1815) and is perhaps the only known example of continental European porcelain with a colonial American history. Consisting of a coffee pot with four cups and saucers, each piece bears the mark that identifies the work of Meissen, the first porcelain manufactory established in Europe. Founded in Dresden, Germany, in 1730 by Augustus the Strong, king of Poland and Saxony, the Meissen factory enjoyed extensive royal patronage and specialized in the production of elegant wares for the European upper-class market.

Continental porcelain was not unheard of in prerevolutionary Charleston. The 1774 inventory of Peter Manigault lists "8 french Plates Dishes & 1 fish Dish" probably procured during Manigault's French travels in the 1750s.[2] The date of Mrs. Motte's coffee service suggests that it was purchased by her brother Miles Brewton (cat. 4), possibly for his elegant new town house on King Street, completed in 1769. During the house's construction, Brewton traveled to London where the specialty ceramic shops enhanced their British wares with selections from France and Germany.[3]

RAL

1. John Austin, *Chelsea Porcelain at Williamsburg* (Charlottesville: University Press of Virginia, 1977), pp. 9–12.
2. Inventory of Peter Manigault, 14 February 1774, Charleston County Inventories (1772–74), p. 409.
3. Aubrey J. Toppin, "The China Trade and Some London Chinamen," *Transactions of the English Ceramic Circle* 3 (1935): 37–56.

113. Fruit cooler, ca. 1795

COMTE D'ARTOIS FACTORY

Paris, France

Porcelain with painted and gilded decoration, 10 ¾ × 7 ½ in.

Marked "CA" (for Comte d'Artois factory) under coronet in red enamel
Historic Charleston Foundation on loan from the estate of
Mrs. John P. Frost
Provenance: Pinckney-Frost family, by descent

During the late eighteenth century, French porcelain became increasingly fashionable in America. For some, it was the close ties, cultural and political, that developed between America and France during the Revolution. For others, it was simply the new classical shapes with bright, decorative gilding that provided the attraction. The letters of Mary Stead Pinckney (d. 1812), written in Paris during her husband's service as the United States ambassador, document the trend. In 1797, she described her visits with other Charlestonians to the Parisian porcelain factories: "Mrs. [Henry] Middleton, Ralph [Stead Izard], Eliza [Izard], myself, and a gentleman to conduct us went yesterday to visit the Angoulême manufactory of china . . . cups & saucers with beautiful miniature figures rivalling the first masters on ivory. Vases from 50 to 1000 louis a pair—an absolute picture . . . we went to see the whole process, from the lump of clay which they were rolling about as if for a tart, till it took the form of the beautiful ware we had so much admired before. . . . If I remain in France I shall certainly visit the manufactory of Sève, which is generally accounted superior to that of Angoulême."[1]

Mrs. Pinckney hoped to procure a set of fashionable china for her cousin, Margaret Izard Manigault. She informed her of recent ceramic purchases of other Americans in Paris, such as Mrs. Edward Rutledge and Mr. Codman of New York: "To the best of my judgement Mrs. E[dward] Rutledge's desert set is Angouleme, & the plates like hers at the manufactory are 6 louis each. Mr. King sent to Mr. Codman, a friend of his in Paris, & acquainted with business, & desired him to send him a table & desert set to cost 250 louis d'ors for the two sets, & to have them both alike, & nothing extraordinary —a little bunch of purple flowers, & a gilt edge—a beautiful desert set (as I wrote Rebecca) only flowers of different colours."[2]

This dessert service bears the mark of the Comte d'Artois factory. Established in 1769, this factory enjoyed the patronage of Charles Philippe, Comte d'Artois, the younger brother of Louis XVI and future King Charles X of France.

RAL

1. Mary Stead Pinckney to Rebecca Izard, 11 January 1797, Paris, as quoted in Charles F. McComb, ed., *Letterbook of Mary Stead Pinckney, November 14th, 1796 to August 29th, 1797* (New York: Grolier Club, 1946), pp. 56–58. For more on French ceramics in America see Alice Cooney Frelinghuysen, "Paris Porcelain in America," *Antiques* 153 (April 1998): 554–63.
2. Mary Stead Pinckney to Margaret Izard Manigault, 21 January 1797, Paris, Manigault Papers, SCL.

114. Sauce tureen, ca. 1800

CROWN DERBY

England

Porcelain with polychrome enamel decoration, 5 ¾ × 8 ⅝ × 4 ⅜ in.

Monogrammed "JCL" (for James and Catherine Lowndes)

The Charleston Museum, transferred from the Carolina Art Association/Gibbes Museum of Art, 1993

Provenance: James Lowndes, by family descent, gift of James Lowndes
to the Carolina Art Association in 1910

This elegant, neoclassical dinner service of James Lowndes (1769–1839) and his wife, Catherine Osborne, exemplifies the best of early nineteenth century ceramics owned by Charlestonians. Made by the English manufactory of Crown Derby, each piece is custom-decorated with the initials "JCL." The son of Rawlins Lowndes and Mary Cartwright, James Lowndes was a member of the South Carolina legislature, and the owner of four plantations on the Ashepoo and Combahee rivers with more than one hundred slaves. He maintained a fashionable town house in Charleston. On 1 December 1799, Lowndes married Catherine Osborne, the daughter of Thomas Osborne and Mary Tookerman. Considering the date of the dinner service, it was probably ordered around the time of their wedding. Today, more than forty pieces of the service survive.

Organized in 1756, the Crown Derby factory was one of the first porcelain manufactories established in England. The company enjoyed broad patronage including the prince of Wales, the duke of Devonshire, and the earl of Shrewsbury. With factories located in Derby and Chelsea, the company also operated a large, fashionable warehouse for retail in London. From its warehouse, Crown Derby catered to the needs of Britain's burgeoning upper-middle class. In 1810, Thomas Soar, one of the factory's specialist enamelers, advertised that he wished

to inform "the Nobility, Gentry, and Public at large, that he enamels Desert, Breakfast, and Tea Services, with arms, crests, cyphers, etc. in the most elegant manner and on the most reasonable terms."[1] Customized decoration such as that on the James and Catherine Lowndes service was extremely rare in America.

RAL

1. William Chaffers, *Marks and Monograms on European and Oriental Pottery and Porcelain* (Los Angeles: Borden Publishing, 1946), pp. 818–29.

115. Soup plate, ca. 1815

FLIGHT, BARR AND BARR
Worcester, England
Porcelain with polychrome enamel decoration, 9 %₁₆ in. (diam.)

Impressed mark: FBB (for Flight, Barr and Barr factory)
Private collection
Provenance: Thomas Lowndes, by family descent

Made by Flight, Barr and Barr of Worcester, the dinner service of Thomas Lowndes (1766–1843) indicates the broad exchange that existed between European and Asian design during the British Regency period.[1] Its decoration imitates the kakiemon style of seventeenth-century Japanese porcelain and was one of the many "Japan" patterns manufactured by Worcester at the turn of the nineteenth century. With its brilliant polychrome enamel decoration, it would have been one of the most expensive patterns available.

Thomas Lowndes was the eldest son of Rawlins Lowndes and Mary Cartwright. On 8 March 1798, he married Sarah Bond I'on, the daughter of Jacob Bond I'on and Mary Ashby. His extensive land holdings included five Lowcountry plantations, a town house on Broad Street, and a summer residence in Flat Rock, North Carolina. Like his brother James (cat. 114), he was a member of the South Carolina legislature, and he also served in the United States House of Representatives from 1801 to 1805.

RAL

1. The partnership of Joseph Flight, Martin Barr, and George Barr in the Royal Worcester Porcelain Works existed from 1813 to 1829.

116. Dinner plate, ca. 1820

China

Porcelain with painted decoration, 9 ⅞ in. (diam.)

Mr. and Mrs. Peter Manigault, Charleston
Provenance: Charles Izard Manigault, by family descent

During his Asian travels Charles Izard Manigault (cat. 21) ordered this armorial dinner service in the brown Fitzhugh pattern that has descended through many branches of the Manigault family. The coat of arms was adapted from the bookplate engraved for Manigault in Australia by Samuel Clayton (cat. 141). The armorial design was expertly copied by specialist enamelers in Canton.

Under the heading "My Dinner Set of China with Arms & crest Painted Brown, Purchased at Canton 1820," Manigault itemized his order for an extensive 381-piece dinner service. In addition to plates of different sizes, bowls, cups, and saucers, the service also included numerous specialized serving pieces including tureens and vegetable, beef, and fish dishes. A dinner service of this quantity and variety was extremely rare in America and indicates the elaborate requirements for elegant dining in early nineteenth century Charleston.

RAL

117. Fruit cooler, ca. 1830

Paris, France

Porcelain with painted and gilded decoration, 15 ¼ × 11 × 8 ⅜ in.

The Charleston Museum, gift of Miss Josephine Pinckney

Provenance: By family descent

By the 1830s, French porcelain was the favored ceramics product in Charleston's elite households. Chinese export porcelain and English-made wares moved into second and third place. The account book of Mary Motte Alston Pringle for the Miles Brewton House documents this trend. In 1836, her inventory of household ceramics included "A Compleat Set French Dinner Desert & Fruit" as her best china along with a set of "Dresden Cups & Saucers" and "Blue India China . . . in daily use." Mrs. Pringle specified that she had obtained her French service locally from Madame Peter Poirier's "Fancy Store" located at 9 Queen Street.[1]

This monumental fruit cooler represents part of a large dinner and dessert service of French porcelain that descended in the Pinckney family. Each piece features a magenta border with gilded anthemia and different, hand-painted botanical scenes. Although several pieces of the Pinckney service resemble shapes provided for other Americans by Marc Schoelcher, one of Paris's most popular mid-nineteenth-century porcelain manufacturers, the service is unmarked, and it is impossible to determine its maker.[2]

RAL

1. Mary Motte Alston Pringle, household inventory book, 1834–65, Alston-Pringle-Frost Papers, SCHS.

2. The author is grateful to Alice C. Frelinghuysen of the Metropolitan Museum of Art for sharing her thoughts on the Pinckney dinner service.

118. Teapot and cup and saucer, ca. 1835

Paris, France

Porcelain with painted and gilded decoration, teapot, 5 ¾ × 9 ¾ × 4 ½ in.;
cup, 2 ⅜ × 3 ⅞ in. (diam.); saucer, 6 in. (diam.)

Historic Charleston Foundation, on loan from the estate of Mrs. John P. Frost
Provenance: Pinckney-Frost family, by descent

This tea service demonstrates the transition
from classical to revival styles that occurred
during the second quarter of the nineteenth
century. Although the shape of the teapot
remains strictly classical, the floral decoration
heralds the return of the looser, more fluid
rococo manner of the mid-eighteenth century.
Traveling Charlestonians were at the vanguard
of these stylistic changes. In 1836, Henry
Middleton consulted his mother, Mary Helen
Hering Middleton, about purchasing a set of
porcelain vases for a relative, writing "would she
wish the classical shape . . . or the Lewis the 14th
or 'Rococo form' now in Vogue?"[1] Such commissions executed by Charlestonians abroad for
their friends and relatives at home were an integral part of the process that kept Charleston
society at the forefront of European taste before
the Civil War.

RAL

1. Quoted in Maurie D. McInnis, "The Politics of
Taste: Classicism in Charleston, South Carolina,
1815–1840" (Ph.D. diss., Yale University, 1996), p. 40.

119. Garden seat, 1850–51

POHING

Jingdezhen and Canton, China

Porcelain with painted and gilded decoration, 18 ¼ × 15 in. (diam.)

Middleton Place Foundation, Charleston

Provenance: Middleton-Manigault family, by descent

During his year in China (see also cat. 86, 126, and 127), Louis Manigault ordered a set of porcelain garden seats from Pohing, one of the Cantonese merchants whose specialty was the porcelain trade. In his journal (cat. 127), Manigault described the process of ordering china in Canton and designing it for the western market: "Almost all the China Ware in Canton comes from Sou-Choo and the north of China. It reaches Canton without being painted as the northern Chinese know not how to paint to suit the Fanquis' [foreigners'] outlandish taste. In Canton, the Chinaware is painted and rebaked. . . . I bought a little supply from one of the largest merchants, Pohing, at 10 Pa My Hay Street. He has every variety of jars, vases, etc. I did not like to go into his shop as I was always tempted to purchase. I bought, amongst other things, six Chinaware Seats with my name in Chinese on one side, and crest and initials on the other. These seats were painted expressly for me."[1] The Manigault garden seats are painted in the rose mandarin pattern that enjoyed great popularity in the mid-nineteenth century.

RAL

1. Louis Manigault, travel journal, 1850, p. 25, private collection (cat. 127).

Manuscripts & Books

120. Rent roll, Charleston, South Carolina, 1753

CHARLES PINCKNEY (1699–1758)

South Carolina Historical Society, Charleston, Benjamin Huger
Rutledge Papers

The 1753 rent roll of Charles Pinckney details
the economic underpinnings of Charleston's
Grand Tour tradition. It meticulously records
the income that Pinckney expected to receive
from his Carolina properties during his five
years abroad. From his plantations and town
rental property, he expected to receive 682
pounds, 11 shillings, and one and one-half
pence in annual income. His elegant town
house on Colleton Square and his house servants were rented to South Carolina royal governor James Glen for one hundred pounds
per annum.[1]

The story of the Pinckney family parallels the
economic ascendancy of Charleston. Charles
Pinckney's father, Thomas, arrived in Carolina
from England in the 1690s, amassing a small
fortune during the colony's first economic
boom. Charles Pinckney studied law at
London's Inner Temple and later became one of
Charleston's most successful lawyers. He was
elected to the South Carolina Commons House
of Assembly (1739–42) and served on the Royal
Council (1742–52). From 1753 to 1758 he served
as the colony's special agent for economic
affairs in London. There his sons, Thomas and
Charles Cotesworth, were placed in England's
most prestigious schools and universities.[2]

RAL

1. See also Charles Pinckney, account book, 1753,
Charles Cotesworth Pinckney Papers, LC.
2. Frances Leigh Williams, *A Founding Family: The
Pinckneys of South Carolina* (New York: Harcourt
Brace Jovanovich, 1978), pp. 3–18.

121. Travel journal, England and Europe, 1774–83

GABRIEL MANIGAULT (American, 1758–1809)

South Carolina Historical Society, Charleston

Gabriel Manigault (1758–1809), the elder son of Peter Manigault and Elizabeth Wragg, was a wealthy rice planter, South Carolina legislator, and amateur architect. Through his many diaries and letters, he was one of the principal chroniclers of late-eighteenth-century Charleston. Educated at home until the age of sixteen, in 1774 he went to Geneva to study with the Reverend Chauvet, a Huguenot clergyman and tutor of other Charlestonians, Francis Kinloch and William Loughton Smith.

Manigault's diary provides a detailed picture of his cultural pursuits in Europe. In Geneva he befriended titled Englishmen also studying there, such as Lord Kingsland and Sir John St. Aubyn. In 1777, he moved to London to begin his legal training at Lincoln's Inn, stopping briefly in Paris to visit the palace at Versailles and to attend a Parisian play. In England, Manigault engaged in all the typical pursuits of Charlestonians abroad. He went to museums and plays, toured royal palaces and gardens, socialized at Vauxhall and Ranelagh, and attended a masquerade ball, dressed as a harlequin. In December 1778, he enjoyed a sociable holiday in the spa town of Bath and later departed for an excursion through Holland, touring all the principal cities between Antwerp and Amsterdam.

Manigault's diary records the remarkable social cohesiveness of Charlestonians abroad. He socialized in both London and Bath with Governor and Mrs. William Bull (cat. 43), Lord and Lady William Campbell (cat. 9 and 10), Mr. and Mrs. Ralph Izard (cat. 11 and 12), and John Hopton (cat. 77), among others. On 19 March 1778, for example, he wrote, "went in the morning in company with Mr. W[alter] Izard, Mr. [John Julius] Pringle, & two other Gentlemen to see Sir Joshua Reynold's, and West's Paintings."

RAL

122. Travel journal, England, 1800–1803

JOHN BLAKE WHITE (American, 1781–1859)

South Carolina Historical Society, Charleston

John Blake White determined as a young man to become an artist. Accordingly, from 1800 to 1803, he studied with Benjamin West in London. White returned to Charleston and studied law, entering the South Carolina bar in 1808. While he relied on his legal work to supply an income, he began painting professionally in 1810 and continued to do so throughout his life, achieving his greatest success in the 1830s with a series of history paintings depicting important American events. White was a director of the South Carolina Academy of Fine Arts, and in 1837 he was elected an honorary member of the National Academy. His works were exhibited at the Boston Atheneum and the Apollo Association.[1] Through his marriage in 1805 to Elizabeth Allston, he became related to fellow Charleston artist, Washington Allston (cat. 34).

During his studies with Benjamin West, White kept a journal recording his travels in London and the English countryside, including a visit to Mr. and Mrs. John Moultrie at Aston Hall in Shropshire (cat. 16). His fellow Americans studying under West included Washington Allston and John Trumbull.

RAL

1. See Mary Ellen Turner, "John Blake White: An Introduction," *Museum of Early Southern Decorative Arts* 16, no. 1 (May 1990): 1–17.

123. Sketchbooks, 1800–1803

JOHN BLAKE WHITE (American, 1781–1859)
Pencil on paper

South Carolina Historical Society, Charleston

John Blake White sketched many of the views he observed during his English travels. Some of the scenes were as ordinary as the view from his window in London or that of the carriage and stable block at one of the hotels where he stayed (illustrated p. 304). Today these images provide remarkable documentation of the everyday life of Charlestonians traveling in England.

RAL

124. Botanical Sketchbook, 1800–1814

JOHN IZARD MIDDLETON (American, 1785–1849)
Pencil, pen and ink, and watercolor on paper, in leather-bound sketchbook

Watermark: J. S. 1797 (John Steele, Chester Co., Pa.)
Folio, each page, 8 × 6 ¼ in.

Inscribed inside front cover: "John Izard Middleton, Charleston, South Carolina, July 16th."
Also bears bookplate: "J. J. Middleton"
Middleton Place Foundation, Charleston
Provenance: Middleton family, by descent

Middleton's botanical sketchbook sheds considerable light on his wide-ranging interests and travels. The core of the book is devoted to botanical drawings in watercolor, many made in his youth near Charleston in 1800 and 1801. There are also four botanical illustrations created in Middlesex, England, in August 1801; more than a dozen plein-air sketches of the English landscape from 1806; another group of botanical watercolors made at Sullivan's Island, South Carolina, in 1811; and finally, several pages of unfinished plein-air sketches as well as lists of topographical measurements and bearings of the South Carolina mountains near Greenville done in 1814.

In his finely rendered botanical studies Middleton takes up a tradition that originated with Pliny the Elder and Dioscorides.[1] By the mid-eighteenth century botany and horticulture enjoyed a tremendous vogue in Europe, as it did in the colonies and early republic. Middleton may have derived his inspiration for his watercolor studies from his brother's copy of Thomas Walter's *Flora caroliniana* (1788) or from the English version of Walter, *The Carolinian Florist,* translated and illustrated by Governor John Drayton in 1798.[2]

Middleton's charming watercolor drawings of flowering plants and trees are delicately and effectively recorded. In the *Nerium oleander,* inscribed "Charleston SC 1801" and "April 30th in fl[ower]" (illustrated p. 306), for example, he shows surprising confidence and ability for so young an artist. Here he makes use of a faint

pencil outline, boldly colors the green leaves and red blossoms while using reserves rather than gouache for his highlights. He illustrates several details of the blossoms at the right. Showing his knowledge of botanical tradition, on another page he refers to the "Sexual System" of Linnaeus, the celebrated Swedish naturalist, while on the *Virginian Scarlet Catch Fly,* he writes "vide Catesby," a reference to Mark Catesby's pioneering volume the *Natural History of Carolina, Florida and the Bahama Islands* (1771), the first major illustrated study of North American flora and fauna.

SRS

1. See the *Natural History* of the Elder Pliny in Latin and the *De materia medica* of Dioscorides in Greek.
2. Henry Middleton's signed copy of *Flora caroliniana,* Thomas Walter (London: John Fraser, Fleet Street, 1788), remains in the library at Middleton Place. John Drayton gave a copy of his first English version of *Flora caroliniana* to the Charleston Library Society in 1798. Governor from 1800 to 1805 and from 1808 to 1810, Drayton was born at the neighboring plantation, Drayton Hall, and during the British occupation of Charleston, studied briefly at Middleton Place with Henry Middleton and his French tutor Fariau. See *The Carolinian Florist of Governor John Drayton of South Carolina,* ed. Margaret Babcock Meriwether (Columbia: South Caroliniana Library, University of South Carolina, 1943), pp. vii, xxviii.

Nerium Oleander
Pentandria Monogynia.

Charleston S.C. 5 ... and grows altov S.C.   April 30th in fl.

125. Travel journal, 1822–48

CHARLES IZARD MANIGAULT (American, 1795–1874)
Asia and Europe

Charleston Library Society

Charles Izard Manigault was one of Charleston's most enthusiastic Grand Tourists. The son of Gabriel Manigault (fig. 19) and Margaret Izard (cat. 79) and grandson of Ralph and Alice DeLancey Izard (cat. 11 and 12), he not only embraced the family tradition of travel and connoisseurship but also extended its scope. Much of his youth was spent in Philadelphia where he was educated at the University of Pennsylvania. Initially interested in mercantile pursuits rather than a planter's existence, from 1817 to 1823 he traveled the Far East (especially China) where his business investments met with varying degrees of success.

After his travels in Asia, Manigault returned to Charleston where he married Elizabeth Heyward, the daughter of Nathaniel Heyward, one of the wealthiest men in Charleston, and commenced the life of a planter, with rice plantations worked by about 100 slaves.[1] Manigault's travel journal covered many years of travel and several different trips. It starts in 1822 in the Far East, but is primarily dedicated to his five trips to Europe between 1828 and 1855. The tradition of keeping a journal when traveling was one well established in his family. As a young man, Manigault heard stories from his father who "long delighted us at home" with sketches, journals, and "instructive conversations" about his

travels.[2] Clearly he valued the stories he heard in his youth, for he mentioned in his own travel journal that he carried those of his father with him so that he could share in his father's observations. In the family tradition he gave to his son Louis his Asian copybook (cat. 126).

MDM

1. See William Dusinberre, *Them Dark Days: Slavery in the American Rice Swamps* (New York: Oxford University Press, 1996).
2. Charles Izard Manigault, "Reminiscences," Manigault Family Papers, SHC-UNC.

126. Copybook, 1817–54

Charles Izard Manigault (American, 1795–1874) and his son
Louis Manigault (American, 1828–99)
East Asia and South America

Private collection
Provenance: By family descent

While European travel provided refinement, sojourns to Asia offered the lure of exoticism, adventure, and the appearance of greater worldliness than those who had never been to such distant places. In 1817, Charles Izard Manigault departed for China, the Philippines, Indonesia, and India. In Canton, he engaged in the China trade, hoping to make his fortune, but six years later he returned to Charleston with the intention of becoming a planter. Nevertheless his adventure created a lifetime of fascinating anecdotes and artifacts that became treasures within his family.

In 1850, Louis Manigault made a similar journey, retracing his father's footsteps. Charles presented his son with this copybook of letters he had kept during his six years in China. Louis employed the copybook much as his father did, for the volume contains one of the most important collections of original bills of sale for an American living in China. In Canton, Manigault purchased porcelain from Pohing (cat. 119); paintings by Tingqua, Sunqua, and Namchong (cat. 86); silver by Cutshing; lacquerware from Chongqua; plus silks and clothing from Aque and Ahoy. In Ningpo, he purchased a set of carved and ivory inlaid furniture consisting of a table and bedstead. Many of these items have remained in the Manigault family to the present day.[1]

RAL

1. Christine H. Nelson, *Directly from China: Export Goods for the American Market, 1784–1930* (Salem, Mass.: Peabody Museum of Salem, 1985), pp. 30–31, 39, 41, 82. For more on the Asian travels of Charles Izard and Louis Manigault see Jane Gaston Mahler, "Huguenots Adventuring in the Orient: Two Manigaults in China," *Transactions of the Huguenot Society of South Carolina* 76 (1971): 1–42.

127. Travel journal, 1850

Louis Manigault (American, 1828–99)
Canton, China

Private collection
Provenance: By family descent

Louis Manigault's travel journal recorded his experiences in Asia and South America. It includes one of the most detailed maps of Canton, depicting the city's mercantile district with its European-style garden adjacent to the trading wharves. Between the wharves and the city walls lay Canton's retail district where Manigault ordered many of the porcelains, silks, silver, and paintings he procured during his Asian journey.

RAL

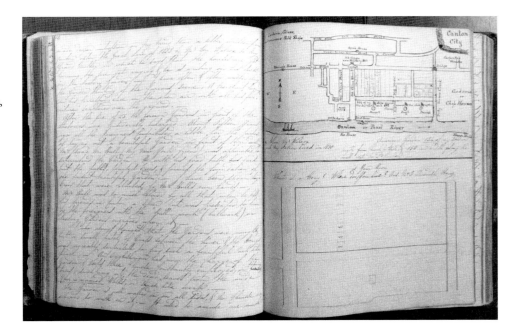

128. "Description of Paintings, at No. 6 Gibbs Street, Charleston, So. Ca., the property of Charles Manigault, 1867."

CHARLES IZARD MANIGAULT (American, 1795–1874)

Private collection
Provenance: By family descent

Charles Izard Manigault was one of Charleston's most important nineteenth-century collectors and art historians. His "Description of Paintings" is a remarkable document, much more than a catalogue of works, for in it he provides a narrative history of each artist and each painting. In his description of the seventeen portraits, most of them of family members, his goal to preserve his family's history and document its importance is clear. The portraits included some of Charleston's most significant commissions from abroad: Allan Ramsay's *Peter Manigault* (fig. 9); Johann Zoffany's *Ralph Izard* (fig. 13); John Singleton Copley's *Mr. and Mrs. Ralph Izard* (cat. 12); Ferdinando Cavalleri's *Charles Izard Manigault and his Family* (cat. 21). Some of the information included in the catalogue he derived from published sources, such as artists' dictionaries.

The real significance of the document rests in the information that would be otherwise lost, such as his descriptions of the acquisition process or the life of each painting. For example, during the Civil War he sent much of his collection to his plantation for safe-keeping, where many suffered damage. The Copley portrait, however, he kept with him at all times, and thus it remained unharmed. His collection also included a number of religious works (cat. 32) and sculptures. His discussion of each provides important insight into how collectors acquired works during this period and the reasons such purchases were made.

MDM

129. *Letters from Italy; describing the customs and manners of that country in the years 1765, and 1766,* 1767

SAMUEL SHARP
Dublin, Ireland

_____

Special Collections, Robert Scott Small Library, College of Charleston
Provenance: Izard family, by descent

Travel books were an integral part of the Grand Tour experience. As continental European travel became popularized and enjoyed by those outside the immediate circle of the British aristocracy, a host of such books began to appear. They supplanted the role of the professional tutors who were hired by English lords as guides for their young sons. Such tutors were known as "bear leaders" for their role in leading their "cubs" around the European continent to complete their education.[1] The earliest guidebooks were written in a highly literary style in imitation of the professorial bear leaders. They were largely devoid of the practical information that characterized later nineteenth-century examples. Among the early guidebooks was this volume on Italy by Samuel Sharp, which belonged to Ralph and Alice DeLancey Izard (cat. 11 and 12). Like a private tutor, it was designed to guide the reader through the major art galleries and tourist attractions of Italy.

RAL

1. Christopher Hibbert, *The Grand Tour* (London: Methuen, 1987), pp. 20–21.

LETTERS

FROM

ITALY,

DESCRIBING THE

CUSTOMS and MANNERS of
that COUNTRY,

In the YEARS 1765, and 1766.

To which is ANNEXED,

An ADMONITION to GENTLEMEN who pass the
ALPS, in their Tour through ITALY.

By SAMUEL SHARP, Esq.

THE THIRD EDITION.

DUBLIN:

Printed for P. WILSON, J. EXSHAW, W. SLEATER,
E. WATTS, D. CHAMBERLAINE, J. POTTS,
and J. WILLIAMS.
MDCCLXVII.

130. *Ponte and Castel S. Angelo,* ca. 1750s
from bound folio of Piranesi etchings

GIOVANNI BATTISTA PIRANESI (Italian, 1720–78)

Etching, 21 ½ × 17 ½ in., in bound folio

Titled: "Vedute del Ponte e Castello Sant' Angelo"
Private collection
Provenance: Joseph Allen Smith, by family descent

When Joseph Allen Smith was in Italy, he assembled an extensive collection of bound folios and prints for the Pennsylvania Academy of the Fine Arts. He also retained a collection for himself. Chief among his personal collections were the bound folios of etchings by Giovanni Battista Piranesi.

Before 1748, Piranesi was at work on the large plates that comprise the *Vedute di Roma,* the sequence of 135 views produced over a thirty-year period that were released individually or in groups. In the eighteenth and nineteenth centuries, these prints were relatively inexpensive compared with paintings and were popular with those on the Grand Tour. Many of these views featured the Roman ruins scattered throughout the city, and they provided an almost encyclopedic rendering of both ancient and modern sights.

Piranesi's earliest images were topographically accurate and were especially valued by scholars and antiquarians for their precision. His *View of the Ponte and Castel S. Angelo* is one of his earlier works with a straightforward depiction of this sweeping landscape view. Centrally placed is St. Peter's, which rises above the bridge but competes with Castel S. Angelo on the right. This latter building, originally the mausoleum of Hadrian and later the papal fortress, was of particular interest to Piranesi, and he devoted several plates to it in his *Le Antichitá Romane* (1756), a publication concerned with archeological inquiries, especially construction techniques and materials.[1]

This bound volume contains prints primarily from the *Vedute di Roma* series, but also has many from *Vasi, candelabri, cippi, sarcofagi, tripodi, lucerne, ed ornamenti antichi* (1778). This latter publication was a collection of individual antiquities both in his collection and in other Italian collections. They ranged from modest cinerary urns to the Warwick Vase (Burrell Collection, Glasgow).

MDM

1. John Wilton-Ely, *The Mind and Art of Giovanni Battista Piranesi* (London: Thames and Hudson, 1978), pp. 25–35.

131. *Grecian Remains in Italy, a Description of Cyclopian Walls, and of Roman Antiquities. With Topographical and Picturesque Views of Ancient Latium.* Printed for Edward Orme, Printseller to His Majesty, Bond-Street; by W. Bulmer and Co. Cleveland-Row, St. James's. 1812–23.

JOHN IZARD MIDDLETON (American, 1785–1849)
Folio, 19 × 13 ¼ in.

Watermarks: Text, E & P, 1805 (Edmeads and Pine, Kent, England), J. Whatman, 1818; plates, J. Whatman Turkey Mills 1818, J. Whatman Turkey Mill 1823
Includes fifty pages of text in seven chapters, with twenty-three hand-colored aquatints and two uncolored line engravings
Middleton Place Foundation, Charleston
Provenance: Middleton family, by descent

Middleton's text demonstrates his mastery of ancient and recent literature on the history of Latium, while the color plates are based on drawings and watercolors he made in Italy in the years 1808–9.[1] By late 1810, W. Bulmer had printed on English paper Middleton's title page (dated 1812), the "Introductory Chapter," and the text of chapters two through five which deal with the cyclopean material and sights between Rome and Albano.[2]

Publisher Edward Orme planned to bring out the entire volume in 1812, but more than a decade of delays occurred. Middleton reported the "first number" being published in 1812.[3] In February of 1812 Edward Dodwell objected to Middleton's plan to include some of Dodwell's drawings in the book. Middleton withdrew the disputed material, reducing the number of illustrations from the forty originally planned to thirty-five. Ultimately only twenty-five plates were published.[4] Judging from the watermarks, no further printing was done until 1818, when the remainder of the text and many plates were published, a delay that may have been exacerbated by the War of 1812. The copper aquatint plates were cut in two groups, in 1811 and 1819, as indicated by their imprint dates, while the pages were probably printed in 1818 and 1823, judging from the watermarks. All this suggests a long campaign to produce the book, with the

final work, as it is known today, not ready to be bound before 1823.

About twenty-five copies of the book are known. Those that have been studied most carefully, at the Museum of Fine Arts in Boston, the South Caroliniana Library, Middleton Place, and the Boston Athenaeum, contain the same twenty-five plates, including twenty-three hand-colored aquatint views and two line engravings of elevations and details marked "A" and "B."

The plates are numbered at the upper right: 2 through 27, with 6, 11, 16, and 23–26 omitted — gaps apparently due to the dispute with Dodwell. All the aquatints are based on Middleton's original drawings except for two views of Albano (numbers 7 and 8), which are credited to Filippo Giuntotardi, an Italian watercolorist with whom he traveled and worked in 1808–9. The aquatint etchings were all made by Mathew Dubourg, a well-known printmaker in London, with the exception of two plates (numbers 5 and 27) by J. Jeakes. The two uncolored line engravings were executed by Swaine.

SRS

132. *Cruchley's New Picture of London, with Superior Coloured Map, Improved to 1835*

G. F. CRUCHLEY, 1835
London, England

Inscribed: "Alicia H. Middleton" and "R. I. Middleton"
Private collection
Provenance: Alicia Hopton Russell Middleton, by family descent

1. Middleton's title page includes a quotation from *The Roman Antiquities* of Dionysius of Halicarnassus in the original Greek. Translated it reads, "That I have indeed made choice of a subject noble, lofty, and useful to many will not, I think, require any lengthy argument, at least for those who are not utterly unacquainted with universal history."
2. J. J. Middleton, *A Letter to a Member of the National Institute at Paris* (Charleston, 1814), p. 9.
3. Petit-Radel confirms this, citing an announcement in the *Journal de Paris* of the appearance of the "first volume" of the work in January 1812. Middleton, *A Letter to a Member*, pp. i, 16.
4. Middleton, *A Letter to a Member*, p. 16.

By the 1830s, the Grand Tour had become an industry for men such as G. F. Cruchley. Located at 81 Fleet Street, London, he specialized in travel books for the "Nobility, Gentry, and Public in general." This London guidebook originally belonged to Alicia Hopton Russell Middleton (cat. 84) and her son Ralph Izard Middleton during their European Grand Tour in the 1830s. It combines brief descriptions of London's major monuments with practical information on postage rates, carriage fares, and the location of banks and churches, and includes a seven-day itinerary titled, "Plan for Viewing the Principal Objects in the Metropolis, in the most advantageous manner and shortest time." The final thirty pages contain a complete catalogue of Cruchley's published works with atlases, travel guides, and itineraries for travel in England and continental Europe written in English, French, German, and Italian.

RAL

133. "Notes on Travel in 1846"

THE REVEREND PAUL TRAPIER (American, 1806–72)

CHARLESTON: *Southern Episcopalian*, 1854

Charleston Library Society

By the mid-nineteenth century, the popularity of Charleston's Grand Tour tradition led the city's press to publish the letters and journals of traveling Charlestonians. *Russell's Magazine,* for example, published numerous articles and letters by Frederick Porcher and James Henry Hammond on their European travels.[1] Such articles provided reminiscences for those who had been to Europe, practical information for those planning to go, and vicarious experiences for those who could not afford the expensive journey.

In 1846, the Reverend Paul Trapier sailed for Europe with his eldest son Paul and his mother-in-law, Mrs. Theodore Dehon. They visited Paris, Brussels, Antwerp, Avignon, Florence, Rome, Naples, Venice, Milan, and Cologne, taking in many of Europe's important cathedrals and other religious sites. In Rome, they attended the inauguration of Pope Pius X about which Trapier wrote:

At an early hour, when we reached the "piazza" in front of St. Peter's, it was already thronged by thousands, who were pouring in from all directions. . . . In due season the papal infantry and cavalry were arranged in open lines, to keep the crowd from intruding upon the pathway of the approaching pageant. Cardinals in their coaches of state, each of them having two, one for his serene self, and another for his suite, with three footmen to the former, and two to the latter, began to arrive in succession through the guarded space, and to alight at the foot of the great staircase to the Vatican, by the side of St. Peter's. . . . The Pope himself was in his state coach, an equipage of which a republican pencil cannot easily paint a picture for democratic eyes, so far did it exceed in gorgeousness the grandest of the sights that we, in our simplicity had ever beheld. . . . Beside him was a Cardinal, and in front of his coach was carved a representation of his tiara, borne by angels. As he passed through the crowds, he bowed repeatedly, and with his two fore-fingers of his right hand, blessed the people.[2]

In 1854, Trapier's letters were published in the South Carolina diocesan journal, the *Southern Episcopalian.* His letters are highly evocative and descriptive, designed to transport the reader to the scene.

RAL

1. F. P. Porcher, "Sketches of Travel," *Russell's Magazine* 3 (May 1858): 130–32; James Henry Hammond, "European Correspondence," *Russell's Magazine* 1 (August 1857): 428–38; (September 1857): 510–20; 2 (October 1857): 37–46; (November 1857): 129–32; (March 1858): 493–99; and Hammond, "Notes on Wine and Vine Culture in France," *Russell's Magazine* 3 (June 1858): 207–13; (July 1858): 338–45; (September 1858): 501–05.
2. Paul Trapier, "Notes on Travel in 1846," *Southern Episcopalian* 2 (June 1855): 105–06; see also Paul Trapier, *Autobiography of the Reverend Paul Trapier* (Charleston: Dalcho Historical Society, 1954), pp. 18–19, 25, 63.

134. *A Handbook for Travellers in Central Italy. Part II. Rome and its Environs.*

London, England: John Murray, 1856

Inscribed: "William Aiken"
Historic Charleston Foundation, transferred by The Charleston Museum
Provenance: By family descent, gift to The Charleston Museum

By the middle of the nineteenth century, guide-books intended for the Grand Tour assumed a form more familiar to modern visitors with information on hotels and restaurants, as well as the locations of bankers, physicians, churches, etc. Other information, however, certainly distinguishes such books from those of today, since many tourists resided in Rome for months and would be able to avail themselves of the teachers of Italian, drawing, painting, dancing, and music who are listed.

This book is one of twelve published by John Murray that survives in the Aiken family library. The titles cover travel in Great Britain, the European continent, Persia, Greece, and Egypt and were purchased on their 1857–58 trip. Annotations in other books in the Aiken library document another Grand Tour by William Aiken in 1826–28, and for both Mr. and Mrs. Aiken in 1848.[1]

Travel books of the 1850s were also buying guides. This volume lists the names and locations of dealers in engravings, antiquities, pictures, cameos, and mosaics. It provides historical information about the sites in Rome as well as guides to the principal museums.

MDM

135. *Biographical Catalogue of the Principal Italian Painters, with a Table of the Contemporary Schools of Italy. Designed as a Hand-book to the Picture Gallery. By a Lady.*

RALPH N. WORNUM
London, England: John Murray, 1855

Inscribed: "Henrietta A. Aiken—Venice October 26th 1857"
Historic Charleston Foundation, transferred by The Charleston Museum
Provenance: By family descent, gift to The Charleston Museum

In addition to guidebooks, travelers on the Grand Tour relied upon more specialized books to assist their lessons about painting and connoisseurship. In the nineteenth century, it was believed that an understanding of the life of the artist was vital to a complete appreciation of the painting. The compact size of this book allowed it to be carried to the gallery.

This volume was purchased by Henrietta Aiken, daughter of Harriett Lowndes and William Aiken when she accompanied her parents on their 1857–58 Grand Tour. Each entry is accompanied by a short biography and a list of the painter's principal works.

MDM

---

1. I would like to thank Marc T. Herndon for the information regarding the Aikens' travels.

Miscellaneous

136. Bookplate of Peter Manigault, ca. 1754

HENRY YATES
London, England
Copper alloy, 4 × 3 in.

Private collection
Provenance: Peter Manigault, by family descent

The son of Gabriel Manigault and Anne Ashby, Peter Manigault (1731–74) went to London at the age of nineteen to study law at the Inner Temple. During his years abroad, Manigault immersed himself in fashionable London society and traveled extensively throughout northern Britain, France, and the Low Countries. After his graduation, Manigault engaged in the customs necessary to secure his status as a gentleman—he had his portrait painted by a popular artist (fig. 9) and hired an engraver to design a stylish plate for the leather-bound books in his library.

The bookplate is signed by Henry Yates, one of London's best eighteenth-century engravers of ephemera. In 1754, Yates was appointed the official engraver of punches at Goldsmiths' Hall.[1] It is notable that the bookplate retains its original paper wrapper, which reads, "For Mr. Manigault to be Left at George's Coffeehouse, Temple bar."

RAL

1. Michael Snodin, "Trade Cards and English Rococo," in *The Rococo in England: A Symposium,* ed. Charles Hind (London: Victoria and Albert Museum, 1986), pp. 95, 99.

137. Pistols, 1756–57

RICHARD WILSON AND JEREMIAH ASHLEY
London, England
Wood, steel, and silver, 6 ¼ × 13 ½ × 2 ½ in.

Marked: "RW" (for Richard Wilson), "London," and "Wilson"
Charleston Library Society, gift of Beatrice St. Julien Ravenel, 1991
Provenance: Charles Pinckney, by family descent

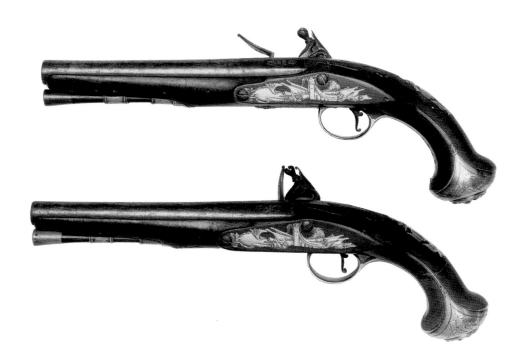

During his five years abroad, Charles Pinckney purchased this handsome set of pistols made by the London gunsmith, Richard Wilson, with ornate silver mounts fashioned by Jeremiah Ashley. A London silversmith, Ashley frequently collaborated with gunsmiths in the creation of expensive, high-style weaponry. The silver mounts are elaborately engraved with baroque-style military trophies and feature classical masks at the termination of the handles.

RAL

138. Watch, ca. 1780–90

GEORGE CURZON ADDIS
London, England
Gold, 2 in. (diam.)

Private collection
Provenance: Nathaniel Russell, by family descent through his younger
daughter, Sarah Russell Dehon

Nathaniel Russell (1738–1820), a New Englander by birth, came to Charleston in 1765 and established himself as a merchant prior to the American Revolution. After the outbreak of the Revolution, Russell marched with the colonial militia, made a substantial financial contribution of eleven thousand pounds to the state government, was selected as an attorney in South Carolina for the United States, and elected to a seat in the third General Assembly in 1779. After the fall of Charleston to the British in May 1780, Russell became a virtual prisoner of war trapped inside the enemy camp, carefully monitored, barred from business, and facing financial ruin.

Despite Russell's devotion to the patriot cause, he seemingly abandoned hope and boarded ship for England where he took the oath of loyalty to the crown. The General Assembly confiscated Russell's property in March 1783. He returned to South Carolina in September of that year, but was forced to spend several months onboard ship petitioning the legislature for permission to return. Russell's dilemma was a common one for Charleston merchants. It is estimated that one-fifth of South Carolina's population became loyalists sometime during the course of the Revolution and nearly five percent of the state's population would go into exile at the end of the war.[1]

Russell may have purchased his handsome gold watch by George Curzon Addis during his 1781–83 residency in London. Addis's London shop was located at 3 Birchin Lane and just down from the Carolina Coffee House at No. 25 Birchin Lane. The Carolina Coffee House provided a lively environment where news from home was exchanged and business affairs conducted.[2]

JTS

1. Robert S. Lambert, *South Carolina Loyalists in the American Revolution* (Columbia: University of South Carolina Press, 1987), p. 306.
2. Bryant Lillywhite, *London Coffee Houses: A Reference Book of Coffee Houses in the Seventeenth, Eighteenth, and Nineteenth Centuries* (London: George Allen and Unwin, 1963), p. 148.

139. Chatelaine, 1792

GREEN AND WARD
London, England
Gold, pearls, enamel, agate; length, 9 ⁷⁄₁₆ in.

Signed: Green and Ward London No. 2426
The Charleston Museum, gift of Mr. and Mrs. Berkeley Grimball
Provenance: Mrs. Gabriel Manigault (Margaret Izard), by family descent

A chatelaine is an ornamental clasp worn at the waist for suspending accessories. This chatelaine was designed for a watch, watch key, and seal. By the late eighteenth century, chatelaines were considered the height of fashion. On 28 September 1792, Mrs. Margaret Izard Manigault ordered her chatelaine from the London firm of Bird, Savage and Bird.

The precise date of order is known because of the remarkable survival of the bill of sale for this object. The watch cost thirty-one pounds, but the accessories brought the total cost to just over fifty pounds. With six rings to suspend chains, this chatelaine could have been quite heavy, but only two rings are utilized, as shown in the bill of sale. The watch has a verge movement and is held in its gilt skeleton case. The reverse side of the face reveals an alternating design of chevrons and flowers, seen under the transparent green enameling. The triple-stranded chain consists of enameled links flanking a string of seed pearls. A locket of hair is seen at the lower end of the chain, perhaps that of her husband. From this locket hang three separate pendants; the central one holds the watch key and carved agate seal. This seal reads *REPONDEZ VITE* across the top and illustrates a bird in flight with a letter in its beak, flying over a landscape.

Chris Loeblein

140. Parure, ca. 1820

French or German principalities
Cut steel, iron, japanned and gilt decoration; tiara width, 7 ¼ in.; necklace length, 18 ⅞ in.; earrings length, 1 ⅜ in.

The Charleston Museum, gift of Mrs. Russel D. Lewis
Provenance: Family of the Reverend James Dewar Simons

Dramatic jewelry designs emerged in the early nineteenth century to accompany the new fashion for Empire-style dresses, with their slender profiles and broad, low necklines. The most distinctive development was the ensemble known as the parure.[1] This parure consists of a tiara, necklace, and pair of drop earrings. Each piece is decorated with Roman heads in relief, in imitation of cameos. These images, as well as the delicate chain and scroll designs, reflect the neoclassic fervor of the period. The metal was japanned to give it a uniform look, highlighted with gilding.[2] A complete parure would include bracelets, rings, and pins as part of an ensemble.

It is notable that a cut steel parure would be found among the effects of a Charleston family. Such jewelry sets were produced to raise money for opposing sides of the Napoleonic Wars. In exchange for gold jewelry, the warring governments of France and Prussia produced iron/steel parures and other adornments to thank their patriotic citizens. It is unknown if Rev. James Dewar Simons ever went to Europe. He died in 1814, at the height of fashion for these parures. His daughter, Mrs. Horatio Allen, traveled in Europe during the 1830s. By that time the fashion for parures was waning.[3] The wars were long over, and the use of gemstones and gold had returned to jewelry.

Chris Loeblein

1. Wendy A. Cooper, *Classical Taste in America, 1800–1840* (Baltimore: Baltimore Museum of Art, 1993), pp. 34–35.
2. Martha Gandy Fales, *Jewelry in America 1600–1900* (Woodbridge, Suffolk: Antique Collector's Club, 1995), p. 120.
3. *Nineteenth-Century Jewelry from the First Empire to the First World War* (New York: Cooper Union Museum for the Arts of Decoration, 1995), p. 4.

141. Bookplate, ca. 1820

SAMUEL CLAYTON (Australian, active early nineteenth century)
Copper, 3 × 2 ½ in.

Signed: S. Clayton New South Wales
Private collection
Provenance: Charles Izard Manigault, by family descent

Engraving from bookplate. Courtesy
of South Carolina Historical Society

During his Asian travels in the 1820s, Charles Izard Manigault commissioned this armorial bookplate. Its engraver was Samuel Clayton, a convicted English forger who was sentenced to life in Australia during its early years as a penal colony. In his 1869 scrapbook, Manigault recalled purchasing several items from Clayton, including engravings of Australian aboriginal chieftains. He wrote, "I also had engraved there, several Hundred of my Coat of Arms, which are now pasted in the Books of my Library. They were engraved for me by one of these talented Convicts, who was too tricky at home to remain."[1] Ironically, Clayton became one of Australia's most important early artists and was commissioned by the Australian government to engrave the first plates for its national currency.

RAL

1. Charles Izard Manigault, scrapbook, 1869, p. 87, private collection.

142. Sewing box, ca. 1820

Canton, China
Lacquer on wood, 8 × 14 ¼ × 10 in.

Monogrammed "MIM" (for Margaret Izard Manigault)
The Charleston Museum
Provenance: Purchased by Charles Izard Manigault for his mother Margaret
Izard Manigault; by descent in the Manigault family to Emma Manigault
Jenkins Gribbin; to Jane Gaston Mahler

This lacquered sewing box was one of the many
presents sent home by Charles Izard Manigault
to his family during his six-year sojourn in Asia.
The top of the sewing box features the initials
"MIM" for his mother, Margaret Izard
Manigault.

RAL

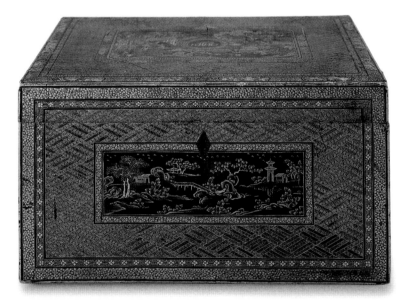

143. *View of the Pantheon*

Mosaic, 1 ¾ × 2 ⁵⁄₁₆ in.

Private collection
Provenance: Charles Izard Manigault, by family descent

144. *View of the Roman Forum*

Mosaic, 3 ¹⁄₁₆ × 4 ½ in.

Private collection
Provenance: Charles Izard Manigault, by family descent

St. Peter's Basilica established a workshop to produce mosaics as early as 1578. In the eighteenth century, Vatican mosaicists began supplementing their official work with *mosaici in piccolo,* or micromosaics. Their clients were cardinals, collectors, and tourists.[1]

Micromosaics are composed of minute tesserae that enabled artists to create detailed pictures, miniatures and jewelry. By the early nineteenth century, the popularity of micromosaics resulted in many more artisans' specializing in micromosaics and the establishment of new private workshops. An 1856 Roman guidebook described the studio of Cavaliere Barber, director of the government's mosaic shop, as "the first amongst the Roman mosaicists . . . well worth a visit."[2] Most commonly the images created for tourists featured views of the ancient Roman monuments.

The Pantheon was one of the most admired and certainly one of the most imitated buildings on the Grand Tour. This great domed temple, built by Emperor Hadrian and restored by Septimus Severus and Caracalla, appeared frequently in souvenir images, such as this micromosaic. While dominated by the Pantheon, this image also shows the fountain added to the piazza in 1575 and the obelisk added to the fountain in 1711.

The micromosaic *View of the Roman Forum* places the spectator at the base of the Capitoline Hill looking toward the Colosseum. In the foreground are three remaining columns of the Temple of Vespasian and Titus, to the right the facade of the Temple of Saturn, and to the left the Arch of Septimus Severus. As is common with *veduta* paintings, two small figures stand admiring the monuments.

These two micromosaics were among many purchased by Charles Izard Manigault, including views of the Colosseum, the Temple of the Sibyl at Tivoli, and the Nymphaeum of Alexander Severus, known as the Temple of Minerva Medica.

MDM

1. Andrew Wilton and Ilaria Bignamini, eds., *Grand Tour: The Lure of Italy in the Eighteenth Century* (London: Tate Gallery, 1996), pp. 284–85.
2. John Murray, *A Handbook for Travellers in Central Italy, Part II, Rome and Its Environs,* 4th ed. (London, 1856), p. xvii. See cat. 133.

145. *Bishop Theodore Dehon,* 1846

Shell with gold mount, 1 ⅞ × 1 ⅝ in.

Historic Charleston Foundation, gift of Mrs. Henry M. Abbot
Provenance: Sarah Russell Dehon, by family descent

Theodore Dehon (1776–1817) was one of Charleston's most eminent nineteenth-century theologians. Born in Boston, he graduated from Harvard in 1795 as the valedictorian of his class. In 1809, he came to Charleston to serve as the rector of St. Michael's Church and was later elected the second Episcopal bishop of South Carolina. His marriage in 1813 to Sarah Russell (1792–1857), the younger daughter of Nathaniel Russell and Sarah Hopton, cemented his ties to the Carolina Lowcountry. In 1817, he died and his wife spent the next forty years of her life living in her father's house as the revered widow of the bishop.

In 1846, Mrs. Dehon accompanied her son-in-law, the Reverend Paul Trapier, to Europe for an extended Grand Tour (cat. 133). In Italy, where artists specialized in engraving cameos for Grand Tourists, she apparently commissioned this cameo portrait of her deceased husband.

RAL

146. Casts of works of art, mid-nineteenth century

Italian

Plaster, 10 ¼ × 6 ¾ × 2 in.

Middleton Place Foundation, Charleston
Provenance: Charles Alston family, by descent

Ancient semiprecious stones, both in intaglio and cameos, were greatly prized by collectors. The fascination for acquiring these miniature sculptures, a tradition that dates to classical antiquity, reached a new fervor in the eighteenth and nineteenth centuries. Collectors sought both originals and casts of gems in other collections.[1] With the growing popularity of gems, casts taken from them became more readily available. Casts expanded to include miniature compositions based on famous works of art. An 1856 Roman guidebook listed several makers of "sulpher casts of medals and small bas-reliefs."[2]

Charlestonians collected these novelties on the Grand Tour. Charles Izard Manigault described this purchase: "[The cameo maker] also makes collections in miniature stamps of plaster of all the celebrated paintings and statues of the ancient and modern school. . . . I bought a collection bound up in books which on opening each side displays little boxes containing these little beautiful representations in Plaster composition. For this I paid $20."[3] Two books of casts preserved from Charles Alston's 1856 Grand Tour purchases feature small gems of famous works of art, including several sculptures by Canova, Raphael's *Transfiguration,* and Domenichino's *Cumaean Sibyl.*

MDM

1. Ian Jenkins and Kim Sloan, *Vases and Volcanoes: Sir William Hamilton and His Collection* (London: British Museum Press, 1996), p. 93.
2. John Murray, *A Handbook for Travellers in Central Italy, Part II, Rome and Its Environs,* 4th ed. (London, 1856), p. 36. See cat. 134.
3. Charles Izard Manigault, travel journal, Rome, February 1830, CLS.

General Bibliography

Amfitheatrof, Erik. *The Enchanted Ground: Americans in Italy, 1760–1980.* Boston: Little, Brown, 1980.

Baker, Paul R. *The Fortunate Pilgrims: Americans in Italy, 1800–1860.* Cambridge: Harvard University Press, 1964.

Bilodeau, Francis W. *Art in South Carolina, 1670–1970.* Columbia: South Carolina Tricentennial Commission, 1970.

Black, Jeremy. *The British Abroad: The Grand Tour in the Eighteenth Century.* New York: St. Martin's Press, 1992.

Black, Jeremy. *The British and the Grand Tour.* London, 1985.

Bowes, Frederick. *The Culture of Early Charleston.* Chapel Hill: University of North Carolina Press, 1942.

Burton, E. Milby. *Charleston Furniture, 1700–1825.* Charleston: The Charleston Museum, 1955.

Burton, E. Milby, and Warren Ripley. *South Carolina Silversmiths, 1690–1860 (revised ed.).* Charleston: The Charleston Museum, 1991.

Carll, M. Allison. "An Assessment of English Furniture Imports into Charleston, South Carolina, 1760–1800." *Journal of Early Southern Decorative Arts* 11, no. 2 (November 1985): 1–18.

Carson, Cary, Ronald Hoffman, and Peter J. Albert. *Of Consuming Interests: The Style of Life in the Eighteenth Century.* Charlottesville: University Press of Virginia, 1994.

Cash, W. J. *The Mind of the South.* New York: Knopf, 1941.

Coclanis, Peter A. *The Shadow of a Dream: Economic Life and Death in the South Carolina Low Country, 1670–1920.* New York: Oxford University Press, 1989.

Edgar, Walter. *South Carolina: A History.* Columbia: University of South Carolina Press, 1998.

Fraser, Walter J. *Charleston! Charleston! The History of a Southern City.* Columbia: University of South Carolina Press, 1989.

Garstung, Donald, ed. *The British Face: A View of Portraiture 1625–1850.* London: Colnaghi, 1986.

Haskell, Francis *Rediscoveries in Art: Some Aspects of Taste, Fashion and Collecting in England and France.* London: Phaidon, 1976.

Haskell, Francis, and Nicholas Penny. *Taste and the Antique: The Lure of Classical Sculpture, 1500–1900.* New Haven: Yale University Press, 1981.

Hibbert, Christopher. *The Grand Tour.* London: Thomas Methuen, 1987.

Jaffe, Irma B., ed. *The Italian Presence in American Art, 1760–1860.* New York: Fordham University Press, 1989.

Jenkins, Ian, and Kim Sloan. *Vases and Volcanoes: Sir William Hamilton and His Collection.* London: British Museum, 1996.

Lively, Susan L. "Going Home: Americans in Britain, 1740–1776." Ph.D. diss., Harvard University, 1997.

Mack, Charles R. and Lynn Robertson, eds. *The Roman Remains: John Izard Middleton's Visual Souvenirs of 1820–1823 with Additional Views in Italy, France, and Switzerland.* Columbia: University of South Carolina Press, 1997.

Manigault, G[abriel] E. "History of the Carolina Art Association," *Year Book, City of Charleston, S.C., 1894* (Charleston: 1895), pp. 243–73.

McInnis, Maurie D. "The Politics of Taste: Classicism in Charleston, South Carolina, 1815–1840," Ph.D. diss., Yale University, 1996.

Miles, Ellen G. *American Colonial Portraits, 1700–1776.* Washington, D.C.: National Portrait Gallery, Smithsonian Institution, 1987.

———, ed. *The Portrait in Eighteenth-Century America.* Cranbury, N.J.: Associated University Presses, 1993.

Miller, Lillian. *Patrons and Patriotism: The Encouragement of the Fine Arts in the United States, 1790–1860.* Chicago: University of Chicago Press, 1966.

Moltke-Hansen, David., ed. *Art in the Lives of South Carolinians.* Charleston: Carolina Art Association, 1979.

O'Brien, Michael, and David Moltke-Hansen, eds. *Intellectual Life in Antebellum Charleston.* Knoxville: University of Tennessee Press, 1986.

Pears, Iain. *The Discovery of Painting: The Growth of Interest in the Arts in England, 1680–1768.* New Haven: Yale University Press, 1988.

Pease, Jane H., and William H. Pease, *Ladies, Women & Wenches: Choice and Constraint in Antebellum Charleston and Boston.* Chapel Hill: University of North Carolina Press, 1990.

Pease, William H., and Jane H. Pease. *The Web of Progress: Private Values and Public Styles in Boston and Charleston, 1828–1843.* New York: Oxford University Press, 1985.

Pinckney, Elise, ed. *The Letterbook of Eliza Lucas Pinckney, 1739–1762.* Columbia: University of South Carolina Press, 1997.

Plumb, J. H. *The Pursuit of Happiness: A View of Life in Georgian England.* New Haven: Yale Center for British Art, 1977.

Powers, Jr., Bernard E. *Black Charlestonians: A Social History, 1822–1885.* Fayetteville: University of Arkansas Press, 1994.

Reinhold, Meyer. *Classica Americana: The Greek and Roman Heritage in the United States.* Detroit: Wayne State University Press, 1984.

Ridley, Ronald T. *The Eagle and the Spade.* Cambridge: Cambridge University Press, 1992.

Rogers, George C., Jr. *Charleston in the Age of the Pinckneys.* Norman: University of Oklahoma Press, 1969.

———. *Evolution of a Federalist: William Loughton Smith of Charleston (1758–1812).* Columbia: University of South Carolina Press, 1962.

Rutledge, Anna Wells. *Artists in the Life of Charleston through Colony and State from Restoration to Reconstruction.* Philadelphia: Transactions of the American Philosophical Society, n.s., 39, no. 2. 1949; reprint, Columbia: University of South Carolina Press, 1980.

Savage, J. Thomas with photography by N. Jane Iseley. *The Charleston Interior.* Greensboro, N.C.: Legacy Publications, 1995.

Severens, Martha R. *The Miniature Portrait Collection of the Carolina Art Association.* Charleston: Gibbes Art Gallery, 1984.

Simon, Robin. *The Portrait in Britain and America with a Biographical Dictionary of Portrait Painters, 1680–1914.* Boston: G. K. Hall, 1987.

Strong, Sir Roy. *The British Portrait 1660–1960,* Woodbridge, Suffolk: The Antique Collectors' Club, 1991.

Stebbins, Theodore E., ed. *The Lure of Italy: American Artists and the Italian Experience, 1760–1914.* New York: Abrams, 1992.

Taylor, Rosser Howard. *Ante-bellum South Carolina: A Social and Cultural History.* Chapel Hill, 1942; reprint, New York: Da Capo Press, 1970.

Vance, William L. *America's Rome.* 2 vols. New Haven: Yale University Press, 1989.

Wilton, Andrew, and Ilaria Bignamini. *Grand Tour: The Lure of Italy in the Eighteenth Century.* London: Tate Gallery, 1996.

Index

Vermeer, Jan, 70
Vernet, 80
Vertue, George, 26
Vesuvius Erupting, 196, 197
Vien, Joseph-Marie, 136
View of the Pantheon, 330, 331
View of the Roman Forum, 330, 331
Vigée le Brun, Louis Elizabeth, 68, 83
    Madame de Stael as Corinne, 68
Virgil, 70, 84
Visconti, Ennio Quirino, 186, 187
Voght, Baron de, 82
Volpato, Giovanni, 43
Voltaire, 68, 80
Vonham, Frederick, 261

Waldo, Samuel L., 34
Wall, William Guy, 71
Walpole, Horace, 175
War of 1812, 75
Washington, George, 5, 7, 38, 98, 123, 223, 224, 278
Washington, William, 34
Watson, Thomas, 276
Watteau, Antoine, 47
Watts, Robert, 112
Webster, Lady, 134, 186
West, Benjamin, 23, 24, 28–33, 41, 48, 71, 100,
    101, 103–106, 128, 152, 158, 241, 302, 303
    Arthur Middleton, His Wife Mary Izard,
        and Their Son Henry
        Middleton, 29, 30, 106, 107
    Death of General Wolfe, 33
    John Allen, 104
    Sibyl, 30
    Signers for Peace, 33
    The Cricketers, 28, 29, 33, 100–102
    Thomas Middleton of Crowfield, 29, 104
    Thomas Middleton of the Oaks, 41, 104, 105,
        152
    Venus and Cupid, 48
    William Middleton, 28
Weyman, Edward, 60
Weyman, Rebecca, 60
Whipham, Thomas, 260, 262

White, John Blake, 17, 128, 303, 304
    Sketchbooks, 303, 304
    Travel Journal, 303
Wickes, George, 266
Wightman, William, 278
Wightman, William May, 38
William, prince of Wales, 10
Wilmer, Mrs. Jonathan R. *See* Wilmer, Sarah
    Reeves Gibbes
Wilmer, Sarah Reeves Gibbes, 178, 179, 239
Wilson, Richard, 198, 322
Wilson, Robert, 76
Wilton, Joseph, 128, 219, 220
    Statue of William Pitt, Earl of Chatham,
        219, 220
Winckelmann, Johann Joachim, 69, 82
Windham, Sir William, 13
Windham, William and James Paine
    Design for a Cabinet at Felbrigg Hall, 13
Winterhalter, Francis Xavier, 35
Winthrop, John, 3
Wollaston, John, 94
    Benjamin Smith (attributed), 94
Wormeley, Ralph, 100, 102, 103
Wormeley, Ralph, Jr., 102
Wragg, Elizabeth. *See* Manigault, Elizabeth
    Wragg
Wragg, Henrietta, 175
Wragg, Joseph, 26
Wragg, Judith DuBose, 26
Wragg, Marie DuBose, 175
Wragg, Samuel, 175
Wragg, William, 175, 177
Wycombe, Lord, 43

Yarnold, Benjamin, 57
Yates, Henry, 321
Young, 233
    John Hopton, 233

Zoffany, Johann, 20, 23, 27, 28, 31, 32, 48, 98,
    126, 31
    Ralph Izard, 27, 48, 310
    Tribuna degli Uffizi, 20

Staff

GIBBES MUSEUM OF ART

Paul Figueroa, Director

Angela D. Mack, Curator of Collections

Stacey Brown, Registrar

Scott Zetrouer, Curatorial Assistant

Greg Jenkins, Preparator

Amy Watson Smith, Curator of Education

Susan Earhart, School Program Coordinator

Joyce Baker, School Program Assistant

Danielle Madore, Studio Program Coordinator

Jennifer Devine, Studio Registrar

Anne Lautz, Administrative Assistant

Barbara Smith, Business Manager

Laurens Bissell, Membership Director

Liz Miller, Membership Assistant

Janis Shields, Public Relations

Lee Breeden, Development Liaison

Nancy Abercrombie, Museum Shop Manager

Kenny Tolbert, Maintenance Assistant

Collette Wright, Security

Tom Bostian, Security

Robert Horsley, Security

Bernard Taylor, Security

Exhibition Associates

Dan Gottlieb, Exhibition Designer

Stephen Hoffius, Associate Editor

Roberta Sokolitz, Associate Editor

Jennie Malcolm, Catalogue Designer

Maurie D. McInnis, Project Consultant

Photograph Credits

Photographs were supplied by the owners of the works and reproduced by permission of the owner, except as indicated in the following additional credits.

Alinari/Art Resource, NY, fig. 84

Jeff Amberg, cat. no. 127

Gavin Ashworth, cat. nos. 90, 105; fig. 39

Dean Beasom, fig. 59

Carolina Art Association/Gibbes Museum of Art, fig. 9, 18, 19, 78

Carpenter Studios, fig. 74

Earl Studio, Tuscaloosa, cat. nos. 32, 86; fig. 85

Giraudon/Art Resource, NY, fig. 46

Allan Hamer, cat. no. 5

Greg Heins, figs. 45, 47, 53, 58

Geri Nolan Hilfiker, cat. nos. 23, 24

Lance Humphries, fig. 13

N. Jane Iseley, fig. 41

Jim Jernegan, cat. no. 138

Tim Martin, cat. nos. 143, 144

David Matthews, cat. nos. 45, 46

David Olin, cat. no. 27

Shelley Paine, cat. no. 75

Réunion des Musées Nationaux Agencephotographique, fig. 7

Rick Rhodes, cat. nos. 3, 4, 7, 9, 10, 15, 18, 21, 26, 29, 30, 31, 33, 36, 37, 39, 40, 41, 42, 43, 44, 47, 50, 53, 54, 55, 57, 58, 59, 62, 63, 64, 65, 66, 67, 73, 74, 76, 77, 87, 88, 89, 91, 93, 94, 95, 96, 97, 98, 99, 100, 102, 104, 106, 107, 108, 111, 112, 113, 114, 115, 116, 117, 118, 119, 130, 137, 139, 141, 142, 145, 146; figs. 2, 11, 14, 20, 29, 30, 33, 36, 37, 60, 69, 77, 79, 90

Terry Richardson, cat. nos. 8, 28, 35, 60, 61, 101; figs. 44, 57, 62

Schwarz Gallery, Philadelphia, cat. no. 38

David Stover Photography, cat. no. 103

Scott Wolff, cat. no. 109